The Supreme Court and McCarthy-Era Repression

The Supreme Court and McCarthy-Era Repression

One Hundred Decisions

ROBERT M. LICHTMAN

UNIVERSITY OF ILLINOIS PRESS
Urbana, Chicago, and Springfield

First Illinois paperback, 2015
© 2012 by Robert M. Lichtman
All rights reserved
Manufactured in the United States of America
1 2 3 4 5 C P 5 4 3 2 1
∞ This book is printed on acid-free paper.

The Library of Congress cataloged the cloth edition as follows:
Lichtman, Robert M.
The Supreme Court and McCarthy-era repression :
one hundred decisions / Robert M. Lichtman.
p.   cm.
Includes bibliographical references and index.
ISBN 978-0-252-03700-9 (hard cover : alk. paper) —
ISBN 978-0-252-09412-5 (e-book)
1. United States. Supreme Court—History—20th century.
2. Civil rights—United States—Cases.
3. United States—Politics and government—1945–1989.
I. Title.
KF8742.L53   2012
342.7308'5026409045—dc23   2011052767

PAPERBACK ISBN 978-0-252-08096-8

To my children, Ellen, David, and Judith,
my grandchildren, Michael and Lilah,
and of course to Susan.

"[I]t is easy to see that it would require an uncommon portion of fortitude in the judges to do their duty as faithful guardians of the Constitution, where legislative invasions of it had been instigated by the major voice of the community."

—Alexander Hamilton, *The Federalist Papers, No. 78*

"The federal judges . . . must know how to understand the spirit of the age, to confront those obstacles that can be overcome, and to steer out of the current when the tide threatens to carry them away, and with them the sovereignty of the Union and obedience to its laws."

—Alexis de Tocqueville, *Democracy in America*

Contents

Author's Note   ix

Introduction: Political Repression and Court-Curbing   1

1. Defining the McCarthy Era   13
2. The Justices of the Vinson Court, *Douds,* and the Start of the Court's McCarthy Era (October Term 1949)   24
3. *Dennis,* the Attorney General's List, Loyalty Programs, Contempts, and More (October Term 1950)   37
4. Deportations, Fallout from *Dennis,* and the Rosenberg Case (October Terms 1951 and 1952, Special Term 1953)   48
5. The Coming of the Warren Court, the *Emspak* Trilogy, and *Brown*'s Consequences (October Terms 1953 and 1954)   64
6. *Nelson, Cole v. Young,* and the Beginning of the Campaign against the Court (October Term 1955)   78
7. The "Red Monday" Decisions, *Jencks,* and a Crescendo of Anti-Court Attacks (October Term 1956)   91
8. *Beilan, Lerner,* and the Court's Shift, Passport Cases, and Congress's Court-Curbing Climax (October Term 1957)   109
9. *Barenblatt, Uphaus,* and the Court in Retreat (October Terms 1958 and 1959)   127

10. *Scales* and *CPUSA, Wilkinson* and *Braden,* and *Konigsberg II* and *Anastaplo*—a Full-Scale Retreat (October Term 1960)   144

11. Frankfurter's Departure, a Near-Decision in *Gibson,* and the Era's End (October Term 1961)   161

    Epilogue: Vietnam War Decisions and Some Observations   171

    Notes   177

    Selected Bibliography   255

    Index of Supreme Court Decisions   267

    Index   273

    Illustrations follow page 90

Author's Note

For those for whom the McCarthy era coincided with formative years, the memories are indelible. As college students, we saw parents' careers disrupted, professors fired, friends drafted into the Army to be faced with punitive discharges, all by reason of transient political associations. As a law student, I eagerly read the Supreme Court's decisions in "Communist" cases and, as a young lawyer in Washington, D.C., heard arguments at the Court. My resolve to write about these cases and the justices who decided them was deferred during decades spent in an all-consuming law practice but never abandoned.

I owe a debt of gratitude to Harold A. Ward, Judge Patricia M. Wald, Marc S. Galanter, Daniel J. Leab, Stephen Weissman, and Jacob Bronstein, each of whom undertook to read my manuscript (or portions of it) and to offer perceptive comment and encouragement. The archivists and librarians at the Library of Congress, Yale University, Princeton University, University of Kentucky, University of Texas, and the San Francisco Public Library gave invaluable assistance. I owe a special debt to Laurie Matheson of the University of Illinois Press for her consistent support and useful advice. And I am profoundly grateful to my family and friends who tolerated me during the years I spent writing this book.

The Supreme Court and
McCarthy-Era Repression

INTRODUCTION

Political Repression and Court-Curbing

The McCarthy era, which began in the late 1940s and continued for more than a decade (years after Senator Joseph R. McCarthy's censure by the Senate in 1954 and his death in 1957), was the longest of the several periods of political repression that punctuate American history. These episodes were largely the products of wars and national crises. The McCarthy era stemmed from a prolonged "Cold War" with the Soviet Union and its satellites following World War II, accompanied by a much shorter "hot" war against two Asian Communist states, the Korean War (1950–53), that resulted in sizable American casualties and ended in a frustrating stalemate.

Repression in a democracy does not fit the classic mold: it is majoritarian, administered by elected officials, and supported by public opinion. Repeatedly, however, the verdict of history, decades later, has been that the perceived internal dangers that generated repression in America were exaggerated and the repressive measures used unwarranted. There is now a consensus, for example, that the nation's security did not require the internment of more than one hundred thousand ethnic Japanese—seventy thousand were American citizens—during World War II. Less than a decade earlier, in 1933, President Franklin D. Roosevelt granted a full pardon to persons convicted under World War I–era sedition statutes. "After each perceived security crisis ended," Justice William J. Brennan Jr., who served during the McCarthy era, observed, "the United States has remorsefully realized that the abrogation of civil liberties was unnecessary. But it has proven unable to prevent itself from repeating the error when the next crisis came along."[1]

While historians may disagree as to precisely which periods of American history may accurately be termed repressive, a fair listing would include:

- the period of the "half war" with France that produced the 1798 Alien and Sedition Acts, authorizing the executive branch to deport aliens deemed dangerous and to prosecute and imprison critics of the government;
- the Civil War period, during which the government suspended the writ of habeas corpus and authorized trial by court-martial for persons deemed disloyal;
- World War I and the "Red Scare" of 1919–20, when hundreds were prosecuted under sedition statutes for speaking in opposition to the war, and aliens associated with socialist and anarchist groups were deported;
- World War II, when the government interned the ethnic Japanese population on the West Coast without charges or hearing and prosecuted for sedition pro-Nazi Americans who spoke in opposition to the war;
- the McCarthy era, when an array of repressive measures, including sedition prosecutions, deportations, and contempt prosecutions for refusal to disclose political associations, was directed at Communists and "subversives";
- the Vietnam War, when the government brought conspiracy prosecutions against antiwar activists and prosecuted antiwar speech under a variety of state and federal statutes.[2]

The historians' verdict on the current "war on terror" is, at this writing, still out. But Congress twice enacted legislation to strip federal courts of jurisdiction in habeas corpus cases brought by alleged terrorists detained at Guantanamo Bay. And warrantless government wiretapping of American citizens took place on an unprecedented scale.[3]

All of these repressive practices posed issues under the Constitution, and over time they became increasingly the subject of litigation, federal and state, with many cases reaching the U.S. Supreme Court. Because each period involved a perceived danger to the nation, with the government's actions justified as necessary to protect the national security and supported by public opinion, Supreme Court justices repeatedly found themselves in an unenviable position, forced to choose in a time of crisis between upholding government action they deemed unlawful or deciding in favor of despised dissidents.

William O. Douglas, a member of the Court for more than three decades, whose tenure encompassed World War II and the McCarthy era, commented: "The Court is not isolated from life. Its members are very much a part of the community and know the fears, anxieties, cravings and wishes of their neighbors. That does not mean that community attitudes are necessarily translated by mysterious osmosis into new judicial doctrine. It does mean that the state of public opinion will often make the Court cautious when it should be bold." Felix Frankfurter, who served on the Court with Douglas, wrote in 1951 during the McCarthy era that "judges, howsoever they may conscientiously seek to discipline themselves against it, unconsciously are too apt to be moved by the deep undercurrents of public feeling." Earl Warren, chief justice for most of the McCarthy years and himself the target of fierce criticism, observed that "always agreeing with the dominant interests would be a serene way of life. It is comforting to be liked, and it would be pleasant to bask in the sunshine of perpetual public favor."[4]

This book is about the situation faced by Supreme Court justices in the McCarthy era, obliged in scores of cases over more than a decade to decide the lawfulness of executive and legislative action directed at alleged Communists and "subversives." The events demonstrate the Court's vulnerability in a time of political repression, when a refusal to acquiesce in the repressive actions demanded by popular opinion may lead to harsh attacks in the press and in the Congress, and may result in legislation to curb the Court and limit its independence. The McCarthy-era court did acquiesce at the outset; but when, in 1956 and 1957, it issued a series of decisions in favor of accused Communists, it triggered a firestorm of public criticism and congressional action that forced it to retreat. The attacks and political pressures deepened existing divisions and rivalries among the justices. The Court's retreat was accomplished almost entirely in 5–4 decisions.

The book's primary focus is the decisions themselves. None is omitted, for even the least important illustrate the character and pervasiveness of the repression and the often conflicting legal principles at issue. The decisions provide the best evidence of the justices' constitutional views—and shifts in views—and their responses to the severe pressures under which they labored.

The Founding Fathers, uncanny as always, accurately foresaw the justices' situation.

The Founding Fathers and Judicial Independence

Judicial independence was debated from the time of the nation's beginning. Thomas Jefferson, when he drafted the Declaration of Independence in Philadelphia in June 1776, included as one of the "repeated injuries and usurpations" inflicted by George III that "[h]e has made Judges dependent on his Will alone, for the tenure of their offices, and the amount and payment of their salaries."[5]

The colonists' grievance was not abstract. Only fifteen years earlier the king had changed the tenure of colonial judges from service during the judge's "good behavior" to service at the king's pleasure. English judges continued under the earlier standard, a 1701 statute providing for service during good behavior with "their Salaries ascertained and established." Colonial judges had received the benefits of this statute until 1761, and, in making the change, the king's obvious intent was to make the judges subservient to the Crown.[6]

In 1787, the framers included in the Constitution presented for ratification by the thirteen states a provision aimed at securing the independence of federal judges, not from the Crown but from the legislative and executive branches. This provision, in Article III, Section 1, guarantees lifetime tenure for both Supreme Court and lower-court judges, subject to a "good Behaviour" limitation, and requires that judges be paid "a Compensation" that cannot be diminished while they hold office.[7]

In *The Federalist Papers*, 78 and 79, Alexander Hamilton explained the rationale for this provision: "[T]he judiciary is beyond comparison the weakest of the three departments of power," lacking "influence over either the sword or the purse" and "ultimately depend[ent] upon the aid of the executive arm even for the efficacy [i.e., enforcement] of its judgments." "[F]rom the natural feebleness of the judiciary," he continued, "it is in continual jeopardy of being overpowered, awed, or influenced by its co-ordinate branches," and "nothing can contribute so much to its firmness and independence as permanency in office."[8]

The tasks the federal judiciary were obliged to perform were likely, in Hamilton's view, to involve it in controversy with "co-ordinate branches." Under "a limited Constitution," he wrote, one containing "specified exceptions to the legislative authority," such as prohibitions against ex post facto laws and bills of attainder, it would be the judges' "duty ... to declare all acts contrary to the manifest tenor of the Constitution void." "[P]ermanent tenure," he said, will encourage "that independent spirit in the judges which must be essential to the faithful performance of so arduous a duty."[9]

More specifically, federal judges would be called upon to make decisions upholding the rights of unpopular minorities against repressive government action. Judicial independence, Hamilton put it, was "requisite to guard the Constitution and the rights of individuals from the effects of those ill humors which the arts of designing men ... sometimes disseminate among the people themselves, and which, though they speedily give place to better information and more deliberate reflection, have a tendency, in the meantime, to occasion ... serious oppressions of the minor party in the community."[10]

The Article III provision, however, did not shield judges from all responsibility for their actions. Judges, Hamilton wrote, "are liable to be impeached for malconduct by the House of Representatives and tried by the Senate; and, if convicted, may be dismissed from office and disqualified from holding any other."[11]

Although Hamilton was not in doubt, the Constitution does not expressly empower federal courts to declare a congressional enactment or an executive-branch action unconstitutional. The principle of judicial review did not become settled until 1803, when Chief Justice John Marshall wrote in *Marbury v. Madison* that "[i]t is emphatically the province and duty of the Judicial Department to say what the law is," and if a statute is in conflict with the Constitution, "the Courts must decide on the operation of each."[12]

Nonetheless, Supreme Court justices are appointed and confirmed by elected officials and are by no means immune from popular pressures. In addition to impeachment and removal by the legislative branch, they are subject to a number of other threats arising both within and outside the Constitution.

Curbing the Supreme Court

Impeachment has proved to be less a threat to federal judges than Hamilton seemed to believe. In 1804, only seventeen years after the Constitution's ratification, the House instituted impeachment proceedings against an associate justice of the Supreme Court, Samuel Chase of Maryland. The charges against Chase, an overbearing Federalist, concerned his partisan actions as a trial judge performing circuit duties (not his concomitant duties as a Supreme Court justice) in prosecutions brought under the Sedition Act of 1798 against critics of President John Adams's administration. The impeachment proceedings against Chase were instituted by a Congress controlled by Jeffersonian Republicans—Adams having been defeated by Jefferson in the election of 1800.[13]

However, Chase, while impeached by the House, was acquitted by the Senate. Six Republicans joined with nine Federalist senators in the thirty-four-member body, precluding the two-thirds majority required to convict. Chase's acquittal became a formidable precedent. "[B]y assuring," Chief Justice William H. Rehnquist wrote nearly two centuries later "that impeachment would not be used in the future as a method to remove members of the Supreme Court for their judicial opinions, it helped to safeguard the independence of that body."[14]

Chase's case marks the only instance in which the House voted to impeach a Supreme Court justice. Eight lower-court judges have been impeached and removed, and two resigned after impeachment; but their offenses were bribery, tax evasion, or some other personal misconduct.[15]

Still, impeachment resolutions are on occasion introduced in the House in response to unpopular decisions by federal judges. A resolution to impeach Justice Douglas was introduced in 1953 after he stayed the execution of convicted spies Julius and Ethel Rosenberg. Calls for the impeachment of judges, without a formal resolution, are common. In the late 1950s, the Court's decisions in school-desegregation and "Communist" cases fueled a right-wing campaign that "blanketed America with 'Impeach Earl Warren' billboards." Judges are not unaware of calls for their impeachment. In 2004, Rehnquist deemed it necessary to warn that "Congress's authority to impeach and remove judges should not extend to decisions from the bench."[16]

Impeachment, however, is not the only means under the Constitution by which Congress can punish the Supreme Court when it makes unpopular decisions. Another method is jurisdiction-stripping. Article III, Section 2, which lists the types of cases to which "[t]he judicial Power" extends, contains a significant limitation: "In all Cases affecting Ambassadors, other public Ministers and Consuls, and those in which a State shall be Party, the supreme Court shall have original Jurisdiction. In all the other Cases before mentioned, the supreme Court shall have appellate Jurisdiction . . . *with such Exceptions, and under such Regulations as the Congress shall make.*" In other words, only two narrow types of cases are assigned to the Supreme Court by the Constitution: cases "affecting Ambassadors" and those in which a State "shall be Party." "In all the other Cases"—comprising almost all of its work—the Court's jurisdiction is "appellate" (*i.e.*, appeals from the decisions of other courts) and by virtue of the "Exceptions clause" is arguably limited to the categories of cases that Congress by statute has assigned to it.[17]

Over the years, Congress has repeatedly expressed its dissatisfaction with Supreme Court decisions by proposing to strip the Court of appellate jurisdiction to decide the same type of case in the future. Congress adopted such a proposal in 1868, when the Court had pending before it *Ex parte McCardle,* a habeas corpus action that challenged the constitutionality of Reconstruction legislation authorizing military trials for civilians charged with fomenting rebellion. McCardle was a Mississippi newspaper editor whose vitriolic writings led to his arrest by military authorities. Two years earlier, the Court had ruled in another case that the government could not suspend habeas corpus in areas where civil courts were functioning. Fearful that it would also invalidate the legislation at issue in *McCardle,* Congress repealed the statute upon which the Court's jurisdiction over McCardle's appeal was founded. The Court immediately dismissed the appeal.[18]

While rarely enacted, jurisdiction-stripping legislation has remained popular with congressional critics of the Court. In the McCarthy era, such legislation came close to being enacted. More recently, the House in 2004 passed by wide margins bills to strip federal courts of appellate jurisdiction in cases involving the Defense of Marriage Act (a federal statute allowing states to refuse to recognize same-sex marriages performed in other states) and the Pledge of Allegiance (this after a federal court of appeals barred public-school recitations of the words "under God" in the Pledge). The bills died in the Senate.[19]

In December 2005, however, shortly after the Court granted review in *Hamdan v. Rumsfeld,* a habeas corpus action brought by a detainee at the Guantanamo Bay prison, Congress passed, and the president signed, legislation to strip federal courts of jurisdiction (except for truncated authority in one court of appeals) over habeas actions by aliens held at Guantanamo. The elected branches' dissatisfaction had begun a year earlier when the Court held that it had jurisdiction to consider challenges to detention at Guantanamo by foreign nationals captured abroad. After the Court agreed to hear Hamdan's specific challenge, jurisdiction-stripping legislation swiftly followed. When the Court then held that the legislation did not apply to pending cases (and, on the merits, sustained Hamdan's challenge to the military commission appointed to try him), the elected branches, in October 2006, enacted a second statute, unequivocally stripping the Court of jurisdiction even over pending cases. But the Court, in this instance, had the last word, invalidating the second statute as violative of the Constitution's guarantee of the habeas corpus remedy.[20]

A third method of curbing the Court is by "packing" it. The Constitution does not specify the number of Supreme Court justices. The current nine was fixed by a statute enacted by Congress in 1869. At other times, Congress has set the number of justices as high as ten and as low as five. Congressional displeasure with the Court's decisions can readily be manifested by an increase in the number of seats and appointment by the president of new and presumably more compliant or right-thinking justices.[21]

Most famously, during the Great Depression of the 1930s, President Roosevelt, his New Deal legislative program stymied by a Supreme Court majority, most of whose members were over age seventy, proposed a "court-packing" plan that would authorize appointment of an additional justice whenever a sitting justice reached age seventy. The proposal met intense criticism and failed—indeed, its legacy has been to discredit any subsequent attempt to respond to unpopular Supreme Court decisions by manipulating the number of justices. Historians have argued, however, that the mere vetting of FDR's proposal was responsible for a sudden and dramatic shift in the Court's decisions, with subsequent rulings uniformly upholding New Deal economic legislation—the so-called "switch in time that saved nine."[22]

Court-curbing efforts have assumed a variety of other forms. Most often, bills or constitutional amendments are introduced to overturn specific decisions. And even introduction of a bill unlikely to pass sends a message.[23]

The executive branch possesses its own means of expressing dissatisfaction with Supreme Court decisions: refusing to enforce them. The Civil War period provided a striking illustration (albeit the order flouted was issued by Chief Justice Roger B. Taney as a circuit judge, not by the full Court). The case involved John Merryman, charged with sabotage and held by the Union Army at Fort McHenry in Baltimore. Merryman's lawyer obtained a writ of habeas corpus, but the Army refused to produce him, contending habeas corpus had been suspended on President Lincoln's authorization. Taney, believing only Congress could suspend the writ, issued an order of attachment for contempt against Fort McHenry's commanding general. Lincoln, however, instructed that the order be ignored. The Court's marshal was stopped at the gate to the fort and was unable to serve Taney's order.[24]

Thirty years earlier, when the State of Georgia in a dispute with the Cherokee tribe defied the Court's orders, the executive branch, in the person of President

Andrew Jackson, took no action. Georgia's defiance could hardly have been more direct: in one case, after it had sentenced a Cherokee man to death and Chief Justice Marshall subsequently issued a writ of error, Georgia executed him anyway. President Jackson reportedly commented, "John Marshall has made his decision, now let him enforce it."[25]

But a short time later, when South Carolina claimed the power to nullify federal laws, Jackson "did an abrupt about-face," embracing the Court. By 1957, when President Dwight D. Eisenhower faced Arkansas's defiance of orders implementing the Court's school-desegregation edict, public perception of the Court's legitimacy left him no option. He sent federal troops to Little Rock to enforce the desegregation orders, telling a news conference that "[t]he courts must be sustained or it's not America."[26]

Yet, the Supreme Court's vulnerability has been evident throughout its history. Eisenhower's statement about Little Rock coincided with Congress's angry assault on the Court in response to its decisions in McCarthy-era "Communist" cases. Justice Robert H. Jackson, whose tenure on the Court spanned World War II and the first part of the McCarthy era, was acutely sensitive to its vulnerability. The Court, he wrote, "has no force to coerce obedience, and is subject to being stripped of jurisdiction or smothered with additional Justices any time such a disposition exists and is supported strongly enough by public opinion. I think the Court can never quite escape consciousness of its own infirmities, a psychology which may explain its apparent yielding to expediency, especially during war time."[27]

The Court in Periods of Political Repression

Implicit in Jackson's comment is that when the Court "yield[s] to expediency," the elected branches have no need to curb it. Put another way, the Court is not necessarily under attack in a time of political repression, for an accommodating Court does not invite attack.

The clearest example is the World War I period. Between 1919 and 1921, the Court issued eight significant decisions in cases instituted by the government against critics of the war under sedition and espionage statutes. It decided all eight cases for the government, uniformly rejecting the defendants' reliance on the First Amendment.[28]

Seven of the cases were criminal prosecutions in which the defendants were charged with disseminating antiwar views in speeches or written materials. The eighth was an administrative proceeding in which the Postmaster General revoked the second-class mailing privilege of a newspaper, the *Milwaukee Leader*, published by German-American Socialists, which took an antiwar stance. One of the criminal cases involved a speech by Eugene V. Debs, a union leader and four-time Socialist Party presidential candidate. Addressing a party convention, Debs's "most egregious statement was '[Y]ou need to know that you are fit for something better than slavery and cannon fodder.'" His ten-year prison sentence was upheld by a unanimous Court in an opinion by Justice Oliver Wendell Holmes.[29]

A second case, *Abrams v. United States*, involved five Russian-Jewish immigrants, self-proclaimed anarchists, who published circulars, one in English and another in Yiddish, and threw some of them from the window of a New York City loft into the street below. The circulars criticized the U.S. government's dispatch of troops to Russia to oppose the Bolshevik revolution and called on readers to "spit in the face the false, hypocritic military propaganda." The Court upheld the defendants' prison sentences, which ranged from three to twenty years.[30]

This decision, however, drew a dissent from Holmes, joined by Justice Louis D. Brandeis, who articulated a clear-and-present-danger test in cases of direct restraints on speech. While this formula later became a fundamental part of First Amendment jurisprudence, the seven-justice majority in *Abrams* paid it little heed.[31]

The World War I decisions, Harry Kalven wrote, are "dismal evidence of the degree to which the mood of society penetrates judicial chambers." Concomitantly, public criticism of the Court was at a low ebb.[32]

In the World War II period, the Court again escaped serious criticism, albeit late in the period it decided several cases against the government. In earlier decisions, it denied habeas corpus protection to German saboteurs landed by submarine in the United States and held for trial by a military commission; declined to review sedition convictions of American Nazis who published a magazine opposed to the war; and, in the first round of Japanese-internment decisions, upheld the convictions of two citizens, one a University of Washington student and the other a member of the Oregon bar, for violating a curfew imposed by the military as a preliminary to internment.[33]

On December 18, 1944, one day after the War Department ordered the release of Japanese internees "whose records have stood the test of Army scrutiny during the past two years," the Court handed down its final Japanese-internment decisions. It upheld the conviction of Oakland-born Fred Korematsu for failing to evacuate the area in which his home was located, in violation of a military order. But it granted habeas corpus relief to Mitsuye Endo, a young Sacramento woman whom the government had interned but now conceded was "a loyal and law-abiding citizen." "There is good reason to believe," Geoffrey Stone wrote, "that the Court intentionally delayed its decision in *Endo* to allow the president rather than the Court to end the internment."[34]

However, in both the Civil War and McCarthy eras, political repression was at times resisted by the Court. In the Civil War period, Congress responded with a jurisdiction-stripping measure passed over President Andrew Johnson's veto (the one aimed at *Ex parte McCardle*) and a statute that temporarily decreased the size of the Court to deny Johnson the opportunity to fill a vacancy. In the McCarthy era, Congress only narrowly failed to enact jurisdiction-stripping legislation and a host of other bills to overturn specific decisions, and one important bill did pass.[35]

Court-Curbing Rationales, Judicial Activism, and Restraint

Over many years, and in widely differing circumstances, the rationales put forward for measures to curb the Supreme Court have remained the same. The justices, it is said, have acted as a "super-legislature," not accountable to the people. They decided "political" questions instead of limiting themselves to "legal" issues. They imposed their own personal preferences, rather than applying the law. "Activist" judges, it is said, must be replaced by judges who are "strict constructionists" and who exercise "judicial restraint."[36]

Complaints such as these, however, have invariably masked disputes over policy. The dispute in the 1930s, for example, was between a conservative Court majority hostile to New Deal economic policies—surely an "activist" Court, given the number of statutes it nullified and the creativity of its rationales—and liberals controlling both elective branches who believed economic reform was essential to combat the Great Depression. Three decades later, the liberal Warren court—which interpreted the Constitution to prohibit "separate but equal" public schools, to impose a "one man, one vote" requirement in elections, and to require specific rules for in-custody interrogation of state criminal defendants—was condemned as "activist" by conservatives who disagreed from a policy standpoint.[37]

When, in 1969, Warren E. Burger succeeded Warren as chief justice, his appointment by President Richard M. Nixon was hailed by conservatives as evidence that "Mr. Nixon had carried out his campaign promise to name 'strict constructionists' to the high court, jurists who . . . would not try to 'legislate' by their decisions." But fourteen years later, and after three more Nixon appointments to the Court and one by his Republican successor, Gerald Ford, an observer concluded that "by almost any measure the Burger Court has been an activist court." "In sixteen terms," Vincent Blasi wrote, "the Warren Court invalidated nineteen provisions of federal statutes; in thirteen terms the Burger Court has struck down twenty-four." The Burger court invalidated 309 state and local statutes on constitutional grounds. Its decisions included *Buckley v. Valeo*, striking down Congress's election-campaign spending limits as violative of the First Amendment, and *Roe v. Wade*, finding in the Constitution a woman's right to an abortion.[38]

In 1986, during Ronald Reagan's presidency, Burger was succeeded as chief justice by Rehnquist, an associate justice for fourteen years and a proven conservative. Rehnquist's seat was filled by Antonin Scalia, a conservative court-of-appeals judge. The Rehnquist court, between 1995 and 2003 alone, invalidated all or part of thirty-three federal statutes. Its Eleventh Amendment jurisprudence, Anthony Lewis wrote, was "breathtaking," "departing from constitutional texts," and "'legislating from the bench'" on a "wholesale" basis. It intervened in the 2000 presidential election, finding an Equal Protection Clause rationale to halt the counting of votes ordered by Florida courts and handing the election to a conservative Republican.[39]

Lewis, commenting on the Burger court in 1983, stated that "the great conflict between judicial 'restraint' and 'activism' is history," for "[w]e are all activists now," adding, "[a]ctivists for what is a different question."[40]

Nevertheless, no Supreme Court justice willingly accepts an "activist" label. Warren, in a 1958 opinion, gave this explanation for his vote to invalidate a federal statute: "The provisions of the Constitution are not time-worn adages or hollow shibboleths. . . . When it appears that an Act of Congress conflicts with one of these provisions, we have no choice but to enforce the paramount commands of the Constitution. . . . We cannot push back the limits of the Constitution merely to accommodate challenged legislation."[41]

Tactical Decision Making and Judicial Independence

Tactical decision making by the Court in the face of threatened court-curbing measures is another matter, for the issue then is preserving the Court's independence. The Court that considered *McCardle* in 1868 probably had not changed the views it expressed two years earlier concerning trials of civilians by military courts; but by acquiescing in Congress's withdrawal of its jurisdiction over McCardle's appeal, it avoided further sanctions. The Court, moreover, did not abandon the fight; only months later, in *Ex parte Yerger*, it held that it did indeed possess habeas jurisdiction but via a different statutory route. Stanley I. Kutler concluded that "in the light of prevailing political passions, the Court's counter-response in the two cases indicates the quintessence of judicial independence and courage, besides being a clever bit of judicial strategy."[42]

In the McCarthy era, the Court, under attack and seeking to placate public opinion and avoid court-curbing legislation, employed a wide range of strategies. It evaded constitutional issues by ruling on narrow nonconstitutional grounds; ordered major cases reargued repeatedly to postpone decisions on inflammatory issues; upheld the constitutionality of repressive statutes but interpreted them as imposing burdens of proof upon the government that it was hard put to sustain; used short, unsigned per curiam opinions to maintain a low profile for controversial decisions; and, when court-curbing legislation was close at hand, retreated (although at most only two justices switched on the closely-divided court), deciding new cases in the government's favor and distinguishing (often unconvincingly) earlier contrary decisions. These tactics, hardly noble, served a purpose. The Court gave substantial if incomplete protection to unpopular dissenters in a period of repression while avoiding more confrontational decisions that would have jeopardized its independence.[43]

Richard M. Fried did not exaggerate much when he wrote: "[I]f anti-Communist extremism was the Dracula prowling the mid-century darkness of American politics, it was the Supreme Court that drove the fatal stake through its heart."[44]

The effort was prodigious. The McCarthy era spanned at least a dozen terms of court (in this reading, from the October 1949 through the October 1961 terms). The Court issued roughly one hundred decisions in "Communist" cases and, rarely unanimous, countless concurrences and dissents. Commencing with the October 1953 term, it took on a simultaneous fight against racial segregation in public schools, a bitter struggle that served greatly to increase its vulnerability. Its decisions in McCarthy-era "Communist" cases, scattered over some thirty volumes of the *United States Reports* and now mostly forgotten, set the stage for a later Court's more successful and straightforward defense of the First Amendment at the time of the Vietnam War.[45]

1

Defining the McCarthy Era

The more remarkable aspect of the McCarthy era is not that political repression occurred but that its duration and scope were so broad. A combination of circumstances and events following World War II, international and domestic, quite predictably held the seeds of repression:

- With the glow of America's victory still fresh and a period of peace and normality in prospect, the Soviet Union, a valued ally in the war, abruptly became a dangerous antagonist, forging a bloc of satellite Communist nations and seeking aggressively to expand its influence throughout the world.[1]
- The confrontation was not only military and economic but also overtly ideological. Soviet Communism proclaimed itself the wave of the future that would engulf and replace American capitalism.
- In the United States there existed a history of hostility to foreign ideologies and Communism in particular (for example, the post–World War I "Red Scare"), along with a visible and outspoken American Communist Party (CPUSA), which endorsed virtually every twist and turn of Soviet policy.[2]
- In the summer of 1948, public concern over Soviet espionage utilizing American Communists was triggered by the testimony of ex-Communist Elizabeth Bentley that she served, until her defection in 1945, as a courier for Soviet spy rings composed largely of American Communists employed in federal agencies. Her testimony was buttressed by that of another ex-Communist, Whittaker Chambers. The individuals they accused included Alger Hiss, a former State Department official who accompanied FDR to Yalta.[3]
- During 1949, control of China, with five hundred million inhabitants, was seized by Chinese Communists, who drove the U.S.-backed Nationalist government from the mainland.[4]

- In September 1949, the Soviet Union exploded an atomic bomb, shattering the American-British nuclear monopoly, an event hastened by Soviet espionage.[5]
- In June 1950, Communist North Korea invaded U.S.-supported South Korea, and the United States intervened militarily. In November, Chinese Communist armies entered the war. A tense and hostile truce ultimately ensued.[6]

While these developments signaled unmistakably that the Soviet Union and its allies threatened America's security on the international scene, other factors, pertinent to an accurate assessment of any internal Communist threat, received less attention—not least the character of the American Communist Party.

The CPUSA was primarily a political organization, one that openly took positions on public issues and often entered candidates in elections for public office. Harvey Klehr and John Earl Haynes wrote in 1992: "The party promoted communism and the interests of the Soviet Union through political means; espionage was the business of the Soviet Union's intelligence services. To see the American Communist Party chiefly as an instrument of espionage or a sort of fifth column misjudges its main purpose." In 1999, following release of the VENONA messages—a trove of coded Soviet messages, intercepted during World War II and decrypted in part, that confirm the involvement of American Communists in Soviet espionage—the historians wrote, "[I]t still remains true that the CPUSA's chief task was the promotion of communism and the interests of the Soviet Union through political means." In the 1948 election, the first presidential election following the end of World War II, the party was an energetic participant, supporting former vice president Henry A. Wallace, the candidate of the newly formed Progressive Party, who received slightly over one million votes, about 2.3 percent of the national total.[7]

Loyalty to the CPUSA on the part of the vast majority of individuals who joined it was demonstrably shallow. The average length of an individual membership was only two or three years; as a result, former members greatly outnumbered current members. Morris Ernst and David Loth, writing in 1952 and using FBI numbers, estimated that "some 700,000 men and women have left the Communist party in this country in the last 30 years." The CPUSA's "peak membership" around 1940 was roughly one hundred thousand; by 1950, membership had fallen to 43,217; by the end of 1951, to 31,608. The "hard core," Ernst and Loth wrote, "has been about 5,000 to 8,000." Only a tiny percentage of American Communists had assisted Soviet espionage, and almost none after World War II ended in 1945.[8]

CPUSA members, in any case, comprised only a fraction of the class of persons who became targets of McCarthy-era repression. Alleged "Communist front" organizations were a greater source. During the 1930s, many hundreds of organizations were formed to oppose fascism or race discrimination, or to support the interests of workers whose leadership often included party members and which cooperated with the party. "Most members of these groups," Geoffrey Stone wrote, "were not Communists, or even Communist 'sympathizers,'" but they "shared many of the same goals." By the time of the McCarthy era, most of the alleged "front" organizations were defunct.[9]

Whether a significant internal Communist threat existed in the postwar years was thus open to question. However, the widespread belief that such a threat did exist, and the related claim that liberal Democrats—New Dealers and their political successors—bore responsibility and could not be trusted to respond adequately, would soon become a reality in American politics. "McCarthyism," Jeff Broadwater believed, was "energized not by opposition to communism but ... by the linkage of Marxism with liberalism." It was also energized by bare-knuckle partisan political tactics.[10]

The Political Reality

Franklin D. Roosevelt died in April 1945, but the American political scene continued long afterward to be dominated by the animosities created during his long period in office. Conservatives viewed the New Deal years, commencing in January 1933, as a series of rebuffs at the hands of planners, intellectuals, and bureaucrats. Powerful right-wing newspaper chains and radio commentators, reflexively hostile to FDR, gave voice to their frustrations. The investigations of the Dies Committee, between 1938 and 1945, and afterward by the permanent House Committee on Un-American Activities (HUAC) convinced them that New Deal agencies employed scores of Communists.[11]

Conservatives were likewise convinced that liberal Democrats were responsible for America's troubles in the international arena. Soviet domination of Eastern Europe, they believed, was attributable to FDR's "sell out" at the Yalta conference, at the urging of advisors (such as Hiss) who were Communists. When China fell to the Communists in 1949, it became an article of faith among conservatives that Communists in the State Department had sabotaged the nationalist government and were responsible for the "loss" of China.[12]

FDR's successor, Harry S. Truman, a moderate selected to replace Henry Wallace on the 1944 Democratic ticket, did not achieve while in office the favorable (no-nonsense, "the buck stops here") reputation he generally enjoys today. In the early days of his presidency, Truman was widely regarded as ineffective and overwhelmed by the responsibilities suddenly thrust upon him. "Not in eighty years, not since Andrew Johnson, Lincoln's successor," David McCullough wrote, "had a President been the target of such abuse." In the first week of October 1946, a month before the congressional elections, his approval rating was 40 percent and, a few weeks later, 32 percent.[13]

In the 1946 elections, the first during Truman's presidency, Republicans gained fifty-five House and thirteen Senate seats, winning control of both houses of Congress for the first time since the 1928 election. In the campaign, the GOP made substantial use of the Communists-in-government issue, and Democratic liberals suffered the brunt of the losses.[14]

In control of Congress, the Republicans seized every opportunity to demonstrate the presence of Communists in the Roosevelt and Truman administrations and in the labor unions that supported them. The antiunion Taft-Hartley Act, enacted over Truman's veto, included a provision that in effect required all union officials to sign a non-Communist oath with penalties for perjury. GOP congressmen Karl Mundt and Richard Nixon sponsored legislation to require the CPUSA and its members to register with the government. HUAC, under its new GOP chairman, J. Parnell Thomas, went to Hollywood to investigate "subversion" in the motion picture industry.[15]

Truman, with the 1948 presidential election looming, sought to defuse the "Communist" issue. In March 1947 he instituted by executive order a "loyalty" program applicable to all federal employees. As an integral part of the program, Attorney General Tom C. Clark prepared a comprehensive list of "totalitarian, fascist, communist, or subversive" groups—by 1950 numbering 197 organizations; membership in or "sympathetic association with" a listed group was often decisive in determining an employee's loyalty. In July 1948, Clark's Justice Department indicted the CPUSA's twelve top officials under the Smith Act for conspiring to teach and advocate forcible overthrow of the government.[16]

At the same time, however, FBI director J. Edgar Hoover, who disliked Truman intensely, decided to go public with Elizabeth Bentley's 1945 revelations and those of Whittaker Chambers, who had given his information to the government in 1939. Hoover delivered the two as "friendly" witnesses to the GOP-controlled HUAC and a counterpart Senate committee, which rushed them to the witness stand.[17]

The Bentley-Chambers disclosures created a sensation. Bentley's charges related to the 1941–44 period. While Chambers split with the Communists earlier, he, like Bentley, named Alger Hiss, with whom he claimed a close personal relationship. The confrontation between the rumpled and troubled Chambers and the elegant and accomplished Hiss, who initially denied even knowing Chambers, was pure drama. Richard Nixon, a HUAC member, built a national reputation on his dogged pursuit of Hiss, aided greatly by covert assistance from Hoover's FBI.[18]

The story of the 1948 presidential election—Truman's seemingly hopeless position; his plucky, shrewd campaign; the overconfidence of his GOP opponent, Governor Thomas E. Dewey of New York; the *Chicago Tribune*'s election-day headline announcing a Dewey victory; and Truman's narrow, late-night win—is political legend. Less well known is the decision by Dewey, a moderate, to forego use of the "Communist" issue as a major weapon against Truman. When one of his opponents for the GOP nomination, former Minnesota governor Harold Stassen, urged outlawing the Communist Party, Dewey disagreed, saying, "You can't shoot an idea with a gun." In a major speech in September, he said, "[I]n this country we'll have no thought police. We will not jail anybody for what he thinks or believes."[19]

"[C]ommunism was not a very great issue in the election of 1948," Earl Latham wrote. "It was on the fringes of the contest, not at the center." Dewey "was no McCarthy," Hugh Scott, the GOP party chairman, said. "He thought it degrading to suspect Truman personally of being soft on Communism. He wasn't going around looking under beds."[20]

The subsequent "triumph of anticommunist politics" stemmed from Truman's 1948 victory. "Smarting from their losses, stung by the knowledge that they had snatched defeat from the jaws of victory," William M. Wiecek wrote, "Republicans determined to regain control of national politics, and seized on anticommunism," which "gave them an impeccably American platform from which to belabor Democrats as tainted with a foreign collectivism." According to Joseph W. Martin Jr., the veteran GOP House leader, Dewey's defeat seemed to prove that "the course of moderation had failed us once again," causing many to turn to "extremism." Robert A. Taft, Martin's bland Senate counterpart, commented in March 1950, only weeks after Joe McCarthy burst onto the national scene, that McCarthy should "keep talking, and if one case doesn't work out he should proceed with another."[21]

The GOP had useful allies in its effort. J. Edgar Hoover made the FBI's resources available to HUAC and McCarthy. Right-wing newspaper chains (Hearst, Patterson-McCormick, Scripps-Howard) trumpeted claims of Democratic perfidy, their reporters often the beneficiaries of Hoover's leaks. And Republicans were joined by a loose amalgam of "professional anti-communists"—Richard Gid Powers called them "counter-subversives." Previously on the fringes of GOP politics, some obviously paranoid about the internal Communist threat, the "counter-subversives" now moved into the GOP mainstream.[22]

No sooner were the 1948 elections over when "the gods showered [the GOP] with golden opportunities." In January 1949, China was "lost"; in March, Judith Coplon, a Justice Department employee, was arrested and charged with spying for the Soviets; in September, the Soviets exploded their first atomic bomb; in January 1950, a federal jury convicted Alger Hiss of perjury; in June, the Korean War began; in July and August, the Rosenberg atomic-espionage case broke and the Rosenbergs were arrested; and in November, the Chinese Communists entered the Korean War.[23]

In the midst of these events, on February 9, 1950, McCarthy, a little-known

Republican senator from Wisconsin, made his Lincoln Day speech to a GOP women's group in Wheeling, West Virginia, a speech written for him by reporters for two right-wing newspapers.[24]

McCarthy's Role

McCarthy held the national spotlight for less than five years before suffering censure by the Senate in December 1954 and subsequent political disgrace, followed in May 1957 by death from liver failure at age forty-eight. He left behind no political movement, organization, philosophy, or significant writings. "If he was anything at all in the realm of ideas, principles, doctrines," Richard H. Rovere, an early biographer, wrote, "he was a species of nihilist; he was an essentially destructive force."[25]

What made McCarthy a force was a rough-hewn and blunt manner, which attracted both captains of industry and blue-collar Americans, and an extra-large ration of gall, ultimately his undoing. Rovere termed him "a skilled manipulator of public opinion, and something like a genius at that essential American strategy: publicity." Robert Griffith, another biographer, cited his "overblown sense of drama" and "talent for political invective." But, as Wiecek observed, McCarthy "opportunistically surfed the wave" of anticommunism; "he was not the wave itself."[26]

The highlights of his career are familiar. Born in modest circumstances in rural Wisconsin in 1908 and supremely ambitious, he was elected to the U.S. Senate in the Republican year of 1946, in part by exaggerating his war record. His first three years in the Senate were notable largely for his devotion to the interests of large corporations—journalists dubbed him "the Pepsi-Cola kid." In January 1950, "[a]s legend has it," searching for an issue upon which to improve his uncertain chances for reelection in 1952, McCarthy seized on a suggestion by Fr. Edmond A. Walsh, a Georgetown University dean, that he make Communists-in-government his issue—and he began with his Wheeling speech.[27]

What McCarthy evidently said in Wheeling (there was dispute later) was: "[W]hile I cannot take the time to name all the men in the State Department who have been named as active members of the Communist Party and members of a spy ring, I have here in my hand a list of 205—a list of names that were made known to the Secretary of State as being members of the Communist Party and who nevertheless are still working and shaping policy in the State Department." He had no such list. On February 10, in Salt Lake City, he placed the number at "57 card-carrying members"; on February 20, on the Senate floor, he referred to 81 "loyalty risks" (but he soon went back to 57). McCarthy never remotely proved these charges. But the specificity of his numbers commanded attention, and by the time his failure of proof began to catch up with his charge, he made a new charge. Announcing in March 1950 that he would identify "the top Russian espionage agent in this country," he named Professor Owen Lattimore of Johns Hopkins University, a well-known Far East expert, author, and occasional State Department consultant.[28]

Senate Democrats, who had regained control in the 1948 elections, concluded that hearings directed to McCarthy's charges—in effect "put up or shut up" hearings—were likely to discredit both McCarthy and GOP red baiting. During April 1950, a special subcommittee of the Senate Foreign Relations Committee, chaired by Millard E. Tydings of Maryland, a conservative Democratic insider, considered McCarthy's accusations in contentious, partisan hearings. The subcommittee's Democratic majority would find his charges false, "perhaps the most nefarious campaign of untruth in the history of our Republic."[29]

But in the interim "counter-subversives" had rallied to McCarthy's support and found a witness for him, Louis F. Budenz, an ex-Communist informer whom the government had used in its Smith Act prosecution of the CPUSA's top leadership. Budenz testified, on the basis of alleged meetings at which he said Party leaders praised Owen Lattimore, that the Johns Hopkins professor was in fact a Party member—one of the Communists who directed the State Department's China policy.[30]

Budenz's uncorroborated testimony was badly impeached at the hearings and rejected by the subcommittee majority. But the Republican members embraced it. "Whatever the probative value of the Budenz testimony," Griffith wrote, "it was greedily seized upon by Republican partisans as proof of G.O.P. charges of long standing, and by the end of April close observers discerned a steady growth of support for McCarthy from within his party." Budenz, Joseph Alsop said, was McCarthy's "rescuer-in-chief."[31]

With the backing of his GOP colleagues, McCarthy took the offensive. In the 1950 elections, he played a major role in the stunning defeat of his adversary, Millard Tydings, in the Maryland senatorial election, utilizing a faked composite photograph, assembled by his aides, that purported to show Tydings in close conversation with former CPUSA boss Earl Browder. McCarthy also appeared prominently in Illinois, where Scott Lucas, the Senate majority leader, was defeated by Everett M. Dirksen, a GOP congressman who ran on the "Communist" issue. A vote for Dirksen, McCarthy said, was a vote against the "Commicrat party."[32]

The Republicans, who gained five Senate and twenty-eight House seats in 1950, assigned McCarthy a major role in the 1952 campaign. Shortly before election day, he appeared on nationwide television to attack the Democratic presidential candidate, Governor Adlai E. Stevenson of Illinois. Seeking to tie Stevenson to the convicted Alger Hiss, McCarthy repeatedly referred to him, in a mischievous manner as if by mistake, as "Alger—I mean Adlai." On election eve, he told a nationwide radio audience that Stevenson was "hopelessly enmeshed in an intrigue to deliver the United States to the control of a Kremlin-directed Communist conspiracy."[33]

The Republicans scored a sweeping victory, electing Eisenhower president and Nixon vice president, and winning control of both houses of Congress. The election results, the *New York Times*'s Arthur Krock wrote, "indicated approval of the objectives of what the Democrats and independents have assailed as McCarthyism." As the new administration took office in 1953, McCarthy, reelected and now chairman of a Senate investigating subcommittee, was at the peak of his power and influence.[34]

But the election of a Republican president led to McCarthy's downfall. He continued to make Communists-in-government charges, notwithstanding that the government was now in GOP hands. As opposition to him began to grow in the Senate, he took on an ill-advised battle with the Department of the Army, precipitated by the Army's refusal to give preferred treatment to G. David Schine, a draftee employed on his subcommittee staff. The dispute led to nationally televised Senate hearings (the so-called Army-McCarthy hearings), the result of which was quickly to turn public opinion against McCarthy.[35]

In December 1954, the GOP-controlled Senate adopted by a wide margin a censure resolution directed to McCarthy's abusive behavior toward other senators and a respected Army general who was a witness before his subcommittee. Although McCarthy remained in the Senate until his death in 1957 and continued to have a faithful and vocal following in many parts of the country, his influence effectively ended with his censure.[36]

McCarthy-era Measures and Supreme Court Cases

The assault on liberal Democratic officeholders, culminating in the GOP's 1952 sweep, would not have been successful if public opinion had not broadly accepted the claim that internal Communist "subversion" posed a real and imminent threat.

Almost certainly the best measure of American public opinion at the time is an in-depth study of attitudes on "communism, conformity and civil liberties" conducted in 1954 by the Fund for the Republic, a unit of the Ford Foundation. The study confirmed the politicians' judgment that public opinion would support virtually any sanction imposed on Communists. Thus, 89 percent of the national cross-section believed that an admitted Communist should be fired from a college teaching job; 68 percent that he should be fired from a clerk's job at a store; and 63 percent that he should be fired as a radio singer. Seventy-seven per cent thought that an admitted Communist should be stripped of American citizenship and 51 percent that he should "be put in jail." And 73 percent thought it a "good idea" for "people to report to the F.B.I. any neighbors or acquaintances whom they suspect of being Communists."[37]

With sanctions against Communists enjoying overwhelming public support, legislators and government officials were quick to oblige. Within a few short years, an elaborate set of loyalty-security procedures, oaths, and penalties was in place at both the national and local levels—laws that would continue in effect long after McCarthy's censure and death. The sweep of these measures and their intrusiveness led to a brisk and continuing flow of cases to the Supreme Court.

Two federal statutes, the Smith Act, a 1940 statute sponsored by Rep. Howard W. Smith, an archconservative Virginia Democrat, and the Internal Security Act of 1950, sponsored by Sen. Pat McCarran, a xenophobic Nevada Democrat, were at the heart of the Justice Department's anti-Communist effort. The Smith Act, which made it a crime to teach or advocate forcible overthrow of the government, was utilized in a wave of prosecutions of CPUSA officials. One hundred twenty-six were indicted and ninety-three convicted. The Supreme Court in several major decisions considered the Smith Act's constitutionality and also the type of proof required to establish a violation.[38]

The Internal Security Act, enacted over President Truman's veto, was a hodgepodge of measures expanding espionage and deportation laws, with key provisions requiring registration of "communist-action" organizations (in other words, the CPUSA), their members, and "communist-front" organizations, and authorizing preventive detention of suspected "subversives." The registration provisions, implemented by a newly created agency, the Subversive Activities Control Board (SACB), led to administrative proceedings against the CPUSA and hundreds of alleged "fronts" and, in 1961, a Supreme Court decision on the statute's constitutionality.[39]

Federal-employee loyalty programs affected a large number of persons. During the six-year period of the Truman administration's program (1947–53), 4,756,705 individuals were screened for "loyalty" by checking their questionnaires against FBI records. As a result, 26,236 cases, most involving alleged association with "subversive" organizations on the attorney general's list, were referred to loyalty boards. Evidence upon which the government relied and the names of its informants were withheld from the accused employees—"hearings" usually consisted only of the employee's attempted proof of his own loyalty—creating legal issues that reached the Supreme Court.[40]

An executive order issued by President Eisenhower in April 1953, which replaced the Truman program, extended to every government agency a 1950 statute, previously applicable only to a small number of "sensitive" agencies, that empowered agency heads summarily to discharge employees in the interest of national security. The Supreme Court in 1956 considered whether Congress had authorized application of the summary-dismissal scheme to employees holding "non-sensitive" jobs.[41]

Three million persons in private industry, whose employers held Defense Department contracts requiring access to classified information, were subjected to loyalty-security screening under the federal Industrial Personnel Security Program. In the late 1950s the Supreme Court considered cases brought by defense-industry employees who had been stripped of clearances essential to their employment on the basis of "confidential" information from unnamed informants.[42]

An additional three million persons were screened by the military services, including all conscripts at a time when a "universal" military obligation existed. The Army, which received virtually all of the conscripts, gave less-than-honorable discharges to those it determined to be security risks. In 1954, abandoning its practice of basing an individual's type of discharge solely upon his record of military service, it began to issue less-than-honorable discharges to draftees on the basis of preinduction political activities—a practice considered by the Supreme Court in a 1958 decision.[43]

Thousands of other individuals, with no connection at all to the federal government, faced deportation or denaturalization (loss of naturalized citizenship) by reason of CPUSA membership. A provision in the same 1940 statute that contained the Smith Act made even past membership in an organization that advocated violent overthrow of the government a ground for deportation; in 1950, the Internal Security Act specifically made CPUSA membership, past or present, an automatic ground for deportation. The Supreme Court adjudicated a heavy stream of political deportation and denaturalization cases throughout the McCarthy era.[44]

Conversely, citizens deemed "subversive" were refused passports necessary for foreign travel. The State Department's Passport Office prevented hundreds of Americans from traveling abroad. The Supreme Court in 1958 decided two cases challenging the department's authority to deny passports on political grounds.[45]

State and local authorities joined actively in the hunt for "subversives." By 1953, thirty-nine states had enacted "little Smith Act" statutes. Some 150 municipalities by 1951 had also adopted some form of ordinance directed at "subversives." The Supreme Court, however, in a much-criticized 1956 decision, held that the Smith Act and other federal anti-"subversion" statutes preempted parallel state or local legislation.[46]

States and localities remained free, however, to impose loyalty-security screening on their own employees and on persons required to obtain state licenses—and they did so with alacrity. About 80 percent of the roughly one million public-school teachers were required to take loyalty oaths, as were a large number of college professors in public institutions. More than two million "nonprofessional" employees were subject to similar requirements. The oaths generally required employees to swear they were not CPUSA members. The Supreme Court in the 1950s decided a series of cases involving loyalty oaths required of public employees and employee discharges stemming from refusals to disclose political associations.[47]

Law school graduates seeking admission to the bar received loyalty-security screening in about one-third of the states. The Supreme Court decided several cases of applicants denied admission to a state bar by reason of past political associations or a refusal to disclose them.[48]

Perhaps the single largest category of "Communist" cases decided by the Court were contempt prosecutions of witnesses before investigative committees—most frequently HUAC. An accused individual, compelled by subpoena to appear, was customarily asked whether he was now or had ever been a member of the Communist Party and (if so) to disclose the names of political associates. Refusals to answer were punished by contempt prosecutions. Witnesses who invoked the Fifth Amendment privilege against self-incrimination usually avoided prosecution but were labeled "Fifth Amendment Communists," resulting in lost jobs and ostracism in the community. In a number of decisions, the Court considered not only Fifth Amendment issues but also the extent to which the First Amendment offered protection to witnesses.[49]

The Era's Duration in the Supreme Court

Cases arising out of McCarthy-era laws and practices were not slow in reaching the Court. During its October 1949 term, the Court ruled on the constitutionality of the non-Communist-affidavit provision of the Taft-Hartley Act. It also issued decisions in three HUAC contempt-of-Congress cases and a deportation case involving a stateless war bride detained at Ellis Island as a security threat.[50]

The heavy flow of "Communist" cases continued throughout the 1950s and into the next decade. The era was by no means over by the October 1960 term—during which President John F. Kennedy took office—when the Court issued fifteen signed decisions in "Communist" cases, including rulings on the constitutionality of key provisions of the Internal Security Act and the Smith Act.[51]

In the October 1961 term, however, the number of "Communist" decisions dropped sharply. And, after the term ended, Felix Frankfurter, who following the surge of court-curbing bills in the Congress became the leader of a five-justice majority that consistently acquiesced in government action, retired due to a stroke. Kennedy appointed in his place Arthur J. Goldberg, a liberal judge more inclined to vote to protect individual rights, tipping the balance on the closely divided Court. In the years that followed, a new majority decided the diminishing number of "Communist" cases overwhelmingly against the government and, unlike in the McCarthy era, frequently on broad constitutional grounds.[52]

There was no bright line, but an observer might fairly say that in the summer of 1962 the Court's McCarthy era, after thirteen terms, came to a close.

2

The Justices of the Vinson Court, *Douds*, and the Start of the Court's McCarthy Era

(OCTOBER TERM 1949)

When, on Monday, October 3, 1949, the Supreme Court convened for its new term, one new justice was present, and the chairs of two other justices were vacant. One of those absent was William O. Douglas who, riding horseback in the Cascade Mountains of Washington state on the final day of his summer vacation, was thrown from his horse and suffered multiple broken ribs and a punctured lung. The other vacant chair, draped in black, belonged to Wiley B. Rutledge, who died three weeks earlier at age fifty-five after a cerebral hemorrhage; his replacement, Sherman Minton, had been nominated by President Truman but not yet confirmed by the Senate. The new justice was Tom C. Clark, whom Truman appointed to fill the seat of Frank Murphy, who died in July at age fifty-nine of a heart attack. Chief Justice Fred M. Vinson, beginning his fourth term as the Court's titular leader, briefly and gracefully eulogized the deceased justices. They had been, by most accounts, the Court's most zealous defenders of civil liberties.[1]

The beginnings of what would soon be a heavy flow of "Communist" cases either awaited action by the Court or was in the pipeline. On October 10, the term's first argument day, the justices heard argument in a lawsuit challenging the constitutionality of the Taft-Hartley Act's non-Communist affidavit requirement. Four days later, at the conclusion of a nine-month trial, a federal jury in New York City found eleven top CPUSA leaders, including Eugene Dennis, its general secretary, guilty of conspiring to teach and advocate forceful overthrow of the government in violation of the Smith Act. "Government attorneys have long been seeking a clear-cut test of the Smith Act," the *New York Times* reported, "and they are confident that the conviction will be upheld when, finally, it is appealed to the Supreme Court."[2]

The Smith Act convictions would not be considered by the Court until the 1950 term, but several defendants in the case were parties to other cases already before the Court. One case involved prison sentences for contempt of court imposed on three defendants for alleged misbehavior during the Smith Act trial. The Court, however, denied review. Another was Eugene Dennis's contempt-of-Congress conviction for failing to appear in response to a HUAC subpoena, which the Court did review.[3]

Dennis's case was one of three contempt-of-Congress cases, all arising from HUAC hearings, decided in the 1949 term. The Court also decided the first of the stream of deportation cases it would review.[4]

The Composition of the Vinson Court

The deaths of Murphy and Rutledge left a Court markedly different from the one that had adjourned the preceding June. The two justices, along with Douglas and Hugo L. Black, had comprised a liberal bloc led by Black, able themselves under the Court's "rule of four" to grant certiorari (plenary review of a case) and with only one added vote to command the result. With their replacement by Clark and Minton, both of whom customarily deferred to government action, a new five-justice conservative majority emerged in "Communist" cases—one that would prevail for the remainder of the Vinson court's tenure—consisting of the new justices, Vinson, and Harold H. Burton, all Truman appointees, and Stanley F. Reed, a Roosevelt holdover. Black and Douglas would continue to cast liberal votes, but now they were often isolated. The votes of the remaining justices, Felix Frankfurter and Robert H. Jackson, were difficult to predict.[5]

At the time of his death, four and one-half years earlier, FDR had chosen seven of the nine sitting justices and promoted an eighth, Harlan F. Stone, a Coolidge appointee, from associate to chief justice. In October 1949, five of his appointees remained, and Stone had been succeeded as chief justice by Vinson. The Vinson court, Michal Belknap wrote, had a "well-deserved reputation for mediocrity." Yet four of its five Roosevelt appointees—Black, Frankfurter, Douglas, and Jackson—were by no stretch of the imagination mediocre. Each was a brilliant jurist who left an imprint on the Court's history.[6]

Black, an Alabama trial lawyer whose soft, Southern drawl masked a steely determination, came by way of the Senate, where he served for ten years prior to joining the Court, at age fifty-one, in August 1937. The son of a small-town shopkeeper, he did not go to college but did attend the law school at the University of Alabama, which then had only forty students in its entering class and three faculty members. A voracious reader, Black was to some "an absolute anomaly—an intellectual leftist liberal from below the Mason and Dixon line." In the Senate, he became a New Dealer and a supporter of FDR's failed "court-packing" plan. When Justice Willis Van Devanter resigned in 1937, giving FDR his first vacancy on the Court, Black received the appointment.[7]

After Black's confirmation by the Senate but before he assumed his seat on the Court, a furor arose stemming from press disclosures of his membership as a young lawyer in the Ku Klux Klan. To quell the furor, Black delivered, two days before the Court's October 1937 term began, an extraordinary radio address to a nationwide audience—reportedly "the largest audience ever to hear a radio speech except for the abdication of Edward VIII"—in which he emphasized that he resigned from the Klan before taking his Senate seat and that his Senate record "refutes every implication of racial or religious intolerance." On the Court, Black was, for more than three decades, with very few exceptions, a champion of the rights of minorities and political dissenters.[8]

"He wrote opinions in a lean, hard-hitting style," C. Herman Pritchett wrote, "which often burned with the fire of an active social conscience." He "brought to the highest Court," Bernard Schwartz said, "a moral fervor rarely seen on the bench." He was "in the battle," Anthony Lewis observed, "not above it . . . a tenacious fighter." In Black's view (never adopted by the Court), the unconditional words of the First Amendment—"Congress shall make no law . . . abridging the freedom of speech, or of the press"—"do mean what they say" and not that Congress may punish speakers when courts find their words dangerous or that suppression is justified by other governmental interests. "[I]t is time enough to step in to regulate people when they *do* something," Black believed, "not when they *say* something."[9]

Frankfurter, FDR's third appointment to the Court (Reed was second), was an Austrian-born Jewish immigrant who did not speak English when he arrived in America at age twelve. Exceptionally bright, he attended Harvard law school and was a prominent member of its faculty, as well as a close advisor to Roosevelt, when FDR appointed him to the Court in 1938, at age fifty-six. The diminutive Frankfurter could be "charming, solicitous, witty, and outgoing," Melvin I. Urofsky wrote, but also "obsequious and fawning," "duplicitous and conniving." Fred Rodell termed him "the jaunty little scholar with the electric charm, the darting mind, and the hosts of high-and-low friends." Indeed, Frankfurter counted as friends not only FDR but also Holmes, for whom he had selected law clerks at Harvard, and Brandeis, with whom he had a three-decades-long "special relationship" ("half brother, half son," Brandeis said).[10]

An energetic supporter of liberal causes as a private citizen (his support for the convicted anarchists Sacco and Vanzetti was a prime example), Frankfurter was widely expected to bring the same viewpoint to his work on the Court. But he held firm opinions "about how the Supreme Court should do its job"—views he liked to attribute to Holmes and Brandeis. "It can never be emphasized too much," he wrote five years after joining the Court, "that one's own opinion about the wisdom or evil of a law should be excluded altogether when one is doing one's duty on the bench. The only opinion of our own . . . that is material is our opinion whether legislators could in reason have enacted such a law." Vincent Blasi termed him "the high priest of judicial restraint."[11]

Frankfurter's tenure was marred by a series of failed attempts to attract other justices to his leadership and points of view—attempts that created animosities within the Court. His initial effort involved Black, whom he undertook to tutor on judicial protocol even before he himself joined the Court. The process was repeated with a series of new justices, including Douglas, Vinson, and Earl Warren, who succeeded Vinson as chief justice. "[M]ost found irritating," Belknap wrote, "the former professor's loquaciousness, arrogance, and habit of lecturing less-learned colleagues on the law." When his advice was spurned, Frankfurter often responded with harsh criticism of his colleague's integrity and motives, voiced privately to other justices or to prominent friends. His antagonism toward Black and (especially) Douglas spanned decades.[12]

Douglas was FDR's next appointee, joining the Court in early 1939. Only forty years old, he was the second-youngest justice in the Court's history. Raised in Yakima, Washington, in genteel poverty by a widowed mother, Douglas attended law school at Columbia and several years later joined the faculty there, subsequently moving to the Yale law school. In 1934 he took a position in Washington, D.C., with the new Securities and Exchange Commission, where he became a commissioner in 1935 and the SEC's crusading chairman two years later. Ambitious and charismatic, Douglas became part of FDR's inner circle, playing in the weekly White House poker game. When Brandeis retired, FDR, who wanted a westerner on the Court, selected Douglas to succeed him. Although Douglas chafed at the relative isolation of a justice's life—in 1944 he received serious consideration in the selection of FDR's running mate and would have welcomed the change—he served for more than thirty-six years on the Court, longer than any other justice.[13]

During his long tenure, Douglas championed First Amendment rights, regularly voting with Black. But he "was a pragmatist," Lucas A. Powe, one of his law clerks, wrote: "[H]e left theory building to others." He focused on outcomes and wrote opinions that were often terse and seemingly hurried. Anthony Lewis, on the occasion of Douglas's retirement, described him as "an innovator who did not care how prickly his ideas or his words were" and "probably as much a loner as any of the 100 men who have so far served on the Supreme Court." Douglas's personal behavior, particularly his divorces and marriages late in life to much younger women, occasioned criticism and strained his close relationship with Black.[14]

Jackson, appointed to the Court by FDR in June 1941 at age forty-nine, was likely the Court's most gifted lawyer. Raised in upstate New York, he spent one year at Albany Law School and another year "reading law" at a Jamestown, New York, law firm, the last Supreme Court justice to qualify for the bar in this fashion. With the coming of the New Deal, Jackson went to Washington, where he became Solicitor General in 1938—arguing so ably before the Court as to elicit Brandeis's comment that "Jackson should be Solicitor General for life"—and Attorney General in 1939. When Chief Justice Charles Evans Hughes retired in 1941, Roosevelt appointed Stone, an associate justice, to replace him, and Jackson to fill Stone's seat. As a justice, Belknap wrote, Jackson "produced opinions that were both masterfully written and of lasting legal significance."[15]

His temporary appointment by Truman in 1945 as the chief U.S. prosecutor at the Nuremberg war crimes trials was a factor in what became a public feud with Black, one that damaged Jackson's reputation. The feud involved both Jackson's ambition to be chief justice and anger over Black's failure to recuse himself in a 1945 case in which his former law partner represented one of the parties. At the time of Jackson's appointment to the Court, press reports suggested that FDR would name him chief justice to replace the retiring Hughes. When, instead, Jackson took an associate justice's seat (with Stone, twenty years older, promoted to chief), he did so in the apparent belief that he was next in line. But Truman was president when Stone died in April 1946 and, amid reports of dissension on the Court, he named the well-respected Vinson, his secretary of the treasury, as chief justice. Jackson, in Europe when he got the news of Vinson's appointment, blamed Black and, distant from friends whose counsel he might otherwise have sought, reacted unwisely. He sent a cable to Truman that condemned Black's action in the 1945 case and then, in disregard of the president's request that he not do so, made public his charges against Black.[16]

Returning from Nuremberg, Jackson resumed his work on the Court, and he and Black restored a degree of civility to their relationship. But in subsequent years, he often allied himself with Frankfurter and shared his colleague's antagonism toward Black and Douglas. In McCarthy-era "Communist" cases, Jackson at times argued that the Communists' conspiratorial methods and goal of forcible overthrow of the government justified withholding from them the usual constitutional protections for speech and association. Yet, at other times, the powerlessness of individuals targeted by the government elicited his sympathy and eloquence.[17]

Reed, the other Roosevelt appointee on the Court, lacked the same flair and intellectual firepower and was also the most conservative of the group on civil liberties issues. One observer termed him "a solid, plodding worker," and another the "most conventionally law-minded of the Roosevelt Justices."[18]

The son of a locally prominent Kentucky family, Reed attended Yale as an undergraduate and studied law at the University of Virginia, Columbia, and the Sorbonne. He entered private practice in Kentucky and then, although a Democrat, went to Washington to work in the Hoover administration. He stayed on when the New Deal arrived, becoming Solicitor General in 1935, a position in which he defended New Deal legislation before an often-hostile Supreme Court, earning FDR's gratitude. Appointed to the Court in January 1938 at age fifty-three, Reed, whose stern countenance belied a kindly nature, earned the affection even of colleagues who disagreed with his views.[19]

As a justice, Reed was, Fred Rodell wrote, "a strong federal-government man, upholding its law and the orders of its administrative agencies, whether directed against wealth or against personal freedom of citizens." He found, Belknap added, "few if any limits to what Congress or the president might do, especially in the interest of national security." Reed deemed the Japanese-internment decisions, even in retrospect, "entirely correct," telling an interviewer, "Yes, these people were taken from their homes and concentrated in concentration camps, in a sense deprived of their property and businesses and homes, etc. But they were recompensed by the Federal Government for some of that loss."[20]

The four Truman appointees were all friends of the president who had worked closely with him either in the Senate or after he was elected president. None was an easterner. "[N]one of them," Urofsky wrote, "proved to be in the same league as the men Roosevelt had named to the bench." Most, Douglas believed, "reflected the small-town attitudes of conformity." "As a group," William Wiecek said, "they made little lasting impress on American public law."[21]

Vinson, like Reed a Kentuckian, served in all three branches of the federal government prior to his appointment as chief justice. The son of a county jailer (reportedly he was born in the front part of the jail), he attended Kentucky Normal College and Centre College, from whose law school he graduated. He was elected to Congress in 1921, becoming expert in tax legislation and later a supporter of the New Deal. Appointed to a federal appellate judgeship by FDR in 1938, Vinson left the bench five years later to direct agencies that managed the Nation's wartime economy. In 1945 Truman appointed him secretary of the treasury. A year later, following Stone's death, the president, convinced of the need to appoint as chief justice "someone off the Court" and aware of Vinson's "reputation as a person who could get along with almost anyone," chose him as Stone's successor.[22]

Vinson's seven-year period as chief justice was not a distinguished one. Belknap thought "he lacked the intellect to command the esteem" of the Roosevelt appointees who regarded him "as an intellectual inferior and a Johnny-come-lately." In Schwartz's view, Vinson "may have been the least effective Court head in the Supreme Court's history." But he was on the winning side, controlling the assignment of opinions, in the overwhelming majority of his Court's decisions. In McCarthy-era "Communist" cases, Vinson and the bloc he led largely acquiesced in government action. In his view, a former law clerk recalled, "[t]he government had to protect itself against communism and if these guys were communists at the trial, those were not tough decisions for him." The Court did not resist the era's repressive practices until Vinson's tenure ended.[23]

Burton, an Ohioan appointed in 1945 to replace the retiring Owen Roberts, was the Vinson court's only Republican. The son of an MIT professor, he was educated in Switzerland (he spoke French fluently) and was a graduate of Bowdoin College and Harvard Law School. A former state legislator and three-term mayor of Cleveland, Burton was elected to the Senate in 1940, compiling a record as a moderate. He served on Truman's Senate committee that investigated waste in wartime procurement, earning Truman's friendship and respect and leading to his appointment to the Court at age fifty-seven.[24]

Burton, Douglas commented, was "as conscientious a man as ever sat on the Court." Conservative in outlook, he regularly sided with Vinson and Reed in "Communist" cases. He "supported national security measures," one observer said, "because he subscribed to Cold War politics." There were, however, exceptions, such as his votes in favor of three organizations listed as "subversive" by the attorney general without a hearing, and former CPUSA members denied admission to state bars. Belknap termed Burton "a plodding pragmatist." But Urofsky thought him "a point of calm and stability, liked and even respected by all his colleagues."[25]

Truman's third selection was Clark, appointed to the Court in 1949 at age forty-nine. A Texan educated at the University of Texas and its law school, he served for six years as civil district attorney in Dallas County. In 1937, Clark came to Washington to work in the Justice Department, where he remained for more than a decade. During World War II, as an attorney prosecuting war frauds, he worked with Truman's investigating committee and, when Truman became president in 1945, was appointed attorney general. In that capacity, he promulgated an expanded attorney general's list of "subversive" organizations and made the decision to prosecute the CPUSA's top officials under the Smith Act. When Frank Murphy died in the summer of 1949, Truman chose Clark, whom Vinson had recommended, as his replacement.[26]

As a justice, Clark consistently voted to sustain the government's actions in "Communist" cases and, when the Court ruled the other way, wrote overwrought dissents. He "brought the fears of the Cold War to the Supreme Court," Richard Kirkendall observed, "and helped to translate them into the law of the land." But Clark wrote for the Court in cases striking down an Oklahoma loyalty oath that made no allowance for individuals who joined "subversive" groups without knowledge of their character and overturning the discharge of a college professor solely for invoking his Fifth Amendment privilege before a congressional committee. Truman later told a biographer, "[Clark] was my biggest mistake . . . about the dumbest man I think I've ever run across."

But Douglas believed that Clark had the "capacity to develop" and "grew in stature" while on the Court.[27]

Sherman Minton was the last, and probably the least distinguished, of Truman's appointees. An Indianan, born on a farm and raised in modest circumstances, he was educated at Indiana University and its law school and obtained a master of laws degree from Yale. Active in Democratic politics, Minton, who bore the nickname "Shay" and chewed tobacco, was elected to the Senate in the Democratic year of 1934; there, he was a staunch New Dealer and a supporter of FDR's "court-packing" bill. He also became a close friend of Truman, occupying an adjacent desk in the Senate chamber. Following his defeat in the 1940 elections, Minton was appointed by FDR to an appellate judgeship in Chicago, where he served until 1949, when Rutledge's death created a vacancy on the Court. Hearing the news, Minton reportedly hurried to Washington, obtained an appointment with Truman, and asked him for the job. Fifty-eight years old, he would serve only seven years.[28]

As a justice, Minton was an almost sure vote for the government, whether the issue was economic regulation or civil liberties. In "Communist" cases, he voted to uphold government action almost without exception. Some observers ascribed to him an adherence to "the philosophy of judicial restraint," not unlike Frankfurter's. But Minton's approach, his biographers conceded, "was hardly as carefully developed or well reasoned as the learned Frankfurter's." Rather, they said, "Minton's version rested on a simple principle that the Court should not undo the actions of the political branches"; his "more simplistic approach led him to read the Constitution almost exclusively as a document for majority will."[29]

These nine justices decided the "Communist" cases before the Court in the 1949 term.

HUAC Contempts

The first of the term's three contempt-of-Congress decisions involved Eugene Dennis. His case did not present the usual refusal to answer an "are you now or have you ever been a member?" question, for Dennis was admittedly a top CPUSA official. In March 1947 he voluntarily appeared before HUAC, which was considering bills to outlaw the CPUSA, but he refused to answer questions concerning his name and the date and place of his birth. HUAC then served him with a subpoena requiring his appearance two weeks later. Dennis's failure to appear led to his contempt conviction and a one-year prison sentence.[30]

The Washington, D.C., jury that convicted Dennis included seven federal-government employees. He had sought on that ground to have his trial moved from Washington but was unsuccessful. He then challenged for cause every prospective juror employed by the federal government. Dennis argued that government employees subject to loyalty screening in their jobs would as jurors be fearful of voting to acquit a known CPUSA official.[31]

The Court, by a 5–2 vote, in an opinion by Minton, joined by Vinson, Reed, and Burton, rejected his argument and affirmed his conviction. Only a year earlier it had held in a routine narcotics case that federal employees were not, absent evidence of "actual bias," disqualified from serving as jurors in criminal cases brought by the federal government. Although Dennis's contention was more narrowly focused—he was a CPUSA official at a time federal employees were subject to discharge if believed to have Communist sympathies—the Court ruled that "while one of an unpopular minority group must be accorded that solicitude which properly accompanies an accused person, he is not entitled to unusual protection or exception."[32]

Jackson, concurring in the result, wrote separately. He had dissented in the 1949 narcotics case, "warn[ing] specifically that the Government in these times is using its power as never before to pry into lives and thoughts of government employees." But he now objected to a "partial repeal" of the earlier holding "for Communists only." "[S]o long as accused persons who are Republicans, Dixiecrats, Socialists, or Democrats must put up with such a jury," he wrote, "it will have to do for Communists." Jackson did not explain how a juror's vote in favor of a Democrat or Republican could jeopardize his employment.[33]

The dissenters were Black and Frankfurter. Black wrote that "[g]overnment employees have good reason to fear that an honest vote to acquit a Communist or any one else accused of 'subversive' beliefs . . . might be considered a 'disloyal' act which could easily cost them their job." Frankfurter, invoking Hamilton's words in the *Federalist Papers,* found it unrealistic to expect "ordinary government employees . . . to exercise that 'uncommon portion of fortitude' which the Founders of this nation thought judges could exercise only if given a life tenure."[34]

The other two contempt-of-Congress decisions stemmed from a single hearing, at which HUAC sought by subpoena to obtain financial records of the Joint Anti-Fascist Refugee Committee (JAFRC), an organization created to assist refugees of the Spanish Civil War, which was placed on the attorney general's list in 1947. In one case the defendant was Helen R. Bryan, JAFRC's executive secretary, who had custody of its records but refused to provide them to HUAC, and in the other Ernestina Fleischman, one of JAFRC's executive-board members, who had neither custody nor control of the records. Each conviction was affirmed by 5–2 vote in an opinion by Vinson.[35]

In *Bryan* the defendant argued, invoking a federal statute, that her compelled HUAC testimony was improperly used as evidence against her at trial. The Court admitted that her case "comes within the literal language of the statute"—"No testimony given by a witness before . . . any committee of either

House . . . shall be used as evidence in any criminal proceeding against him in any court." But it refused to read the statute literally because, it said, that "is contrary to the congressional intent and leads to absurd conclusions." In his dissent Black, joined by Frankfurter, chided the majority for its "refusal to abide by this congressional mandate."[36]

In *Fleischman*, the Court ruled that an individual board member, even one without custody or control of subpoenaed records, has a duty to do "all he can" to assure compliance and that "the burden was upon [Fleischman] to present evidence to sustain such a defense." In dissent Black, again joined by Frankfurter, responded that "[r]efusal to comply with a subpoena to produce papers can be punished only if the witness has power to produce. It is a complete defense for him to show that the papers are not in his possession or under his control."[37]

The term's most significant contempt-of-Congress cases were two the Court declined to review—the convictions of Dalton Trumbo and John Howard Lawson, two of the Hollywood Ten, left-wing directors and screenwriters who defied HUAC's 1947 investigation of the film industry. Their cases presented a basic issue: whether an individual may be compelled by a congressional committee, consistently with the First Amendment, to disclose CPUSA membership—an issue the Court would not decide until 1959. At the justices' conference on April 1, 1950, four voted to grant certiorari; but at a second conference a week later, one of the four, Jackson, switched, leaving Black, Frankfurter, and Douglas one vote short. On May 13, Frankfurter wrote to Jackson, asking his vote in favor of rehearing in the two cases and citing the "intrinsic importance" of the question presented—to no avail.[38]

Deportation—Ellen Knauff's Case

Knauff, an exclusion case, was by no means a typical McCarthy-era deportation proceeding.[39]

Ellen Knauff, born a German Jew, escaped Hitler's Germany at age nineteen by marrying a Czech citizen, moving to Prague, and obtaining Czech citizenship. In 1939, following a divorce, she fled to England, joined the Royal Air Force, and in 1946 was honorably discharged. She returned to Germany to work for the American military government and married a discharged American serviceman employed by the Army in Germany—a marriage approved by American military officials. Knauff, who lost her Czech citizenship when she remarried and was stateless, arrived in New York in August 1948 with other war brides to pursue American citizenship. However, with no reason given, she was denied entry and held at Ellis Island to await deportation back to Germany. In May 1949, the Court granted review of her habeas corpus action, and Jackson as circuit justice ordered her release on bail.[40]

The issue before the Court was whether the government, acting under wartime regulations, lawfully excluded Knauff, without charges or a hearing, upon the attorney general's representation that her entry would be "prejudicial to the interests of the United States" and that he acted on the basis of confidential information "the disclosure of which would be prejudicial to the public interest." The issue was complicated by the War Brides Act, enacted in 1945, which as a reward to American servicemen made inapplicable to their alien brides a number of immigration restrictions, arguably including the regulations relied upon by the government.[41]

The Court, however, by a 4–3 vote, sustained the government's action. In an opinion by Minton, it ruled that the attorney general (it was Clark) acted pursuant to valid wartime regulations still in force and that his action was "final and conclusive." The Court stated: "[I]t is not within the province of any court, unless expressly authorized by law, to review the determination of the political branch of the Government to exclude a given alien." Nor, it held, did Congress create an exception for war brides.[42]

Black, Frankfurter, and Jackson dissented. The War Brides Act, Frankfurter argued, may readily be interpreted to provide an exception for war brides from the procedures utilized. Jackson, joined by the other dissenters, wrote that he was unwilling to "find that Congress has authorized an abrupt and brutal exclusion of the wife of an American citizen without a hearing." He added: "The plea that evidence of guilt must be secret is abhorrent to free men, because it provides a cloak for the malevolent, the misinformed, the meddlesome, and the corrupt to play the role of informer undetected and uncorrected."[43]

Knauff's odyssey, however, was not over. Although she was returned to Ellis Island, her cause elicited support from the *St. Louis Post-Dispatch*, leading to the introduction of private bills in her behalf in both houses of Congress. Her lawyers filed a new habeas corpus action based upon the pendency of the private bills and the executive's unwritten practice of not deporting aliens who are the subjects of private bills. But, in May 1950, immediately after a lower-court decision adverse to her, the government rushed Knauff to the airport to be placed aboard a flight to Frankfurt. With twenty minutes left before the flight departed, Jackson signed a stay order pending Supreme Court review. "To stand between the individual and arbitrary action by the Government," he wrote, "is the highest function of this Court."[44]

The Justice Department, under pressure, agreed in January 1951 to give Knauff a hearing before an Immigration & Naturalization Service (INS) inquiry board. When she first sought entry, then–Attorney General Clark had charged in an internal letter that she "was formerly a paid agent of the Czechoslovakian Government and reported on American personnel assigned to" the Army unit in Germany for which she worked. At the INS hearing, the government produced as a witness a former Czech military officer who testified that Knauff was present on several occasions at the Czechoslovak Liaison Mission in Frankfurt—she testified she was there to try to maintain her expiring Czech passport. The officer, who had worked at the mission, said he had been told by a colleague that Knauff was "a very valuable source of information." The inquiry board ruled against her, but an INS appeals board found that "all we have in this case is hearsay, uncorroborated by direct evidence." When J. Howard McGrath, Clark's successor as attorney general, approved the appeals board's decision, Knauff "came ashore at Manhattan from Ellis Island."[45]

The Court's decision, Jackson wrote later, "was a near miss, saved by further administrative and congressional hearings from perpetuating an injustice."[46]

Taft-Hartley Non-Communist Oath—*Douds*

Douds was the term's most important decision.[47]

Section 9(h) of the Taft-Hartley Act, assertedly aimed at preventing "political strikes" by Communist-dominated unions, made it next to impossible for CPUSA members to hold union office. The mechanism employed was an oath: in order to utilize essential federal labor-law remedies, a union was required to file with the NLRB affidavits signed by each of its officers stating that "he is not a member of the Communist Party or affiliated with such party" and "does not believe in . . . the overthrow of the United States Government by force or by any illegal or unconstitutional methods."[48]

A six-justice Court, in an opinion by Vinson, upheld this provision against a claim that it infringed the First Amendment rights of union officers. The Court found that Congress's power to regulate interstate commerce authorized it to prevent "political strikes" and that it "could rationally find" that the CPUSA, unlike other political parties, used union leadership positions to obstruct commerce for "political advantage."[49]

The Court recognized that the statute "undeniably discouraged the lawful exercise of political freedoms," but it declined to apply a clear-and-present-danger test "requiring a showing of imminent danger to the security of the Nation." The oath provision, it stated, "is designed to protect the public not against what Communists . . . advocate or believe, but against what Congress has concluded they have done and are likely to do again." Where "particular conduct" is thus regulated and "the regulation results in an indirect, conditional, partial abridgment of speech," the Court said, a balancing test should be used "to determine which of these two conflicting interests demands the greater protection"—a test it then decided in the government's favor.[50]

Jackson's opinion, concurring in part, bluntly stated his view that different rules may be applied to Communists. "If the statute before us required labor union officers to forswear membership in the Republican Party, the Democratic Party or the Socialist Party," he began, "I suppose all agree that it would be unconstitutional." However, notwithstanding that "those Communist Party activities visible to the public closely resemble those of any other party," he found "a rational basis upon which Congress reasonably could have concluded that the Communist Party is something different in fact from any other substantial party we have known, and hence may constitutionally be treated as something different in law." He identified at length the Party's "distinguishing characteristics," including the Communist movement is "dominated and controlled by a foreign government," "the Party's goal . . . is to seize powers of government by and for a minority," and "[e]very member of the Communist Party is an agent to execute the Communist program."[51]

But Jackson and Frankfurter, who also concurred in part, while agreeing that the "membership" and "affiliation" portions of the oath were valid, disagreed with respect to the "beliefs" portion—that the oath taker "does not believe in" forcible overthrow of the government. Jackson denied that government has "any power, on any pretext, directly or indirectly to attempt foreclosure of any line of thought"; Frankfurter added that "probing into men's thoughts trenches on those aspects of individual freedom which we rightly regard as the most cherished aspects of Western civilization."[52]

Only Black found the entire oath incompatible with the First Amendment. Responding to the claim that the CPUSA may be treated differently because it is controlled by a foreign power, he characteristically invoked history: "This was the precise reason given in Sixteenth-Century England for attainting all Catholics unless they subscribed to test oaths wholly incompatible with their religion. . . . And in our own country Jefferson and his followers were earnestly accused of subversive adherence to France."[53]

◇ ◇ ◇

The Court adjourned for its summer recess in early June. Its "Communist" decisions had made no political waves. In five signed decisions, it sustained the government's actions in all five.

By the time the Court began a new term in October, the Korean War had begun, the Rosenbergs had been arrested, and Congress had passed Pat McCarran's Internal Security Act of 1950 over Truman's veto. Most of the bill's provisions, the president said in his veto message, "have no relation to . . . real dangers"; its registration provisions, he predicted, would cause "no serious damage to the communists, much damage to the rest of us." But the vote to override was decisive, 57–10 in the Senate and 248–48 in the House. During the thirty-day grace period allowed under the new law, not a single organization came forward to register voluntarily.[54]

3

Dennis, the Attorney General's List, Loyalty Programs, Contempts, and More

(OCTOBER TERM 1950)

The flow of "Communist" cases quickened in the 1950 term, and the scope of the cases widened greatly. The Court continued to acquiesce in the government's actions, but not entirely.

During the term the Court addressed basic issues relating to the attorney general's list of "subversive" organizations and the federal-employee loyalty program. It considered contempt convictions arising from the refusal of three witnesses to give information to a federal grand jury in Colorado. It decided the first of a stream of state and city public-employee discharge cases, this one involving Los Angeles city employees. And it decided a First Amendment case in which a left-wing soap-box orator was prosecuted for refusing a demand by police that he stop speaking and two lawsuits for monetary damages brought under an 1871 civil-rights statute by individual targets of repressive action.[1]

By far the most important decision of the term, however, was *Dennis v. United States*, which reviewed the Smith Act convictions of the CPUSA's top officials. The First Amendment issue in *Douds* was the validity of a "partial sanction" for CPUSA membership, not a direct penalty. In *Dennis*, a direct criminal sanction—prison—punished speech and association. The clear-and-present-danger test was held inapplicable in *Douds*; but in *Dennis* its application was seemingly mandated, unless the law was to be changed.[2]

As the term began, Attorney General McGrath announced "immediate steps" to enforce the newly enacted Internal Security Act. The Justice Department commenced "a country-wide round-up" of eighty-six alien Communists, aimed at deporting them if accepted by their countries of origin and "failing that, to put them under the six-month detention provided in the security act." The Subversive Activities Control Board (SACB), the new agency created by the Internal

Security Act, began to compile, the *New York Times* reported, "a new and better official blacklist of subversive organizations."[3]

The Attorney General's List and the Federal-Employee Loyalty Program—*Joint Anti-Fascist, Bailey*

The first cases triggered by the old list of "subversive" organizations, the one compiled by the attorney general, had already worked their way to the Court. Three alleged Communist "front" organizations, placed on the list in 1947 without hearing or an opportunity to object, had sued for a declaration that the listings were unlawful. A related case involved the firing of Dorothy Bailey, an $8,000-a-year employee of the U.S. Employment Service, on loyalty grounds. Bailey was charged with being a Communist and active in a Communist "front" on the basis of undisclosed information supplied by FBI informants whom the government refused to identify, and whom she was thus unable to confront or cross-examine. The cases bristled with due process and First Amendment issues.[4]

The Court's decisions, however, did not resolve any of the constitutional issues. In *Joint Anti-Fascist,* which dealt with the attorney general's list, the Court ruled by 5–3 vote in favor of the three listed organizations (JAFRC, National Council for American-Soviet Friendship, and International Workers Order), but the justices could not agree on a rationale. Each member of the five-justice majority (Black, Frankfurter, Douglas, Jackson, and Burton) wrote a separate opinion, and only one of the five opinions attracted the vote of a second justice. In *Bailey,* the Court affirmed by 4–4 vote a lower-court decision upholding Bailey's firing and, in accordance with its practice when equally divided, issued no opinions.[5]

The opinions of the majority justices in *Joint Anti-Fascist* presented a variety of rationales. Burton's opinion was premised on a narrow, technical ground: the attorney general had prevailed in the lower court on a motion to dismiss, and a procedural rule required that in deciding such motions allegations in the complaints—here, the organizations' denials of Communist affiliation— be presumed true, making the attorney general's listing decisions arbitrary. Frankfurter's more straightforward rationale was that the listing procedure denied procedural due process: "[D]esignation has been made without notice, without disclosure of any reasons justifying it, without opportunity to meet the undisclosed evidence or suspicion on which designation may have been based, and without opportunity to establish affirmatively that the aims and acts of the organization are innocent." Douglas agreed. Jackson believed that a hearing was required, not for the organizations' benefit, but in order that federal employees who were organization members, and who might lose their jobs if the organizations were listed, could challenge the designations.[6]

Black alone argued that "with or without a hearing" the attorney general's list was constitutionally invalid. "[T]he system adopted effectively punishes many organizations and their members merely because of their political beliefs and utterances," he wrote, and "[t]his cannot be reconciled with the First Amendment." Moreover, he added, "officially prepared and proclaimed blacklists possess almost every quality of bills of attainder, the use of which was from the beginning forbidden to both national and state governments."[7]

The dissenters, Reed joined by Vinson and Minton, found no violation of either the organizations' or the employees' rights. In their view, listing by the attorney general was "'[a] mere abstract declaration' by an administrator regarding the character of an organization, without the effect of forbidding or compelling conduct" by it. Further, to allow the organizations to participate in the listing determination, Reed said, "would amount to interference with the Executive's discretion."[8]

The switched vote that turned the 5-3 majority in *Joint Anti-Fascist* into a tie vote in *Bailey* was Burton's. Although, as a result of the tie, no opinions were issued in the case, *Bailey* was discussed in the *Joint Anti-Fascist* opinions. Douglas described how Bailey's loyalty board, charged with evaluating the FBI informants' credibility, did not know their identity. "Without knowing who her accusers are," he said, "[Bailey] has no way of defending. She has nothing to offer except her own word and the character testimony of her friends." In Reed's view, however, the Constitution required "no more" than that the employee have a "fair opportunity to explain his questioned activities."[9]

The outcome in *Joint Anti-Fascist* was simply that the lower-court judgments dismissing the lawsuits at the outset were reversed, and the cases could now proceed in the trial court. Bailey's firing, on the other hand, was sustained.[10]

Though its actual impact was minimal, *Joint Anti-Fascist* aroused public concern. Government attorneys announced the next day that membership in the three organizations "would continue to carry weight in Federal employes' [sic] loyalty investigations." The *New York Times*, terming the decision "a bombshell," warned that it "clears the way for any of the 130 organizations on the official subversive list to demand a trial in Federal Court." Its influential columnist Arthur Krock wrote that the president was not "necessarily" obligated to comply with *Joint Anti-Fascist*'s "limitation on procedure" unless he "chooses to accept the limitation."[11]

Attorney generals continued for some time to add organizations to the list of "subversive" organizations without affording them a hearing. In April 1953, however, Eisenhower's attorney general, Herbert Brownell, in the process of adding sixty-two organizations, announced that "the organizations would have the right to protest such designation and ask for a hearing." The first "listing" hearing, obtained by the Independent Socialist League, which sought to remove itself from the list, did not take place until 1955.[12]

Grand-Jury Contempt—*Blau, Rogers*

The term's three contempt decisions, involving Patricia Blau, her husband Irving Blau, and Jane Rogers, arose out of proceedings before a federal grand jury in Denver. Each defendant refused to provide information concerning the Communist Party of Colorado, invoking the Fifth Amendment privilege against self-incrimination.[13]

Patricia's case was the subject of a rare unanimous decision by the Court in a "Communist" case. The facts were uncomplicated: Patricia, a witness before the grand jury, declined to answer a series of questions about the state Party—such as "Were you ever employed by the Communist Party of Colorado?" and "Do you know the names of any persons who might now have the books and records of the Communist Party of Colorado?"—on the ground that her answers might tend to incriminate her. The district judge, however, found the privilege inapplicable and held Patricia in contempt, sentencing her to a year in prison.[14]

The Court, eight justices (Clark did not participate) joining in a short opinion by Black, reversed. So long as the Smith Act was on the books, it found, Patricia "reasonably could fear that criminal charges might be brought against her if she admitted employment by the Communist Party or intimate knowledge of its workings." It was "immaterial," Black wrote, whether her admissions "by themselves" would have supported a conviction, so long as they "would have furnished a link in the chain of evidence needed" to prosecute her under the Smith Act.[15]

Although the decision was unanimous and in accord with settled principles of law, it caused public consternation. The ruling, the *Times* reported, "has brought questions, confusion, even dismay in some quarters. . . . There was wonder over the implications of the ruling." A *Los Angeles Times* political cartoon, reprinted in the *Times,* showed a hand carrying the sickle of "Communist Infiltration" entering America's august courts. Government attorneys told the press that "[p]rosecution of twenty-four persons pleading self-incrimination" would proceed because their cases "may not be identical with Mrs. Blau's." HUAC's acting chairman announced that he "does not believe [the decision] is applicable to witnesses cited for contempt of Congress."[16]

Irving Blau's case, decided a month later, was only slightly less clear cut than Patricia's, and the Court, by a 6–2 vote, reversed his conviction also. In an even shorter opinion by Black, the Court held, on the authority of Patricia's case, that the district court should have sustained Irving's Fifth Amendment–privilege claim when he refused to answer questions about the activities and records of the Communist Party of Colorado. But in his case there was a second refusal. Patricia had sought to evade service of the grand jury's subpoena, and Irving refused to disclose his wife's whereabouts to the grand jury, invoking the privilege that protects confidential spousal communications. This privilege claim too, the Court ruled, should have been sustained. Minton, joined by Jackson, dissented.[17]

In the third case, however, where the defendant, Jane Rogers, claimed the Fifth Amendment privilege only after first admitting her party affiliation, the Court, by a 5-3 vote in an opinion by Vinson, affirmed her conviction. Rogers testified she was formerly treasurer of the Communist Party in Denver and in possession of its books and records, but she refused to identify the person to whom she had turned over the records, stating, "I don't feel that I should subject a person or persons to the same thing that I'm going through." Jailed overnight, she was again asked the question and again refused to answer, this time claiming her Fifth Amendment privilege. But the Court held she had waived the privilege when she admitted her party affiliation and activities. "Disclosure of a fact waives the privilege as to details," it said, and once Rogers disclosed she had been Party treasurer, "disclosure of acquaintanceship with her successor" did not "increas[e] the danger of prosecution."[18]

In dissent Black, joined by Frankfurter and Douglas, argued that Rogers did not waive the privilege but rather asserted it "at the first moment she became aware of its existence." "Moreover," he added, "today's holding creates this dilemma for witnesses: On the one hand, they risk imprisonment for contempt by asserting the privilege prematurely; on the other, they might lose the privilege if they answer a single question."[19]

The outcome in *Rogers* was reached belatedly, for at the justices' conference a majority voted to reverse Rogers' conviction. Black prepared an opinion of the Court, not a dissent. But two of his majority—Jackson and Reed—deserted him, and Vinson's dissent became the majority opinion.[20]

Civil Actions for Monetary Damages

Two civil actions for damages under a Reconstruction-era statute originally aimed at the Ku Klux Klan—one against members of the Tenney committee, a "little HUAC" committee of the California legislature, and the other against individuals who broke up a public meeting held in opposition to the Marshall Plan—were rejected.[21]

The first lawsuit, brought by a former CPUSA member who had been summoned before the Tenney committee seemingly to silence his criticism, was easily disposed of. By an 8-1 margin, the Court, in an opinion by Frankfurter, held that Congress did not intend the 1871 statute to create civil liability on the part of legislators acting in an official capacity.[22]

In the second lawsuit, plaintiffs—members of a Democratic club in Los Angeles at which the anti-Marshall Plan meeting was held—alleged that five individuals wearing American Legion caps "by force and threats of force, did assault and intimidate plaintiffs and those present at the meeting and thereby broke up the meeting." The Court, by a 5–3 vote, held, in an opinion by Jackson, that in the absence of any claim that defendants acted to deprive plaintiffs of equal protection under the law, the 1871 statute was not violated. The Court saw only "a lawless political brawl, precipitated by a handful of white citizens against other white citizens." The dissenters interpreted the statute more broadly.[23]

The two decisions suggested that individuals seeking monetary damages commanded less sympathy from the Court than those seeking only to ward off adverse government action.

"Heckler's Veto"—*Feiner*

Irving Feiner's conviction presented classic First Amendment issues. A college student, he was arrested while speaking to a crowd on a Syracuse street corner to publicize a local meeting of Young Progressives of America, an organization that supported Henry Wallace's presidential bid. His speech, which included sharp criticism of the president ("President Truman is a bum") and the American Legion ("a Nazi Gestapo organization") and, before a racially mixed audience, an exhortation to black Americans ("negroes don't have equal rights; they should rise up in arms and fight for their rights"), induced a hostile reaction from some audience members and a police order to stop speaking. When Feiner refused to be silenced, he was convicted of disorderly conduct and given a thirty-day jail sentence. Black was "convince[d]" that Feiner was "sentenced to the penitentiary for the unpopular views he expressed."[24]

The Court, however, by a 6–3 vote in an opinion by Vinson, affirmed his conviction, finding that the police "were motivated solely by a proper concern for the preservation of order" and that their actions were not "a cover for suppression of [Feiner's] views and opinions." "[W]hen as here," it said, "the speaker passes the bounds of argument or persuasion and undertakes incitement to riot," police are not "powerless to prevent a breach of the peace." But Douglas, joined by Minton, stated in dissent that the record showed merely "an unsympathetic audience and the threat of one man to haul the speaker from the stage." "It is against that kind of threat," he wrote, "that speakers need police protection." "Here," Black added, "the policemen did not even pretend to try to protect [Feiner]."[25]

Feiner, Urofsky wrote, "validated the so-called 'heckler's veto,' by which evidence or fear of hostile audience reaction justifies silencing the speaker."[26]

State Loyalty Oaths and "Innocent Members"—*Garner*

Garner v. Board of Public Works, which reviewed the firing of seventeen Los Angeles city employees for refusing to sign a loyalty oath or a separate non-

Communist affidavit, proved particularly troublesome for the Court. In conference, five justices voted to reverse the state court's judgment sustaining the firings. But when the decision was issued, five justices had voted to affirm; two voted to affirm as to two employees and reverse as to the remaining fifteen; and two to reverse as to all seventeen. A Douglas opinion, which began as an opinion of the Court, ended up a dissent joined only by Black. An opinion by Clark, which began as a dissent, emerged as the Court's opinion.[27]

The oath, contained in a 1948 city ordinance, was unusually broad in scope, covering present, past, and future periods. All city employees were required to swear that they do not, have not, and will not "advise, advocate or teach" or hold membership in any organization that "advises, advocates or teaches" violent overthrow of the government. The affidavit referred to the CPUSA by name and required an employee to state "whether he is now or ever was a member" and, if so, the dates of membership. Two employees took the oath but refused to sign the affidavit; the other fifteen refused to do either.[28]

Seven justices (all except Black and Douglas) found the affidavit valid, merely an inquiry aimed at determining the employee's fitness to hold his job. "[P]ast loyalty," the Court said, "may have a reasonable relationship to present and future trust." The firing of the two employees who refused to execute the affidavit (notwithstanding they took the oath) was therefore affirmed.[29]

The fifteen employees who refused both to take the oath and to execute the affidavit were, anomalously, treated more generously, both by Frankfurter and Burton who voted in their favor and by the five-justice majority, which affirmed all of the firings. Frankfurter found the oath invalid because it failed to exclude "innocent" membership: "The oath . . . excludes from city employment all persons who are not certain that every organization to which they belonged . . . at any time since 1943 has not since that date advocated [violent] overthrow." Burton deemed the oath invalid because its retroactive character "leaves no room for a change of heart."[30]

The Court more or less agreed. While not invalidating the oath, it said it had "no reason to suppose" that the city would interpret the oath "adversely" to "those persons who during their affiliation with a proscribed organization were innocent of its purpose, or those who severed their relations with any such organization when its character became apparent." It "assume[d]" the fifteen employees would be given "an opportunity to take [the oath] as interpreted and resume their employment."[31]

Douglas, joined by Black, found the entire scheme unlawful as a bill of attainder. He relied on two post–Civil War decisions, which invalidated "test oaths" of loyalty to the Union imposed upon various professions. The same principle applied, Douglas said, whether the oathtaker "is a professional man, a day laborer who works for private industry, or a government employee."[32]

Garner sent a clear signal that loyalty-oath schemes cannot punish "innocent" membership. But at the same time it held that a non-Communist affidavit may properly be demanded of any city employee, whatever the nature of his job, to assist the city in determining whether he is "trustworthy" or "fit"—a rationale that would assume increased importance in later years.[33]

Dennis—The Smith Act and the First Amendment

Dennis was the term's climactic decision.

The trial under the Smith Act of the CPUSA's top officials, held at the Foley Square courthouse in lower Manhattan, was political theater. The defendants and their attorneys behaved belligerently, and the trial judge, Harold R. Medina, "combative, abrasive, sarcastic, hypersensitive," responded in kind. Medina held several of the defendants in contempt during the trial and, when it ended, imposed prison terms for contempt on each defense attorney. To control picketing or demonstrations outside the courthouse, New York City's police commissioner assigned four hundred police officers "to every session of the proceedings"—"the largest detail in police history to a court case"—and had "two patrol wagons . . . parked near the court house." The outcome of the nine-month trial, given the intensity of anti-Communist sentiment, was a foregone conclusion: the jury returned guilty verdicts after only seven hours' deliberation, and Medina sentenced all but one of the defendants to five-year prison terms.[34]

The *Dennis* defendants were *not* charged with attempting or conspiring to overthrow the government by force and violence. Rather, the indictment charged that they conspired to do two things:

> [first] to organize as the Communist party of the United States of America a society, group, and assembly of persons *who teach and advocate* the overthrow and destruction of the Government of the United States of America by force and violence, and

> [second] knowingly and willfully *to advocate and teach* the duty and necessity of overthrowing and destroying the Government of the United States by force and violence

in violation of the Smith Act. The prosecution's evidence did not show advocacy of acts of violence or sabotage. Instead, as Douglas, who alone among the justices read the record, wrote in his dissent:

> So far as the present record is concerned, what [defendants] did was to organize people to teach and themselves teach the Marxist-Leninist doctrine contained chiefly in four books: *Foundations of Leninism* by Stalin (1924); *The Communist*

Manifesto by Marx and Engels (1848); *State and Revolution* by Lenin (1917); *History of the Communist Party of the Soviet Union* (B.) (1939).

The books could be found in any large library.[35]

"[S]uperhuman wisdom and equanimity" would have been required, one observer wrote, for the Court, near the apex of the McCarthy era, to nullify Congress's law designed to deal with an internal Communist threat and to free the CPUSA's top officials. At the justices' conference, only Black and Douglas voted to reverse the convictions. In his contemporaneous notes, Douglas observed: "The amazing thing about this conference on this important case was the brief nature of the discussion—Those wanting to affirm had minds closed to argument or persuasion. The conference discussion was largely *pro forma*. It was the more amazing because of the drastic revision of the 'clear & present danger' test which affirmance requires."[36]

When the 6-2 decision was announced on June 4, Vinson, writing for a plurality of four justices, did apply a clear-and-present-danger test, but as Douglas forecast the test was drastically revised. Because, Vinson said, Holmes and Brandeis "were not confronted with any situation comparable to the instant one—the development of an apparatus designed and dedicated to the overthrow of the Government, in the context of world crisis after crisis"—he would not utilize their formulation that "no danger flowing from speech can be deemed clear and present, unless the incidence of the evil apprehended is so imminent that it may befall before there is opportunity for full discussion," a standard obviously not met. Instead, he adopted the modification of Judge Learned Hand, who wrote the court of appeals' decision in the case: "In each case [courts] must ask whether the gravity of the 'evil,' discounted by its improbability, justifies such invasion of free speech as is necessary to avoid the danger." Employing this modification, Vinson found that "the requisite danger existed" and the restriction of speech was justified. The element of imminence was thus removed from the test.[37]

Jackson, concurring separately, was more direct. He believed the clear-and-present-danger test was outdated and not worth revising. Holmes and Brandeis served on the Court, he said, "before the era of World War II revealed the subtlety and efficacy of modernized revolutionary techniques used by totalitarian parties." The Holmes-Brandeis test, in his view, should be "save[d]" for "the kind of case for which it was devised"—trivial situations—"[w]hen the issue is the criminality of a hot-headed speech on a street corner, or circulation of a few incendiary pamphlets, or parading by some zealots behind a red flag, or refusal of a handful of school children to salute our flag."[38]

Frankfurter, in his concurring opinion, urged near-complete deference to Congress's judgment in passing the Smith Act. Even in free-speech cases, he wrote, "reconcil[ing] competing interests is the business of legislatures, and the balance they strike is a judgment not to be displaced by ours, but to be respected unless outside the pale of fair judgment." "History teaches," he warned, "that the independence of the judiciary is jeopardized when courts become embroiled in the passions of the day"—a consideration never far from his thoughts.[39]

Douglas's dissent argued simply that the defendants' advocacy presented no danger. "This record," he stated, "contains no evidence whatsoever showing that the acts charged, *viz.*, the teaching of the Soviet theory of revolution with the hope that it will be realized, have created any clear and present danger to this Nation." Even if, he continued, the Court were to take judicial notice of every event relevant to an internal Communist threat, it could only find that "[f]ree speech has destroyed [the CPUSA] as an effective political party." American Communists, he said, "are miserable merchants of unwanted ideas; their wares remain unsold." "How it can be said," he concluded, "that there is a clear and present danger that this advocacy will succeed is, therefore, a mystery."[40]

Black, whose view of the First Amendment did not allow even a clear-and-present-danger limitation on speech, took a long-term view of the situation, expressing hope that "in calmer times, when present pressures, passions and fears subside, this or some later Court will restore the First Amendment liberties to the high preferred place where they belong in a free society."[41]

The *Dennis* decision, unsurprisingly, was widely hailed. Attorney General McGrath called it "a good day for loyal citizens and a bad day for the conspirators." "The First Amendment," the *Times* commented, "was designed to preserve our freedom and not to serve the purposes of a furtive conspiracy allied with foreign Governments to overthrow all freedom." The *Washington Post* termed the decision "the most important reconciliation of liberty and security in our time." And the *Los Angeles Times* added, "We are fighting Communism with blood and money on both sides of the world; now the Supreme Court permits us to fight it at home." "What the American press found most heartening about the *Dennis* decision," Michal Belknap observed, "was the fact that it seemed to pave the way for total destruction of the CPUSA."[42]

The Justice Department moved quickly to follow up on its victory. Two weeks later, it announced the indictment, on similar Smith Act charges, of twenty-one lesser CPUSA officials—soon to be dubbed "second-string Communists." The prosecutions were filed in New York City, Philadelphia, Chicago, and San Francisco. James M. McInerney, an assistant attorney general, estimated the number of Communists who ultimately would be indicted at "nearer 2,500 than 25,000." Actions would be begun, he said, in about forty judicial districts.[43]

The Court, in a related action the same day it decided *Dennis*, refused to review the contempt convictions and prison sentences imposed by Judge Medina on six attorneys for the *Dennis* defendants. Black and Douglas dissented from the Court's action—which may have encouraged the attorneys to petition for rehearing.[44]

Another consequence of *Dennis* was that, when the Court's formal mandate issued a few weeks later, four defendants jumped bail and became fugitives. Bail in the amount of $80,000 was forfeited, and bench warrants were issued for their arrest. The FBI announced that its "full facilities" were being employed in the search. The four defendants' flight would later generate additional work for the Court.[45]

The Court's decisions during the 1950 term proved only marginally more controversial than in the placid 1949 term. If *Joint Anti-Fascist* and *Blau (Patricia)* evoked criticism, *Dennis*, an unqualified win for the government in the term's most significant and most visible case, readily compensated. The 4–4 vote in *Bailey*, while not pretty, allowed the federal-employee loyalty program to continue unchanged. And *Garner* signaled the Court's willingness to uphold the numerous state and local loyalty programs. *Dennis* and *Garner* showed how isolated Black and Douglas were.

Nor had the series of events that fueled the McCarthy era ended. During the course of the term, the Chinese Communists entered the Korean War; the 1950 elections—in which McCarthy's doctored photograph drove Millard Tydings from the Senate—were held; and Julius and Ethel Rosenberg were convicted of conspiracy to commit espionage and sentenced to death.[46]

4

Deportations, Fallout from *Dennis*, and the Rosenberg Case

(OCTOBER TERMS 1951 AND 1952, SPECIAL TERM 1953)

The Court's decisions in the 1951 and 1952 terms again largely sustained government action. Deportation issues predominated, with the Court issuing seven signed decisions in deportation cases over the two-year span. Three other decisions were spawned by *Dennis*, two relating to punishment of *Dennis* defense attorneys. The Court also ruled on the validity of a loyalty oath required of Oklahoma's public-school teachers and on New York City's loyalty program for its teachers. And it considered for the first time loyalty measures applied by the Army to its draftees—in this case, a medical doctor.[1]

In June 1953, at the end of the 1952 term, the imminent execution of Julius and Ethel Rosenberg gave rise to a wrenching series of events. Two days after the Court began its summer recess, Douglas granted a stay of execution. The stay was sought by a stranger to the litigation on the basis of a legal issue not raised by the Rosenbergs' own attorneys, whose repeated efforts to obtain Supreme Court review had narrowly failed. Vinson, unwilling to allow postponement of the executions until the new October term, convened a special term the next day. The Court heard hurried oral argument and, sharply divided, vacated Douglas's stay. Frankfurter was unable to complete his dissenting opinion until after the Rosenbergs had been executed—a circumstance, he wrote, that "has the appearance of pathetic futility. But history also has its claims."[2]

The 1952 term encompassed the election in November of a Republican president and a GOP-controlled Congress, following a campaign in which Democrats were repeatedly accused of being "soft" on Communism. Joe McCarthy, reelected, assumed the chairmanship of a Senate investigating subcommittee. In 1953 McCarthy-era politics reached their high-water mark.[3]

Deportation—Seven Decisions

Three of the Court's seven "Communist" deportation decisions were issued in the 1951 term. The first, *Harisiades v. Shaughnessy*, decided three cases presenting the same issue: whether the government, acting under a 1940 statute, could constitutionally deport a resident alien because of CPUSA membership that ended prior to the statute's enactment.[4]

The three individuals were Peter Harisiades, a Greek national, who came to the United States in 1916 at age thirteen, and whose fourteen-year party membership ended in 1939; Luigi Mascitti, an Italian national, who arrived in 1920 at age sixteen and resigned from the party in 1929 after a six-year membership; and Dora Coleman, born in czarist Russia, who arrived in 1914 at age thirteen and was a party member during three short intervals, the most recent ending in 1937 or 1938—the Court termed her activities "not significant." Two of the three were married to American citizens, and all had American-born children.[5]

The Court, by a 6-2 vote in an opinion by Jackson, sustained the deportations, rejecting the aliens' constitutional claims. The Due Process Clause, Jackson wrote, did not shield an American citizen "from conscription and the consequent calamity of being separated from family, friends, home and business while he is transported to foreign lands to stem the tide of Communism," and "[i]f Communist aggression creates such hardships for loyal citizens, it is hard to find justification for holding that the Constitution requires that its hardships must be spared the Communist alien." As to retroactive application of the 1940 statute, the Court found that the Constitution's ex post facto clause applied only to criminal laws and that deportation, "however severe its consequences, has been consistently classified as a civil rather than a criminal procedure."[6]

In dissent Douglas, joined by Black, argued that resident aliens are entitled to due process protection and "unless they are free from arbitrary banishment, the 'liberty' they enjoy while they live here is indeed illusory." "Banishment," he wrote, "may deprive a man and his family of all that makes life worth while."[7]

A second decision the same day, *Carlson v. Landon*, involving five current CPUSA members, addressed the issue of bail pending deportation. The new Internal Security Act conferred discretion on the attorney general to detain party members awaiting deportation without bail. The five individuals, each a resident alien subject to a deportation order who had been free on bail, were taken into custody following the effective date of the act.[8]

The Court, by 5-4 vote in an opinion by Reed, upheld the detentions without bail. Due process, it found, was not denied "where there is reasonable apprehension of hurt from aliens charged with a philosophy of violence against this Government." Nor was the Eighth Amendment's ban on "excessive bail" violated, it said, because the Amendment "fails to say all arrests must be bailable" and "does not require that bail be allowed under the circumstances of these cases."[9]

The four dissenters stated different rationales. Frankfurter contended the act did not confer discretion on the attorney general to adopt a "blanket" policy of "denying bail to all active Communists"—"an abstract, class determination, not an individualized judgment." Burton disputed the Court's Eighth Amendment holding: "The Amendment cannot well mean that, on the one hand, it prohibits the requirement of bail so excessive in amount as to be unattainable, yet, on the other hand, under like circumstances, it does not prohibit the denial of bail, which comes to the same thing."[10]

Before *Carlson* was announced, Frankfurter tried vainly to persuade Jackson to join his opinion, a switch that would have changed the outcome. He explained to Jackson, "I do this not because I give a damn about these aliens even though I, though perhaps not you, might reflect, 'there but for the grace of something or other go I.' . . . It is because the Rule of Law seems to me more and more under threat."[11]

United States v. Spector, decided a month later, presented an atypical alignment of justices. The case involved an Internal Security Act provision that made it a felony for an alien subject to a deportation order to "willfully fail or refuse to depart from the United States within a period of six months from the date of such order . . . or willfully fail or refuse to make timely application in good faith for travel or other documents necessary to his departure." Efroim Spector, who immigrated from czarist Russia in 1913 and was ordered deported in 1930 for advocating forceful overthrow of the government, was indicted for failing to make "timely application" for necessary travel documents. A lower court dismissed the indictment, finding the words of the statute unconstitutionally vague.[12]

The Court, however, by a 5–3 vote, upheld the statute. Douglas, joining Vinson, Reed, Burton, and Minton, wrote the Court's terse opinion holding the provision not unduly vague "when viewed in its statutory setting." It declined to consider a second issue—whether the statute was unconstitutional "because it affords a defendant no opportunity to have the court which tries him pass on the validity of the order of deportation"—because Spector failed to raise it.[13]

This second issue was the basis for Jackson's dissent, joined by Frankfurter. "The crime consists of two elements," he wrote, "one, an outstanding order for deportation of an alien; the other, the aliens' willful failure to leave the country or take specified steps toward departure." But under the statute, Jackson said, the first element was not tried by a court; rather, there was an "administrative determination" by an INS official, "which then becomes conclusive upon the criminal trial court." Congress cannot, he argued, "subdivide a charge against an alien and avoid jury trial by submitting the vital and controversial part of it to administrative decision . . ." As to Spector's failure to raise the issue, Jackson (in a barb aimed at Douglas) said he "abstain[ed] from comment on this new squeamishness whereby the Court imprisons itself within counsel's argument." Black dissented on the vagueness ground.[14]

The decision was not inconsequential in its impact. The Justice Department estimated that "about 3,000 aliens, particularly 2,147 from Communist-dominated countries, could be affected by the ruling."[15]

During the 1952 term, two decisions reviewed the attorney general's exclusion from the United States, without charges or a hearing, of resident aliens seeking to return home. In both cases the excluded alien was held at Ellis Island and the attorney general relied on the regulation upheld by the Court in 1950 in Ellen Knauff's case. But in *Kwong Hai Chew v. Golding*, an 8–1 decision in the alien's favor, written by Burton, the Court distinguished *Knauff* on the ground that she was an "alien entrant" while Chew, a Chinese immigrant who resided in New York, was a "lawful permanent resident." It noted that Chew's job as a ship's steward required, and he had received, clearance from the Coast Guard. The attorney general's regulation, the Court held, applied to "'excludable' aliens" and did not authorize Chew's detention "without notice of the charges against him and without opportunity to be heard in opposition to them."[16]

Five weeks later, however, the Court, dividing 5–4, upheld the exclusion of Ignatz Mezei, a stateless Gibraltar-born cabinetmaker who had resided in Buffalo, New York, for twenty-five years. Mezei left the United States in 1948 to visit his ailing mother in Romania; denied entry there, he remained in Hungary for nineteen months until he was granted a visa by the American consul in Budapest and returned to New York. But he was detained without charges at Ellis Island as a security threat. Twice he was deported, once to France and once to Britain, and each time he was refused permission to enter; in all, seventeen countries refused to receive him. After twenty-one months on Ellis Island, Mezei sought his release on bail, and, when the government refused to divulge any evidence proving him a danger, the lower courts granted him a "conditional parole on bond."[17]

The government appealed this ruling to the Court and won. A five-justice majority, in an opinion by Clark, viewed the case as governed by *Knauff*. Mezei's twenty-five-year residence in Buffalo counted for nothing. *Kwong Hai Chew* was not applicable, the Court said, because Mezei's history "drastically differs": while Chew "pursued his vocation" at sea with "full [Coast Guard] security clearance," Mezei "simply left the United States and remained behind the Iron Curtain for 19 months." The Court shrugged off his rejection by other countries and indefinite detention at Ellis Island: "Congress may well have felt . . . that an alien in [Mezei's] position is no more ours than theirs."[18]

Jackson, joined by Frankfurter, viewed Mezei as a resident alien entitled to due process and delivered a stinging dissent. Mezei, he wrote, "who seems to have led a life of unrelieved insignificance, must have been astonished to find himself suddenly putting the Government of the United States in such fear that it was afraid to tell him why it was afraid of him. . . . [I]f the Government has its way he seems likely to be detained indefinitely, perhaps for life, for a cause known only to the Attorney General." Black, joined by Douglas, dissented separately.[19]

Mezei's case did not end with the Court's decision. A month later, after the *New York Times* interviewed him at Ellis Island, Attorney General Brownell told a bar group that he would study the case, and in February 1954 Mezei was accorded a hearing before an INS inquiry board. There, he denied he was ever a CPUSA member, although he admitted having been president for six months of a Buffalo branch of the International Workers Order, which offered life insurance and health benefits to workers but was listed as "subversive" by the attorney general (IWO was one of the three organizations in *Joint Anti-Fascist*). The government, however, produced two ex-Communist witnesses who testified that Mezei was a CPUSA member from 1924 to 1934, and the inquiry board ruled against him. But, in August, Brownell decided nonetheless to release Mezei "on parole," and, the *Times* reported, he "boarded a train for Buffalo, where he has a wife and four children."[20]

On the same day it decided *Mezei*, the Court ruled on a technical issue concerning the procedure for obtaining judicial review of a deportation order. Prior to 1946, the only remedy was a habeas corpus action; but in that year, Congress enacted the Administrative Procedure Act (APA), which granted judicial review to any person adversely affected by "agency action" unless a statute "preclude[s] judicial review." The APA remedy afforded a significant benefit: while a habeas corpus action required that the alien be in government custody, an APA proceeding allowed him to challenge his deportation order without having to wait to be arrested.[21]

The case before the Court was William Heikkila's APA challenge to his deportation order. Born in Finland and brought to the United States at the age of three months, Heikkila was a CPUSA member between 1929 and 1939. His action sought a declaration that the Internal Security Act provision authorizing his deportation was unconstitutional. The Court, however, in a 7–2 decision written by Clark, held the APA did not apply to deportation orders because an applicable statute "preclude[d] judicial review." The statute it relied on stated that the attorney general's decision ordering deportation is "final."[22]

Frankfurter, joined by Black, dissenting, argued that an attorney general's deportation orders are not final but rather "are voluminously challenged and frequently set aside" in the courts (in other words, in habeas corpus actions).[23]

INS's efforts to deport Heikkila continued years after the Court's decision. In 1958, with his case pending before a federal district court, INS agents arrested him as he left work (he was a draftsman for a San Francisco engineering firm), flew him on a U.S. Border Patrol plane to Vancouver, and held him there to await a flight to Europe. He landed in Helsinki, *Time* magazine reported, "with $11.50 in cash, no luggage, no topcoat." The district judge in Heikkila's case was outraged, and INS had to bring him back to the United States. Heikkila died two years later, still resisting deportation.[24]

The seventh deportation decision, issued the final day of the 1952 term, reversed the criminal conviction of Harry Bridges, the head of the West Coast longshoremen's union (the ILWU), for fraud in obtaining naturalized citizenship. The government had been trying since 1938 to deport the Australian-born Bridges, who entered the United States in 1920, on the ground he was a CPUSA member—which he denied. After a deportation order against him was reversed by the Court in 1945, Bridges applied for and obtained citizenship. But in 1949, the government prosecuted him for an alleged false statement in his naturalization proceeding—that he never belonged to the CPUSA—obtaining a conviction and five-year prison sentence. His conviction, if upheld, would lead automatically to loss of citizenship.[25]

The specific question before the Court was a mundane statute-of-limitations issue: the three-year limitations period for the crime had expired, and prosecution was barred, unless a wartime suspension-of-limitations statute applied. The Court, by a 4–3 vote in an opinion by Burton, held it did *not* apply. The suspension provision, it said, covered only "war frauds of a pecuniary nature or of a nature concerning property." Reed, joined by Vinson and Minton, dissented.[26]

After the decision, an INS official "hinted that there would probably still be an effort to deport Bridges." A new proceeding to revoke his citizenship, the official said, was not foreclosed by the decision. The government's effort ended in 1955 when a district judge, disbelieving its witnesses, found that the evidence Bridges was a CPUSA member was not (as required) "clear and convincing."[27]

State Loyalty Programs—*Adler, Wieman*

In *Adler v. Board of Education,* the Court considered a challenge to New York's "Feinberg Law," which authorized firing public-school teachers for membership in organizations listed as "subversive" by the state board of regents. The state said it was concerned that "propaganda can be disseminated among the children by those who teach them" and "is sufficiently subtle to escape detection in the classroom."[28]

In a 6–3 decision written by Minton, the Court upheld the law. Teachers, it found, "have no right to work for the State in the school system on their own terms. . . . [T]hey are at liberty to retain their beliefs and associations and go elsewhere." The Court added that "[o]ne's associates, past and present . . . may properly be considered in determining fitness and loyalty."[29]

Frankfurter dissented on a technical ground—ripeness. The lawsuit was filed, he said, immediately after the Feinberg Law was enacted, and the Court should refrain from deciding difficult constitutional questions on the "bare bones" of the statute without a trial record.[30]

Black and Douglas based their dissents on the First Amendment, with Douglas describing the prospect faced by New York's teachers: "Youthful indiscretions, mistaken causes, misguided enthusiasms—all long forgotten—become the ghosts of a harrowing present. Any organization committed to a liberal cause, any group organized to revolt against an hysterical trend, any committee launched to sponsor an unpopular program becomes suspect. These are the organizations into which Communists infiltrate . . . A teacher caught in that mesh is almost certain to stand condemned."[31]

The lead plaintiff in the case, Irving Adler, a math teacher at a Manhattan high school, was one of an estimated 378 New York City teachers "ousted by dismissal, resignation or early retirement" as "subversives." The city reinstated Adler's pension in 1977.[32]

In *Wieman v. Updegraff*, the Court, without dissent, struck down Oklahoma's loyalty oath because the words of the oath, requiring public employees to deny affiliation with any organization "officially determined" by the attorney general to be a "communist front or subversive organization," had no "innocent member" exception.[33]

As a result, the Court held, in an opinion by Clark, Oklahoma's oath "offends due process." Membership in a "subversive" group "may be innocent," Clark wrote, quoting FBI director J. Edgar Hoover's statement that "one of the great weaknesses of all Americans, whether adult or youth, is to join something." A group may be innocent at the time of affiliation, Clark said, only later to be turned "toward illegitimate ends" or a group "formerly subversive" may later free itself "from the influences which originally led to its listing." The Court described "the consequences visited upon a person excluded from public employment on disloyalty grounds": "In the view of the community, the stain is a deep one; indeed, it has become a badge of infamy."[34]

Frankfurter and Black wrote concurring opinions, each joined by Douglas. Black compared the McCarthy era to an earlier period of repression: "[T]he present period of fear seems more ominously dangerous to speech and press than was that of the Alien and Sedition Laws. Suppressive laws and practices are the fashion."[35]

Dennis's Aftermath

On the day it decided *Dennis*, the Court refused, with three dissenting votes (one unannounced), to review the contempt convictions of the *Dennis* defense attorneys; but it changed its mind at the start of the 1951 term. The switch was a consequence of Jackson's changed vote, which he explained in a memorandum to his colleagues: "The Government has instituted a program which threatens to put in the courts in different parts of the country many prosecutions of Communists. . . . If there are to be fair trials of these cases, it is indispensable that competent and fearless counsel represent the accused. . . . I think the difficulties of obtaining counsel in these cases has increased since we denied review and that it threatens to become impossible." He now proposed a "limited review" in the *Dennis* attorneys' case. The Court would only consider whether, under a rule of criminal procedure, it was proper for Medina, the trial judge, to decide the contempt charges summarily himself or whether the charges should instead have been decided by a judge "other than the accusing one and after notice, hearing, and opportunity to defend."[36]

Notwithstanding that its goal was to encourage lawyers to undertake "Communist" cases, the Court's 5–3 decision, *Sacher v. United States*, which Jackson wrote, upheld the *Dennis* lawyers' contempt convictions. The focus of the dispute was Medina's decision to await completion of the trial before punishing the attorneys for contempt. It was undisputed that he could have punished them summarily if he "had acted at once upon occurrence of each incident." But, the attorneys argued, after the trial ended there was no reason why another judge, one not personally involved, should not have heard and decided the contempt charges.[37]

The Court rejected this argument. If it were to require that summary punishment "be imposed only instantly upon the event," it said, there would be "an incentive [for the judge] to pronounce, while smarting under the irritation of the contemptuous act, what should be a well-considered judgment." However, given the Court's goal of encouraging lawyers to serve as defense counsel, it added this unusual assurance: "That there may be no misunderstanding, we make clear that this Court, if its aid be needed, will unhesitatingly protect counsel in fearless, vigorous and effective performance of every duty pertaining to the office of the advocate on behalf of any person whatsoever."[38]

Black, Frankfurter, and Douglas dissented. Frankfurter emphasized Medina's role in instigating the lawyers' contempts. "The conduct of the lawyers," he wrote, "had its reflex in the judge," who "acted as the prosecuting witness." Any reason for summary action, moreover, "ceased after the trial had terminated."[39]

Abraham J. Isserman, one of the *Dennis* lawyers whose contempt conviction was affirmed, was the subject of another decision by the Court during the 1952 term. This time the issue was disbarment. Isserman had been a member of the New Jersey bar, and New Jersey disbarred him after his contempt conviction was upheld. The Court maintained a Supreme Court bar, to which lawyers were admitted on the basis of membership in a state bar, and, under its rules, disbarment by a state resulted automatically in disbarment by the Supreme Court unless "good cause to the contrary" was shown. The issue in Isserman's case was whether there was "good cause" why he should not be disbarred in the Supreme Court.[40]

The Court split 4–4 on this issue, which under its rules resulted in disbarment. Vinson, joined by Reed, Burton, and Minton, rejected the view that Isserman, having received a six-month prison sentence for contempt and suffered disbarment by New Jersey, "has already been punished enough for his contempt." "There is no vested right in an individual to practice law," Vinson wrote.[41]

Jackson, joined by Black, Frankfurter, and Douglas, found "good cause" for withholding disbarment in the severe punishment already imposed. He added, "On the occasions when Isserman has been before this Court, or before an individual Justice, his conduct has been unexceptionable and his professional ability considerable."[42]

The same day, with Black and Douglas dissenting, the Court refused to review Isserman's New Jersey disbarment.[43]

A third *Dennis*-related decision, *Stack v. Boyle*, involved bail prior to trial for twelve "second-string" CPUSA officials indicted on the West Coast in the wave of Smith Act prosecutions that followed *Dennis*. The government opposed any bail on the ground that four *Dennis* defendants had jumped bail. It asked the Court to assume that each defendant "is a pawn in a conspiracy and will, in obedience to a superior, flee the jurisdiction." A lower court fixed bail in the "uniform amount" of $50,000 for each of the twelve defendants—an amount they contended was excessive.[44]

A unanimous Court, in an opinion by Vinson, vacated the lower court's ruling, holding that each defendant must receive an individualized bail determination. The Court extolled the importance of pretrial bail: "This traditional right to freedom before conviction permits the unhampered preparation of a defense, and serves to prevent the infliction of punishment prior to conviction.... Unless this right to bail before trial is preserved, the presumption of innocence, secured only after centuries of struggle, would lose its meaning." Bail "for any defendant," it said, "must be based upon standards relevant to assuring the presence of that defendant . . . to be applied in each case to each defendant."[45]

Vinson's lofty words may have reflected a concern similar to Jackson's fear that "Communist" defendants would be unable to obtain counsel. The availability of pretrial bail, like the right to counsel a basic attribute of American criminal justice, would soon be spotlighted in numerous Smith Act prosecutions.

Loyalty of an Army Doctor

The case of Stanley Orloff, a New York psychiatrist drafted into the Army, was indeed "a novel case." Too old for the general draft, Orloff was inducted under a statute subjecting medical doctors to the draft if they had received professional training at government expense. The statute contemplated that the doctors would serve as commissioned officers, and this had been the Army's unvarying practice. But when Orloff refused to answer questions concerning membership in organizations on the attorney general's list and invoked his "constitutional privilege" when asked if he had ever been a CPUSA member, the Army denied him a commission. However, it kept him as a private and assigned him duties as a medical lab technician. Orloff sued, arguing the Army was obligated either to grant him a commission or to discharge him.[46]

The Court, by a 6–3 vote in an opinion by Jackson, rejected Orloff's argument. "It is obvious," it found, "that the commissioning of officers in the Army is a matter of discretion within the province of the President as Commander in Chief." And while the doctor-draft statute intended that doctors be assigned medical duties, it said, the Army had "now" assigned Orloff "medical duties in the treatment of patients within the psychiatric field."[47]

In dissent Frankfurter, joined by Black and Douglas, argued that the doctor-draft law required that a doctor refused a commission "be discharged from the Army because Congress imposed the condition of such a commission on drafting doctors above the general draft age." Black in a separate dissent wrote that Orloff "is being held in the Army not to be used as a medical practitioner, but to be treated as a kind of pariah in order to punish him for having claimed a privilege which the Constitution guarantees."[48]

Orloff's case, while unusual, was not unique. Five weeks prior to the Court's decision, AP reported that a New Haven doctor, Charles A. Nugent, was drafted as a private and assigned to basic infantry training because of his refusal to list organizations to which he had belonged. An AP photo showed Nugent shoveling coal at a Massachusetts induction center.[49]

Rosenberg—The "Race for Death"

The espionage-conspiracy convictions of American Communists Julius and Ethel Rosenberg and their death sentences, the occasion for protests at home and abroad, were defining events of the era. At the Court, the case laid bare (perhaps more than any other) the pressures under which the justices labored and the divisions among them.

The case involved transmission to the Soviets of technical information relating to the atomic bomb, America's most valuable military secret, obtained by David Greenglass, an Army enlisted man assigned during World War II to work at the Los Alamos laboratory. Greenglass, Ethel Rosenberg's younger brother, and his wife, Ruth, became the prosecution's principal witnesses. While their testimony evidenced Julius's guilt, the evidence against Ethel showed not much more than that she knew and approved of her husband's activities. "From the very first," Ronald Radosh and Joyce Milton wrote, "the government's interest in Ethel was based less on her own alleged complicity than on the possibility that the threat of prosecuting her could be used to pressure her husband into a full confession." Following a series of ex parte discussions with government lawyers, the trial judge, Irving R. Kaufman, sentenced both Rosenbergs, parents of two small boys, to death.[50]

In their yearlong effort to obtain Supreme Court review, the Rosenbergs' lawyers submitted a stream of petitions for certiorari, rehearing, habeas corpus, and, near the end, stay of execution. The first of these, a certiorari petition filed in June 1952—arguing the case was tantamount to a treason prosecution but did not satisfy constitutional standards for proving treason—was denied in October, with Black, Frankfurter and Burton voting to grant it. Douglas, who could have provided a fourth (and decisive) vote, voted to deny review.[51]

The attorneys then mounted a collateral attack on the convictions, filing a § 2255 motion (a statutory form of habeas corpus for federal prisoners) in the district court, alleging misconduct by the prosecution. U.S. Attorney Irving Saypol, in the midst of the Rosenberg jury trial, had called a press conference— resulting in a front-page story in the *Times*—to announce the indictment for perjury of William Perl, Julius's college classmate, for falsely denying to a grand jury that he knew Julius and others in the case. Perl, Saypol told the press, had been expected to testify in the Rosenberg trial and to corroborate testimony by the Greenglasses but now, he implied, had backed out. The lower courts denied the Rosenbergs' motion, although the court of appeals termed Saypol's action "wholly reprehensible."[52]

The § 2255 appeal reached the Court in late March 1953. At the justices' conference on April 11, Frankfurter told his colleagues, "You have a duty to consider how this [death] sentence, and this Court, will stand in the light of history if you leave the cloud of these allegations hanging over the trial." The justices, however, again voted to deny review, over Black's and Frankfurter's objections. Frankfurter asked for time to decide whether to write a statement to accompany the Court's order.[53]

His decision *not* to write a statement was communicated in a memorandum three days prior to the justices' May 23 conference. "Considering the siege of fear which so extensively holds otherwise sensible people in its grip," Frankfurter explained, "it may well be that by setting forth the truth about Saypol's inexcusable conduct I might help make a hero of him." "[A]n even more important consideration," he said, was that criticism of Saypol might "lead high-minded and patriotic laymen who do not understand these things to believe that I implied that the Rosenbergs were convicted though innocent."[54]

On the day before the conference, Douglas circulated what Frankfurter termed a "bombshell memorandum," one that "obviously requires a reopening of the discussion at Conference." Douglas not only changed his position, providing a third vote in favor of review, but also said he would attach to the Court's order denying review a statement that he "agree[d] with the Court of Appeals that some of the conduct of the United States Attorney was 'wholly reprehensible' but believ[ed], in disagreement with the Court of Appeals, that it probably prejudiced the defendants seriously." He would, in other words, state that Saypol's misconduct "probably" deprived the Rosenbergs of a fair trial. Frankfurter, while personally critical of Douglas's action, used his memorandum to seek a fourth vote in favor of review. He wrote to Burton, arguing, unsuccessfully, that the Court should not "place itself in the position of being heedless to the pronouncement of a member of the Court that the pair were sentenced to death after a trial that violated the requisites of a fair trial." He also tried to persuade Jackson; but Jackson, who believed Douglas was grandstanding to a liberal audience in a case he knew the Court would not review, responded only with vitriol.[55]

The May 23 conference was chaotic. Douglas's memorandum, Jackson said, placed the Court "in an impossible position"—a member of the Court ready to say publicly "that the Rosenbergs had not had a fair trial"—and compelled him now to vote in favor of review. With the requisite four votes in hand, the discussion turned to scheduling argument. But after "quite some little time," according to Frankfurter, Douglas interjected that his memorandum was perhaps "badly drawn," that he "hadn't realized it would embarrass anyone," and "[h]e would just withdraw his memorandum if that would help matters." With that, Jackson switched his vote back, denying review. "And so Douglas," Frankfurter wrote, "when it was clear that the Rosenberg case would be heard because of [his] ... memorandum, kept it from being heard."[56]

A hectic series of events followed. Judge Kaufman selected the week of June 15 for the execution, and prison officials fixed June 18 as the execution date. On June 12, the Rosenbergs' lawyers sought a stay of execution from Jackson, the circuit justice, who referred the application to the full Court with a recommendation that it hear oral argument on the application. The next day, at their Saturday conference, the justices, by a 5–4 vote, with Douglas joining Vinson, Reed, Clark, and Minton, rejected Jackson's recommendation. A stay without oral argument was then denied, again by a 5–4 vote—this time with Douglas in favor and Burton opposed.[57]

On Monday, June 15, the Court convened to issue orders implementing these rulings and to announce its recess until October. Before the justices could leave their seats, John F. Finerty, a veteran attorney belatedly added to the Rosenberg defense team, asked leave to file an original petition for habeas corpus, arguing Saypol made "knowing use" of perjured testimony. That afternoon the justices voted 7–2 (the two were Black and Frankfurter) to deny Finerty's request. The Court then began its summer recess.[58]

The Rosenbergs were now reduced to seeking stay relief from individual justices. On Tuesday morning, June 16, Douglas received stay applications not only from the Rosenbergs' lawyers but also from Fyke Farmer, a Nashville attorney, on behalf of Irwin Edelman who appeared as "next friend" to the Rosenbergs. Edelman was "a self-styled pamphleteer and soapbox orator" from Los Angeles, "a loudmouth and eccentric" expelled from the CPUSA in 1947, who had been critical of the Rosenberg defense. Farmer had discerned a new issue which, the preceding day, he tried to argue to Judge Kaufman; but Kaufman refused to hear him, terming him and Edelman "interlopers" and "intruders."[59]

The new issue presented to Douglas related to the lawfulness of the death sentences. The indictment charged a conspiracy, from June 1944 to June 1950, to violate the Espionage Act of 1917; that statute authorized the trial judge acting alone to impose the death penalty. But in August 1946, Congress enacted the Atomic Energy Act, which authorized the death penalty for transmitting atomic data to foreign nations "only upon recommendation of the jury and only in cases where the offense was committed with intent to injure the United States." Because, Farmer contended, the Atomic Energy Act became effective during the course of the alleged conspiracy, its penalty provision applied; and since the Rosenberg jury did not recommend the death penalty and the indictment did not charge an "intent to injure the United States," Kaufman's imposition of the death penalty was unlawful.[60]

Douglas, impressed by Farmer's argument, worked on the issue all day and into the night. He spoke with several other justices: Vinson, who said that Farmer lacked standing to raise the issue; Frankfurter, who said the issue seemed to be "one that should be looked into" and advised him to do "what your conscience tells you, not what the Chief Justice tells you"; and Black, who read his opinion and offered encouragement. But Jackson, according to the FBI, aware Douglas was giving serious consideration to Farmer's application, "recommend[ed]" that Vinson meet privately with Attorney General Brownell; the two did meet and discussed reconvening the entire Court to overturn the stay if Douglas granted it. "Vinson said that if a stay is granted," the FBI reported, "he will call the full Court into session Thursday morning to vacate it."[61]

At noon on Wednesday, June 17, Douglas released his decision staying the Rosenbergs' executions, scheduled for the following day, until the applicability of the Atomic Energy Act's penalty provisions "can be determined," first by the lower courts. "I merely decide," he wrote, "that the question is a substantial one which should be decided after full argument and deliberation." He added: "I have serious doubts whether this death sentence may be imposed for this offense except and unless a jury recommends it." Upon releasing his ruling, Douglas left by car for the West Coast.[62]

Within hours, the government filed an application, signed by Brownell, asking the Court "to convene a special term to review" Douglas's stay order. An hour later, the Court announced that "[t]he Chief Justice directs that the Supreme Court will convene a special term of the Court on Thursday, June 18, at noon, in order that" Brownell's application "may be considered." Douglas got the news in Uniontown, Pennsylvania, on his car radio.[63]

On Thursday, the Court heard nearly three hours of sometimes-unruly oral argument. Farmer used his allotted seventeen minutes to argue the Atomic Energy Act issue. But Emanuel Bloch, the Rosenbergs' lead attorney, declined even then to embrace Farmer's argument, and Finerty spent time assailing Saypol and Brownell. Jackson, with lives at stake, inquired of counsel whether Irwin Edelman was the same individual "before this court last year in a vagrancy case."[64]

At the justices' conference that afternoon and the following morning, the discussion was heated, with raised voices heard outside the conference room. "We heard Frankfurter screaming in a loud voice," a law clerk recalled. "[W]e couldn't articulate exactly what it was, but it was Frankfurter's voice." Black said, according to Clark's notes, "This is a race for death.... This will be a black day for the Court. I *plead* that it not be decided today." Burton, Frankfurter reported, "said in effect that he would make a fifth if there were four votes either for upholding Douglas' action or for vacating [the stay] and making some other arrangements for hearing full arguments on the Atomic Energy Act point." But in the end, Frankfurter wrote, "there were only three—Black, Douglas and I."[65]

After the Friday morning conference, the justices took the bench to deliver their ruling. A per curiam order, written and read by Vinson and concurred in by six justices, vacated Douglas's stay. The new issue had been considered "on its merits," Vinson said, and found "not substantial." "The Atomic Energy Act did not repeal or limit the provisions of the Espionage Act." "[F]ull opinions," he announced, would be filed later. Jackson and Clark read short, concurring opinions, in which the same six justices joined.[66]

Frankfurter submitted a memorandum stating he would write more fully "[i]n due course," but Black and Douglas read dissenting opinions. When he issued his stay, Douglas said, "I knew only that the question was serious and substantial. Now I am sure of the answer. I know deep in my heart that I am right on the law." He thought it "too elemental for citation of authority that where two penal statutes may apply—one carrying death and the other imprisonment—the court has no choice but to impose the less harsh sentence." Black could find no "prior instances where vacation stays [stays granted during a summer recess] of individual Justices have been set aside by the full Court before the next regular term [in October]." "Surely," he wrote angrily, "the Court is not here establishing a precedent which will require it to call extra sessions during vacation every time a federal or state official asks it to hasten the electrocution of defendants"[67]

With the stay vacated, the Rosenbergs' execution was rescheduled for 11:00 P.M. that night. Their attorneys, however, deemed it unseemly that the Rosenbergs (Jews, albeit confirmed Marxists) be electrocuted on the Jewish Sabbath, and Judge Kaufman reportedly agreed. But the executions were not postponed; rather, the time was advanced by three hours so that the Rosenbergs could be executed minutes before Friday sundown. The FBI set up a "secret command post" at Sing Sing prison where they were held "should either of them show signs of wanting to confess." The executions were marked by vigils at the White House, where pickets "march[ed] four deep" and near Union Square in Manhattan where an estimated five thousand gathered, and by clemency pleas from abroad. President Eisenhower, refusing clemency, stated that "by immeasurably increasing the risk of atomic war the Rosenbergs may have condemned to death tens of millions of innocent people all over the world."[68]

Two opinions were filed later. Frankfurter's June 22 opinion addressed "the sole issue" whether the Atomic Energy Act claim upon which Douglas based his stay "was sufficiently serious to require the judicial process to run its course with the deliberation necessary for confident judgment." He concluded that "the claim had substance and that the opportunity for adequate exercise of the judicial judgment was wanting." Vinson's July 16 "opinion of the Court" explained that the Court refused to delay the Rosenbergs' executions because it had a "duty to see . . . that the punishments prescribed by the laws are enforced with a reasonable degree of promptness and certainty."[69]

"[T]he imposition of the death sentence and the Government's determination to see it carried out were powerfully and broadly supported in all parts of the United States," Arthur Krock wrote in the *Times*. Indeed, when the Court vacated Douglas's stay, Rep. Frank L. Chelf, a Kentucky Democrat, rushed to the House floor, interrupting debate, to announce what he "just read on the ticker tape." "Praise God, from whom all blessings flow," he said, "We thank the Supreme Court."[70]

Douglas's stay, Krock wrote, "enabled the enemies of this nation to besmirch" American justice, and "angry disagreement" with his action "is obviously widespread." In the Congress, within hours after Douglas acted, Rep. W. M. Wheeler, a Georgia Democrat, introduced a resolution calling for his impeachment—one specification charged treason—as House members "cheered and applauded." Chauncey W. Reed, the Republican chairman of the House Judiciary Committee, announced that Wheeler's resolution would receive a "prompt hearing." A special five-member subcommittee held hearings on June 30. But with Douglas's stay by then vacated, the Rosenbergs dead, and the issue of judicial independence starkly presented, the resolution was killed by the full committee. Still, Douglas, as he later wrote, had been "denounced" in the press by many members of Congress and "temporarily became a leper whom people avoided..." "It hurts," he said, "when old friends cut one down."[71]

American justice did not cover itself with glory in *Rosenberg*. The prosecutors were guilty of misconduct, the defense lawyers barely competent, Judge Kaufman's death sentence for Ethel "a grave miscarriage of justice," and the Supreme Court's performance patently inadequate. Frankfurter termed the "manner in which the Court disposed of" the case, "[t]he merits ... aside," "one of the least edifying episodes in its modern history." Douglas's assessment was that the justices "certainly were aware of the hysteria that beset our people, and that hysteria touched off the Justices also. I have no other way of explaining why they ran pell-mell with the mob in the Rosenberg case and felt it was important that this couple die that very week—before the point of law on the legality of their sentence could be calmly considered and decided by the lower courts." But Douglas himself on two occasions could have assured a review on the merits and failed to do so. And Frankfurter, in one observer's words, only "saw review as an opportunity for the Court to affirm the convictions and quiet the national controversy surrounding the case."[72]

Rosenberg was of a piece with the Court's other "Communist" decisions in the 1951 and 1952 terms. Nine other signed decisions, including five in deportation cases, sustained the government's actions. The four decisions against the government were all based on narrow grounds unlikely to generate controversy.

5

The Coming of the Warren Court, the *Emspak* Trilogy, and *Brown*'s Consequences

(OCTOBER TERMS 1953 AND 1954)

Vinson's July 16 *Rosenberg* opinion was his last. On September 8, 1953, he died in his home, at age sixty-three, of a massive heart attack. Vinson's death was received with an outpouring of praise for him from Eisenhower, Truman, and many of the justices. The *New York Times* cited "his exceptional ability as a negotiator, a trouble-shooter, a reconciler of conflicting views." News stories that reported his death also speculated on his successor, with the name of three-term California governor Earl Warren, who only a few days earlier announced he would not seek another term, most prominently mentioned.[1]

Shortly after his election, Eisenhower had assured Warren, whom he had "long respected" and also owed a political debt, that he would offer him "the first vacancy on the Supreme Court." In August 1953, the president offered him in the interim the post of solicitor general; Warren accepted and was preparing to come to Washington when Vinson died. Eisenhower had not intended to make Warren chief justice; but he and Attorney General Brownell could not find a sitting justice whom they wished to promote, and Warren insisted that "[t]he first vacancy means the first vacancy." On September 30, five days before the start of the Court's new term, the president announced his selection of Warren to be chief justice.[2]

The genial, bluff sixty-two-year-old Warren, a native Californian, was the son of a thrifty Norwegian immigrant who worked in the car-repair shops of the Southern Pacific railroad. A graduate of the University of California at Berkeley and its law school, he became interested in Republican politics when Hiram W. Johnson, an energetic reformer, was governor. First a prosecutor in Alameda County (largest city Oakland), Warren became its district attorney in 1925; he was elected state attorney general in 1938 and governor in 1942. A successful and popular governor with wide bipartisan appeal, he was twice easily reelected. One of his few failures as governor was the defeat of his proposal for a state system of compulsory health insurance, opposed successfully by organized medicine. When Warren ran for vice president in 1948 as Dewey's running mate, Truman commented, "He's a Democrat and doesn't know it."[3]

Warren's years in elective office encompassed World War II. In early 1942, as state attorney general, he "played a pivotal role" in the decision to intern the ethnic Japanese population on the West Coast. He told a House committee that "when we are dealing with the Caucasian race" there are "methods" to determine loyalty, but "when we deal with the Japanese . . . we cannot form any opinion that we believe to be sound." Only at the end of his life did Warren acknowledge fault, writing in his memoirs that he "deeply regretted the removal order and my own testimony advocating it. . . . It was wrong to react so impulsively, without positive evidence of disloyalty." Earlier, in private conversation, he admitted to his colleague on the Court, Arthur J. Goldberg, "You know, in retrospect, that's one of the worst things I ever did."[4]

Pending Senate confirmation, Warren was given a recess appointment, enabling him to join the Court at the outset of the new term. As a justice, he combined traditional values—his "great strength," Justice Potter Stewart observed, "was his simple belief in the things that we now laugh at: motherhood, marriage, family, flag, and the like"—with the skills and insights of a successful politician. "Warren's forte," Bernard Schwartz wrote, "was not so much intellect as it was leadership." While never a scholar, he became an outstanding chief justice—"the Super Chief," his colleague William J. Brennan Jr. termed him—due to his uprightness and ability to lead and persuade. His offhand (perhaps simplistic) remarks at a farewell party in Sacramento revealed his sympathies: "I am glad to be going to the Supreme Court because now I can help the less fortunate, the people in our society who suffer, the disadvantaged." "Most often," Anthony Lewis wrote, "his sympathy lay with the individual victims of governmental restraints."[5]

Before joining the Court, Warren, in one biographer's view, had been "as militant an anti-Communist as those he associated with McCarthyism." But on the Court, he saw at first hand the impact of an overwhelmingly anti-Communist public opinion on the civil liberties of individuals. Guided at the outset by Frankfurter, he was initially hesitant in "Communist" cases. But within a few years, he "moved toward Black and Douglas," Michal Belknap wrote, "beginning to exhibit the concern for individual rights that would become the hallmark of the Warren Court."[6]

Warren's first two Court terms were dominated by the school-desegregation cases—*Brown I* in May 1954, holding racial segregation in public schools violative of the Equal Protection Clause and, a year later, *Brown II*, ordering that desegregation proceed with "all deliberate speed"—and marked by a diminution, temporary only, in the number of decisions in "Communist" cases. These two categories of decisions—desegregation cases and "Communist" cases—separate at the outset, would in time become interrelated, first on the political scene, where both fueled bitter criticism of the Court and court-curbing legislation, and later, as southern states employed against the NAACP (which fostered desegregation litigation) the same techniques used against accused Communists, in the Court's decisions themselves.[7]

1953 Term—*Barsky* and *Galvan*

In the 1953 term, the Court issued signed decisions in only two "Communist" cases. Both were decided in the government's favor by a divided Court, and the new chief justice voted with the majority each time.

In *Barsky v. Board of Regents* the Court considered New York's suspension of a medical doctor's license solely because of his contempt-of-Congress conviction for refusing to produce to HUAC the records of an alleged Communist "front." Edward K. Barsky, a physician and surgeon since 1919, had gone to Spain during its civil war to provide medical services for the loyalist side; upon his return, he became chairman of JAFRC, later placed on the attorney general's list of "subversive" organizations (an action reviewed in the Court's 1951 *Joint Anti-Fascist* decision). In 1945 Barsky refused to comply with HUAC's subpoena for JAFRC's financial records and, convicted of contempt, received a six-month prison sentence. The state board of regents, authorized by statute to discipline medical doctors convicted of "a crime," then suspended Barsky's medical license for six months—the penalty recommended by a ten-doctor "Grievance Committee."[8]

The Court, by a 6–3 vote in an opinion by Burton, upheld the board's action. New York's regulatory scheme for the practice of medicine, it found, reasonably made "the conviction of any crime a violation of its professional medical standards . . . leaving it to a qualified board of doctors to determine initially the measure of discipline to be applied to the offending practitioner." At the Court's conference, according to Douglas's notes, Warren viewed the case as open-and-shut: the "stat[ute] [is] not vague—power to discipline is present."[9]

Frankfurter, Black, and Douglas dissented. Frankfurter deemed the board's action "arbitrary." Revocation of a medical license, he wrote, "must have some rational relation to the qualifications required of a practitioner"; here, there was a "partial destruction of a man's professional life on grounds having no possible relation to fitness, intellectual or moral, to pursue his profession." "When a doctor cannot save lives in America because he is opposed to Franco Spain," Douglas said, "it is time to call a halt and look critically at the neurosis that has possessed us."[10]

The term's other "Communist" decision, *Galvan v. Press*, was a deportation case that in most respects was a replay of *Harisiades*—in other words, a longtime resident alien deported for having once been a Communist Party member. Born in Mexico, Galvan entered the country in 1918 at age seven and later worked in California as a laborer for a food company. He had an American wife and four sons born in the United States. He joined the wartime party in 1944 and ended his membership in 1946 or 1947. Galvan contended he had been an "innocent" member, unaware of the Party's advocacy of violence.[11]

The Court, however, by a 7–2 vote in an opinion by Frankfurter, upheld his deportation. "Congress," it found, "did not exempt 'innocent' members of the Communist Party." A separate provision of the act did exempt "innocent" members of organizations forced to register as Communist "fronts"; the absence of similar language with respect to the CPUSA, the Court reasoned, meant that no exemption for "innocent" Party members was intended. "It is enough," the Court said, "that the alien joined the Party, aware that he was joining an organization known as the Communist Party which operates as a distinct and active political organization, and that he did so of his own free will."[12]

In dissent Black, joined by Douglas, citing the First Amendment and the prohibitions against bills of attainder and ex post facto laws, was "unwilling to say . . . that despite these constitutional safeguards this man may be driven from our land because he joined a political party that California and the Nation then recognized as perfectly legal." For "an act which he had no possible reason to believe would subject him to the slightest penalty," Black wrote, Galvan "now loses his job, his friends, his home, and maybe even his children, who must choose between their father and their native country."[13]

In a per curiam ruling during the 1953 term, the Court rejected further punishment for Harry Sacher, one of the *Dennis* defense lawyers, faced with disbarment from practice before the federal district court in Manhattan. The district judge, who ordered Sacher's disbarment at a time his *Dennis* contempt conviction was on appeal, could not have known, the Court said, that he "would be obliged to serve, as he did, a six months' sentence for the same conduct for which it disbarred him." "[W]e are of the opinion," it concluded, "that permanent disbarment in this case is unnecessarily severe." Reed and Burton disagreed. "Disbarment is not punishment for contempt," Reed wrote, "but a cleansing of the bar by ousting."[14]

The *Sacher* per curiam was written by Warren, and Frankfurter sent a "Dear Chief" note expressing "satisfaction" in the decision which, he said, "vindicates the Court as free from the enveloping influence of unreason of our day."[15]

His note to Warren was a reflection of the relationship that initially developed between the two men. Frankfurter, Schwartz wrote, "made a massive effort to cultivate the new Chief Justice," showering him with notes, memoranda, and articles "intended to inculcate the Frankfurter view." But within a few years their relationship soured. "[I]n the end," Anthony Lewis said, Warren "found Black a more congenial personality: easier in manner, less awesome in intellectuality, more understanding of others' views." He also came to regard as just the case outcomes urged by Black.[16]

1954 Term—Harlan for Jackson, *Emspak* and *Peters*

Warren's cautious approach in "Communist" cases changed with his turnabout in *Emspak v. United States*. An unexceptional contempt-of-Congress case, *Emspak* was argued during the 1953 term, and at the justices' conference six voted to affirm the conviction. The primary issue was whether Julius Emspak, a left-wing union official, who in refusing to answer HUAC's questions invoked "primarily the first amendment supplemented by the fifth," had adequately claimed his Fifth Amendment privilege. According to Douglas's notes of the conference, Warren, speaking first, had no doubt the conviction should stand: "Congress had power to create the committee—its motives are beyond question—questions are in scope of [authorizing] resolution—gets down to whether the man claimed his privilege—no clear intention to claim his privilege—his lawyer was there." Emspak "wanted to eat this pie and have it," Warren continued, according to Burton's notes—in other words, he wanted neither to answer the questions nor to appear to hide behind the Fifth Amendment—and "[w]e should not condone that action." Black, Frankfurter, and Douglas were likely dissenters. Warren assigned the opinion to Reed.[17]

However, Reed in his draft opinion not only rejected Emspak's Fifth Amendment claim but also decided, broadly in the government's favor, an issue the Court had thus far avoided deciding—whether the First Amendment precluded Congress from compelling an individual to disclose "Communist" associations. Black complained in an April 1954 memorandum and asked that the other justices "not go along with [Reed's] opinion until its devastating effect on free speech and press can be pointed out in dissent." At a May conference, Black moved to have *Emspak* reargued the following term; his motion carried, with only Reed and Minton opposed.[18]

Before the case could be reargued, however, Jackson died. He had participated in *Emspak* during the 1953 term. But at the end of March 1954, he experienced a "mild" heart attack, recovering enough to be present on May 17 when *Brown I* was announced. On October 9, at the start of the new term, he suffered a second and fatal heart attack. He was sixty-two. As in Vinson's case, Eisenhower and other dignitaries paid him tribute; his fellow justices accompanied the casket to Jamestown, New York, his hometown. Initial speculation on his successor centered on John Foster Dulles (the secretary of state), Dewey, and Brownell, all New Yorkers. On November 8, Eisenhower selected another New Yorker,

John Marshall Harlan, whom he had appointed to a federal court of appeals ten months earlier.[19]

The fifty-five-year-old Harlan was the grandson and namesake of the Justice Harlan who alone dissented in *Plessy v. Ferguson*, the 1896 decision upholding "separate but equal" public facilities (and overruled in *Brown I*), famously stating that "[o]ur Constitution is color-blind." The younger Harlan, the son of a successful Chicago lawyer, was educated at Princeton, Oxford (he was a Rhodes Scholar), and New York Law School. At the time of his appointment to the court of appeals, he was a prominent Wall Street trial lawyer, primarily representing large financial interests.[20]

Harlan brought to the Court formidable legal skills and a superb character. "Skepticism and open-mindedness were his characteristics," Nathan Lewin, a former law clerk, observed. While his writing lacked flair, Harlan, in Norman Dorsen's view, "produced opinions that for consistent professional competence have not been exceeded . . . by any Supreme Court Justice since Brandeis." He was, Schwartz said, "plainly one of the best, if not the best, lawyer on the Court"; and while patrician in manner, "underneath was a warm nature that enabled him to be close friends with those with whom he disagreed intellectually, notably Black." Harlan's colleague, Potter Stewart, lauded "his freedom from all guile, his total decency."[21]

A conservative in the classic sense, naturally inclined to a philosophy of judicial restraint, Harlan replaced Jackson as Frankfurter's principal ally on the Court—wags referred to him as "Frankfurter without mustard" or "Frankfurter-lite." The two formed the "consistent core," Belknap wrote, "of a shifting restraintist bloc." But although, as a court-of-appeals judge, Harlan "almost mechanically upheld" the Smith Act convictions of thirteen "second-string" CPUSA officials, he was by no means an assured vote for the government in "Communist" cases. In a 1957 Smith Act decision, his opinion for the Court reversed the convictions of another group of "second-string" party officials and construed the act as requiring proof of advocacy "to *do* something . . . rather than merely to *believe* in something"—a requirement prosecutors proved unable to meet. And he wrote a 1956 decision holding that a statute authorizing summary dismissals of federal employees on loyalty grounds in a handful of "sensitive" agencies could not be extended indiscriminately by executive order to all government employees—a decision one historian termed "lethal to the loyalty-security program."[22]

The Court delayed reargument in *Emspak* because of Congress's delay in confirming Harlan's nomination. In late November 1954, shortly after Eisenhower announced the nomination, Senator James O. Eastland of Mississippi, a ranking member of the Judiciary Committee and a harsh critic of the Court following *Brown I*, requested that a Senate vote be deferred until the new Congress convened in January 1955. The Democrats had narrowly regained control of the Senate in the 1954 elections, and in the new Congress Eastland would become chairman of the Judiciary Committee. Harlan was not confirmed until March 1955, with nine Democrats from Deep South states voting against him.[23]

Emspak was reargued in April, together with two other contempt-of-Congress cases presenting similar issues—*Quinn*, involving another official of Emspak's left-wing union, and *Bart*, in which the defendant was an official of the *Daily Worker*, the CPUSA's newspaper. At the justices' conference, Warren reversed his earlier position, as described in Douglas's notes: "CJ—refers to his vote in Emspak last year and growing doubts about it—now he has changed his position . . . not necessary to reach the First Amend[ment]." Warren explained, according to Burton, that "we can dispose of these cases on the slipshod method of the committee in questioning." A majority of the justices now favored reversal. Warren assigned the opinions to himself.[24]

Emspak, *Quinn*, and *Bart* were decided on May 23. The Court, in opinions by Warren, reversed all three contempt-of-Congress convictions, by a 6–3 or 7–2 vote, holding that the witness's Fifth Amendment privilege claim excused his refusal to answer. In *Quinn*, which Warren made the lead opinion, the witness had refused to answer whether he was a CPUSA member. Appearing before HUAC without a lawyer the day after another union official, Thomas J. Fitzpatrick, refused to testify, Quinn "adopt[ed] as his own the grounds relied upon by Fitzpatrick." Fitzpatrick had invoked "the first and fifth amendments" or "the first amendment in the Constitution, supplemented by the fifth amendment." The Court held that Quinn's claim of Fifth Amendment privilege was sufficient: "The mere fact that Fitzpatrick and [Quinn] also relied on the First Amendment does not preclude their reliance on the Fifth Amendment as well." The Court added as a "second ground" that "[a]t no time did the committee specifically overrule his objection based on the Fifth Amendment; nor did the committee indicate its overruling of the objection by specifically directing [Quinn] to answer." "[A] clear disposition of the witness' objection," it held, "is a prerequisite to prosecution for contempt."[25]

In *Emspak*, where the witness relied "primarily" on the First Amendment "supplemented" by the Fifth in refusing to answer sixty-eight questions about his "associations and affiliations," the Court held, citing *Quinn*, that his privilege claim was sufficient. Responding to the government's contention that Emspak deliberately masked his Fifth Amendment claim to avoid public scorn—a contention that initially impressed Warren—the chief justice wrote: "[I]f it is true that in these times a stigma may somehow result from a witness's reliance on the Self-Incrimination Clause, a committee should be all the more ready to recognize a veiled claim of the privilege. Otherwise, the great right which the Clause was intended to secure might be effectively frustrated by private pressures."[26]

In *Bart*, the last of the trilogy, the Court elaborated on the committee's obligation to make explicit its denial of an objection. Bart had objected on pertinency grounds to answering questions about his name as a child when he came to the United States, before he legally changed it, and on Fifth Amendment grounds to questions concerning the Communist Party in Ohio. The Court found that HUAC failed to "directly overrule" his objections and that absent "a clear-cut ruling," evidence of "the requisite intent" to commit a criminal contempt was lacking.[27]

Reed, Minton, and Harlan were dissenters. Reed converted his earlier draft opinion for the Court to a lengthy dissent in *Quinn* and *Emspak*. He saw "a calculated effort by Messrs. Quinn, Emspak and Fitzpatrick to hinder and delay a congressional committee in its effort to bring out facts" in order to legislate.[28]

The holdings in the three cases were narrow and easily complied with by the committees. The *Times* reported a "consensus of lawyers and interested officials" that the decisions "would in no way restrict the investigating functions of Congressional committees." "A specific direction to answer a question," the *Times* said, "is standard with many Congressional committees." But the *Washington Evening Star* voiced "concern over the extent to which the court is going in the matter of dubious pleas of self-incrimination."[29]

Peters v. Hobby, decided the final day of the 1954 term, was the ultimate narrowly based decision. At its outset, however, the case had seemed the perfect vehicle, chosen by ex–New Deal lawyers at the Arnold, Fortas & Porter law firm, to challenge anew the constitutionality of federal-employee loyalty procedures, sustained by a 4–4 vote in *Bailey* in 1951, that allowed firings based on undisclosed information supplied by unnamed informants.[30]

John P. Peters was hardly a typical government employee. A professor of medicine at Yale, he was appointed a special consultant to the U.S. Public Health Service "because of his eminence in the field of medical science." The position, advisory only and nonsensitive, required his presence in Washington only four to ten days annually. In 1949, after he answered "a detailed interrogatory" concerning his "associations and affiliations," an agency loyalty board found "no reasonable grounds" for belief Peters was disloyal. But, in 1951, when the standard was changed to "reasonable doubt" as to loyalty, a new proceeding was instituted. Peters was charged with membership in the CPUSA and other proscribed organizations and association with Communists and "sympathizers." At a hearing before his agency's loyalty board, he denied CPUSA membership under oath and answered the other charges; his testimony was supported by eighteen witnesses and forty affidavits—the "only evidence" received at the hearing. Neither the names of the informants whose reports gave rise to the charges nor the substance of their reports was disclosed to him. The agency board determined "on all the evidence" that there was "no reasonable doubt" as to Peters's loyalty.[31]

However, in early 1953, the Loyalty Review Board, an interagency board created by Truman's executive order, on its own motion conducted a "post-audit" and held another hearing. Again Peters testified and was supported by other witnesses, and again he presented the only evidence at the hearing. But the review board, presumably on the basis of confidential information, found "a reasonable doubt" as to his loyalty. He was dismissed from his position and "barred from the Federal service" for three years. Peters's lawsuit alleged that these procedures infringed his Sixth Amendment right "to be confronted with the witnesses against him" and denied him due process of law under the Fifth Amendment.[32]

Oral argument for the government was presented by an assistant attorney general, Warren E. Burger (later chief justice), because the solicitor general, Simon E. Sobeloff, a former Maryland appellate judge, refused to sign its brief or argue its case. Burger ran into trouble when he told the justices that the informants' information, relied upon by the review board, would not be part of the record before the Court and could not be disclosed to it without a presidential order. Peters's counsel, Thurman Arnold, a former federal appellate judge, also had difficulty at the argument. Asked whether the review board was authorized by Truman's executive order to review Peters's case, he said he hoped the Court would decide the case on constitutional grounds. Frankfurter responded, "This Court reaches constitutional issues last, not first."[33]

At the justices' conference, Warren stated it was unnecessary to reach constitutional issues because the executive order did not authorize the review board to decide cases in which the agency board had ruled in the employee's favor. "Counsel did not raise the point," he said, "but that does not bar us." Frankfurter, Clark, and Harlan agreed. Black and Douglas urged reversal on constitutional grounds; but Black said he "will acquiesce if [a] majority wants to go on the procedural point."[34]

The Court's opinion, which Warren again assigned to himself, was joined by five other justices. It held that the review board's action overturning an agency-board determination in favor of the employee "was so patently in violation of the Executive Order . . . that the constitutionality of the Order itself does not come into issue." This limitation on the review board's authority, it said, was a "safeguard" which assured that a favorable determination by an employee's "co-workers in the department . . . his peers" would not be overturned "by political appointees who perhaps might be more vulnerable to the pressures of heated public opinion."[35]

The dissent, Reed joined by Burton, challenged the Court's reading of the executive order, pointing out that during a single year the review board had "post-audited" more than five thousand cases decided favorably to employees by agency or regional loyalty boards.[36]

The Court's holding was so limited as to have virtually no effect. Truman's executive order had been superseded in April 1953 by Eisenhower's executive order that abolished the Loyalty Review Board. Moreover, the decision left unchanged the government's practice of relying on undisclosed evidence and unnamed informants in loyalty cases. "A decision on the regulations," Douglas had warned Black, "would . . . be tantamount to a victory for the government" because "their system of the Faceless Informer would continue."[37]

But to Warren his alternatives may have seemed even less attractive. If he reversed on constitutional grounds, his decision would likely have been joined only by Black and Douglas. Clark was an architect of the Truman loyalty program; Minton had voted in *Bailey* to uphold it; and Frankfurter and Harlan were unlikely to join a controversial constitutional decision when a nonconstitutional ground was available. In fact, even though decided on the narrowest of grounds, *Peters* drew a sour reaction the next day from the *Times*'s Arthur Krock, who termed it "an interesting reminder of the breadth of [the Court's] assumption of judicial supremacy in our government system."[38]

But, as Krock's reaction indicated, *Peters,* while narrowly based, was not meaningless. Nor was the *Emspak* trilogy. That the government lost all four signed decisions in "Communist" cases during the 1954 term was a message that the Warren court would protect the rights even of accused Communists.

The government also lost two other "Communist" cases in per curiam rulings during the 1954 term, both involving lawyers. On rehearing, the Court set aside its 1953 disbarment of *Dennis*-lawyer Abraham Isserman. Its earlier action, by 4–4 vote following Isserman's disbarment in New Jersey, had led to a change in the Court's rules to require that disbarment in the Supreme Court be supported by a majority of the justices participating. The new order, by 4–3 vote and written by Black, stated that a majority "do not find ground for disbarment of Isserman." Burton, joined by Reed and Minton, dissented. The Court's ruling presaged Isserman's reinstatement to the bar of the federal district court in Manhattan in 1959 and the State of New Jersey in 1961.[39]

In the other per curiam ruling, written by Warren, the Court unanimously reversed the denial of Ben G. Levy's application to join the bar of the federal district court in Houston because he associated with an individual "generally considered to be a member of the communist party." The record, the Court said, "discloses no sufficient grounds" for denying the application. Levy, a transplanted New Yorker, later founded an ACLU chapter in Houston and served on a Texas appellate court.[40]

Brown and "Communist" Influences

Whatever initial uncertainty Warren may have shown in "Communist" cases, his handling of the school-desegregation cases was from the start sure-handed. In historic litigation fraught with emotion, and with the justices sharply divided when he arrived, Warren achieved a unanimous Court, in both *Brown I* and *II*, with all nine justices joining in a single opinion written by him and none filing a separate opinion.

The five school-desegregation cases, brought by the NAACP's Legal Defense and Education Fund headed by Thurgood Marshall, were ready for decision during Vinson's final term. A series of conferences disclosed the divisions on the Court, with a narrow majority apparently ready to ban segregation in public schools. Frankfurter believed that a decision by a fragmented Court—"a flurry of conflicting opinions that would confuse and anger the American people," as Richard Kluger put it—would be disastrous. He persuaded his colleagues the cases should be reargued the following term. By then, Warren had replaced Vinson. Frankfurter, in a letter to Reed three days after *Brown I* was announced, described what had been avoided: "I have no doubt that if the *Segregation* cases had reached decision last Term there would have been four dissenters—Vinson, Reed, Jackson and Clark—and certainly several opinions for the majority view."[41]

Warren obtained unanimity, Schwartz wrote, by emphasizing to his colleagues "the ultimate human values," that "[s]egregation could be justified only by belief in the inherent inferiority of blacks." He eased the concerns of justices from southern states—Reed and Clark (Black's vote evidently was never in doubt)—by stressing the need for caution in the Court's decision. In time Reed was the lone holdout; Warren met with him privately and often, finally telling him, "Stan, you're all by yourself in this now. You've got to decide whether it's really the best thing for the country." Jackson had considered a separate concurring opinion, but his initial heart attack intervened; when Warren brought the opinion in *Brown I* to his hospital room, Jackson approved it.[42]

The opinion Warren wrote was succinct and straightforward. "Separate educational facilities," it held, "are inherently unequal." "To separate [black children] solely because of their race generates a feeling of inferiority . . . that may affect their hearts and minds in a way unlikely ever to be undone." *Plessy v. Ferguson*, now overruled, had termed it a "fallacy" that "the enforced separation of the two races stamps the colored race with a badge of inferiority."; "[i]f this be so," *Plessy* said, "it is . . . solely because the colored race chooses to put that construction upon it." The Warren court responded by quoting the contrary finding of a Kansas court in one of the five cases before it, stating that "[w]hatever may have been the extent of psychological knowledge at the time of *Plessy v. Fer-*

guson, this finding is amply supported by modern authority." In a supporting footnote—footnote 11—it cited six books and articles on the psychological effects of racial segregation, adding a "see generally" reference to Gunnar Myrdal's monumental work, *An American Dilemma*. Footnote 11 would become a focal point for criticism of the decision.[43]

On the question of implementation, the Court ordered reargument the following term, a delay that served to diminish the decision's immediate impact in southern states and was likely a factor in persuading Clark and Reed to join Warren's opinion. Due to the delay in Harlan's confirmation, *Brown II* was not handed down until May 31, 1955.[44]

In it the Court remanded the cases to the respective district courts and conferred discretion upon them to shape the relief ordered in the light of local conditions. But it required the school systems to "make a prompt and reasonable start toward full compliance" with *Brown I* and to enter "such orders and decrees" as are necessary "to admit to public schools on a racially nondiscriminatory basis with all deliberate speed the parties to these cases." The final five words reflected caution: only "the parties" to the five cases—that is, the named plaintiffs, a handful of black children in each case—were required to be admitted "with all deliberate speed."[45]

While widely hailed, the decisions were also, unsurprisingly, harshly criticized. Some criticized the Court for activism. The *Washington Evening Star*, for example, stated the day after *Brown I*: "In effect, nine men have concluded that segregation in the public schools is a bad thing and have asserted the power to outlaw it." Herman Talmadge, Georgia's arch-segregationist governor, charged that the Court had "usurped from the Congress and the people the power to amend the Constitution" and urged defiance: "[T]he people of Georgia," he said, "will not comply with the decision of the court."[46]

Mississippi's Eastland, in a speech on the Senate floor ten days after *Brown I*, attributed the decision to Communist influences. "Everyone knows," he said, "that the Negroes did not themselves instigate the agitation against segregation. They were put up to it by radical busybodies who are intent upon overthrowing American institutions." The Court, he continued, "has been indoctrinated and brainwashed by left-wing pressure groups." Eastland cited an award given Black in 1945 by the Southern Conference for Human Welfare, "a notorious Communist-front organization," at a dinner also attended by Minton. Douglas had urged recognition of Communist China, he said, a "spectacle . . . for a man who sits on the highest tribunal of our country . . . openly to espouse the cause of our greatest enemy." Frankfurter and Reed, he recalled, had been character witnesses for Alger Hiss. Turning to footnote 11, Eastland condemned the Court's "resort to the unprecedented, unsound, and irrelevant authority of a group of recent partisan books on sociology and psychology." "What is to prevent the Court," he asked, "from citing as an authority in some future decision the works of Karl Marx?"[47]

Eastland was not done with footnote 11. Returning to the Senate floor two months later, he charged that authors cited in the footnote "have veered far to the left in their associations and writings." One, he said, was associated with the Institute of Pacific Relations, "a Communist-run and Communist-directed organization which engineered the betrayal of China to communism"; another was a professor at Howard University, "a socialistic Negro college in the Nation's Capital"; and Myrdal was "a Swedish Socialist politician." In May 1955, a few days prior to *Brown II*, Eastland, who was the Judiciary Committee chairman, introduced a resolution to authorize his committee "to investigate the extent and degree of participation by individuals and groups identified with the Communist conspiracy, Communist-front organizations, and alien ideologies, in the formation of the 'modern scientific authority' upon which the Supreme Court relied in the school integration cases."[48]

The goals of Eastland and his allies were evident. As George Lewis explained, "By claiming that the Supreme Court was in some way communist-tainted—or, certainly, that *Brown* was promoting communist ideas—they were turning what had been perceived as a peculiarly southern problem of race relations into a predicament of truly national proportions," as well as creating "a convenient rationale . . . for resisting *Brown*." In the Congress, however, few outside the South supported Eastland's charges—a situation that would shortly change.[49]

McCarthy's Censure and 1954 Anti-"Subversive" Laws

During the course of the Court's 1953 and 1954 terms, the face of McCarthy-era politics was altered, but not its substance. The Republican-controlled Senate censured McCarthy in December 1954, largely destroying his political influence. But "[e]ven while the Senate was debating what to do about Joe McCarthy," Robert Griffith wrote, "it was rushing through, virtually unopposed, a wide variety of so-called anti-subversive bills"—the *Times* counted eight. Nor was McCarthy condemned by the Senate for making false or reckless accusations of Communist ties. Rather, the censure resolution introduced by Ralph Flanders, a Vermont Republican, cited him for conduct "unbecoming a member of the United States Senate" and "contrary to senatorial traditions"—that is, "for transgressing the rules and the spirit of the club to which he belonged." "We have condemned the individual," Herbert Lehman of New York said, "but we have not yet repudiated the 'ism.'"[50]

The Republicans' 1954 election campaign distanced itself from McCarthy but not his message. The GOP adopted a strategy, in Richard Nixon's words, of "ignoring McCarthy, emphasizing vigorously the Administration's anti-Communist record, and attacking the other side for its past and present softness on the issue."[51]

Senate Democrats, led by Hubert H. Humphrey, responded to the "soft on Communism" charge by introducing on the Senate floor, on August 12, the "Communist Control Act of 1954," a mischievous piece of legislation that "outlawed" the CPUSA and stripped it of its "rights, privileges, and immunities" under federal and state law. Earlier legislation stopped short of outlawing the party, largely because FBI director Hoover expressed concern that it would be driven underground. But Humphrey told the Senate, "I am tired of reading headlines about being 'soft' toward communism," "tired of reading headlines about being a leftist," "tired of having people play the Communist issue as though it were a great overture," "I want Senators to stand up," he said, "and to answer whether they are for the Communist Party, or are against it." In an election year, not a single senator voted against the legislation; it became law less than two weeks later.[52]

Not every event, however, furthered repression. In the November 1954 elections, the Democrats won both houses of Congress, gaining nineteen seats in the House and one in the Senate, and several liberal Democratic candidates for the Senate, including Paul Douglas of Illinois and Joseph C. O'Mahoney of Wyoming, won in the face of red-baiting campaigns against them.[53]

The justices found encouragement in a surprising January 1955 speech by Harry P. Cain, a former Republican senator and a Subversive Activities Control Board member, who voiced sharp criticism of the federal loyalty-security system. Frankfurter sent a copy of the speech to Burton, who found it a "fearless, objective and constructive treatment of the subject . . . and unfortunately rare."[54]

6

Nelson, Cole v. Young, and the Beginning of the Campaign against the Court

(OCTOBER TERM 1955)

The flow of decisions in "Communist" cases became heavier in the 1955 term, with the Court handing down nine signed decisions. The government won three, including a major decision upholding the Immunity Act of 1954 (one of Congress's election-year anti-"subversive" efforts), but two of the cases it lost generated the most discussion, almost all critical of the Court. The year 1956 marked the onset of the spate of court-curbing bills Congress would consider.

The nine decisions ran the gamut of government action against "subversives": two contempt cases, one of them against a defense lawyer; a deportation and a denaturalization case; the SACB's order directing the CPUSA to register under the Internal Security Act; one case each involving federal and state public-employee loyalty programs; a private-employer firing upheld by state courts; and the criminal conviction (and lengthy prison sentence) of Steve Nelson, a CPUSA official, under a state sedition statute.[1]

The *Nelson* decision, which effectively invalidated on federal-preemption grounds more than forty state sedition statutes, gave segregationists in and outside the Congress "a second theme for their chant" and led to an anti-Court alliance between southern Democrats and conservatives outside the South, mostly Republicans. Even before *Nelson* was decided, Howard W. Smith of Virginia, the House Rules Committee chairman and author of the Smith Act, had introduced an anti-preemption bill at the behest of private employers. Smith's bill, HR 3, while written in general terms, was intended to nullify Supreme Court decisions holding state labor laws preempted by federal law, deemed more favorable to unions. After *Nelson*, HR 3 attracted a widened group of supporters. As Walter F. Murphy wrote, "[T]he segregationists could curb the Court," "[t]he ultra-security-conscious could revitalize state sedition laws," and employers "could get the specter of federal supremacy removed from their legal closets."[2]

During the term, Warren continued his move toward the Black-Douglas wing of the Court, voting with them in eight of the nine decisions. Frankfurter, in the majority in eight of the nine, was at the Court's center.

Contempts—*Ullmann* and *Cammer*

The one "Communist" decision in which Warren deserted Black and Douglas was *Ullmann v. United States,* where the Court upheld the contempt conviction of a defendant who refused to testify before a federal grand jury, invoking his Fifth Amendment privilege, despite having received a grant of immunity under the Immunity Act of 1954. The act authorized federal prosecutors in national-security cases to override a witness's privilege claim by granting him immunity from "penalty or forfeiture" concerning any matter as to which "he is compelled, after having claimed his privilege against self-incrimination, to testify or produce evidence." In 1896 the Court upheld a similar statute directed to testimony before the Interstate Commerce Commission. But the present defendant, William Ludwig Ullmann, an ex-Treasury Department employee accused by Elizabeth Bentley of having supplied information to her spy ring, argued that the immunity given him under the act was inadequate because it did not shield him from state prosecution or from a range of noncriminal sanctions imposed upon Communists.[3]

The Court, by 7–2 vote in an opinion by Frankfurter, rejected Ullmann's argument. Relying on the 1896 decision, it held that "the immunity granted need only remove those sanctions which generate the fear justifying invocation of the privilege." "Immunity displaces the danger," it said, and "[o]nce the reason for the privilege ceases, the privilege ceases." As to the threat of state prosecution, the Court construed the act as barring state as well as federal prosecution.[4]

Douglas's dissent, in which Black joined, contended that the immunity grant failed to eliminate Ullmann's need for the privilege because it did not cover numerous "disabilities imposed by federal law" upon Communists, such as ineligibility for certain types of employment or to obtain a passport, which "are forfeitures . . . as much protected by the Fifth Amendment as criminal prosecution itself." Nor was Ullmann protected against "the curse of infamy," Douglas stated, which follows upon exposure as a Communist. The Fifth Amendment, he said, "protects the conscience and the dignity of the individual . . . against the compulsion of government," conferring a "right of silence."[5]

In a less significant contempt case, involving a district judge's far-fetched application of a federal statute, the Court unanimously reversed the conviction. The defendant, Harold I. Cammer, was the attorney for Ben Gold, a union official who, after decades as a CPUSA member, resigned from the Party and a few days later signed a Taft-Hartley non-Communist affidavit. The government moved to prosecute Gold for filing a false affidavit and, after two federal grand juries in New York declined to indict him, obtained an indictment from a Washington, D.C., grand jury, thirteen of whose twenty-two members were government employees. The Court had held in 1950, in Eugene Dennis's contempt-of-Congress case, that government-employee jurors were not subject to challenge "solely by reason of their employment" but that defendants could show a juror's "actual bias." Cammer directed a letter and questionnaire to the grand jurors to ascertain whether any of them "might be influenced by bias or fear to indict persons charged with having had some association with the Communist Party."[6]

For sending these communications, a district judge found Cammer guilty under a federal statute that authorized a court to punish as criminal contempt "[m]isbehavior of any of its officers in their official transactions." The Court, however, in an opinion by Black, had no difficulty concluding that "a lawyer is not a court 'officer' within the meaning of" the statute. Unlike "marshals, bailiffs, court clerks or judges," it said, "a lawyer is engaged in a private profession."[7]

Deportation and Denaturalization—*Jay, Zucca*

Jay v. Boyd addressed a statutory procedure under which the attorney general was authorized to suspend a deportation order if the alien met specified criteria—for example, deportation would "result in exceptional and extremely unusual hardship." The alien in question, Cecil Reginald Jay, a Briton who entered the United States in 1914, was a CPUSA member from 1935 to 1940, and for that reason was ordered deported. The attorney general did not personally exercise discretion in suspension-of-deportation cases; rather, under regulations he promulgated, a hearing was conducted by an INS "special inquiry officer" whose decision could be appealed to an appeals board. In Jay's case the inquiry officer found the statutory criteria were met but refused on the basis of undisclosed "confidential information" to suspend deportation. The appeals board rejected Jay's appeal "in light of the confidential information available."[8]

The issue before the Court was the validity of the attorney general's regulation authorizing INS officials to rely on "confidential information" if they found that disclosure "would be prejudicial to the public interest." The Court, by a 5–4 vote, in an opinion by Reed, upheld the regulation and INS's refusal to suspend Jay's deportation. "[S]uspension of deportation," it said, "is not given to deportable aliens as a right, but by congressional direction, it is dispensed according to the unfettered discretion of the Attorney General."[9]

Warren, Black, Frankfurter, and Douglas dissented. Warren stated that a proceeding where "subordinate hearing officers" can deny relief based on undisclosed "confidential" information "is not an administrative hearing in the American sense of the term. It is no hearing." Black wrote that "this condemnation of Jay on anonymous information is not unusual—it manifests the popular fashion in these days of fear."[10]

United States v. Zucca, a denaturalization case, also involved the government's unwillingness to disclose "confidential" information. The defendant, Ettore Zucca, allegedly a CPUSA member from 1925 to 1947, acquired citizenship in 1944. The government charged that he obtained citizenship by fraud because at his naturalization hearing he falsely denied membership in any organization that teaches or advocates overthrow of the government. The lower courts, however, dismissed the government's lawsuit for failure to file an "affidavit showing good cause" for cancellation of citizenship, a prerequisite under the applicable statute.[11]

The Court, in a 5–3 decision written by Warren, affirmed. "The natural meaning of the language used" in the statute, it said, "is that filing of the affidavit is a procedural prerequisite to maintenance of the suit." "[T]he affidavit," it added, "must set forth evidentiary matters showing good cause for cancellation of citizenship."[12]

Clark's dissent, joined by Reed and Minton, made plain that the government's reluctance to disclose "evidentiary matters" explained its failure to comply with the affidavit requirement. Party membership, he wrote, "can be proved only from the testimony of other members concerning attendance at meetings, payment of dues, etc.," and if "the testimony and identity of undercover agents . . . must be disclosed in any affidavit, the Government must choose between foregoing denaturalization cases and drying up its source of information before the proceeding can be brought."[13]

In another deportation case, the Court was divided 4–4 and issued no opinion. The issue was substantial: whether a "Communist" alien, held in custody, was entitled to participate in his deportation proceeding. David Hyun, a Korean native who came to Hawaii in 1924, was arrested in 1950 and, charged with CPUSA membership, held in California for deportation proceedings. In his deportation case, the government took the depositions of witnesses in Hawaii; but Hyun, in custody, was unable to attend, lacking the money either to send a lawyer or to pay for his and his guards' transportation to Hawaii (as the government demanded). The INS hearing officer, "relying only" on the deposition testimony of two Hawaii witnesses, found Hyun deportable. A lower court held that his "financial inability" to attend the depositions did not amount to a denial of due process. The Court, equally divided, affirmed without opinion.[14]

CPUSA v. SACB—The First Time

The CPUSA's challenge to the SACB's order under the Internal Security Act, directing the Party to register with the attorney general as a "Communist-action" organization and to disclose the names and addresses of its members, was seemingly the most important case on the Court's docket. Registration triggered a range of sanctions not only on the party but also its members. The case posed First and Fifth Amendment issues; guilt had been determined by an administrative agency, not a jury. Black was only half joking when he told his colleagues, "This act violates almost all of the Bill of Rights, except for the quartering of troops." But, in the end, as in *Peters,* the Court sidestepped the constitutional issues, reversing the SACB's order and remanding the case to it on a point of procedure—three of the twenty-two government witnesses before the SACB had perjured themselves in other proceedings.[15]

The justices did not come easily to this outcome. At an inconclusive conference in November 1955, four justices (Warren, Black, Douglas, and Burton) expressed "very grave doubts" about the act's constitutionality. "This is not a registration statute," Warren said, "it is a death penalty statute." But Clark argued that the Court could "uphold it as a registration act"—it had upheld other registration schemes—and "carve out the sanctions as to members" for decision in later cases. Minton's view was less nuanced: "The party's purpose is to destroy us. . . . I would not be sorry if the whole party was destroyed, and the members too."[16]

A second conference in March again seemed inconclusive until Warren announced: "I have decided to reverse on Matusow's evidence." He was referring to ex-Communist Harvey Matusow, one of the government's witnesses before the SACB, who recently had recanted his testimony as a prosecution witness in both a Smith Act and a Taft-Hartley false-affidavit prosecution. The CPUSA had sought unsuccessfully to "adduce additional evidence" of perjuries, not only by Matusow but also two other government witnesses, Paul Crouch and Manning Johnson, and the government did not deny the perjury allegations. Frankfurter and Harlan agreed with Warren's disposition. Clark's agreement was conditional: "If we pass on the constitutionality of the board, etc. I would be willing to reverse on Matusow's testimony."[17]

Warren assigned the opinion to Frankfurter, who, however, omitted the constitutional issues entirely, deciding only on the perjurious-witness ground. His draft opinion, which he thought was for a unanimous Court, gave him "deep satisfaction," he told his colleagues, because "[t]his action will afford a striking demonstration of the Court's regard for the moral requirements in the administration of law touching the most despised group in the community." But Clark protested, stating his "understanding that the majority agreed to pass upon the constitutional issues." "I find no case in the history of this Court," he said, "that dodges the constitutional issues . . . on such a flimsy pretext."[18]

Frankfurter's opinion, for a six-justice majority, began with an answer to Clark. Citing *Peters,* he wrote that "the case must be decided on a non-constitutional issue, if the record calls for it, without reaching constitutional problems." And the record called for it, he found, because the SACB's report "contained 36 references to the testimony of Crouch, 25 references to the testimony of Johnson, and 24 references to the testimony of Matusow." Frankfurter concluded, "When uncontested challenge is made that a finding of subversive design by [the Party] was in part the product of three perjurious witnesses, it does not remove the taint for a reviewing court to find that there is ample innocent testimony to support the Board's findings." The board, he said, must "reconsider its original determination in light of the record as freed from the challenge that now beclouds it."[19]

In dissent Clark, joined by Reed and Minton, stated that "[t]he action today is taken merely for delay and can result only in the Board reaffirming the action."[20]

The decision also generated criticism outside the Court. "Justice Department lawyers said they were 'astounded' by the majority opinion," the *Washington Post* reported, and "[s]ome declared it may prove to be the most important Communist victory in the past decade." An Alabama congressman, George W. Andrews, interrupted debate on the House floor to announce that the SACB had "suspended all pending cases" because of the Court's action; he asked, "How much longer will this Congress continue to permit the Supreme Court to usurp the powers of Congress, write the laws of this land, destroy States rights, and protect the Communist Party?"[21]

Private-Employee Firing—*Black v. Cutter Laboratories*

Some cases are not worth the effort. Doris Brin Walker, a CPUSA member and an attorney who chose to work as a clerk-typist at Cutter Laboratories, a Berkeley pharmaceutical firm, was president of her union local when Cutter fired her. The employer's motive was disputed: the union argued she was fired for union activities, the employer that she was fired because of her party membership. The dispute was arbitrated under a collective bargaining agreement and pursued in the California courts.[22]

The arbitrators found Walker was fired for union activities and that her party membership was a pretext—the company had known of it for over two years and took no action. But the California Supreme Court ruled that "it must be accepted as conclusively established that a member of the Communist Party cannot be loyal to his private employer as against any directive of his Communist master" and that Walker's "reinstatement . . . would serve no cause save that of the Communist conspiracy."[23]

The Court ended up dismissing the appeal, by 5–3 vote, in an opinion by Clark, finding that the state court's decision "involves only California's construction of a local contract under local law, and therefore no substantial federal question is presented." The dissenters, Douglas joined by Warren and Black, saw a First Amendment issue.[24]

Public-Employee Loyalty Programs—State and Federal

Both of the Court's two decisions involving public-employee firings, by contrast, were significant.

In *Slochower v. Board of Higher Education*, the Court reviewed New York City's discharge of a college professor for invoking his Fifth Amendment privilege before a congressional committee. Under a provision in the city's charter, Harry Slochower, for more than two decades a professor of German at Brooklyn College, was fired automatically when he pleaded the Fifth Amendment in response to questions by the Senate Internal Security Subcommittee (SISS) concerning Communist affiliations. He told the SISS at the 1952 hearing that he was not a CPUSA member and would answer all questions about his political affiliations after 1941. He refused, however, to answer questions about affiliations in 1940 and 1941, stating he had testified earlier before a college faculty board with respect to that period. In his lawsuit, Slochower argued that "the mere claim of privilege" under the Fifth Amendment was not "a reasonable basis" for firing him and that his dismissal denied him due process of law.[25]

The Court, by 5–4 vote in an opinion by Clark, agreed. It "condemn[ed] the practice of imputing a sinister meaning to the exercise of a person's constitutional right under the Fifth Amendment." Analogizing the case to *Wieman*, where a loyalty oath failed to distinguish "innocent" membership, the Court stated that the city's charter provision compelled Slochower's termination even if his Fifth Amendment plea "resulted from mistake, inadvertence or legal advice conscientiously given, whether wisely or unwisely." His firing, moreover, was based on "events occurring before a federal committee" "wholly unrelated to his college functions," not in the course of an inquiry by the city, as in *Garner*, "to determine the qualifications of its employees."[26]

Reed, joined by Burton and Minton, dissented, as did Harlan separately. It was "reasonable," Reed wrote, for the city "to require its employees either to give evidence regarding facts of official conduct within their knowledge or to give up the positions they hold." The witness's Fifth Amendment privilege, he said, "protects him against prosecution but not against the loss of his job."[27]

Slochower was reinstated following the Court's decision, but Brooklyn College's president, Harry D. Gideonse, announced he was suspending him and would bring new charges. Slochower chose to resign and to pursue a new career "practicing psychoanalysis."[28]

The federal-employee loyalty case, *Cole v. Young*, considered the meaning of an opaque federal statute. The employee, Kendrick Cole, an inspector in the Food and Drug Administration's New York district, was charged with "a close association with individuals reliably reported to be Communists" (people he hiked with) and a "sympathetic association" with a listed "subversive" organization (a group called Nature Friends of America). He initially declined to answer these charges and was immediately fired by his department head, the secretary of Health, Education, and Welfare. A World War II veteran, Cole was entitled under the Veterans' Preference Act, a wartime statute giving veterans preferred treatment in government employment, to appeal his dismissal to the Civil Service Commission. The CSC, however, rejected his appeal on the ground that the Veterans' Preference Act did not apply to loyalty discharges. Cole had been discharged, the government said, under the Act of August 26, 1950, which provided that an agency head may summarily suspend an employee and terminate his employment "whenever he shall determine such termination necessary or advisible in the interest of the national security . . . and such determination . . . shall be conclusive and final"—in other words, no CSC appeal.[29]

The 1950 act by its terms applied only to eleven "sensitive" agencies (for example, the Atomic Energy Commission, the military departments), but one of its provisions authorized the president to extend it to other departments as he "deem[s] necessary in the best interests of national security." Eisenhower, in the 1953 executive order that established his administration's loyalty-security program, extended the 1950 act to every job in the federal government. The question before the Court was whether the president was authorized by the 1950 act to extend it to employees in nonsensitive positions, such as Cole.[30]

The Court by a 6–3 margin, in an opinion by Harlan, answered no. The 1950 act, it found, applied only to government activities "directly concerned with the Nation's safety" and to employees in "'sensitive' position[s]." The Court emphasized that summary dismissal under the 1950 act was not the government's only avenue for removing employees on loyalty grounds. Nonsensitive employees such as Cole could be dismissed under "general personnel laws," as was the practice under the Truman loyalty program, instituted three years before the 1950 act was passed.[31]

Clark's dissent, joined by Reed and Minton, viewed the matter more gravely. The Court, he wrote, "has stricken down the most effective weapon against subversive activity available to the Government." Its decision, he feared, "might leave the Government honeycombed with subversive employees."[32]

Government officials, however, reacting to the Court's decision, did not express alarm. "The officials," the *Times* reported, "see no difficulty in using regular personnel procedures to get rid of unreliable employees in non-sensitive areas." Attorney General Brownell promptly announced that employees suspended from nonsensitive jobs in seventeen pending loyalty cases had been restored to their positions.[33]

But the decision generated sharp criticism in the Congress, and legislation to overturn *Cole* was introduced in both houses of Congress. In the Senate, Karl Mundt, a South Dakota Republican and a leading red-hunter, termed it a "travesty" when "six men in black robes can nullify our every effort and expose the internal workings of our Government to the stealthy espionage and sabotage of Communist agents whose services the government cannot now terminate unless the agency in which they work be designated 'sensitive' or unless their individual positions are classified as 'sensitive.'" His bill proposed to amend the 1950 act to make it expressly applicable to employees holding nonsensitive jobs. Joe McCarthy introduced similar legislation, as did Eastland, SISS's chairman, and Francis E. Walter, a Pennsylvania Democrat and HUAC's chairman. Walter's bill, within a few weeks, gained the endorsement of the Eisenhower administration.[34]

State Sedition Statutes—*Nelson*

Nelson generated much greater criticism.

Steve Nelson, the CPUSA's top official in western Pennsylvania, was convicted of violating Pennsylvania's Sedition Act. From the start his prosecution was a circus: in an August 1950 raid on the Communist Party's Pittsburgh office, Michael A. Musmanno, a county judge and Democratic candidate for lieutenant governor, acting as a "private prosecutor," "select[ed] at random several arms full of subversive literature to be used as evidence." At Nelson's trial more than fifteen months later, the ambitious Musmanno, by then having won election to the state Supreme Court, was the principal prosecution witness. Another prosecution witness was Matt Cvetic, whose alleged exploits as an undercover FBI informant inside the party in Pittsburgh were the subject of a motion picture, *I Was a Communist for the FBI*, released several months before the trial and widely exhibited. In the film a character modeled on Nelson was portrayed as a "murderous, swinish Moscow flunky." Unable to obtain counsel, Nelson defended himself. Convicted, he received a twenty-year prison sentence.[35]

The Court's decision, in April 1956, however, was concerned only with the state's little-used sedition statute, one of an assortment of statutes in forty-two states that criminalized sedition, anarchism, or syndicalism. Like many of the others, Pennsylvania's act was directed at incitement—"[a]ny writing ... or conduct ... [t]o encourage any person to take measures ... with a view of overthrowing ... the Government of this State or of the United States." Nelson's prosecution was directed exclusively at sedition against the federal government. But the state's sedition law, the Supreme Court of Pennsylvania held, had been superseded by the Smith Act, and "[f]ederal pre-emption could hardly be more clearly indicated."[36]

The Court, by a 6–3 vote, agreed, holding Pennsylvania's law preempted with respect to sedition directed at the federal government. In an opinion by Warren, it found the federal scheme "so pervasive"—citing the Smith Act, the Internal

Security Act of 1950, and the Communist Control Act of 1954—that "[l]ooking to all of them in the aggregate, the conclusion is inescapable that Congress has intended to occupy the field of sedition." Enforcement of state laws, it said, "would conflict with the operation of the federal plan." Nor was the Court "unmindful of the risk of compounding punishments"—not an abstract issue because Nelson had also been convicted, in August 1953, of violating the Smith Act, and the Court had decided to review the case.[37]

Reed's dissent, in which Burton and Minton joined, argued that Congress had not expressed any intention to exclude parallel state laws—Rep. Howard Smith stated, in a letter read to the Court at oral argument, that he did not have "the remotest idea" the Smith Act would nullify state laws—and the Justice Department assured the Court that the operation of state laws had not "interfered with, embarrassed, or impeded the enforcement of the Smith Act."[38]

A filing by the attorney generals of thirty-four states urging rehearing received substantial coverage in the press. A *Boston Herald* commentator, noting the filing, spoke of "a rising revolt against the Supreme Court . . ." The *Houston Chronicle* termed the filing "significant" and said that "[t]hose who think that it is only the South which is upset over U.S. Supreme Court rulings are wrong." The Court, however, denied rehearing.[39]

Nelson's Aftermath—The Campaign to Curb the Court

Widespread denunciation, not only of *Nelson* but the Court itself, followed—in the Congress, the press, by influential organizations—and was accompanied by the introduction of dozens of court-curbing bills. The *Times*'s Arthur Krock saw "[t]he most determined effort since 1938 . . . to check and reverse the trend of Supreme Court decisions." The *Times* reported in May 1956 that "[a]bout seventy" anti-Court legislative proposals had been introduced in the Congress. The attacks on the Court continued throughout the spring and into the summer.[40]

On April 11, a week after *Nelson* was decided, Joe McCarthy in a Senate speech called the decision a ruling "that aid[s] the Communist Party." By virtue of *Nelson*, he said, "the States would be powerless to protect themselves if the Federal Government were overthrown by the Communist conspiracy." He introduced a bill providing in substance that "no Federal antisubversion statute shall be construed to deprive the States of jurisdiction to enforce their own antisubversion or antisedition statutes." Styles Bridges, an influential New Hampshire Republican, joined by eleven other Republicans and three southern Democrats, sponsored similar legislation.[41]

In the House on April 16, Noah Mason, an arch-conservative Illinois Republican, joined by Virginia's Howard Smith and seven other southern Democrats, took the floor to condemn *Nelson* and the Court. Mason urged passage of Smith's anti-preemption bill, HR 3, which he said would go "a long way toward stopping [the Court's] rapidly increasing usurpation of States' rights." He also voiced criticism of *Brown*: "Under the 10th amendment to the Constitution, control over the public schools was specifically reserved to the States.... [I]t is the function and the responsibility of the States to provide schools, to regulate them, and to have full control over them." Mississippi's William M. Colmer found it "most refreshing to see that the gentleman, from one of our so-called Northern States, has so much in common with so many from the so-called Southern States here today."[42]

On May 10, speakers in both Houses pressed for passage of HR 3. In the Senate, Harry F. Byrd of Virginia, chairman of the Finance Committee and sponsor with eleven other senators of a companion bill to HR 3, emphasized that "general" anti-preemption legislation was needed, not merely a bill to overturn *Nelson*. "[I]f our form of government is to be preserved," he said, "the preemption doctrine must be outlawed." In the House, Paul Brown of Georgia, affirming his support for the bill, stated that *Nelson*'s impact "cannot be limited" to Pennsylvania "any more than the ill effects of the abandonment of judicial precedent in the segregation cases can be limited to one subject or one State." The *Chicago Tribune* in an editorial praised Byrd's speech and his bill.[43]

McCarthy, appearing before Eastland's SISS in May and June, attacked the Court on a variety of grounds, including the justices' lack of prior judicial experience. Warren, McCarthy said, "had no judicial experience"; his "entire experience was as a politician." The two senators agreed that "there is just one pro-Communist decision after another from this court," with Eastland asking:

> EASTLAND: What other explanation could there be except that a majority of that court is being influenced by some secret, but very powerful Communist or pro-communist influence?
>
> McCARTHY: It is impossible to explain it. Either incompetence beyond words, Mr. Chairman, I would say, or the type of influence which you mentioned.[44]

The judicial-experience issue was debated in the Senate in connection with a bill introduced by George A. Smathers, a Florida Democrat, to require that all future Supreme Court appointees have at least five years' prior judicial experience. "[M]ost members of the Senate," Smathers said, "and certainly many of the American people would prefer that we begin to get better trained legal minds to serve us on the Supreme Court of the United States." John C. Stennis of Mississippi "agree[d] wholeheartedly," noting that he was himself the "author of a bill on the same subject matter."[45]

Lawyer groups joined the chorus. The National Association of Attorneys General, appearing before the Senate Judiciary Committee, urged passage of HR 3. Smith's bill was also approved, for the second consecutive year, by the American Bar Association's House of Delegates at its August meeting. At the same meeting, the Delegates rejected a resolution that urged "willing compliance" with *Brown*. A month earlier, with Warren and Burton present on the dais, the ABA's president, E. Smythe Gambrell of Atlanta, pointedly told a circuit judicial conference that judges were not "free agents, licensed to roam at will, remaking the law in any image they may choose and jousting at every windmill they may encounter."[46]

Criticism voiced by James F. Byrnes, a former member of the Court, more recently the governor of South Carolina, was doubtless especially unwelcome to the Court's current members. Byrnes's May 18 article in *U.S. News & World Report* (its cover story), titled "The Supreme Court Must Be Curbed," appealed to "the court of public opinion" to "urge the Congress to act before it is too late." "The present trend," he wrote, "brings joy to Communists and their fellow travelers who want to see all power centered in the Federal Government because they can more easily influence one Government in Washington than the 48 governments in 48 states." But Byrnes's ire was directed primarily at *Brown*. Southerners feared, he said, that the "purpose" of those seeking public-school integration was "to break down social barriers in childhood and the period of adolescence, and ultimately bring about intermarriage of the races."[47]

The Conference of State Governors, by an "almost unanimous vote," adopted a resolution stating that the governors are "gravely concerned" by the Court's preemption decisions. They "recommended to the Congress that Federal laws should be so framed that they will not be construed to pre-empt any field against state action unless this intent is stated"—a fair description of HR 3.[48]

On June 12 Eastland's Senate Judiciary Committee favorably reported a companion bill to HR 3, and on June 25 the House Judiciary Committee approved HR 3, but with an amendment limiting its application to sedition laws. The Justice Department had opposed the bill in the form proposed by Smith largely because, aside from sedition and labor law, no one could predict with any assurance the areas of law that would be impacted. The railroad industry, for example, long regulated under federal law, was fearful that state regulation might be superimposed and sought language excluding railroads from the bill. The House committee's action also reflected the efforts of its chairman, Emanuel Celler, a Brooklyn liberal, who, unable to stop the bill, sought to limit its scope. The House Democratic leadership refused to bring the limited bill to the floor under a rule permitting it to be amended, and Smith, forced to choose between a sedition-only bill or waiting until next year—after the November elections—chose to wait.[49]

The bills to overrule *Cole v. Young*, while supported by the Eisenhower administration, made little progress before the session ended. In the Senate, the bills received hearings and were reported by SISS but not by the full Judiciary Committee; in the House, the Post Office and Civil Service Committee, after brief hearings, took no action before Congress adjourned, on July 27.[50]

The Court's antagonists, Walter Murphy observed, "had only lost a little time; and if the Warren Court continued its indicated trend of decisions, this might turn out to have been no real loss at all."[51]

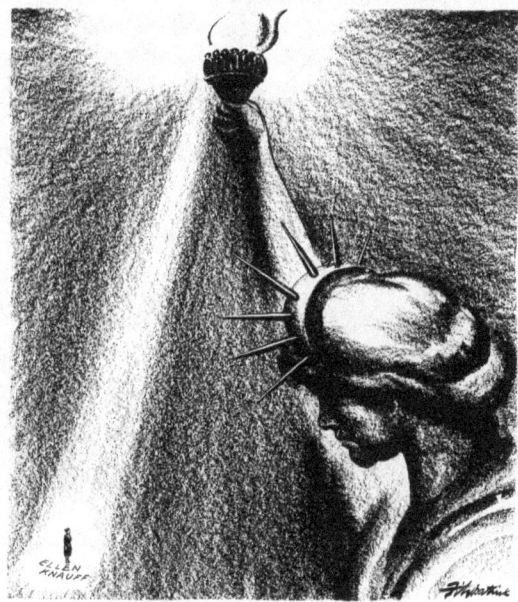

"Unto the Least of These." Fitzpatrick cartoon, *St. Louis Post-Dispatch*, November 4, 1951. After Ellen Knauff, a stateless war bride held on Ellis Island as a threat to national security, lost her appeal to the Supreme Court, she was admitted to the United States due largely to the efforts of the *St. Louis Post-Dispatch*, which carried this celebratory cartoon. Source: *St. Louis Post-Dispatch*, State Historical Society of Missouri.

"Leggo!—You're Interfering with Our Rites." Herblock cartoon, Washington Post, June 6, 1957. Cartoonist Herblock and the *Washington Post*, one of the few newspapers to defend the Court when it was under attack, published this cartoon following the widely criticized *Jencks* decision. Copyright by The Herb Block Foundation.

The justices of the Warren Court in a 1953 photo. In front, from left to right: Felix Frankfurter, Hugo L. Black, Earl Warren, Stanley F. Reed, and William O. Douglas. In back, from left to right: Tom C. Clark, Robert H. Jackson, Harold H. Burton, and Sherman Minton. © Bettmann/CORBIS

Felix Frankfurter, an intellectual force positioned at the Court's center, more than any other justice determined its direction in "Communist" cases and ultimately led its retreat. © Oscar White/CORBIS

Hugo L. Black, leader of the Court's liberal bloc, believed that the unconditional language of the First Amendment's free-speech guarantee meant what it said.
© Oscar White/CORBIS

William O. Douglas, like Black a First Amendment champion, shown in 1949 while recuperating from injuries sustained in a horseback-riding accident.
© Bettmann/CORBIS

Robert H. Jackson (center), shown with Black (left) and Frankfurter (right) at Chief Justice Vinson's funeral in 1953, was antagonistic to Black and Douglas and often allied with Frankfurter. Source: Getty Images

Earl Warren, chief justice for most of the McCarthy era, was initially hesitant in "Communist" cases but masterful from the outset in handling the Court's school-desegregation decisions.
© Bettmann/CORBIS

Fred M. Vinson was chief justice during the early part of the era; under his leadership the Court largely acquiesced in government action. © Oscar White/CORBIS

Tom C. Clark, prone to overwrought dissents when the government lost a "Communist" case, shown shaking hands with President Truman after being sworn in as a justice in 1949; Vinson (far right), Vice President Alben W. Barkley (second from left), and House Speaker Sam Rayburn (third from right) look on. © CORBIS

John M. Harlan, a conservative who wrote the Court's much-criticized 1957 *Yates* opinion, shown shortly after he joined the Court in 1955.
© Bettmann/CORBIS

William J. Brennan Jr., a Democrat appointed to the Court by President Eisenhower in 1956, joined its liberal bloc and wrote its controversial *Jencks* opinion.
© CORBIS

Potter Stewart, an Ohio Republican appointed to the Court in 1957, was a member of Frankfurter's five-justice majority, which carried out the Court's retreat.
© Bettmann/CORBIS

Arthur J. Goldberg, then Secretary of Labor, shown with President Kennedy in August 1962, three weeks before his appointment to replace Frankfurter, a change that tipped the Court's balance. © Bettmann/CORBIS

Eleven top Communist Party officials (Eugene Dennis, its general secretary, is second from left), being taken from the Foley Square courthouse in handcuffs after their conviction under the Smith Act in 1949; the Court's *Dennis* decision was handed down two years later. © Hulton-Deutsch Collection/CORBIS

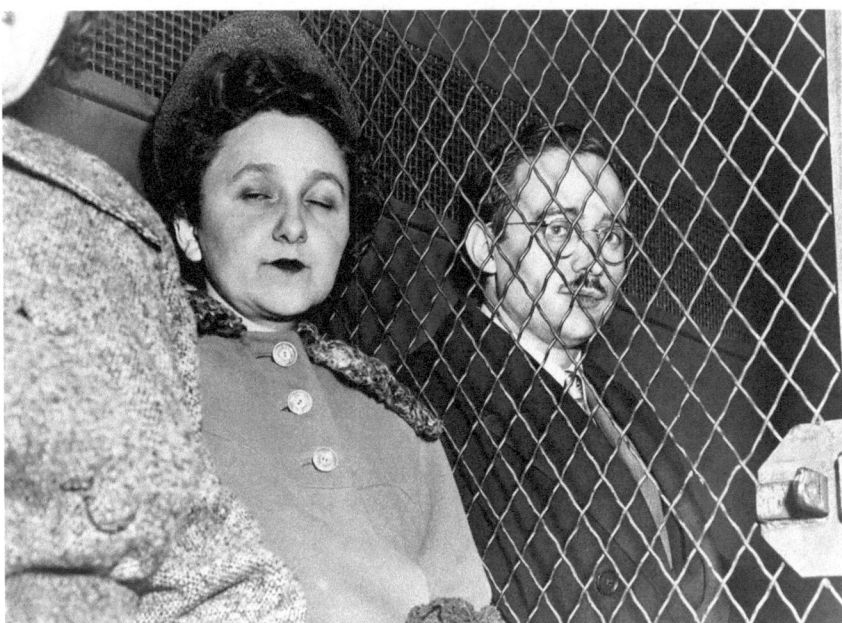

Julius and Ethel Rosenberg, convicted of espionage conspiracy and sentenced to death, being transported in a U.S. Marshal's van on June 17, 1953, the day Justice Douglas issued a short-lived stay of execution. © Hulton-Deutsch Collection/CORBIS

Oleta O'Connor Yates, a Communist Party official in California and the lead defendant in the Court's 1957 *Yates* decision, shown in 1954 addressing dock workers in San Francisco. © Bettmann/CORBIS

Clinton Jencks, a union organizer in New Mexico's copper mines, shown here with his wife Virginia on the set of *Salt of the Earth*, a 1953 film made by blacklisted Hollywood talent in which both appeared; Jencks was the defendant in one of the Court's most criticized decisions. Source: Wisconsin Center for Film and Theater Research

Willard Uphaus, a pacifist and Methodist lay preacher, shown at a 1956 HUAC hearing, was imprisoned for contempt by the State of New Hampshire in a case that proved unusually divisive for the justices. © Bettmann/CORBIS

Republican Senator William E. Jenner (left), shown with Attorney General Herbert Brownell (center) and FBI director J. Edgar Hoover at a 1953 Senate Internal Security Subcommittee hearing, sponsored legislation to strip the Court of jurisdiction in five subject areas. © Bettmann/CORBIS

Senator Joseph R. McCarthy, shown in conversation with subcommittee counsel Roy M. Cohn at the 1954 Army-McCarthy hearings, provided the face and the tone for the era. © Bettmann/CORBIS

One of the ubiquitous "Impeach Earl Warren" signs, this one along U.S. Highway 10 in Wisconsin in 1966. © Bettmann/CORBIS

As Senate majority leader, Lyndon Johnson, shown with Hubert Humphrey in a 1964 photo, staved off anti-Court legislation during a climactic five-day period in 1958; Humphrey as a senator sponsored the mischievous Communist Control Act of 1954. © Bettmann/CORBIS

7

The "Red Monday" Decisions, *Jencks*, and a Crescendo of Anti-Court Attacks

(OCTOBER TERM 1956)

The Court's level of resistance to repressive McCarthy-era government action reached its zenith in the 1956 term. There were no sweeping constitutional holdings. "Procedural fault-finding and statutory interpretation," Robert G. McCloskey wrote, "are still the order of the day." But the Court's direction was unmistakable. So also was the intensity of the anti-Court reaction and the impetus given by its decisions to court-curbing legislation.[1]

The Court issued eleven signed decisions in "Communist" cases, and the government lost them all. Four were issued the same day, June 17, 1957, a day critics called "Red Monday." Two other significant cases were decided in per curiam opinions, again adversely to the government. Lucas Powe termed the Court's performance "nothing short of astounding."[2]

The decisions, once more spanning the spectrum of anti-"subversive" actions, seemed to indicate diminished concern by the Court for adverse reaction. Among several decisions relating to Smith Act prosecutions, one, *Yates v. United States*, not only reversed the convictions of fourteen CPUSA officials but also made it more difficult (nearly impossible as it turned out) for the government to secure future Smith Act conspiracy convictions. A contempt-of-Congress decision, *Watkins v. United States*, sharply criticized the procedures employed by HUAC and indeed the entire House. Both *Watkins* and a decision in a state contempt case stated that the First Amendment imposed limits on committees seeking to compel disclosure of a witness's political associations. And the Court twice overturned a state's refusal to admit former Communists to the practice of law, angering bar groups.[3]

The decision, however, that most inflamed the Court's critics was *Jencks v. United States*, which reversed the conviction of a union official for filing a false non-Communist affidavit—one of four decisions involving Taft-Hartley's affidavit requirement. *Jencks*'s holding that the defendant was entitled to examine reports to the FBI by two prosecution witnesses raised the specter of Communists rummaging through the FBI's confidential files—a view fostered by inflammatory language in Clark's dissent. Legislation curtailing the decision was enacted before the justices returned from their 1957 summer vacation.[4]

The Court's opinion in *Jencks* was written by a new member, William J. Brennan Jr., formerly a justice of the New Jersey Supreme Court, selected by Eisenhower to replace Minton who retired for medical reasons. Brennan, a Democrat, joined the Court under a recess appointment two weeks after the term began and promptly aligned himself with the Black-Douglas-Warren wing, restoring the four-justice liberal bloc lost when Frank Murphy and Wiley Rutledge died in the summer of 1949. Eisenhower gained another appointment when Reed retired in February 1957 and this time chose a justice more attuned to his views, Charles E. Whittaker, a federal judge from Missouri. But Whittaker did not join the Court until late March and had almost no impact on its direction during the term.[5]

The November 1956 elections brought remarkably little change to the political landscape. Eisenhower won reelection in a landslide, but Democrats continued narrowly to control the Congress, winning a two-vote margin in the Senate and a thirty-three-vote margin in the House. Nor did the political situation change in May 1957 when Joe McCarthy died of liver failure, a consequence of excessive drinking. In recent months, the *New York Times* said, "his once powerful voice had virtually no influence on his colleagues." It cited his vote against Brennan's confirmation, the only negative vote cast.[6]

Brennan and Whittaker for Minton and Reed

Brennan was largely unknown in Washington when Eisenhower chose him. On September 7, when Minton, ill with pernicious anemia, announced his decision to retire, the president, with election day only weeks away, told Attorney General Brownell that he wished to appoint a Democrat, to show the nonpartisan character of his judicial appointments, and that he preferred a Catholic. The Court had not had a Catholic member since Murphy's death seven years earlier, and the influential Francis Cardinal Spellman of New York had raised the issue with the president. Brennan met both criteria, and, given recent criticism of Warren's lack of prior judicial experience, his nearly eight-year tenure on state courts was a plus. Minton, the retiring justice, received little attention; when he commented that "[t]here will be more interest in who will succeed me than in my passing," the *Times* called it "the most pertinent comment on his public career."[7]

Brennan was born in Newark, the son of an Irish-immigrant father who worked as a coal stoker before becoming a union official and then, as Newark's public safety director, the city's "dominant politician." Young Brennan attended the University of Pennsylvania's Wharton School of Finance and Harvard Law School. After military service in Washington during World War II and private practice in Newark, he became a state superior court judge in 1949, joining the state's supreme court in 1952. Brownell later claimed that before recommending Brennan to Eisenhower, he "read all his published opinions"; but Brennan was a lifelong Democrat with a liberal bent, as not only his judicial opinions but also two speeches he gave critical of government anti-"subversive" policies revealed. He had an affable manner and exceptional charm—"a magnetic personality," Linda Greenhouse said.[8]

At fifty years old—its youngest member—Brennan brought to the Court energy ("probably the hardest worker among the Brethren"), a considerable intelligence, and, particularly in later years, an uncanny ability to stitch together majorities. He served on the Court more than thirty years and became, in Powe's view, "the most important jurist of the second half of the century." Brennan quickly became Warren's closest colleague, entrusted with important opinions. In McCarthy-era "Communist" cases, he was, with Warren, Black, and Douglas, consistently on the side of the individual. Frankfurter, who had been Brennan's teacher at Harvard, failed to secure his allegiance on the Court, reportedly quipping, "I always encouraged my students to think for themselves, but Brennan goes too far."[9]

Whittaker was another matter. While conscientious to a fault, he was overwhelmed by the work of the Court—perhaps "the worst Justice of the century" in Bernard Schwartz's view. His story nonetheless was compelling. Born on a Kansas farm, he left high school at age sixteen. But three years later, he went to Kansas City, where he managed to enroll in the University of Kansas City Law School, a night school, at the same time working as a law-firm office boy and completing his high-school studies. As a lawyer, he built a successful practice representing corporations. In 1954, Eisenhower appointed him to the federal district bench and, two years later, the court of appeals. When Reed retired after nineteen years on the Court (giving as his reason, "Because I'm 72 years old"), Brownell, asked by the president to recommend individuals with judicial experience and deeming the Midwest "underrepresented on the Court," chose the fifty-six-year-old Whittaker.[10]

Whittaker served only five years. "[H]e was not fitted intellectually or physically for the job," Leon Friedman wrote. Faced with difficult and complex issues, he was often simply unable to decide. As Douglas recalled, "Whittaker would make up his mind on argument, only to be changed by Frankfurter the next day. In Conference, Whittaker would take one position when the Chief or Black spoke, change his mind when Frankfurter spoke, and change back again when some other Justice spoke." Enormously hardworking, he reached a state of exhaustion, was hospitalized, and retired in March 1962. During his tenure, he wrote five opinions of the Court in "Communist" cases, none significant. Conservative in outlook, however, his vote was decisive in the government's favor in a number of major decisions decided by 5–4 vote. In the 1956 term, joining the Court late in the term, he participated in only one of its decisions in "Communist" cases.[11]

Smith Act-related—*Yates, Mesarosh, Kremen*

The Court decided two cases in which "second-string" CPUSA officials were convicted of conspiracy to violate the Smith Act in prosecutions modeled on *Dennis*.

Mesarosh v. United States, decided at the start of the term, was a prosecution of five western Pennsylvania CPUSA officials, one of them Steve Nelson (whose real name was Mesarosh), resulting in five-year prison sentences. After the Court granted review, the solicitor general moved to remand the case to the trial court in Pittsburgh for "further proceedings" in view of perjuries before other tribunals by a prosecution witness, Joseph D. Mazzei. The government didn't confess error. While admitting that Mazzei, a long-time paid FBI informer, committed repeated perjuries subsequent to the Smith Act trial—including testimony before a Senate committee that the CPUSA planned "the liquidation of Senator Joseph McCarthy"—the government insisted that his trial testimony "was entirely truthful and credible." His "untrue statements" in other forums, it said, "might have been caused by a psychiatric condition, and . . . such condition might have arisen subsequent to" the trial. The government seemingly intended on remand to seek a determination that Mazzei's trial testimony was untainted.[12]

The Court, however, by 5–3 vote in an opinion by Warren, reversed the convictions and ordered a new trial. Emphasizing the significance of Mazzei's trial testimony in convicting the defendants, it found that his "credibility has been wholly discredited" by the government's disclosures and that "[t]he dignity of the United States Government will not permit the conviction of any person on tainted testimony." The Court invoked its "supervisory jurisdiction" in federal criminal cases (not the Constitution), stating that its duty "is to see that the waters of justice are not polluted."[13]

Harlan, joined by Frankfurter and Burton, dissented, arguing that the Court should simply have granted the solicitor general's motion and remanded the case to the trial court.[14]

Yates, decided on "Red Monday," was a conspiracy prosecution of West Coast CPUSA officials. The fourteen defendants were convicted, as in *Dennis*, of "conspiring (1) to advocate and teach the duty and necessity of overthrowing the Government . . . by force and violence and (2) to organize, as the [CPUSA], a society of persons who so advocate and teach." Initially, in conference, there were four votes to affirm the convictions, three to reverse, and two justices (Frankfurter and Harlan) not ready to vote. But after Minton and Reed left the Court and Burton switched sides, only Clark was for affirmance. A seven-justice Court, in an opinion by Harlan, reversed all fourteen convictions and held, in the case of five defendants, that the evidence was insufficient to allow a retrial.[15]

Harlan's thirty-nine-page opinion—Michal Belknap called it "complex, scholarly, and painfully dull" and Harry Kalven "at first acquaintance . . . a sort of *Finnegan's Wake* of impossibly nice distinctions"—first held that the charge of conspiring to "organize" the CPUSA was barred by the three-year statute of limitations. Organizing the party, the Court said, was not "a continuing process," as the government contended; rather, giving the Smith Act, a criminal statute, the narrower of two plausible interpretations, "organize" meant the CPUSA's formation in 1945, when it changed from its wartime Communist Political Association format—six years before the indictment was returned.[16]

The Court next found that the trial judge improperly withheld from the jury's consideration the question whether the defendants' advocacy had the capacity to incite, to "stir listeners to forcible action." Both sides had requested, but the judge refused, an instruction like one given in *Dennis*, instructing the jury that the defendants' advocacy must be "not of a mere abstract doctrine of forcible overthrow, but of action to that end, by the use of language . . . calculated to incite persons to such action." An instruction of this kind was essential, the Court held, because the Smith Act did not prohibit "advocacy and teaching of forcible overthrow as an abstract principle, divorced from any effort to instigate action to that end." This distinction, it said, was "consistently recognized" in the Court's First Amendment decisions, and to avoid a serious constitutional issue it assumed that Congress did not intend to "disregard a constitutional danger zone so clearly marked."[17]

The most significant difference between *Yates* and *Dennis*, however, was not the jury instruction but that the *Yates* court read the trial record and considered the sufficiency of the evidence. Having concluded that only advocacy capable of instigating action was made unlawful by the Smith Act, it measured the evidence in the fourteen-thousand-page record against that standard. What it found, Harlan wrote, was that "instances of speech that could be considered to amount to 'advocacy of action' are so few and far between as to be almost completely overshadowed by the hundreds of instances in the record in which overthrow, if mentioned at all, occurs in the course of doctrinal disputation so remote from action as to be almost wholly lacking in probative value." The prosecution's evidence, as in *Dennis*, consisted in large part of passages in texts. In ordering the acquittal of five defendants, the Court found that "[s]o far as this record shows, none of them has engaged in or been associated with any but what appear to have been wholly lawful activities." As to the remaining nine, the Court allowed them to be retried under "proper legal standards."[18]

Only three of the justices in the majority subscribed to Harlan's opinion in its entirety. Black and Douglas would have gone farther, acquitting all fourteen defendants. Black cited "the routine introduction in evidence of massive collections of books, tracts, pamphlets, newspapers, and manifestoes." "Guilt or innocence," he said, "may turn on what Marx or Engels or someone else wrote or advocated as much as a hundred or more years ago." Burton rejected the Court's interpretation of the term "organize." Clark alone would have affirmed.[19]

Press reaction to the decision expressed puzzlement at the distinction it drew between abstract advocacy and incitement to action. "Who," the *Los Angeles Times* asked, "would be able to tell when a man who advocates the overthrow of the Government by force and violence, is advocating it as an abstract matter, and when he is trying to start a revolt?" The *New York Daily News* called the decision "a masterpiece of hair-splitting," which "turns on the proposition that teaching or advocating the Government's violent overthrow is not criminal unless you also tell how the job is to be done."[20]

The Justice Department, faced with *Yates's* insistence upon proof of advocacy to "*do* something, now or in the future, rather than merely to *believe* in something," soon admitted that "we cannot satisfy the evidentiary requirements laid down by the Supreme Court" and dismissed the charges against the remaining *Yates* defendants. It also dismissed other Smith Act conspiracy cases pending in eight cities. There remained prosecutions under the Act's "membership" clause, which criminalized membership in a group organized to teach or advocate forceful overthrow. Two membership-clause cases reached the Court during the 1956 term, but in June the Court ordered them reargued the following term.[21]

In the third Smith Act-related case, Shirley Kremen, described by *Time* magazine as a twenty-one-year-old "onetime campus radical," and Samuel I. Coleman, a New York CPUSA "functionary," were charged with harboring two fugitive Smith Act defendants—Robert G. Thompson, a *Dennis* defendant who jumped bail when the Court affirmed his conviction, and Sidney Steinberg, a "second-string" CPUSA official who fled after his indictment. The FBI found the four living in a remote cabin in the Sierra Nevada mountains and arrested them.[22]

The issue before the Court concerned the bureau's warrantless search of the cabin and seizure of its "entire contents"—hundreds of mundane items (for example, phonograph records from Edith Piaf to Brahms, a mandolin and mandolin picks, prescription drugs, hot water bottles, pipes and pipe cleaners, cigarettes, Kleenex, shampoo, toothbrushes and toothpaste, lipstick, coat hangers) transported two hundred miles to the FBI's San Francisco office. Some of the items were introduced in evidence at the trial. In conference, six justices voted to reverse the convictions on Fourth Amendment grounds. Warren believed "the wholesale removal was illegal—too highhanded to tolerate," and Harlan found the search "beyond the pale." But agreeing on an opinion was more difficult.[23]

Douglas, given the assignment by Warren, wrote a draft opinion holding the search and seizure unlawful on two grounds. First, the FBI agents "had ample time to obtain a search warrant" and "[h]aving the time, it was their duty to obtain a search warrant." Second, "no search warrant could be justified which ... authorized a seizure of the entire contents of the cabin." Frankfurter and Harlan, however, each prepared a separate concurring opinion, leaving only three justices (Warren, Black, and Brennan) who would join Douglas's opinion.[24]

Harlan's draft concurrence came as a personal disappointment to Douglas, who wrote to him:

> I was greatly surprised and grieved that you did not bring me your problems in *Kremen* nor saw fit to discuss them with me.... It so happens that you are the critical member, for without you there is no Court opinion in *Kremen*. Felix could not, in view of his intense hostility, ever join me in an important constitutional case. I had hoped you could. Certainly your arrival here seemed to bring a fresh breeze into an atmosphere where too much suspicion and distrust prevailed.... And it hurts me to see you play the game that has brought the Court into disrepute.

Harlan sent an immediate handwritten reply: "Nothing could have been farther from my mind than the things you say.... I am very fond of you personally."[25]

In the end, Warren, with difficulty, brokered a per curiam opinion, largely written by Harlan, which all six justices in the majority joined. The opinion stated only that "[t]he seizure of the entire contents of the house and its removal some two hundred miles away ... are beyond the sanction of any of our cases." The Court appended a complete list of the items seized—in very small print it consumed ten pages in the *United States Reports*. The "F.B.I. inventory," Harlan told Douglas, "seems to me to be the best substitute for argument as to the unreasonable character of the seizure."[26]

Clark and Burton filed a dissenting statement, arguing that the items admitted in evidence "were legally seized" and "if any items were illegally seized their effect should be governed by the rule of harmless error since there was ample evidence of guilt otherwise."[27]

Contempt—*Watkins* and *Sweezy*

Like earlier reversals of contempt-of-Congress convictions, *Watkins*, a "Red Monday" decision, was directed to a procedural flaw, easily remedied by the committees. But this time the Court lectured the Congress at length, warning that congressional investigations must have a legislative purpose and "there is no congressional power to expose for the sake of exposure"—HUAC's long-standing practice.[28]

The witness, John T. Watkins, a former official of a left-wing union, took a nuanced position before HUAC. He denied past or present CPUSA membership but admitted that from 1943 to 1946 he cooperated with the party. He was willing to identify former associates who he believed were still party members but refused to name others who, although once members, had "long since removed themselves from the Communist movement." He declined to invoke the Fifth Amendment but challenged the relevance of the questions "to the work of this committee" and its "right to undertake public exposure of persons because of their past activities."[29]

The Court's discursive opinion, written by Warren and joined by five others on a seven-justice Court (only Clark dissented), emphasized that Congress's investigations "must be related to, and in furtherance of, a legitimate task of the Congress" and not "conducted solely for the personal aggrandizement of the investigators, or to 'punish' those investigated." The Bill of Rights imposed additional limitations: the Court reaffirmed the right of witnesses to invoke the Fifth Amendment and said that investigations being "part of lawmaking" were "subject to the command" of the First Amendment.[30]

The Court's holding, however, was narrow. Because "[n]o witness can be compelled to make disclosures on matters outside" a committee's "legislative sphere," it said, a person forced "to make this choice is entitled to have knowledge of the subject to which the interrogation is deemed pertinent." It demanded clarity in Congress's authorizing resolutions—criticizing the vagueness of the authorizing resolution for HUAC—and stated that HUAC's "duty" when Watkins objected to questions as not pertinent was "to state for the record the subject under inquiry at that time and the manner in which the propounded questions are pertinent thereto." Because it failed to do so, Watkins was "not accorded a fair opportunity to determine whether he was within his rights in refusing to answer" and his conviction was "necessarily invalid."[31]

In dissent, Clark condemned "the mischievous curbing of the informing function of the Congress."[32]

In the state contempt case, *Sweezy v. New Hampshire*, another "Red Monday" decision, six justices seemed to agree that the one-man investigating unit violated the witness's First Amendment rights but could not agree on an opinion or even a rationale.[33]

The hearings were conducted by the state's attorney general, Louis C. Wyman, whom the state legislature authorized in a 1951 statute "to determine whether subversive persons... are presently located within this state." Wyman subjected the witness, Paul M. Sweezy, an economist and self-styled "socialist" and "classical Marxist," to a wide-ranging interrogation. Although he responded to most of Wyman's questions—he emphatically denied CPUSA membership—Sweezy refused on both pertinency and First Amendment grounds to answer whether his wife and another individual were active in the state's Progressive Party and whether in a lecture at the University of New Hampshire he advocated Marxism and said that "Socialism was inevitable in America." A state court ordered Sweezy jailed "until purged of the contempt."[34]

Warren's plurality opinion, in which Black, Douglas, and Brennan joined, stated that "there unquestionably was an invasion of [Sweezy's] liberties in the areas of academic freedom and political expression"—rights "enshrined in the First Amendment." But his opinion, as in *Watkins*, was based on a pertinency rationale. The authorization given Wyman by the legislature, Warren said, was so broad that there could be no "assurance that the questions [Sweezy] refused to answer fall into a category of matters upon which the legislature wanted to be informed when it initiated this inquiry." In these circumstances, he concluded, "the use of the contempt power, notwithstanding the interference with constitutional rights," denied him due process.[35]

Frankfurter, joined by Harlan, concurred in the result but viewed the pertinency issue as "a matter for the decision of the [state] courts." He relied instead on the First Amendment. With regard to the questions about Sweezy's university lecture, he condemned "the grave harm resulting from governmental intrusion into the intellectual life of a university." And, as to the questions about Progressive Party membership, he emphasized that they did not relate to the CPUSA: "Whatever... the justification for not regarding the Communist Party as a conventional political party, no such justification has been afforded in regard to the Progressive Party." Balancing "the right of a citizen to political privacy" and "the right of the State to self-protection," Frankfurter ruled in the citizen's favor.[36]

Clark, joined by Burton, dissented, striking the same balance in the state's favor.[37]

Douglas, in a note to the file, explained why Warren's opinion did not adopt a First Amendment rationale: "The Chief Justice had tried to get a court on the First Amendment. He proposed to write the opinion on that ground. He tells me that Frankfurter would not agree to it. So in a canvas of the Court he decided the only way he could get an opinion of the court was on the relevancy of the questions to the legislative inquiry." Frankfurter, Douglas wrote, "misle[d] the C.J., getting him to write on a secondary ground, and then he himself writing on the ground the C.J. wanted to put his opinion on."[38]

Bar Admission—*Schware* and *Koenigsberg*

Schware v. Board of Bar Examiners was unanimous. The record, the Court said, showed Rudolph Schware "to be a man of high ideals with a deep sense of social justice." New Mexico's bar examiners, however, had denied him admission on the ground he failed to demonstrate "the requisite moral character for admission to the Bar." They cited his admitted membership in the CPUSA between 1932 and 1940; two arrests, one for criminal syndicalism during a 1934 strike and the other in 1940 for recruiting volunteers for the loyalists during the Spanish Civil War; and his use of an alias at places of employment in the 1930s.[39]

The Court, in an opinion by Black, joined by Warren, Douglas, Brennan, and Burton, found "no evidence in the record which rationally justifies a finding that Schware was morally unfit to practice law" and that New Mexico's action denied him due process. Schware joined the CPUSA, it said, at a time "when millions were unemployed and our economic system was paralyzed [and] many turned to the Communist Party out of desperation or hope." His "past membership in the Communist Party," the Court held, "does not justify an inference that he presently has bad moral character." Nor did the "mere fact that a man has been arrested" show "he has engaged in any misconduct." And Schware's use of an alias, in an "attempt to forestall anti-semitism in securing employment or organizing his fellow workers," was not "wrong."[40]

The second bar-admission case, *Konigsberg v. State Bar of California*, was more difficult for the Court because Raphael Konigsberg, unlike Schware, refused to answer whether he had been a CPUSA member. The bar examiners denied him admission on the ground he failed to prove both "good moral character" and that he did not advocate overthrow of the government "by unconstitutional means." The Court, however, dividing 5–3, again in an opinion by Black joined by Warren, Douglas, Brennan, and Burton, found that "the evidence does not rationally support the only two grounds upon which the [bar examiners] relied."[41]

Its reasoning paralleled *Schware*. Forty-two individuals who had known Konigsberg "attested to his excellent character," the Court found, and "not a single person has testified that Konigsberg's character was bad or questionable in any way." A witness did testify that Konigsberg attended meetings of a CPUSA unit in 1941. But "[e]ven if it be assumed" he was a CPUSA member in 1941, the Court said, "the mere fact of membership" would neither "support an inference that he did not have good moral character" nor "provide a reasonable basis for a belief that he presently advocates overthrowing the Government by force."[42]

Harlan, joined by Clark, dissented, contending that Konigsberg's "failure to answer was the reason for exclusion." His refusal to answer, Harlan said, "made it impossible [for the state] to proceed to an affirmative certification that he was qualified." Frankfurter dissented on a technical ground.⁴³

Burton's vote was decisive. "I developed my conviction in this case," he told Black, "*only after reading the entire record* which left no doubt in my mind as to [Konigsberg's] genuineness and moral character."⁴⁴

Loyalty Program—*Service*

Service v. Dulles, the final "Red Monday" decision, set aside the State Department's discharge on loyalty grounds of John Stewart Service, a foreign service officer and one of the "China hands" whose advice, in the view of conservatives, led to the "loss" of China.⁴⁵

The loyalty proceedings stemmed from Service's involvement in the 1945 *Amerasia* case. That controversy followed upon the discovery of hundreds of classified documents, all bearing the State Department's stamp, in the offices of *Amerasia*, a small-circulation magazine directed to Asian affairs and evidently under the control of Communists. Service, while not a Communist, had furnished some of his own State Department reports to *Amerasia*'s editor; he was arrested and charged with espionage. A federal grand jury, however, declined to indict him.⁴⁶

Four successive departmental loyalty proceedings were instituted against Service, and all were decided in his favor by the State Department's loyalty board. But Truman's Loyalty Review Board conducted a "post-audit" of the last determination—the procedure later held unlawful in *Peters v. Hobby*—and its adverse ruling led to Service's immediate firing by Secretary of State Dean Acheson.⁴⁷

The Court's decision could hardly have been narrower in scope. In firing Service, Acheson invoked the so-called McCarran Rider, a statute which authorized him "in his absolute discretion" to terminate an employee "whenever he shall deem such termination necessary or advisable in the interests of the United States." The State Department, however, had adopted regulations affording procedural protections to employees in loyalty cases—regulations not complied with in Service's case. The question before the Court was whether the secretary was bound by departmental regulations when a statute conferred "absolute discretion" upon him.⁴⁸

The Court unanimously, in an opinion by Harlan, answered this question in the affirmative. While "under the McCarran Rider the Secretary was not obligated to impose upon himself these more rigorous substantive and procedural standards," the Court said, "neither was he prohibited from doing so ... and having done so he could not, so long as the Regulations remained unchanged, proceed without regard to them."⁴⁹

Supervising Deportees—*Witkovich, Sentner*

In *United States v. Witkovich*, the Court construed an Internal Security Act provision requiring "supervision" of persons who had been subject to a final order of deportation for more than six months. For the first six months, the act authorized detention without bail—as in *Carlson v. Landon*. But afterward the alien became subject to "supervision" and was required by the act "to give information under oath"

> as to his nationality, circumstances, habits, associations, and activities, and such other information, whether or not related to the foregoing, as the Attorney General may deem fit and proper.

Willful failure "to give information" was made a crime punishable by imprisonment.[50]

George I. Witkovich, ordered deported in 1953 for CPUSA membership, was indicted in 1955 for willful failure "to give information" to INS. The government, after trying unsuccessfully to deport him to Yugoslavia, had entered an "order of supervision" and questioned him about his activities. Witkovich, a pressman for a Slovenian-English newspaper in Chicago, refused to answer such questions as "Do you subscribe to the Daily Worker?" and "Are you now a member of the Communist Party of U.S.A.?" and "[D]o you know [a series of named individuals]?" A lower court, however, held that the attorney general's power of "supervision" was limited to assuring that the alien "is available for deportation" and, since the questions Witkovich refused to answer were not related to his availability for deportation, dismissed the indictment.[51]

The Court, by a 6–2 vote, in an opinion by Frankfurter, agreed. The government's broad reading of its power of "supervision," it said, raises "issues touching liberties that the Constitution safeguards." To avoid a constitutional issue, it construed the statute as authorizing only "questions reasonably calculated to keep the Attorney General advised regarding the continued availability for departure of aliens whose deportation is overdue."[52]

Clark, joined by Burton, dissented, warning that "[s]everal thousand alien Communists who have been finally ordered deported will from now on, due to the Court's decision today, be under virtually no statutory supervision."[53]

Three weeks later, in a one-sentence per curiam order citing *Witkovich*, the Court affirmed a lower-court decision that nullified several paragraphs of an "order of supervision" for Antonia Sentner. Sentner, a resident of St. Louis for thirty-nine years, had been ordered deported in 1953 for CPUSA membership. The paragraphs at issue required her to terminate her party membership, refrain from associating with any party member (her husband was a Party official), not violate the Smith Act, and "conduct herself in a lawful and orderly manner."

In dissent, Clark and Burton contended that the Court, without hearing "the Government's side," had "enlarge[d] its holding in *Witkovich*."[54]

Taft-Hartley Affidavits—*Jencks*, *Gold*, and More

Taft-Hartley's non-Communist affidavit requirement for union officials, and denial of statutory remedies to non-complying unions, gave rise to *Jencks* and three other decisions during the term.

In response to Taft-Hartley, union officials who were CPUSA members sometimes adopted "a 'resign and sign' strategy," that is, they formally resigned from the Party and signed non-Communist affidavits. Ben Gold, the president of the Fur and Leather Workers Union, a union expelled by the CIO as Communist-dominated, signed a non-Communist affidavit only days after resigning from the CPUSA; he had been a member for thirty years. The government, charging that his resignation was a pretext, obtained his conviction for filing a false affidavit. But Gold challenged his conviction on the basis of FBI contacts with jury members. During his trial in Washington, D.C., an advertisement appeared in local newspapers in support of Hugh Bryson, an official of another left-wing union also charged with filing a false affidavit—a case with no connection to Gold's. However, after a juror in Gold's trial reported that she received a copy of the advertisement in the mail, an FBI agent "visited" three of the Gold jurors or their families, while the trial was in progress, inquiring "whether they had received any 'propaganda' literature."[55]

The Court, in a per curiam ruling written by Warren and joined by five other justices, held that the Bureau's contacts with the Gold jurors constituted "official intrusion into the privacy of the jury" and required a new trial. The dissenters, Reed, Burton, and Clark, argued that the FBI contacts had no "adverse" consequences.[56]

In a second case, the Court reviewed a National Labor Relations Board ruling that refused a statutory remedy to the Mine, Mill & Smelter Workers, another left-wing union expelled by the CIO, on the ground it was not in compliance with Taft-Hartley's affidavit requirement because Maurice Travis, its secretary-treasurer, had filed a false affidavit. The Court, however, held unanimously, in an opinion by Douglas, that the only sanction for filing a false Taft-Hartley affidavit was criminal prosecution. "[T]here is no indication," it said, "that Congress meant to impose on a union the drastic penalty of decompliance 'because its officer had deceived the union as well as the Board by filing a false affidavit.'"[57]

The NLRB had imposed an identical penalty against Ben Gold's Fur and Leather Workers' union, premised on Gold's filing of a false affidavit. In a companion decision, also unanimous and written by Douglas, the Court, citing *Mine-Mill*, overturned that ruling too.[58]

Jencks was of much greater consequence. Clinton Jencks was a union organizer and president of a Mine-Mill local in New Mexico. Prior to his indictment, he had appeared in the role of a union organizer in *Salt of the Earth,* a 1953 film made by blacklisted Hollywood talent about a Mine-Mill strike in Hanover, New Mexico. The making of the film was marked by government interference and a movie-industry boycott. "Since Jencks was a minor [union] functionary," Ellen Schrecker wrote, "it was clear that the furor about *Salt of the Earth* had prompted" his indictment.[59]

At his trial in 1954, prosecutors charged that the non-Communist affidavit Jencks filed in April 1950 was false. They relied on the testimony of two paid undercover FBI informers, both ex-Communists. J.W. Ford testified concerning Jencks's association with the CPUSA in 1948 and 1949, and Harvey Matusow recounted "several conversations" with Jencks in July or August 1950, shortly after he filed the affidavit at issue, in which the context indicated both were Party members. A year after Jencks's trial, Matusow made his well-publicized recantation, which included disavowal of his testimony against Jencks. During the periods covered by their trial testimony, both Matusow and Ford had given reports to the FBI. Defense counsel moved the trial judge to compel the government to produce the reports, a motion summarily denied.[60]

The Court, in a 7–1 decision, found that the defense was entitled to obtain Matusow's and Ford's reports to the FBI in order to impeach their trial testimony. The government, relying on a 1953 precedent, had argued that the defense was obligated first to show inconsistency between the reports and the witness's testimony. But the Court, in Brennan's opinion for five justices, responded that "the accused is helpless to know or discover conflict without inspecting the reports" and need only show that the reports concerned "the events and activities as to which [the witnesses] testified at the trial." Nor, it held, must the reports be produced to the trial judge *in camera* (in private) "for his determination of relevancy and materiality" because "only the defense is adequately equipped to determine the effective use for purpose of discrediting the Government's witness."[61]

The Court recognized that "protection of vital national interests may militate against public disclosure of documents in the Government's possession." But, it said, the government could not both prosecute a defendant and withhold documents material to his defense. Rather, it held, "criminal actions must be dismissed when the Government, on the ground of privilege, elects not to comply with an order to produce, for the accused's inspection and for admission in evidence, relevant statements or reports in its possession of government witnesses touching the subject matter of their testimony at the trial."[62] Burton, joined by Harlan, concurred in the result but argued that the trial judge should "before disclosing the privileged material to the defendant . . . pass on the question by examining *in camera* the portions claimed to be privileged."[63]

Clark's dissent condemned the Court's decision in extravagant terms and invited congressional action: "Unless the Congress changes the rule announced by the Court today, those intelligence agencies of our Government engaged in law enforcement may as well close up shop, for the Court has opened their files to the criminal and thus afforded him a Roman holiday for rummaging through confidential information as well as vital national secrets."[64]

Given Matusow's recantation, the government was unable to retry Jencks. He later pursued an academic career and taught economics at San Diego State University.[65]

The Anti-Court Backlash and Court-curbing Legislation

"[T]he decisions of the 1956 Term," Walter Murphy wrote, "transformed congressional criticism into militant opposition." The opposition extended beyond Congress to the press, bar, and state judiciary. Even Eisenhower, usually noncommittal, ventured that "possibly in their latest series of decisions there are some that each of us has very great trouble understanding."[66]

The press sharply criticized the term's major decisions. *Watkins*, the *Washington Evening Star* wrote, will likely "cripple the investigative function of Congress." The *Cleveland Plain Dealer* said about *Yates*: "Well, Comrades, you finally got what you wanted. The Supreme Court has handed it to you on a platter." Referring to the four "Red Monday" decisions, the *Chicago Tribune* stated, "The Supreme Court managed to perform major services for Communists and loyalty risks on the Federal payroll and at the same time to diminish substantially the power of Congress to deal effectively with any of them." By its decision in *Jencks*, the *New York Herald-Tribune* wrote, the "Supreme Court is in effect destroying the essence of the FBI." The *New York Daily News* suggested that "if a movement should start in Congress to impeach one or more of the learned justices, it might have much popular support."[67]

The legal profession continued its criticism of the Court and support of court-curbing legislation. At the American Bar Association's annual meeting in New York City, its president, David F. Maxwell of Philadelphia, criticized *Schware* and *Konigsberg*, calling it "particularly relevant" that a bar applicant had once been a Communist.[68]

The ABA's 1957 meeting was bifurcated and, after a short recess, reconvened in London, with Warren, Harlan, and Clark in attendance. There, Herbert R. O'Conor, a former U.S. Senator, presenting the report of the ABA's committee on Communist tactics, strategy, and objectives, told its House of Delegates that national security may be endangered if courts "lean too far backward in the maintenance of theoretical individual rights." Not only *Jencks* legislation was needed, he said (to vigorous applause), but also legislation to overturn *Cole v.*

Young, *Witkovich*, *Yates*, *Watkins*, and *Slochower*. Warren, angered by the report, which he later termed "a diatribe against" the Court "charging it with aiding the Communist cause," and believing it was submitted at the well-publicized London session "designedly to besmirch the Court," resigned his membership in the ABA. The ABA told the press that he had been dropped from membership for "non-payment of dues."[69]

The National Association of Attorneys General, convened in Sun Valley, Idaho, heard its president, Louis C. Wyman (the New Hampshire official in *Sweezy*), charge that the Court's decisions "have set the United States back twenty-five years in its attempt to make certain that those loyal to a foreign power cannot create another Trojan horse here." The association called for immediate legislation "to reaffirm and reactivate Federal and state internal security controls."[70]

The Conference of Chief Justices, composed of chief justices of state supreme courts, formed a committee to study the role of the judiciary in the distribution of power between state and federal governments. The committee's chairman, John R. Dethmers of the Michigan Supreme Court, cited *Nelson* as an example of "what disturbed conference members," asking, "Can't a state protect itself against seditious activities?"[71]

The Court made its own situation worse by an end-of-the-term decision that had nothing to do with Communists but gave added fuel for criticism. Reviewing a conviction for a brutal rape in the District of Columbia, for which Andrew Mallory, a nineteen-year-old African-American, had been sentenced to death, the Court unanimously ordered a new trial because police failed to arraign him before a judicial officer "without unnecessary delay" as directed by a federal criminal rule. The police instead had interrogated Mallory until a confession, admitted in evidence at his trial, was obtained. Criticism of *Mallory* placed the Court on the side not only of accused Communists but also, as Assistant Attorney General Warren Olney told the *Evening Star*, "real hardened professional criminals who will take advantage of" the decision.[72]

Criticism of *Jencks* had the most immediate results. The FBI threatened—Hoover "is understood to have passed the word," the *Times* said—to "withdraw from the prosecution of certain spy and other criminal cases" if necessary "to protect confidential sources of its files." Attorney General Brownell stated that "law enforcement would be 'almost impossible' unless Congress limited the scope of the decision." The White House announced it "would 'urge' Congressional adoption of legislation" directed at *Jencks*.[73]

The administration's bill curtailed the decision by requiring *in camera* inspection by the trial judge and limiting disclosure to statements "signed by the witness, or otherwise adopted or approved by him as correct." If the government refused disclosure, the trial judge was to strike the witness's testimony or at most declare a mistrial, but not to dismiss the case as *Jencks* required. On

July 1 and 2, less than a month after the decision, the Judiciary committees in both Houses approved the bill.[74]

Objections by Senate liberals, however, stalled the process, and, with the session nearing its close, the Senate passed a compromise bill. But the House passed the Administration bill by a 351–17 margin.[75]

A conference version, close to the administration bill, easily cleared both Houses prior to adjournment and became law on September 2. While the new statute accepted *Jencks*'s basic principle—that the defense is entitled to inspect statements of prosecution witnesses relating to their trial testimony—it substantially limited the decision by mandating prior *in camera* inspection by the trial judge, defining producible "statements" narrowly, and not requiring dismissal of the case if the government refused to produce the statements.[76]

When the legislation passed, Frankfurter told Brennan, *Jencks*'s author, that he considered himself at fault for the uproar over *Jencks*. "I very largely blame myself for all the dust that the case kicked up," he wrote; "if I had not allowed my good-colleagueship to suppress my good sense, the rumpus would have been avoided." "For if I had had my wisdom govern," he said, "I would have written a short concurrence with your opinion sticking my pen into Tom [Clark]'s hot air and puncturing his balloon, by stating the exact narrow holding of the decision and exposing the non-holding . . . That's what I should have done, just as I did it in *Watkins* & *Sweezy*."[77]

The enactment of *Jencks* legislation by no means put an end to calls for anti-Court action by the Congress. Indeed, the House Judiciary Committee formed a special subcommittee to review recent "controversial" Supreme Court decisions and to suggest legislative action.[78]

H.R. 3, Howard Smith's anti-preemption bill, which overruled *Nelson* (and more), was reintroduced in the 85th Congress in 1957. While Emanuel Celler succeeded in holding the bill in the Judiciary Committee for over a year, the House would approve it in 1958.[79]

Legislation to overturn *Cole v. Young* was reported favorably by the House Post Office and Civil Service Committee. Seizing upon a bill that had passed the Senate, the House committee substituted the language of Francis Walter's bill extending the 1950 summary-termination statute to nonsensitive federal employees.[80]

In July 1957, William E. Jenner, Republican of Indiana and SISS's former chairman, introduced the most far-reaching of the court-curbing bills. His bill, S 2646, stripped the Court of appellate jurisdiction in five categories of cases, each the subject of a recent decision. The Court would be denied authority to review cases involving contempt of Congress, the federal loyalty-security program, state antisubversive statutes, measures adopted by boards of education to deal with subversion among teachers, and admission to the practice of law in any state. Jenner accompanied the introduction of his bill with an extended, decision-by-decision attack on the Court—decisions, he said, that had severely damaged "our legislative barriers against communism and subversion." "[W]e in Congress," he concluded, "must fulfill our plain duty and act immediately in the way the Constitution empowers us to act, to repair as much of the damage as we can and prevent even worse damage in the future."[81]

Within days, Jenner's bill was accorded a hurried hearing before Eastland's SISS and reported favorably. Only two witnesses testified, Jenner and Benjamin Mandel, SISS's research director, who produced *Daily Worker* articles to support Jenner's statement that the CPUSA "has been dancing with joy" over the Court's decisions. The following week, Eastland sought approval of the bill by the full Judiciary committee. But Thomas C. Hennings Jr., a liberal Missouri Democrat, citing the absence of opposition witnesses at SISS's hearing, proposed that the bill be kept until the next session so that full hearings could be held and all interested parties allowed to appear. Jenner's motion to table Hennings's proposal failed by one vote, and further hearings on the bill were postponed to 1958.[82]

Only *Jencks* legislation had been enacted when Congress adjourned at the end of August 1957, but other court-curbing bills, including Jenner's bill, were very much alive when Congress returned at the start of the new year.

Nonetheless, the 1956 term was exceptional in the history of the Court. In the heart of the McCarthy era, and in the face of harsh congressional and public condemnation, the Court decided case after case in favor of despised dissidents. The justices seemed even less divided than in past years—in the three most important and most-criticized decisions, *Yates*, *Watkins*, and *Jencks*, Clark was a lone dissenter, and several less important decisions were unanimous. The "Red Monday" decisions, in Geoffrey Stone's view, "marked the end of the Cold War in the Supreme Court."[83]

But the flow of "Communist" cases did not diminish and what in fact followed was a five-year period of retreat by the Court from the decisions of the 1955 and 1956 terms. In that period, it decided in the government's favor major constitutional issues it had sidestepped for years.[84]

"The decisions of [the 1956] term," Senator Hennings wrote shortly after the term ended, "have not put an end to the hysteria which exists in our nation. In fact, the immediate result of many of the decisions has been to fan the existing fires of fear and hate."[85]

8

Beilan, *Lerner*, and the Court's Shift, Passport Cases, and Congress's Court-Curbing Climax

(OCTOBER TERM 1957)

The effects of the anti-Court campaign began to be reflected in the Court's decisions during the 1957 term. "The anti-Court bills," Lucas Powe wrote, "caused Frankfurter to get religion again." The justice believed, Powe explained, that Congress was questioning "whether an independent judiciary might be too high a price to pay when the cost was the eradication of the loyalty-security program.... Frankfurter was ready to save the Court; prudence dictated the Court yield in this area." This view, almost incontrovertible in succeeding terms, was only partially confirmed in the 1957 term.[1]

The continued heavy flow of "Communist" cases produced fourteen signed decisions and two via per curiam opinions. The outcomes were mixed, but they revealed a shift in the Court's direction. The government prevailed in two state public-employee loyalty cases (decisions that reduced *Slochower* to insignificance) and three criminal contempt cases (in one the justices had decided for the defendant the preceding term but Frankfurter switched sides after reargument). However, it lost five deportation decisions, two decisions testing the State Department's authority to deny passports on political grounds, and two narrow rulings invalidating state laws that conditioned the receipt of government benefits on signing a non-Communist oath. It also lost the two per curiam decisions—one reviewing the issuance of less-than-honorable Army discharges to "subversive" draftees and the other a contempt-of-Congress case against *Dennis* lawyer Harry Sacher.[2]

Frankfurter was on the winning side in all but one of the decisions, including all five—four by 5–4 vote—in the government's favor. In those decisions, he led a five-justice bloc that included Harlan, Burton, Clark, and Whittaker. However, Frankfurter was also the swing vote against the government, joining Warren, Black, Douglas, and Brennan, in the passport cases and in a deportation decision that undercut his own 1954 opinion in *Galvan v. Press* (holding that "innocent" CPUSA membership was no defense to deportation).³

In the two Smith Act membership-clause cases held over from the preceding term, the Court dodged the complex statutory and constitutional issues presented by summarily reversing the convictions on *Jencks* grounds. The solicitor general had confessed error.⁴

Segregation-related issues were again prominent. The Court handed down the first of its decisions in cases where southern states used against the NAACP techniques borrowed from the campaign against Communist "subversion." It held unanimously that Alabama's demand for NAACP membership lists infringed the members' "freedom of association" under the First Amendment. Just before the term began, the president dispatched federal troops to Little Rock to enforce court orders, defied by Arkansas's governor, to desegregate the city's public schools—a controversy that would require a decision of the Court at a special term the following September.⁵

The anti-Court campaign in the Congress gained in strength. The passport decisions in fact gave rise to a new set of bills, along with a presidential message calling for prompt congressional action. A seemingly unstoppable coalition of southern Democrats and conservatives outside the South pressed for enactment of an assortment of court-curbing bills. Jenner's jurisdiction-stripping bill, in modified form, emerged from the Senate Judiciary Committee. Smith's anti-preemption bill, HR 3, was passed by the House, as were bills to overturn *Cole v. Young*, *Yates*'s interpretation of the term "organize," and *Mallory*. The climax came in August 1958 in a series of debates and tense votes in the Senate during the final five days of the session. Due to the wizardry of the majority leader, Lyndon B. Johnson, and the rush to adjourn in an election year, the Court, quite incredibly, escaped.⁶

Contempt—*Yates, Brown, Green,* and *Sacher*

Oleta O'Connor Yates, a CPUSA official in California, was a defendant not only in the Smith Act conspiracy decision bearing her name, but also in a criminal contempt case arising out of the same trial. When she took the witness stand in her own defense at the 1952 trial, Yates refused on two occasions, separated by several days, to answer the prosecution's questions whether various individuals were Party members. On the first occasion, the trial judge, William C. Mathes, held her in both civil contempt, ordering her jailed until she answered (a seventy-day confinement until the trial ended), and criminal contempt, imposing at the end of the trial a three-year prison sentence (set aside, however, by a court of appeals in 1955). On the second occasion, Yates refused to answer eleven questions, and Mathes held her in criminal contempt for each refusal imposing eleven concurrent one-year prison sentences.[7]

Only Yates's eleven one-year sentences were before the Court. By a 6–3 vote, in an opinion by Clark, it held that her refusals to answer constituted contempt but "only one contempt." Where a witness declines to answer "within a generally defined area of interrogation," the Court said, "the prosecutor cannot multiply contempts by further questions within that area." It reversed Yates's convictions on ten counts and remanded for resentencing on the remaining count, noting that in imposing a one-year sentence Mathes's judgment may have been "affected" by his belief that she "had committed 11 separate contempts."[8]

Douglas, joined by Warren and Black, dissented, arguing that all eleven counts should be dismissed.[9]

Remanded to Judge Mathes, the case returned to the Court before the term ended because Mathes, ignoring the Court's "gentle intimations," again imposed a one-year sentence on the remaining count. In a per curiam opinion written by Frankfurter, the Court found, by a different 6–3 vote, that Yates "has in fact spent seven months in jail in the course of these proceedings" and the time she "has already served in jail is an adequate punishment for her offense." Clark, Burton, and Whittaker dissented.[10]

Yates's contempt case had reached the Court the preceding term and was voted upon by the justices at that time. An opinion by Reed affirming her conviction and, upon his retirement, a nearly identical opinion by Burton were circulated. But Frankfurter wanted the case reargued. He wished to "re-examine the record" in the light of an opinion he was writing reversing a contempt conviction in another "Communist" case, *Brown v. United States*—an opinion in which he was to be joined by Warren, Black, Douglas, and Brennan. "If I find the *Yates* case falls within what I deem to be the governing considerations in *Brown*," he told his colleagues, "I will have to change my position. In that case there will be a majority for reversal in *Yates*."[11]

In the end, both *Yates* and *Brown* were reargued in the 1957 term. Yates's conviction was again affirmed, and Frankfurter again wrote the Court's opinion in *Brown*. But this time he wrote *affirming* Brown's conviction and was joined by Burton, Clark, Harlan, and Whittaker.[12]

Stefena Brown's contempt conviction arose in a denaturalization proceeding. Born in Poland, she obtained American citizenship in 1946. The government sought to strip her of citizenship on the ground she obtained it by fraud, having testified falsely at her naturalization hearing that she had not been a member of the CPUSA or any other organization "teaching opposition to organized government" during the preceding ten years. In fact, the government charged, she had been a CPUSA member from 1933 to 1937. Brown testified that, although she was a Young Communist League member from 1930 to 1935, her Communist activities ended at that time, more than ten years prior to the naturalization hearing. On cross-examination, the government asked whether she had ever been a CPUSA member, and she refused to answer, invoking her Fifth Amendment privilege. The trial judge ruled Brown had "abandoned" the privilege by taking the witness stand and found her guilty of criminal contempt.[13]

Frankfurter, in his draft opinion the preceding term, found that reversal of Brown's conviction was compelled by a 1919 decision of the Court requiring proof of "obstruction to the court in the performance of its duty." After reargument, however, he deemed this precedent inapposite and addressed the constitutional issue in the case: whether Brown could invoke the Fifth Amendment after taking the witness stand and giving exculpatory testimony. In a criminal case, the answer plainly would have been "no." Although denaturalization was a civil proceeding, the Court held the same rule applied and Brown "could not take the stand to testify in her own behalf and also claim the right to be free from cross-examination on matters raised by her own testimony on direct examination."[14]

In dissent Black, joined by Warren and Douglas, argued that the practice in criminal cases "is itself debatable and should not be carried over to any new area absent the most compelling justification." Brennan relied on the 1919 precedent.[15]

In a third criminal contempt case, Gilbert Green and Henry Winston, *Dennis* defendants who jumped bail and remained at large until their surrender more than four years later, were summarily held in contempt by a federal judge and sentenced to three years' imprisonment. The defense argued that the Constitution barred prosecution for a crime punishable by more than one year's imprisonment without indictment by a grand jury and trial by a jury.[16]

Harlan, writing for the same five-justice majority as in *Brown*, rejected this contention. He relied on "a long and unbroken line of decisions" establishing that "criminal contempts are not subject to jury trial as a matter of constitutional right." And, given these decisions, he said, it would be "anomalous" to conclude that criminal contempts are subject to the Constitution's indictment-by-grand-jury guarantee.[17]

Black, dissenting, joined by Warren and Douglas, argued that summary punishment for criminal contempt "stands as an anomaly in the law" and "the time has come for a fundamental and searching reconsideration of the validity of this power." Brennan believed the evidence did not prove guilt beyond reasonable doubt.[18]

In a final contempt ruling, the Court, by a 6–2 vote, in a per curiam opinion, reversed the contempt-of-Congress conviction of *Dennis* attorney Harry Sacher. His conviction stemmed from SISS hearings investigating informer Harvey Matusow's recantation—hearings intended to prove Matusow's action was part of a Communist plot. Sacher was defense counsel in a Smith Act case in which Matusow, a prosecution witness, recanted his testimony, resulting in a new trial for two CPUSA officials. After answering questions about Matusow, Sacher refused to state whether he himself was or had been a CPUSA member, objecting that the questions were "not pertinent to anything with which this committee is concerned." The subcommittee claimed the questions were pertinent to proposed legislation to bar Communist lawyers from practicing in federal courts. Convicted, Sacher was sentenced to six months in prison.[19]

The Court, however, citing *Watkins*, ruled that while SISS was authorized to inquire about Matusow's recantation, its authorized "scope of inquiry" did not extend to bills to bar Communist lawyers. Clark and Whittaker dissented.[20]

Frankfurter, the per curiam's author, sought a low profile for the decision, rebuffing Douglas's request for "a full dress opinion." Harlan urged "holding up announcement of the decision pending the present flurry in Congress."[21]

Loyalty Discharges, a How-to Guide—*Beilan* and *Lerner*

In *Slochower,* two years earlier, the Court ruled that New York City could not lawfully discharge a public employee solely for invoking the Fifth Amendment before a Senate committee. It did, however, suggest an exception to its ruling: the result might be different if the employee refused to answer the same questions asked by his employer to evaluate his "qualifications" for the job. In *Beilan* and *Lerner,* the "qualifications" exception swallowed *Slochower*'s rule.[22]

Herman A. Beilan had taught in the Philadelphia public schools for twenty-two years when, in 1952, summoned to the superintendent's office, he refused to say whether "he had been the Press Director of the Professional Section of the Communist Political Association in 1944." Nor, he added, would he answer other questions "of this type." No action was taken against Beilan until, more than a year later, he was called before a HUAC subcommittee and invoked the Fifth Amendment in response to questions about Communist activities. Five days afterward, the board of education instituted proceedings to fire him for "incompetency" for refusing to answer the superintendent's questions.[23]

The Court, by 5–4 vote, in an opinion by Burton, upheld Beilan's discharge. The superintendent's questions, it said, were "relevant to the issue of [his] fitness and suitability to serve as a teacher." It explained: "The Board ... took care to charge [him] with incompetency, and not with disloyalty. It found him insubordinate and lacking in frankness and candor—it made no finding as to his loyalty." *Slochower*, the Court said, "envisioned and distinguished the situation now before us."[24]

In a companion case, Max Lerner, a subway conductor, was discharged pursuant to New York's Security Risk Law. While he worked in a "major artery" in

New York City's transportation system, Lerner's "daily task was simply to open and shut subway doors." Brought before a city agency, he refused to answer whether he was a CPUSA member, invoking the Fifth Amendment. Lerner was discharged on the basis of the agency's findings that he was of "doubtful trust and reliability" and thus a security risk and that his "continued employment would endanger national and state security." Although these findings were based solely on his refusal to answer and Fifth Amendment plea, a state court found that Lerner was not fired for pleading the Fifth Amendment but for his "lack of candor" in refusing to give information about himself.[25]

The Court affirmed, again by 5–4 vote, in an opinion by Harlan. Unlike *Slochower*, it said, the agency's decision was not based on Lerner's invocation of the Fifth Amendment "in a federal inquiry having nothing to do with" his qualifications for employment but rather in a state "inquiry into fitness of its employees." Although the state did base his firing on the ground that he was "in effect" a security risk, the Court continued, it did not "equate this ground for dismissal with 'disloyalty.'"[26]

Douglas, joined by Black, dissenting, responded that "[t]he fitness of a subway conductor for his job depends on his health, his promptness, his record for reliability, not on his politics or philosophy of life. The fitness of a teacher for her job turns on her devotion to that priesthood, her education, and her performance in the library, in the laboratory, and the classroom, not on her political beliefs." To be sure, he said, "[a] teacher who is organizing a Communist cell in a schoolhouse or a subway conductor who is preparing the transportation system for sabotage" would be "unfit"; but there is "no such evidence in the records before us," "only a bare refusal to testify." Warren and Brennan dissented separately.[27]

Douglas's dissent cited *NAACP v. Alabama*, decided the same day, in which the Court struck down an Alabama court's order compelling disclosure of NAACP membership lists. Harlan, who wrote for a unanimous Court in *NAACP*, found that "compelled disclosure of affiliation with groups engaged in advocacy" may constitute an "effective . . . restraint on freedom of association." Past disclosures of the identity of NAACP members, he said, "has exposed these members to economic reprisal, loss of employment, threat of physical coercion, and other manifestations of public hostility." *NAACP v. Alabama*, Douglas wrote in *Beilan-Lerner*, "gave protection" against "governmental probing into political activities and associations of one dissident group of people," and the Court "should do the same here."[28]

Beilan and *Lerner* provided states and cities with a how-to guide. When firing employees who plead the Fifth Amendment, they taught, public agencies should use words such as "fitness," "candor," "reliability," and "trust," and never mention the Fifth Amendment.

Deportation/Denaturalization—*Rowoldt* and More

"Communist" aliens fared well in the 1957 term.

The case of Charles Rowoldt, an elderly Jewish alien who immigrated from Germany in 1914 and was briefly a CPUSA member in 1935, may have had special resonance for Frankfurter, himself a turn-of-the-century Jewish immigrant from a German-speaking country. Rowoldt's CPUSA membership, in the depths of the Depression, was likely not atypical. Testifying at his deportation hearing (the only evidence on this issue), he explained his motive for joining: "[T]he Communist Party . . . had one aim—to get something to eat for the people. . . . Even at the few communist meetings I attended, nothing was ever said about overthrowing anything. All they talked about was fighting for the daily needs." Rowoldt was ordered deported in 1951.[29]

The Court, by 5–4 vote in an opinion by Frankfurter, reversed because the record failed to show that Rowoldt had a "meaningful association" with the CPUSA. In *Galvan*, three years earlier, the Court ruled, also in a Frankfurter opinion, that under the Internal Security Act it did not matter if the alien was unaware the Party advocated forcible overthrow and "[i]t is enough" that he joined "aware that he was joining an organization known as the Communist Party which operates as a distinct and active political organization, and that he did so of his own free will." Rowoldt's membership seemed to fall within the capacious *Galvan* standard.[30]

Frankfurter's rationale relied on the "spirit" (but not the words) of what he termed the "alleviating Amendment of 1951 as expounded by its sponsor, Senator McCarran." That amendment—which excused from deportation persons who were members of a proscribed organization when under age sixteen or "for purposes of obtaining employment, food rations, or other essentials of living"—mandated, he said, "the kind of meaningful association" not shown by Rowoldt's "unchallenged" testimony.[31]

Harlan, dissenting, joined by Burton, Clark, and Whittaker, argued that McCarran's "ameliorating amendment" was intended to benefit only persons "*excluded* from entry . . . because they had joined totalitarian organizations in *foreign countries*." He cited McCarran's reference to persons who became Hitler Youth members "during infancy."[32]

Bonetti v. Rogers presented the kind of narrow, this-case-only issue—the Court termed the facts "rare and novel"—that Frankfurter preferred when the Court decided a "Communist" case against the government. But in *Bonetti* he sided with the government, and Burton and Whittaker were the swing votes in the Court's decision overturning Frank Bonetti's deportation order.[33]

Bonetti, a Los Angeles resident, came from France in 1923. He joined the

CPUSA in 1932 but in 1936 "voluntarily ceased paying dues and left the Party." In 1937 he went to Spain to fight in the Spanish civil war, "abandoning all rights of residence here." Fifteen months later, however, in 1938, Bonetti was admitted to the United States "for permanent residence as a quota immigrant." In 1951, he was ordered deported for having been a CPUSA member. The issue before the Court was whether the words of the statute—requiring deportation if the alien was a Party member "at the time of entering the United States, or has been at any time thereafter"—applied to both of Bonetti's entries or only the last one. If the latter, he was not deportable, for he was neither a Party member in 1938 nor afterward.[34]

The Court, by 6–3 vote in an opinion by Whittaker, chose the narrower interpretation. The statute, it found, referred only to "the entry under which [Bonetti] claims the status and right of lawful presence that is sought to be annulled by his deportation." Since he "claims no right of lawful presence" under his 1923 entry, the Court said, his 1938 entry "constituted 'the time of entering the United States,' within the meaning" of the statute.[35]

In dissent Clark, joined by Frankfurter and Harlan, argued that the statute applied "to membership after *any* entry—including the first as well as the last."[36]

Whittaker wrote for a unanimous Court in a third deportation case, this one a criminal prosecution. Knut Einar Heikkinen, born in Finland and editor of a Finnish-language newspaper in Wisconsin, was ordered deported in 1952 by reason of CPUSA membership between 1923 and 1930. He was prosecuted under the statute, upheld by the Court in 1952 in *Spector*, making it a felony for an alien subject to a deportation order to either willfully fail to depart or willfully fail "to make timely application in good faith for travel or other documents necessary" to departure within six months after issuance of the deportation order. Indicted for both offenses, Heikkinen was convicted and received a five-year prison sentence.[37]

The Court had little difficulty in reversing his conviction because of the government's failures of proof. As to the failure-to-depart charge, it held, the government was required to prove, and did not, that some country "was willing, in that [six-month] period, to receive" Heikkinen. And, as to his alleged failure to apply for necessary travel documents, the Court cited a letter INS had written to him advising that "[a]rrangements to effect your deportation . . . are being made and when completed you will be notified when and where to present yourself for deportation." "Surely," it found, Heikkinen "was justified in relying upon the plain meaning of those simple words, and it cannot be said that he acted 'willfully' . . . until, at least, they were in some way countermanded, which was never done within the prescribed period."[38]

Denaturalization actions, which entailed loss of citizenship often followed by deportation, received close scrutiny at the Court. In *Schneiderman* in 1943,

Bridges in 1953, and *Zucca* in 1956, the Court decided denaturalization cases against the government and in favor of accused Communists. Since 1943 it required the government to bear "the heavy burden of proving its case by 'clear, unequivocal, and convincing' evidence which does not 'leave the issue in doubt.'" In the 1957 term, in two cases involving Michigan Communists, the Court held the government failed to sustain its burden of proof.[39]

The facts in the two cases were similar. Stanislaw Nowak came to the United States from Poland in 1913 at age ten; Rebecca Maisenberg immigrated from czarist Russia in 1912 when she was eleven. Both were naturalized in 1938, under a pre–World War I statute. Nowak, a union organizer, was then elected and served for years as a Democratic state senator; Maisenberg ran unsuccessfully for office on the Communist Party ticket. In the early 1950s, the government filed suits to denaturalize them. Because, it charged, both were CPUSA members when they obtained citizenship in 1938, their negative answers to a question in a petition for naturalization form ("Do you belong to or are you associated with any organization which teaches or advocates anarchy or overthrow of existing government in this country?") were false, and, in addition, their party memberships showed that in the five years preceding their applications they were not "attached to the principles of the Constitution" as the statute required.[40]

The Court, by identical 6–3 votes in opinions by Harlan, ruled in Nowak's and Maisenberg's favor. The question on the form, it found, was "not sufficiently clear." "Nowak could reasonably have interpreted [the question] as a two-pronged inquiry relating simply to anarchy." Nor did party membership "of itself" prove a lack of "attach[ment] to the principles of the Constitution." The government, the Court held, was obligated to prove in addition, and did not, "that Nowak knew of the Party's illegal advocacy." Maisenberg's case, it held, was governed by *Nowak*. Burton, Clark, and Whittaker dissented.[41]

The two decisions, the *New York Times* reported, "will apparently have only limited effects" because persons applying for citizenship "are now required to answer a specific question about Communist party membership."[42]

Passports—*Kent* and *Dayton*

As a corollary to deporting aliens for past or present CPUSA membership, the government sought to prevent citizens with left-wing associations—not only CPUSA members—from going abroad. The State Department's Passport Office and its chiefs, Ruth Shipley and, starting in 1955, Frances G. Knight, spearheaded this effort. Those denied passports (unlike the usually faceless individuals in deportation cases) were often renowned artists, such as singer-actor Paul Robeson, blacklisted at home but employable in Europe, and playwright Arthur Miller, invited to attend a Brussels premiere of *The Crucible*, and scientists, such as Linus

Pauling, asked to lecture abroad. Leonard Boudin, a lawyer who represented many of the individuals denied passports, was himself denied a passport.[43]

For many years, Stanley I. Kutler wrote, "passports generally were not necessary for foreign travel," and citizens who did seek passports received them "as a matter of right." In June 1952, however, Congress made it unlawful during "any national emergency proclaimed by the President" for a citizen to leave or enter the United States "unless he bears a valid passport," and President Truman soon issued the requisite proclamation. In August 1952, the State Department adopted regulations barring the issuance of passports to current or "recently terminated" CPUSA members, persons "who engage in activities which support the Communist movement," and persons "as to whom there is reason to believe . . . that they are going abroad to engage in activities which will advance the Communist movement." "At any stage of the proceedings," the regulations stated, an applicant "may be required" to sign a non-Communist affidavit.[44]

In *Kent v. Dulles,* the Court considered the State Department's denial of a passport to Rockwell Kent, a painter and "one of America's foremost artists." The feisty seventy-five-year-old Kent, a self-styled socialist who denied being a Communist, had been a member of at least eighty-five alleged Communist-front organizations (the FBI's count in 1951). The Passport Office asked him to sign a non-Communist affidavit and, when he refused, declined to process his application further.[45]

The Court, in a 5–4 decision written by Douglas and joined by Frankfurter, Warren, Black, and Brennan, held the regulations invalid because Congress had not authorized the State Department to withhold passports from citizens on the basis of political affiliations. The government relied on a 1856 statute— "The Secretary of State may grant and issue passports . . . under such rules as the President shall designate and prescribe"—along with precedent that issuing passports is "a discretionary act." But the Court, noting that the secretary's discretion had been exercised "quite narrowly" in the past, declined to find that Congress, when it made passports a prerequisite for foreign travel, intended to give him "unbridled discretion" to deny a passport "for any substantive reason he may choose."[46]

The Court's interpretation of the statutes had a constitutional underpinning: "The right to travel is a part of the 'liberty' of which the citizen cannot be deprived without the due process of law under the Fifth Amendment. . . . Travel abroad, like travel within the country, may be necessary for a livelihood. It may be as close to the heart of the individual as the choice of what he eats, or wears, or reads. Freedom of movement is basic in our scheme of values." Where such basic rights are involved, it said, "we will construe narrowly all delegated powers that curtail or dilute them."[47]

Clark, writing for the four dissenters, reviewed the same legislative history and found that "the Secretary was intended to exercise his traditional passport function in such a manner as would effectively add to the protection of this country's internal security."[48]

A companion case, *Dayton v. Dulles*, presented somewhat different circumstances. Weldon Bruce Dayton, a physicist, sought a passport to travel to India to engage in experimental research at an institute associated with the University of Bombay. Although he willingly executed a non-Communist affidavit, his application was denied by the Secretary of State on the ground that issuance of a passport to him "would be contrary to the national interest." This decision, he was told, was based on his association with Communists and "persons suspected of being part of the Rosenberg espionage ring" and on his "alleged presence" at a New York apartment "allegedly used for microfilming material obtained for use of a foreign government." Although given a hearing, Dayton was refused access to the "confidential reports of investigation" relied on by the State Department.[49]

The Court ruled in Dayton's favor, again by 5–4 vote, in a short opinion by Douglas. The principal issue argued by the parties, Douglas wrote, was "whether the hearing accorded [Dayton] satisfied the requirements of due process," but "[a] majority of the Court thinks we need not reach that constitutional question." Since Dayton was denied a passport "for reasons which we have today held [in *Kent*] to be impermissible," he said, the Court would base its decision on the same ground. Clark, joined by the other *Kent* dissenters, stated in a one-paragraph dissent that the Secretary was authorized to deny a passport to an applicant "who is going abroad with the purpose of engaging in activities that would advance the Communist cause."[50]

The short opinions in *Dayton* gave only a hint of the events that preceded the decision. At their conference, the justices had not only discussed the due process issue but, according to Douglas's notes, seven justices were ready to decide for Dayton on that ground. In addition to the four-member liberal bloc, Frankfurter condemned the secretary's denial of a passport for "reasons known only to him"; Harlan "reverses—can't have a hearing which is not a hearing"; and Whittaker said, "It violates due process to deny [a] passport on confidential information." Douglas accordingly drafted an opinion based on the due process ground. "It is the essence of a fair hearing," he wrote, "that the citizen be given the right to be apprised of the evidence used to deny him his constitutional rights and to rebut it if he can." Clark drafted a full dissent, arguing that the ruling "would place the Secretary in the intolerable position of necessarily sacrificing the national interest no matter how he turned, either by issuing the passport or disclosing the secret information."[51]

Support for Douglas's opinion, however, evaporated. Frankfurter soon circulated a draft opinion concurring in the judgment on *Kent* grounds and declining to reach the constitutional issue. Harlan, joined by Whittaker, circulated a similar concurrence and then both became dissenters, even after the Court's decision was limited to *Kent* grounds. The refusal by Frankfurter (one of the five-justice *Kent* majority) to join Douglas's opinion was decisive. Douglas capitulated, advising his colleagues: "There are only four for the opinion in this case as last circulated—namely the Chief Justice, Justice Black, Justice Brennan and myself. Since we are in the minority and since this is a constitutional issue, we have decided to defer to the majority of the Court and accordingly not to reach the constitutional question."[52]

The Court's limited rationale, however, did little to mitigate the criticism generated by the two decisions. The *Times*'s Arthur Krock repeated with approval Rep. Kenneth Keating's comment that "[w]e cannot allow individual citizens [to travel abroad] without let or hindrance, spewing out their anti-American vitriol everywhere." David Lawrence wrote in *U.S. News & World Report*, "If the Supreme Court had ruled that treason now is lawful, it could not have dealt a more devastating blow to the safety of the people of America." The day after the decisions were issued, Francis Walter, HUAC's chairman, introduced legislation to overturn them; so, a day later, did Eastland, characterizing the Court's action as "again lavishly deferring to communism." Eisenhower urged corrective legislation, stating that "[e]ach day and week that passes without it exposes us to great danger."[53]

The State Department, however, in compliance with the decisions, issued a passport to (among others) Paul Robeson, ending a lengthy battle. He expected to leave for London in two weeks, Robeson told the *Times*. His plans reportedly included "discussions with British producers about a London presentation of 'Othello.'"[54]

Loyalty Oaths and Government Benefits—*Spieser*

California's constitution, which provided honorably discharged veterans a tax exemption for $1,000 of property, was amended in 1952 to deny the exemption to any person who "advocates the overthrow" of the federal or state government by force or violence. An implementing statute required a person claiming the exemption to show, by signing an oath on his property-tax return, that he does not advocate forcible overthrow. Lawrence Spieser and Daniel Prince, honorably discharged World War II veterans, refused to execute the oath and, denied the tax exemption, challenged the state's scheme.[55]

The Court, by a 7–1 vote in an opinion by Brennan, held the scheme unlawful. It was not unlawful because it punished speech—the Court "assume[d] without deciding" that the state could punish advocacy of forcible overthrow—but because of the state's "method for determining" when a claimant may be denied the exemption.[56]

The problem identified by the Court was that the state placed on the applicant the burden of proving his claim of exemption. As a consequence, it found, where speech "falls close to the line separating the lawful and the unlawful," self-censorship was likely. It explained: "The man who knows that he must bring forth proof and persuade another of the lawfulness of his conduct necessarily must steer far wider of the unlawful zone than if the State must bear these burdens." The scheme, the Court said, "can only result in a deterrence of speech which the Constitution makes free." Only Clark dissented, terming the Court's rationale "wholly novel doctrine, unsupported by any precedent."[57]

A companion decision involved two Unitarian churches, which claimed a tax exemption for real property used exclusively for religious worship but refused to sign the oath. The Court, by the same 7–1 vote, again in an opinion by Brennan, ruled in the churches' favor for the reasons stated in *Speiser*.[58]

Black, joined by Douglas, in a concurring opinion for both cases, commented that the cases offered "just another example of a wide-scale effort by government in this country to impose penalties and disabilities on everyone who is or is suspected of being a 'Communist' or who is not ready at all times and all places to swear his loyalty to State and Nation."[59]

Less-than-honorable Military Discharges—*Harmon*

While the Army for a number of years had issued less-than-honorable discharges to conscripts deemed security risks, in 1954 it began for the first time to base such discharges on preinduction activities. The Army explained that the persons thus discharged "limit [their] usefulness to the United States Army by acts or affiliations, past or present, over which [they] had complete control." Although this practice drew criticism and was abandoned in 1956, the Army "refused," the *Times* reported, "to upgrade several hundred less-than-honorable discharges it had given previously to security risks."[60]

Two of the individuals in question, John Henry Harmon III and Howard D. Abramowitz, sued the Secretary of the Army to obtain honorable discharges. Abramowitz had served in Korea, was decorated with a Silver Star, and was honorably separated when his active-duty obligation ended. But while in an inactive reserve status, he was given an "undesirable" discharge because of alleged Communist activities prior to his Army service. Harmon, despite an "excellent" service record, was issued an "undesirable" discharge (later changed to a general discharge under honorable conditions) because of alleged associations with Communists prior to his induction.[61]

At oral argument, the solicitor general's office conceded the secretary's action was not legally sustainable but argued that the courts lacked jurisdiction to remedy the situation. "You mean you're wrong but the courts can't do anything about it," Brennan asked a Justice Department lawyer. "That's right," the lawyer answered. "You say this is beyond the legal authority of the Secretary of the Army," Frankfurter said. "Why, then, hasn't the Department of Justice so informed the Department of the Army?" "It has," the lawyer replied, but the Army would not admit the discharges were invalid. The lower courts agreed with the government that the courts lacked jurisdiction. Harmon and Abramowitz had unsuccessfully appealed their discharges to an Army review board, and a statute made the board's findings "final subject only to review by" the Secretary of the Army.[62]

The Court, by an 8–1 vote in a per curiam opinion, invalidated the less-than-honorable discharges. Frankfurter had told his colleagues that he placed "great importance" in "having a unanimous disposition of the discharge cases expressed in a single document" and "[t]hat involves, inevitably, a per curiam with a minimum of exposition." The opinion was a less-than-graceful committee effort—a draft by Whittaker, edited by Frankfurter, with suggestions by Black and Brennan.[63]

On the issue of jurisdiction, the Court ruled that if the secretary "exceed[ed] his powers," then "his actions would not constitute exercises of his administrative discretion, and . . . judicial relief from this illegality would be available." On the merits, it relied on statutory language providing that the Army review board's decision "shall be based upon all available records of the [Army] relating to the person requesting such review." "We think the word 'records,'" it said, "means *records of military service*, and that the statute, properly construed, means that the type of discharge to be issued is to be determined solely by the soldier's military record in the Army."[64]

Clark, again alone in dissent, stated that the issuance of military discharges was entrusted by Congress to the executive branch and that "[a]t no time until today have the courts interfered in the exercise of this military function." His hometown *Dallas Morning News* said that the decision "seems to make the United States Army a potential haven for Communists and other undesirable characters."[65]

The Court-Curbing Bills and Lyndon's Miracle

Throughout the spring and summer of 1958, an assortment of court-curbing bills moved through the congressional maze. House members overwhelmingly supported anti-Court legislation. In the Senate, liberal Democrats aided by a few Republican moderates opposed the legislation but were outnumbered by the bills' supporters. Eastland, an implacable foe of the Court, chaired the Judiciary Committee, to which most of the bills were referred. Johnson, the Senate majority leader, was largely silent on the issue, although as a likely candidate for the 1960 Democratic presidential nomination he would need the support of liberal Democrats.[66]

Jenner's bill, S 2646, stripping the Court of jurisdiction in five subject areas in which it had decided "Communist" cases against the government, was "the most fundamental challenge to judicial power," Walter Murphy wrote, since the days of FDR's court-packing proposal. Eastland's SISS, following perfunctory hearings the preceding year, held full hearings on the bill. An array of veterans' organizations, right-wing groups, and southern lawyers supported the measure, but the ACLU, NAACP, Americans for Democratic Action, and AFL-CIO were opposed. The Eisenhower administration announced its opposition but made little or no effort to persuade Republicans in the Congress. The ABA's House of Delegates adopted a weakly worded resolution opposing the bill.[67]

To enhance his bill's chances, Jenner compromised. John Marshall Butler (the Maryland Republican elected by McCarthy's 1950 campaign against Millard Tydings) offered a substitute bill, which was reported favorably by the Judiciary Committee in May. Under the substitute, the Court would be stripped of jurisdiction in only one subject area, state bar-admission cases; but other provisions overturned *Watkins, Nelson,* and *Yates* (both its interpretation of the term "organize" and its holding that the Smith Act did not bar abstract advocacy).[68]

HR 3, which nullified both *Nelson* and federal-preemption decisions affecting state labor laws, also progressed. Smith obtained hearings on his bill in May before Celler's House Judiciary Committee, and the Committee approved it in June. *Nelson*-only bills (in other words, directed to state sedition laws only), supported by the Eisenhower administration, were reported favorably by both the House and Senate Judiciary Committees. On July 17, HR 3 passed the House by a 241–155 margin.[69]

Other anti-Court bills, more narrowly focused, cleared the House even more easily. The bill to reverse *Cole v. Young,* a substitute for a different bill the Senate had approved, passed the House on July 10 by a 298–46 vote and proceeded to a House-Senate conference. A bill to overturn *Yates's* interpretation of "organize" was passed by the House without a roll-call vote. And a *Mallory* bill, making confessions admissible in criminal trials notwithstanding a delay in arraigning the defendant, was passed by a 294–79 vote. The Senate Judiciary Committee approved the bill, with an amendment, on August 8.[70]

Because the Court's passport decisions were not issued until mid-June, proponents of legislation to overturn them faced severe time constraints. Nonetheless, the House Foreign Affairs Committee held hearings in July and August, and a bill was favorably reported by the Committee and passed by the House, without a roll-call vote, on August 23. In the Senate, the Foreign Relations Committee conducted hearings in July but took no action.[71]

Lyndon Johnson kept the anti-Court bills from reaching the Senate floor until late in the session. Then, under pressure from the bills' supporters and assured by his floor managers, Hubert Humphrey and Thomas Hennings, that they had the votes to defeat at least the measures deemed most objectionable (the Jenner-Butler bill and HR 3), he allowed several of the bills to reach the floor. On August 19, "after months of maneuver," Anthony Lewis reported, "the Senate was at last into its promised great debate on the Supreme Court."[72]

The *Mallory* bill, certain to pass, came first. Debate centered on the Senate Judiciary Committee's insertion of the word "reasonable" in the bill, so that only confessions made during a "reasonable delay" in arraigning the suspect were admissible. Over conservatives' objections, the Committee amendment was agreed to by a 41–39 vote, after which the bill passed by a 65–12 margin. The difference in wording from the House-passed bill, however, necessitated a House-Senate conference.[73]

On August 20, the Senate considered the Jenner-Butler bill. Jenner, explaining why he introduced his bill, referred to "a long line of cases, involving Communists and subversive activity, in which the Court had accepted, point after point, the legal propositions advanced by the Communists." Hennings responded that the bill seeks "to visit retribution" on the Court for past decisions and presaged "future attempts to strip the Court of its jurisdiction whenever there is disagreement with its decisions." The vote came on Hennings' motion to table the bill. His motion prevailed, and the bill died by a 49–41 vote.[74]

In the early evening the Senate turned to S 654, a *Nelson*-only bill, and, more important, to a motion by John L. McClellan, an Arkansas Democrat, to amend the bill by adding the text of HR 3 to it. The vote on McClellan's amendment—a vote on HR 3—was not simply a reprise of the Jenner-Butler vote. Because HR 3 overturned federal-preemption decisions adverse to employers, it drew support from the Chamber of Commerce, National Association of Manufacturers, and American Farm Bureau, all of whom lobbied for it intensively. When Hennings moved (as in the Jenner-Butler debate) to table McClellan's amendment, his motion was defeated by a 46–39 vote. An immediate motion to reconsider failed by a 47–40 margin. Passage of the bill, including HR 3, was now imminent.[75]

Johnson, surprised by the turn of events, moved to adjourn the Senate until noon the next day. "It is 11:30 in the evening," he said. "I think Members are ready to go home." But McClellan and Jenner, with victory at hand, opposed adjournment and demanded a roll-call vote on Johnson's motion. As the roll call proceeded, Johnson conspicuously noted on a tally sheet the names of senators who voted against him; his motion passed easily.[76]

After a few choice words to Humphrey whose vote count proved inaccurate, Johnson retreated to his office in the Capitol, taking with him Humphrey and the *Times*'s Lewis, a liberal who he knew opposed anti-Court legislation. There, scotch-and-soda in hand, Johnson delivered, in Robert Caro's description, an "awesome" monologue, continuing into the early-morning hours: "[N]ot only a step-by-step exegesis of the complicated parliamentary maneuvers that alone could stop the bill from passing, but an exposition of why it should be stopped, an exposition so passionate that from that day forward, Anthony Lewis would believe in Lyndon Johnson's commitment to liberal causes." "What an opportunity," Harry McPherson later wrote explaining Johnson's motives, "to defeat a bad bill, save the Court, and win the embarrassed thanks of the Senate liberals! It was worth doing."[77]

When proceedings resumed the next day, the Senate debated a motion by John Carroll, a Colorado liberal, to send the bill back to committee. At the same time, Johnson "talked to senators from both parties, arguing, cajoling, pleading, even threatening." In the roll-call vote that followed, three conservatives, one of them Everett Dirksen, the GOP whip, supporters of the bill only hours earlier, switched sides. Another supporter, Robert Kerr of Oklahoma, stayed outside the Senate chamber. But two moderates, previously opposed to the bill, defected. When Johnson's count showed he needed one more switch, he turned to Wallace Bennett, a conservative Utah Republican and a strong supporter of Vice President Richard Nixon's 1960 presidential bid. Johnson told Bennett that as matters stood the vote would be a tie and, in Caro's words, "a tie vote would have to be broken by Nixon, and no matter how Nixon voted . . . the vote would hurt Nixon's chances to become President: he would have to antagonize either liberals or conservatives." With Bennett voting in favor of Carroll's motion, the bill was sent back to committee by a 41–40 vote, killing it. "The final result," Lewis wrote in the *Times* the next morning, "was one of the great triumphs of Mr. Johnson's career as a Senate strategist."[78]

Nor did any of the other anti-Court bills, caught in the end-of-session stampede, become law. The *Nelson*-only bill, which passed the House and would easily have passed the Senate, was yoked to HR 3 and sent back to committee. A bill overruling *Cole v. Young* was agreed on by House-Senate conferees and approved by the House on August 22. But after a conversation on the Senate floor between Johnson and the Senate and House committee chairmen, Olin D. Johnston of South Carolina and Tom Murray of Tennessee, the conference bill was not called up in the Senate. And the *Yates*-"organize" and passport bills, both passed by the House, were not reported out of committee in the Senate.[79]

There remained the *Mallory* bill, which had passed both Houses but with a slight difference in wording. On August 23, a conference version was reported and quickly approved by the House. But the conferees had added language not contained in either the House or Senate bill—a technical violation of a Senate rule. The bill died in the Senate on John Carroll's point of order, at 4:10 A.M. on Sunday August 24, in the final minutes of the session.[80]

By then the Court was well into its summer recess. With help from Lyndon Johnson and no small amount of luck, it had dodged, for the moment, all of the legislative bullets. The justices, however, had little cause for celebration for, as Warren later wrote, "[s]ome of this legislation, evoking as it did the atmosphere of Cold War hysteria, came dangerously close to passing."[81]

9

Barenblatt, Uphaus, and the Court in Retreat

(OCTOBER TERMS 1958 AND 1959)

Events moved quickly at the Court following Congress's adjournment on August 24, 1958. Four days later, convened in a special term, it heard argument in the Little Rock school-desegregation controversy. On September 29, it issued an unprecedented joint opinion by all nine justices, declaring that the constitutional rights of black students "are not to be sacrificed or yielded to the violence and disorder which followed upon the actions of the Governor and Legislature."[1]

The special term completed, Harold Burton, suffering from Parkinson's disease, announced his retirement from the Court, at age seventy, after thirteen years as a justice. He was, the *Times* said, "[a] pleasant, soft-spoken gentleman who has moved quietly through American public life." His successor, nominated by Eisenhower the following day, was Potter Stewart, also an Ohio Republican, only forty-three years old, and a federal court-of-appeals judge. Stewart joined the Court on October 14 under a recess appointment.[2]

The 1958 congressional elections, held on November 4, resulted in a sweeping victory for the Democrats and reduced anti-Court ranks in the Congress. Democrats gained forty-nine seats in the House and sixteen in the Senate, giving them their widest margins since the New Deal. Newly elected Senate liberals included Eugene McCarthy of Minnesota, Philip Hart of Michigan, and Ernest Gruening of Alaska. Wisconsin's William Proxmire, elected in 1957 to complete Joe McCarthy's unexpired term, was easily reelected to a full term, prompting his Republican opponent to charge that Soviet premier Nikita Khrushchev "won a great victory at the polls yesterday." The diminution in the number of anti-Court members was significant: of the forty-one senators who supported the Jenner-Butler bill in the August 20 roll-call vote, four were defeated and two, including Jenner himself, retired and were replaced by moderate Democrats.[3]

The Court, however, conscious of its recent escape from punitive legislation, quickened its retreat from "Red Monday." The flow of decisions in "Communist" cases, heavy in each of the preceding two terms, slowed in the 1958 term, when the Court issued seven signed decisions, and even more so in the 1959 term, with only two signed decisions and two via per curiam opinions. During the 1958 term, the government prevailed in two major constitutional decisions, and in the 1959 term it won every one of the handful of cases decided.[4]

Frankfurter was now a reliable vote for the government and, more clearly than before, the leader of a five-justice conservative majority in "Communist" cases, with Stewart replacing Burton. In two 1958-term criminal cases (not "Communist" cases) presenting issues under the 1957 *Jencks* statute, he wrote opinions seemingly intended to placate Congress by construing the statute to require production of only a narrow category of statements by government witnesses. He assigned a noteworthy decision in the 1959 term to Harlan who, writing for the five-justice majority, upheld the denial of Social Security benefits to an elderly alien deported to Bulgaria by reason of past CPUSA membership.[5]

The most important decisions, both by 5–4 vote, were *Barenblatt v. United States* and *Uphaus v. Wyman*, in which the Court decided in the government's favor a constitutional issue it had nibbled at, but avoided deciding, for years: whether legislative committees may, consistent with the First Amendment, compel witnesses to disclose "Communist" associations. *Barenblatt* was another HUAC contempt-of-Congress case, and, as in earlier cases, nonconstitutional issues were also presented. But this time the Court chose to decide on constitutional grounds. *Uphaus* seemed indistinguishable from *Sweezy* (it involved a New Hampshire adult-camp director's refusal to provide information to Louis Wyman's one-man committee). But Frankfurter and Harlan, who in *Sweezy* joined in a concurring opinion that sustained the witness's refusal to answer on First Amendment grounds, created the majority in *Uphaus* reaching the opposite result.[6]

The conservative *U.S. News & World Report* welcomed the two decisions. The Court has begun "what is being interpreted as a strategic retreat," it commented, and "[t]he question now is raised whether the Court is starting to make a turn to the 'right.'" A "[n]ew line-up" of justices and a "new majority within the Court" has emerged, the magazine said, one "that may lead the Court away from the line of congressional fire."[7]

The only significant decision against the government during the two terms was *Greene v. McElroy*, which addressed but did not decide the constitutional issue whether the government could revoke a security clearance essential to an individual's job on the basis of "confidential" reports not disclosed to him. The Court simply held (as in the passport cases) that the secretary lacked authorization to do so.[8]

Smith Act "membership" clause cases returned to the Court, but it twice postponed a decision. In the 1958 term, it ordered the cases reargued in the 1959 term, and in the 1959 term it again ordered them reargued (along with another longstanding case, *CPUSA v. SACB*, challenging the registration provisions of the Internal Security Act) at the start of the 1960 term.[9]

Stewart for Burton

When Burton met with the president and Attorney General William P. Rogers in July 1958 to discuss his intended resignation, Eisenhower's "biggest concern was that Burton's successor be sufficiently conservative," and "the only person they discussed" was Potter Stewart. Yet Stewart was no doctrinaire conservative. Asked by the press about his "judicial philosophy," he answered, "I don't really know what it is. I'd like to be thought of as a lawyer"[10]

Born into an accomplished and successful Cincinnati family—his father, James Garfield Stewart, was a justice of the Supreme Court of Ohio and a former mayor of Cincinnati—Stewart received a private-school education and graduated from Yale's college and law school. After serving in the Navy during World War II, he practiced with a large Cincinnati law firm and was active in local politics. Handsome, bright, and articulate, Stewart was named to the court of appeals in 1954, at age thirty-nine. When, four years later, Eisenhower appointed him to the Supreme Court, the press found him "urbane, suave, and disarming in his answers."[11]

An "extremely able" justice (Douglas's assessment), Stewart had a gift for pithy phrases—most famous was his remark in a 1964 opinion about hard-core pornography, that he would not attempt to define it "[b]ut I know it when I see it." He "rate[d] high," one observer said, "on intellect, lucidity, and judicial candor." Stewart gained a reputation as the "swing man" on an otherwise equally divided Court. But in "Communist" cases, he voted far more often for the government. During the 1958 and 1959 terms, his votes largely paralleled Frankfurter's and were decisive in *Barenblatt*, *Uphaus*, and several other 5–4 decisions won by the government.[12]

Committee-Contempts—*Barenblatt*, *Uphaus*, and More

As in prior years, the Court in the 1958 and 1959 terms decided several committee-contempt cases—the archetypal McCarthy-era offense.

The first, and easiest for the Court, involved the contempt-of-Congress conviction of Abram Flaxer, head of the left-wing United Public Workers, who failed to produce to SISS lists showing the names and addresses of union members employed by state or local governments. Flaxer did not deny that the information was available to him, and when asked how long it would take to prepare the lists, he replied, "I imagine it could be done within a week." The chairman then ordered him to produce the list "within 10 days from this date." "[T]his date" was October 5, 1951, and Flaxer's indictment specified October 5 as the date of his contempt.[13]

A unanimous Court, however, in an opinion by Douglas, "read the record as showing no default on that date." "[T]o say the least," it said, "there was ambiguity in [the committee's] ruling on the time of performance. The witness could well conclude, we think, that he had 10 days more to consider the matter.... Certainly we cannot say that [Flaxer] could tell with a reasonable degree of certainty that the Committee demanded the lists this very day, not 10 days hence."[14]

In another case in which witnesses may have been misled, the Court, again unanimous, reversed the contempt convictions of three witnesses before Ohio's "little HUAC" commission for refusing to answer questions about alleged Communist activities. But the Court affirmed the conviction of a fourth witness by a 4–4 vote (Stewart did not participate, his father having ruled on the case in the Ohio Supreme Court). The four witnesses had been informed by the commission that they could rely on the privilege against self-incrimination in Ohio's constitution, and they invoked the privilege in refusing to answer. But Ohio also had an immunity statute, and although the commission never mentioned the statute to the witnesses, the Ohio Supreme Court upheld their contempt convictions on the ground that the witnesses were presumed to know Ohio law and thus to know that the immunity statute "deprived them of the protection of the privilege."[15]

The Court held, in an opinion by Brennan, that the Ohio Supreme Court's judgment denied due process to the witnesses and that to sustain it "would be to sanction an indefensible sort of entrapment by the State—convicting a citizen for exercising a privilege which the State had clearly told him was available to him."[16]

However, in the case of one question to the fourth witness—Joseph Stern refused to answer the question "Where do you reside, Mr. Stern?"—the commission directed him to answer after he claimed the privilege. Clark, joined by Frankfurter, Harlan, and Whittaker, voted to affirm Stern's conviction for this single refusal. "There was no 'entrapment' in the above question," Clark wrote, "since it was made clear, even without reference to the Ohio immunity statute, that as to that question the privilege was not available." But Brennan, joined by Warren, Black, and Douglas, thought it "obvious that Stern was as much 'entrapped' as the others."[17]

Barenblatt and *Uphaus* presented more far-reaching issues. Lloyd Barenblatt, a thirty-one-year-old psychology instructor at Vassar College (until he received

HUAC's subpoena), was convicted of contempt-of-Congress for refusing to answer five questions—including whether he was, while a graduate student at the University of Michigan, a member of "the Haldane Club of the Communist Party." Barenblatt did not invoke the Fifth Amendment, relying instead on his First Amendment rights. He also contended, with an eye to *Watkins*, that HUAC's authorizing resolution was impermissibly vague, that HUAC failed adequately to inform him of the pertinency of its questions, and that its goal was merely exposure.[18]

The five-justice majority, however, in an opinion by Harlan, affirmed his conviction. Addressing the narrower issues, the Court upheld the HUAC authorizing resolution it had criticized in *Watkins*. The resolution's "proper meaning," it now found, was "not to be derived alone from its abstract terms" but also from HUAC's history, which showed the House had given HUAC "pervasive authority to investigate Communist activities in this country." The Court also rejected Barenblatt's pertinency claim. HUAC was investigating communism in education, it said, and Barenblatt, "unlike Watkins," refused "to answer questions as to his own [CPUSA] affiliations, whose pertinency of course was clear beyond doubt."[19]

Whether the First Amendment protected his refusal to answer, the Court held, turned on a balancing test: "Where First Amendment rights are asserted to bar governmental interrogation resolution of the issue always involves a balancing by the courts of the competing private and public interests at stake in the particular circumstances shown." On the government's side of the balance, it said, Congress has "wide power to legislate in the field of Communist activity," a power that "rests on the right of self-preservation." It noted that the Court "has consistently refused to view the Communist Party as an ordinary political party." On the other side of the balance, Barenblatt's interests, never specifically described, were dismissed as "subordinate to those of the state." In answer to his claim that HUAC's goal was merely exposure, a purpose proscribed by *Watkins*, the Court now ruled that "the Judiciary lacks authority to intervene" on the basis of Congress's "motives."[20]

Harlan, the opinion's author, two years earlier had joined Frankfurter's opinion in *Sweezy* that found the First Amendment violated by the investigator's questions. But Sweezy, Harlan now explained, was questioned about his university lecture even though he "had not been shown ever to have been connected with the Communist Party" and about the Progressive Party which was "then on the ballot as a normal political party in some 26 states. "This is a very different thing," he said, from HUAC's inquiry "into the extent to which the Communist Party has succeeded in infiltrating our universities."[21]

Black, joined by Warren and Douglas, delivered an angry dissent. HUAC's authorizing resolution, he said, was not only unconstitutionally vague, but the vagueness problem was compounded by the Court's balancing test, which required Barenblatt to weigh the balance "at the time of his interrogation." He criticized the Court's dismissal of Barenblatt's side of the balance while "on the other side the demands of the Government are vastly overstated and called 'self preservation.'" He condemned the very idea of a balancing test, "[t]he notion that despite the First Amendment's command Congress can abridge speech and association if this Court decides that the governmental interest in abridging speech is greater than an individual's interest in exercising that freedom."[22]

Black also challenged the Court's rationale that "the ordinary rules and requirements of the Constitution do not apply" because Communists "do not constitute a political party but only a criminal gang." The CPUSA cannot be thus outlawed, he said, because "mixed among those aims of communism which are illegal are perfectly normal political and social goals. And muddled with its revolutionary tenets is a drive to achieve power through the ballot, if it can be done." "[M]any Communists," he said, "undoubtedly hoped to accomplish its lawful goals through support of Communist candidates," and "[t]o attribute to them, and to those who have left the Party, the taint of the group is to ignore both our traditions that guilt like belief is 'personal and not a matter of mere association'" and the fact that members of a political party "'notoriously do not subscribe unqualifiedly'" to all of its asserted principles.[23]

Brennan, dissenting separately, contended that "no purpose for the investigation of Barenblatt is revealed by the record except exposure purely for the sake of exposure. This is not a purpose to which Barenblatt's rights under the First Amendment can validly be subordinated."[24]

Uphaus presented similar issues. Willard Uphaus, a Methodist lay preacher who held a doctorate from Yale and had taught in its divinity school, was executive director of World Fellowship, variously described as a "pacifist organization" and "an interfaith group set up to address major world problems." The group maintained an adult summer camp in New Hampshire at which lecturers addressed the camp's guests—Brennan described it as "some sort of assemblage that was oriented toward the discussion of political and other public matters." The camp drew the attention of Louis Wyman following reports that Uphaus and some of the speakers had "a history of association with 'Communist front' movements" and had "followed the 'Communist line.'"[25]

Wyman issued subpoenas to the group demanding the names of "all persons who attended the camp" in 1954 and 1955. When Uphaus, sixty-five years old and described by the *Times* as a "slightly-built man with a shock of unruly white hair and a gentle voice," refused to provide the names, he was held in contempt by a state court and ordered jailed until he complied.[26]

The Court, by the same vote as in *Barenblatt*, in an opinion by Clark, sustained the contempt order. Uphaus's First Amendment contention was, as in

Barenblatt, subjected to a balancing test. New Hampshire's investigation, the Court found, was "undertaken in the interest of self-preservation . . ." The record shows, it said, that Uphaus had "participated in 'Communist front' activities" and that at least nineteen speakers he invited "had either been members of the Communist Party or had connections or affiliations with it or with one or more of the organizations cited" in the attorney general's list. On Uphaus's side of the balance, the Court, noting that state law required World Fellowship to maintain a guest register open to inspection by police, found only "the interest in associational privacy of persons who, at least to the extent of the guest registration statute, made public at the inception the association they now wish to keep private." *Sweezy*, it added, was distinguishable, "since World Fellowship is neither a university nor a political party."[27]

Brennan's dissent, in which Warren, Black, and Douglas joined, found the record "affirmatively shows that the investigatory objective was the impermissible one of exposure for exposure's sake." The "damaging effect" of exposure "on the persons to be named in the guest list is obvious," he wrote, and "there is really nothing against which" their rights "can be balanced."[28]

Earlier Brennan had tried to persuade Frankfurter that exposure was the state's sole objective, asking him to read Wyman's report. But Frankfurter was unpersuaded, citing "the respect to be accorded the determination of a State." He assured Brennan, however, that "there isn't a man on the Court who personally disapproves more than I do of the activities of all the un-American Committees, of all the Smith [Act] prosecutions, of the Attorney General's list, etc., etc."[29]

The Court sustained Uphaus's confinement "until he produces the documents called for in the subpoenas," observing that if he "chooses to . . . obey the order of New Hampshire's courts, he need not face jail." The state courts in December 1959 ordered Uphaus imprisoned for one year or until he complied. He filed a new appeal to the Court and a motion to obtain his release on bail, but in September 1960 the Court denied him bail, by a 6–3 vote.[30]

The names of NAACP members, however, continued to be viewed very differently. The Court, in the 1959 term, decided *Bates v. City of Little Rock* in which, as in *NAACP v. Alabama* in 1958, it unanimously rejected the efforts of a southern jurisdiction to compel disclosure of NAACP members' names. Local NAACP officials had been convicted of violating city license-tax ordinances when they refused to provide the names of persons who paid dues or made contributions. The Court, in an opinion by Stewart, found it "now beyond dispute that freedom of association for the purpose of advancing ideas and airing grievances is protected" by the Constitution and held that the cities "failed to demonstrate a controlling justification for the deterrence of free association which compulsory disclosure of the membership lists would cause."[31]

Deportation—*Nestor* and More

The government won both of the Court's two deportation decisions in the 1958 and 1959 terms plus a third decision in which a deportee, already exiled to a foreign country, was stripped of Social Security benefits. In each case the vote was 5–4.

In *Niukkanen v. McAlexander*, Frankfurter effectively abandoned his position in *Rowoldt*, two years earlier, that the government must show a "meaningful association" with the CPUSA in order to obtain deportation on the basis of past Party membership. Willia Niukkanen, a fifty-year-old Portland, Oregon, house painter, was born in Finland when his Finnish parents (who resided in the United States) returned for a visit; they brought him to the United States when he was nine months old. Niukkanen married an American citizen and served honorably in the U.S. Army. While two ex-Communists testified he was a CPUSA member from 1937 to 1939, they admitted he was attracted by "the sufferings of the people in the depression" and that overthrow of the government was not discussed at the Party meetings he attended. Niukkanen's own testimony confirmed that "the only thing I heard in those days was more relief and more work." But when asked whether he had been a CPUSA member, he answered, "Knowingly, I haven't, no." The district judge found that he "perjured himself" by this answer and sustained the deportation order.[32]

In a per curiam ruling, written by Frankfurter for the five-justice majority, the Court upheld Niukkanen's deportation. Whether he is "saved from" deportation by *Rowoldt*, Frankfurter wrote, "turns on evaluation of the testimony before the District Court," and that "largely depends on the credibility of the testimony on which the district judge based his judgment." The district judge found Niukkanen perjured himself, he said, and the Court "cannot say" that his findings were "clearly erroneous."[33]

In dissent Douglas, joined by Warren, Black, and Brennan, found the case "on all fours" with *Rowoldt*. The "whole of this record" shows, he wrote, that Niukkanen "was caught up in a movement whose ideology he did not understand and whose leaders spoke in terms of bread for the hungry, and jobs for the unemployed." As in *Rowoldt*, Douglas concluded, Niukkanen's association with the Party was "'wholly devoid of any "political" implications.'"[34]

Before *Niukkanen* was issued, Frankfurter, in a memorandum to the other justices, blamed Douglas's dissent for forcing him to "put on record that Niukkanen was found to be a perjurer." He had "benevolently" tried to avoid this "disclosure," he said, in order not to "prejudice what I had hoped would be a successful effort to get a private bill for the relief of Niukkanen," but "[t]he dissent leaves me no choice." Three weeks after the Court's decision, Senator Wayne Morse of Oregon did introduce a private bill for Niukkanen—"[T]his Capitol dome is not going to fall," Morse told the Senate, "if this house painter in Portland, Oreg., remains in the United States"—and as late as 1975 Oregon legislators continued to do so.³⁵

Kimm v. Rosenberg affirmed, in a per curiam opinion written by Clark, INS's rejection of Diamond Kimm's request for suspension of deportation. He was not eligible for this relief, INS said, because he failed to prove he was of "good moral character" and not a member of the CPUSA, prerequisites to a suspension. Born in Korea in 1901, Kimm entered the United States as a student in 1928 and studied geology at the University of Southern California. Unable to return to Korea because of hostilities there, he remained in the United States and, during World War II, worked as a chemist and then briefly in the Office of Strategic Services. After the war, he was ordered deported because he was no longer a student. At his suspension hearing, Kimm presented evidence of his good character, and there was no suggestion he was a Communist. But "apparently at random, and out of the blue" (Brennan's description), he was asked whether he was a CPUSA member and invoked the Fifth Amendment, resulting in INS's finding that he was ineligible for suspension of deportation.³⁶

The decision turned on a burden-of-proof issue. The Court found that the statute governing suspension of deportation, "in contrast to the statutory provisions governing deportation, imposes the general burden of proof upon the applicant." Whether Kimm "was justified in his personal refusal to answer," it said, "this did not relieve him under the statute of the burden of establishing the authority of the Attorney General to exercise his discretion in the first place."³⁷

Douglas, in a dissent joined by Warren and Black, argued that the statute "says nothing about the need of an alien to prove he was never a Communist." "[N]o one has said or intimated" Kimm was a Communist, Brennan added.³⁸

Kimm was deported to North Korea about 1965.³⁹

Social Security benefits due another deportee, Ephram Nestor, were terminated under a 1954 statute directing that "no monthly benefit... shall be paid" to an individual deported under specified sections of the Immigration and Nationality Act. Not all deportees were covered; but the statute did apply to persons deported on the basis of unlawful entry, certain crimes such as narcotics addiction, and CPUSA membership.⁴⁰

Nestor, who came to the United States from Bulgaria in 1913, became eligible for Social Security benefits in November 1955 and, based on his earnings over almost nineteen years, received a monthly payment of $55.60. In July 1956, however, he was deported to Bulgaria for having been a CPUSA member from 1933 to 1939, and his benefits were terminated. Nestor sued for restoration of his benefits, and a district judge ruled that he had been stripped of "an accrued property right" and deprived of due process.⁴¹

The government appealed and won. The five-justice majority, in an opinion by Harlan, held that Nestor had no property right in his benefits, for "[t]o engraft upon the Social Security system a concept of 'accrued property rights' would deprive it of the flexibility and boldness in adjustment to ever-changing conditions which it demands." While due process, the Court continued, precluded "patently arbitrary classification, utterly lacking in rational justification," it was not "irrational for Congress to have concluded that the public purse should not be utilized to contribute to the support of those deported on the grounds specified in the statute." Responding to the dissenters, the Court added that the 1954 statute was neither a bill of attainder nor an ex post facto law because punishment is an "[e]ssential" element of both and termination of Social Security benefits was not "'punishment' in the constitutional sense."[42]

In dissent Douglas found the statute "a classic example of a bill of attainder" and that "[c]utting off a person's livelihood by denying him accrued social benefits" was indeed punishment. Brennan, arguing that the statute was also an ex post facto law, took note of Nestor's situation: "His predicament is very real—an aging man deprived of the means with which to live after being separated from his family and exiled to live among strangers in a land he quit 47 years ago. The common sense of it is that he has been punished severely for his past conduct."[43]

Loyalty discharges—*Greene, Vitarelli, Nelson/Globe*

Federal and state loyalty-discharge cases continued to reach the Court, now including cases of private-company employees discharged as a result of the government's revocation of their security clearances.

When William L. Greene, an aeronautical engineer, lost his clearance in late 1951, he was an executive, earning $18,000 per year, with ERCO, a company engaged in classified work for the armed services. ERCO's principal contract was for a flight simulator Greene had designed. Before reaching the Court, his case proceeded through more than four years of hearings before security boards, reviews, and determinations by defense officials, ending adversely to him. ERCO had been compelled to fire Greene at the outset, and, without a security clearance, he was unable to find employment as an aeronautical engineer. Eventually he did find work as an architectural draftsman at a salary of $4,700 per year.[44]

The government presented no witnesses at the hearings afforded Greene and relied entirely on "confidential reports" not disclosed to him. The security boards saw the reports but neither the informants nor the investigators who "took their statements." The charges, of which Greene was informed in summary fashion, stemmed largely from a five-year marriage that ended in 1947. He was charged with having "sympathetically associated" with Communists, including his ex-wife; having Communist publications in his home; attending a dinner given by a Communist "front"; being a member of a bookshop group listed by the attorney general; investing $1,000 in a radio station whose stockholders were reportedly "Communists or pro-Communists"; and having contacts with Soviet embassy officials in the 1944–47 period. Greene responded that, except for his contacts with Soviet officials for the purpose of selling ERCO products to the Soviet government (an explanation corroborated by ERCO executives), all of the actions charged were attributable to his relationship with his ex-wife and that "basic disagreements" with her had led to the breakup of their marriage.[45]

The principal issue in the case was the government's near-total reliance on "confidential" informants whom Greene was unable to confront or cross-examine. The Court, by an 8–1 vote in an opinion by Warren (joined, however, by only four other justices), found that the clearance program was not "the creature" of any statute or presidential executive order and that "in the absence of explicit authorization from either the President or the Congress the [military departments] were not empowered to deprive [Greene] of his job in a proceeding in which he was not afforded the safeguards of confrontation and cross-examination." The Court did not decide that Greene had a constitutional right to these safeguards, although it cited the "relatively immutable" principle that "the evidence used to prove the Government's case must be disclosed to the individual so that he has an opportunity to show that it is untrue." Rather, it held, the Department of Defense has not been delegated "authority to bypass these traditional and well-recognized safeguards in an industrial security clearance program which can operate" to deny individuals "the opportunity to follow chosen private professions."[46]

While Warren's opinion did not dwell on the constitutional safeguards, he still said too much for Frankfurter, Harlan, and Whittaker. They concurred in the judgment only, agreeing that the department's action was not authorized but "intimating no views as to the validity of [its] procedures."[47]

Clark, again a lone dissenter, expressed "hope that the winds may change," for "[i]f they do not the present temporary debacle will turn into a rout of our internal security."[48]

There was a companion case to *Greene*. Charles Allen Taylor, a lathe operator for Bell Aircraft, which manufactured government aircraft, was also fired after losing his security clearance, and his case raised similar issues. But when the Court granted review of Taylor's case, the government restored his clearance, and at the oral argument the Solicitor General stated that the findings of the security boards that denied him clearance would be "expunged" and he would be given "compensation for wages lost" during the time he was unemployed. The Court, in a per curiam ruling, dismissed Taylor's case as moot.[49]

Bills to overturn *Greene* were quickly introduced in both houses of Congress. Francis Walter's bill was intended "specifically to overcome this decision so that the Department of Defense may have congressional authority to safeguard our industrial establishments, without disclosing information injurious to our national security." The Eisenhower administration, however, issued a remarkable executive order establishing new industrial security procedures. "For the first time in any government security program since World War II," Anthony Lewis wrote in the *Times*, "the presumption will be that suspects are entitled to confront and cross-examine their accusers. The use of confidential informants is to be the exception, not the rule."[50]

Vitarelli v. Seaton presented much narrower issues. The Court held unlawful the firing of William Vincent Vitarelli, an Interior Department employee, on loyalty-security grounds without affording him procedural protections provided in the department's own regulations. Vitarelli, who held a doctorate from Columbia, had been employed as a $6,140-per-year teacher on the Pacific island of Koror in the Palau District, a trust territory administered by the United States. Because he lacked either civil service or Veterans' Preference Act protection, the secretary of the Interior could have fired him for no reason. Instead, although his job was surely nonsensitive, the department instituted a loyalty-security proceeding against him. The principal charge was that from 1941 to 1945 he had been in "'sympathetic association'" with three named persons "alleged to have been members of or in sympathetic association with" the CPUSA and "had concealed from the Government the true extent of these associations." After a security-board hearing in which the only witnesses were those Vitarelli produced, the secretary, in September 1954, fired him "in the interest of national security."[51]

The department had adopted regulations for loyalty-security proceedings, and the Court held, in an opinion by Harlan, that "[h]aving chosen to proceed against [Vitarelli] on security grounds" the secretary was "bound" by the regulations "even though without such regulations he could have discharged [Vitarelli] summarily." The regulations plainly were not complied with. Vitarelli's 1954 dismissal, the Court ruled, was "illegal."[52]

Thus far the Court was unanimous. But in October 1956, the department, seeking to bolster its legal position in Vitarelli's lawsuit, had issued a revised termination notice, backdated to September 1954, firing him without giving any reasons. The Court, dividing 5-4, refused to give effect to this maneuver, finding that "its sole purpose was an attempt to moot [Vitarelli's] suit ... by an 'expunging' of the grounds which brought" the department's regulations "into play." It ordered Vitarelli reinstated "subject of course to any lawful exercise of the Secretary's authority hereafter to dismiss him."[53]

This result was unsatisfactory to Frankfurter who, joined by Clark, Whittaker, and Stewart, insisted that the department's 1956 action effectively fired Vitarelli and that he should not be reinstated even temporarily.[54]

In subsequent years, Vitarelli, described by the *Honolulu Star-Bulletin* as "a Quaker and peace activist," continued his work in education in Palau, retiring in 1970.[55]

That *Beilan* and *Lerner* rendered *Slochower* a dead letter was confirmed unequivocally in *Nelson v. County of Los Angeles*. There, the Court sustained the firing of two social workers, Thomas A. Nelson and Arthur Globe, after they invoked the Fifth Amendment in response to a HUAC subcommittee's questions about CPUSA membership. Even the veneer of *Beilan* and *Lerner*—where the questions were asked by public employers ostensibly to ascertain the employee's fitness—was absent, for here as in *Slochower* the questions were asked only by a congressional committee.[56]

The two social workers, however, had been ordered by the County to answer HUAC's questions relating to CPUSA membership and were fired for "insubordination." A second ground was violating a state statute that made it their "duty" when subpoenaed by a congressional committee to answer questions about CPUSA membership and mandated that an employee who refused to answer be "dismissed from his employment." Nelson, a permanent hire, received a hearing prior to his discharge, but the only issue at the hearing was whether he had in fact refused to answer. Globe, a temporary employee, was "summarily discharged."[57]

The Court affirmed Nelson's discharge by a 4–4 vote (Warren did not participate) without opinion and sustained Globe's discharge by a 5–3 vote in an opinion by Clark. It rejected Globe's contention, relying on *Slochower,* that he was fired for invoking his Fifth Amendment privilege. The statute in *Slochower,* the Court said, created a "'built-in' inference of guilt derived solely from a Fifth Amendment claim"; Globe's discharge, on the other hand, was based "solely on employee insubordination for failure to give information which we have held that the State has a legitimate interest in securing." Globe's case, the Court held, "is controlled by" *Beilan* and *Lerner*.[58]

Dissenting, Black, joined by Douglas, stated "that the State took Globe's job away from him only because he claimed his privilege under the Federal Constitution." Brennan found Globe's case "substantially identical" to Slochower's because "the California statute contains the identical vice of automatic discharge for a Fifth Amendment plea made before another body, not concerned with investigating the 'fitness' of the employee involved."[59]

The *New York Times* in an editorial termed the decision "regrettable." Recalling that Jenner's court-curbing bill sought to overturn *Slochower,* it wrote that "[w]hat Senator Jenner was unable to achieve the Supreme Court has now virtually accomplished on its own."[60]

In still another loyalty case, the Court, after argument, in a per curiam ruling, remanded for "further consideration." A Washington state statute required public employees to affirm "[t]hat I am not a subversive person or a member of the Communist Party or any subversive organization" and provided that "refusal to answer on any grounds shall be cause for immediate termination of such employee's employment." Two University of Washington professors challenged the statute on the ground that "no hearing is afforded at which the employee can explain or defend his refusal to take the oath." The Court (Black and Douglas dissenting) found that the state courts failed to "pass on this point" and remanded to allow consideration of the issue.[61]

Disciplining Smith Act Counsel—*Sawyer*

In *Sawyer* the Court reviewed discipline imposed by Hawaii upon defense counsel in a Smith Act conspiracy trial in Honolulu. The alleged misconduct took place not in the courtroom but in a speech by the lawyer, while the seven-month trial was in progress, at a meeting in support of the defendants 180 miles away. Hawaii suspended the lawyer, Harriet Bouslog Sawyer, from the practice of law for one year.[62]

Sawyer's speech, as recorded in the notes and memory of a local journalist, condemned Smith Act prosecutions: "[S]he wanted to tell about some rather shocking and horrible things that go on at the trial"; "men in power are trying to put men in jail because of their thoughts and books written before he was born"; "there's no such thing as a fair trial in a smith act case." Sawyer also criticized the evidentiary rules in conspiracy cases: "all rules of evidence have to be scrapped or the government can't make a case"; "they widened the rules and tell what other people did years ago . . . including the kitchen sink." Sawyer's speech, the Hawaii bar charged, imputed unfairness to the trial judge, Jon Wiig, and impugned the integrity of the federal district court.[63]

The Court, dividing 5–4, reversed. Brennan wrote an opinion, in which Warren, Black and Douglas joined; Stewart, the fifth vote for reversal, concurred only in the result. The case turned on the implications to be drawn from Sawyer's speech. Brennan's plurality opinion argued that "lawyers are free to criticize the state of the law" and may also "criticize the law-enforcement agencies of the Government . . . without by that token impugning the judiciary." He found "no support for any further factual inference than that [Sawyer] was voicing strong criticism of Smith Act cases and the Government's manner of proving them and that her references to the happenings at the Honolulu trial were . . . not a reflection in any wise upon Judge Wiig personally or his conduct of the trial."[64]

Frankfurter, however, joined by Clark, Harlan, and Whittaker, found the speech to be "no abstract attack on the state of the law" but rather "a plainly conveyed attack on the conduct of a particular trial, presided over by a particular judge." He implied, moreover, that although Sawyer was not charged "in terms" with intending to influence the trial's outcome, this was indeed her intention, for her "attacks on fairness ... were made while the jury was open and receptive to media of communication."[65]

In his short concurring opinion, Stewart simply responded to Frankfurter. "[I]f it had been charged or found" that Sawyer attempted to interfere with a fair trial, he wrote, "this would be the kind of a case to which the language of the dissenting opinion seems largely directed." But, he said, "that was not the charge here, and it is not the ground upon which [she] has been disciplined."[66]

Interpreting the Jencks Act

The 1957 *Jencks* statute was before the Court in two routine criminal cases, one for tax evasion and the other charging a fraud in interstate commerce. Frankfurter, writing in both cases for the five-justice majority, assured Congress that the Court would interpret the new law to require that only a narrow class of witnesses' statements be produced.[67]

In the first case, *Palermo v. United States*, the justices were unanimous that the statement—an IRS agent's six-hundred-word summary of his three-and-a-half-hour conference with the witness—was not producible under the statute, but the five-justice majority did not stop there. It announced that *Jencks* was not a constitutional ruling but merely "prescribe[d] procedures for the administration of justice in the federal courts" in the absence of a statute. It held that the procedures prescribed in the new statute were "exclusive" and that "statements of a government witness made to an agent of the Government which cannot be produced under the terms of [the new law] cannot be produced at all." It emphasized Congress's intent that production be limited to "those statements which could properly be called the witness' own words" and warned that if lower courts "disregarded the command of Congress," "there is always the safeguard of this Court's reviewing power."[68]

In the second case, *Rosenberg v. United States*, the justices were unanimous that the statement—a key witness's letter to prosecutors admitting to memory loss in the period since the alleged fraud—should have been produced, but the majority found that the prosecution's failure to do so was harmless error. There was no harm, it said, because the witness disclosed the "same information" at the trial.[69]

Brennan, joined by Warren, Black, and Douglas, concurred in the result in *Palermo* and dissented in *Rosenberg*. "*Jencks* was not put on constitutional grounds, for it did not have to be," he wrote in *Palermo*, but the Sixth Amendment's confrontation requirement was "close to the surface of the decision." Nor should the Court have decided that procedures under the statute were exclusive, he said, thereby "stripping" trial judges "of all discretion to make nonqualifying reports available in proper cases." In *Rosenberg*, Brennan opposed application of the harmless-error doctrine, stating that producible statements "must be given to the defense . . . for only the defense can fully appreciate their possible utility for impeachment."[70]

Court-Curbing Bills in the 86th Congress

While the anti-Court forces in the Congress were thinned in the 1958 elections, they remained formidable. In the House, the *Times* reported at the start of the new Congress, the campaign for court-curbing legislation enjoyed "apparently good prospects of success." In the Senate, it said, while the outlook "is not yet clear, the chances are that new pressures will result in passage of some of the measures, probably in modified form."[71]

Bar groups again provided support for the anti-Court bills. A resolution by the Conference of Chief Justices in August 1958, too late to affect the outcome the preceding year, was embraced by the Court's opponents in the new Congress. The state chief justices, by a 36–8 margin, urged the Court to exercise "judicial self-restraint" and to recognize "the difference" between that which "the Constitution may prescribe or permit" and "that which . . . a majority of the Supreme Court . . . may deem desirable or undesirable." Virginia's Harry F. Byrd told the Senate that "certainly, never before in the history of American jurisprudence . . . has such powerful criticism of the Supreme Court of the United States come forth from such high and respected authority."[72]

The ABA's House of Delegates, in February 1959, approved (with only slight changes in language) the recommendations of its committee on Communist tactics, strategy, and objectives. "Many cases," the committee found, "have been decided in such a manner as to encourage an increase in Communist activity in the United States"—it listed no fewer than 24 "principal" cases. The committee urged the adoption of bills to overrule *Nelson*, *Cole v. Young*, and *Witkovich*; to amend the Smith Act to redefine "organize" and ban abstract advocacy of forcible overthrow; and to authorize the secretary of state to withhold passports "based upon confidential information." The ABA's action, Anthony Lewis commented, "added up to a charge that the court has been soft on communism." Only days later, Eastland took the Senate floor to trumpet the ABA's new criticism.[73]

Aided by the bar groups' support, court-curbing legislation was again successful in the House, but less so in the Senate. In February 1959, a bill to overturn *Yates*'s interpretation of the Smith Act term "organize" was favorably reported by the Judiciary Committee and, less than two weeks later, passed by the House without debate. Smith's HR 3 was approved by the Judiciary Committee in June and passed by the House, by a vote of 225 to 192, the same month. The *Mallory* bill, which passed both Houses a year earlier only to die on a technicality, again passed the House, by a 262-to-138 margin.[74]

Passport legislation was reported by the Foreign Affairs Committee on September 4 and passed by the House four days later by a wide margin. But committee liberals had succeeded in gaining procedural rights for persons refused passports. Under the bill applicants were assured a hearing, and in order to deny a passport, the secretary of state was required to find that the applicant was a CPUSA member or had engaged in "Communist" activities *after 1950*. A denial, moreover, was "subject to judicial review on the record—in other words, the secretary had to disclose to a reviewing court (and the applicant) evidence to support denial. In the Senate, however, a bill sponsored by Republican Kenneth Keating of New York and Thomas J. Dodd, a Connecticut Democrat, which denied judicial review and authorized the secretary to withhold information from the applicant, was reported favorably by the Judiciary Committee.[75]

Walter's bill to provide the authorization found lacking in *Greene* was passed by the House in February 1960—passing without debate when opponents failed to notice it on the House's consent calendar. Unlike Eisenhower's executive order, issued three weeks later, the bill gave the secretary of defense unfettered authority to rely on "confidential" information.[76]

All of the House-passed bills, however, died in the Senate. Most never made it out of committee, and none had reached the Senate floor for a vote when, on September 1, 1960, the 86th Congress adjourned. A presidential election was only two months away.[77]

The Court's retreat, and the increased dominance of Frankfurter's five-justice majority, coincided with a diminishing political threat to the Court. But in the succeeding term, which saw a sharp spike in the number of "Communist" decisions, the Court would continue its retreat, ruling in the government's favor in almost every significant case.

10

Scales and *CPUSA*, *Wilkinson* and *Braden*, and *Konigsberg II* and *Anastaplo* —a Full-Scale Retreat

(OCTOBER TERM 1960)

The 1960 term saw a sudden and final outpouring of decisions in "Communist" cases—fifteen signed decisions. The government prevailed in nine (a tenth had a mixed result), every one over the dissenting votes of Black, Warren, Douglas, and Brennan. The decisions included *Scales*, which upheld the constitutionality of the Smith Act's "membership" clause, and *CPUSA v. SACB*, which sustained the registration provisions of the Internal Security Act. Decisions in two contempt-of-Congress cases confirmed that after *Barenblatt* the First Amendment posed no obstacle to committees seeking to compel disclosure of "Communist" affiliations. And in two bar-admission decisions, the Court ruled in effect that states may deny admission to any applicant who refuses to answer questions about his political associations. Of the five cases decided against the government, only one—a largely unnoticed companion case to *Scales*—had any continuing significance.[1]

The results of the November 1960 elections were inconclusive. Democrat John F. Kennedy was elected president, but his popular-vote margin was only 112,000 out of 68 million votes cast. The Democrats retained control of the Congress but by a diminished margin, losing twenty seats in the House and one in the Senate. Given its shaky mandate, there was little prospect that the Kennedy administration would spend scarce political capital to resist McCarthyism. In fact, Joseph P. Kennedy, the president's father and the family patriarch, had been Joe McCarthy's friend and a contributor to his campaigns; Robert F. Kennedy, JFK's brother and closest confidant, had served on the staff of McCarthy's subcommittee. As for JFK himself, "McCarthyism," Arthur M. Schlesinger, Jr. wrote, "simply did not strike him as one of 'his' issues." At his first news conference following the election, the president-elect announced he would continue

J. Edgar Hoover as FBI director—in Hoover's view, the CPUSA was as great a threat as ever.[2]

Coincident with the election, the Court considered Willard Uphaus's new appeal and his imprisonment. The Court's denial of bail to this gentle, scholarly old man, who refused as a matter of conscience to reveal names, may have contributed to increased tensions among the justices. Frankfurter, who voted against Uphaus at every stage, received sharp criticism in letters from old and valued friends. In one reply letter he testily defended himself as one "who has done far more to promote civil liberties long before he ever came to this Court than is true of some of those whose rhetoric appeals to you more." In November Douglas advised his colleagues that due to Frankfurter's "continuous violent outbursts against me in Conference," he would no longer attend conferences (he soon relented), and in April, Warren, responding in open court to Frankfurter's dissent to the Court's reversal of a criminal conviction, accused him of "degrading this court."[3]

Uphaus's appeal was dismissed by the Court on November 14 in a one-sentence per curiam order. No more was needed after Brennan circulated a draft opinion stating the appeal did not present "a substantial federal question." Frankfurter wrote the per curiam order in the margins of Brennan's draft. Black, Warren, and Douglas dissented. Black, noting that New Hampshire's attorney general, Louis Wyman, asserted a right to renew his investigation, said "a distinct possibility exists that this man [Uphaus] who, at least so far as these records show, has never committed a single crime, nor even so much as an immoral act, faces imprisonment for the rest of his life." Douglas's dissent reargued the 1959 *Uphaus* decision, invoking *NAACP v. Alabama* as governing precedent. "What we there said was not designed . . . as a rule for Negroes only," he wrote, and "[a]ll groups—white or colored—engaged in lawful conduct are entitled to the same protection against harassment as the N.A.A.C.P. enjoys."[4]

The dichotomy between NAACP and "Communist" decisions in fact began to crumble in the 1960 term, with the Court's unanimity in NAACP cases the first consequence. One of the term's NAACP decisions reviewed a 1958 Arkansas statute requiring each public school teacher in the state to submit an affidavit identifying every organization to which he or she belonged in the previous five years. The state, taught by *Beilan* and *Lerner*, argued that it wasn't trying to identify NAACP members but rather to appraise each teacher's fitness. Frankfurter, joined by Clark, Harlan, and Whittaker, agreed, finding that the teachers' privacy interests did not "overbalance" the state's interest in evaluating its teachers. But Stewart defected, joining Warren, Black, Douglas, and Brennan. This transient majority, in an opinion by Stewart, held that the statute's "comprehensive interference with associational freedom goes far beyond what might be justified in the exercise of the State's legitimate inquiry into the fitness and competency of its teachers."[5]

More Contempt Cases—*Wilkinson, Braden, et al.*

Committee-contempt cases flooded the Court. It issued five signed decisions in contempt cases, two involving successive witnesses at the same HUAC hearing in Atlanta.[6]

Frank Wilkinson, a forty-three-year-old political activist from California who had been an "unfriendly" witness at earlier HUAC hearings, came to Atlanta as the representative of a group advocating HUAC's abolition. Arriving at his hotel, he was served with a HUAC subpoena ordering him to appear as a witness. At the hearing, Wilkinson declined to answer questions, invoking the First Amendment, and was indicted for contempt for refusing to answer the question, "Are you now a member of the Communist Party?" He argued that he was not subpoenaed for a valid legislative purpose but rather to expose him to public censure because of his anti-HUAC activities.[7]

The Court's usual five-justice majority, in an opinion by Stewart, affirmed Wilkinson's conviction and one-year prison sentence. As to his claim that he was subpoenaed for advocating HUAC's abolition, the Court found "nothing to indicate that it was the intent of Congress to immunize from interrogation all those (and there are many) who are opposed to the existence of [HUAC]." "Moreover," it said, "it is not for us to speculate as to the motivations that may have prompted the decision of individual members of the subcommittee to summon [Wilkinson]." Rejecting Wilkinson's First Amendment contentions as having been "throughly canvassed by us in *Barenblatt*," the Court stated that "it is the nature of the Communist activities involved . . . that establishes the Government's overbalancing interest."[8]

Black's dissent, joined by Warren and Douglas, argued that the case "involves nothing more nor less than an attempt by [HUAC] to use the contempt power of the House of Representatives as a weapon against those who dare to criticize it." Turning again to *Barenblatt*'s balancing test, he said that where First Amendment freedoms "are left to depend upon a balance to be struck by this Court in each particular case, liberty cannot survive. For under such a rule, there are no constitutional rights that cannot be 'balanced' away." Brennan wrote that HUAC's "dominant purpose" was to harass Wilkinson and "expose him for the sake of exposure.[9]

Carl Braden preceded Wilkinson to the witness stand at HUAC's hearing. Several years earlier, Braden, then a copyeditor at the *Louisville Courier-Journal*, and his wife Anne, both pro-integration activists, were nominal purchasers of a home in a whites-only neighborhood, which they then conveyed to a black family. After the home was destroyed by dynamite, the Bradens were made defendants in a Kentucky sedition case—prosecutors charged the bombing was a Communist plot intended to aggravate racial tensions. Carl was convicted and received a fifteen-year prison sentence—set aside, however, following the Court's *Nelson* decision.[10]

Prior to the hearing, Braden helped circulate petitions in opposition to state sedition laws and to HUAC's hearing. Summoned as a witness, he refused to answer six questions concerning his political associations—one asked whether he was a CPUSA member when he signed a letter urging opposition to bills in Congress to overrule *Nelson*—and was convicted of contempt.[11]

The Court, by the same 5–4 vote, again in an opinion by Stewart, affirmed his conviction. Braden's principal contentions, it said, had been disposed of in *Barenblatt* and *Wilkinson*. It gave short shrift to his added claim that in refusing to answer at the hearing he had reasonably relied on *Watkins* (*Barenblatt* had not yet been decided) "in good faith on the advise [sic] of competent counsel." "His mistaken view of the law," the Court held, "is no defense."[12]

Black, joined by Douglas and Warren, wrote that when "this Nation . . . begins to send its dissenters, such as Barenblatt, Uphaus, Wilkinson, and now Braden, to jail, the liberties indispensable to its existence must be fast disappearing." Douglas, joined by the other three dissenters, argued that Braden was "entitled to rely" on *Watkins* and *Sweezy* when he refused to answer.[13]

Decisions rubberstamping HUAC did not come easily for justices on either side of the Court's divide. Stewart, when he read his *Wilkinson* and *Braden* opinions aloud in the courtroom, added that "[o]f course" they "do not imply any personal views as to the wisdom or unwisdom of the creation or continuance of this committee"—words omitted from his printed opinions. Black's dissents, Anthony Lewis wrote in the *Times*, were "passionate and despairing." More than forty contempt-of-Congress cases were pending in lower courts, Lewis reported, and "certainly" the defendants' "chances look dimmer."[14]

McPhaul v. United States, in which the contempt charged was a failure to produce documents demanded by HUAC, presented only a narrow procedural issue. HUAC's 1952 subpoena sought records of the Civil Rights Congress, a group that became defunct in 1956 but once actively supported black and left-wing causes (Paul Robeson was a prominent supporter) and was listed as "subversive" by the attorney general. The subpoena was served on Arthur M. McPhaul, a CRC official in Detroit, who appeared at the hearing but did not produce any records and refused to answer questions about them, invoking his Fifth Amendment privilege. At his trial for contempt, McPhaul argued that the government failed to prove either that the records were in existence or were within his possession or control. The trial judge ruled, however, that in the absence of any explanation from McPhaul the records would be deemed both "in existence [and] subject to [his] control . . ."[15]

The issue before the Court was whether it was the Government's obligation to prove the subpoenaed records existed and were within McPhaul's control. The five-justice majority, in an opinion by Whittaker, held it was not. Once the government presented "a *prima facie* case" that McPhaul refused to produce the records, it said, "[t]he burden then shifted to [him] to present some evidence to explain or justify his refusal."[16]

The four dissenters, in an opinion by Douglas, argued that the Court's action "dispensed with" the presumption of innocence by "shifting the burden to a witness" to show "he is not able to produce the documents."[17]

The defendant in a fourth HUAC contempt-of-Congress case, Bernhard Deutch, freely disclosed his own political associations but refused to inform on others—a position that may have led Stewart to switch sides in an otherwise unremarkable case.[18]

The questioning of Deutch, a twenty-four-year-old University of Pennsylvania graduate student, concerned his undergraduate years at Cornell. He admitted he had been a CPUSA member at Cornell—he was no longer a member, he said, although "I am a Marxist today—I don't want to deny that"—and explained that "about all that happened were bull sessions on Marxism, and some activities like giving out a leaflet or two." "[T]he organization," he said, was now "completely defunct." However, when HUAC asked about persons he had associated with as a Party member, Deutch refused to answer, saying he would not "trade my moral scruples by informing on someone else."[19]

The Court, in an opinion by Stewart, joined by Warren, Black, Douglas, and Brennan, reversed Deutch's conviction on pertinency grounds. The subject of HUAC's inquiry was unclear: the trial judge thought it was "the infiltrating of Communism into educational and labor fields"; but the Court concluded the subject was Communist activities in the Albany (N.Y.) area, particularly infiltration of labor unions. Having so concluded, the decision was easy because, as the Court stated, "the questions which [Deutch] was convicted of refusing to answer obviously had nothing to do with the Albany area or with Communist infiltration into labor unions. It can hardly be seriously contended that Cornell University is in the Albany area."[20]

Harlan, dissenting, with Frankfurter, argued that "[p]ertinency . . . is to be judged not in terms of the immediate probative significance of a particular question to the matter under authorized inquiry, but in light of its tendency to elicit information which might be a useful link in the investigatory chain." Whittaker, joined by Clark, charged that the Court "grossly misread this record."[21]

In the fifth decision, the Court unanimously reversed the contempt convictions of two witnesses before Ohio's "little HUAC" commission, while affirming in part by 4–4 vote (Frankfurter recused himself) the convictions of three others. Each of the witnesses, alleged Ohio Communists, refused to answer questions, invoking the privilege against self-incrimination. But, with some exceptions, "instead of overruling the objection or in any way directing the witness to answer the question, the Commission gave every indication that it sustained, or at least acquiesced in, the objection."[22]

The Court, in an opinion by Whittaker, held that a finding of contempt when the commission appeared to sustain or acquiesce in the witnesses' objections "would deeply offend traditional notions of fair play and deprive them of due process." It reversed the convictions of two witnesses who had not been directed to answer. But the other three witnesses had been directed to answer one or more questions, and their convictions for refusing to answer those questions were affirmed without opinion by an equally divided Court.[23]

Two Denaturalization Cases

Neither of the Court's two decisions in denaturalization cases, one in the government's favor and one against, was of doctrinal consequence.

The first involved Gus Polites, a native of Greece who immigrated to the United States in 1916 and was a party member from 1931 to 1938. He obtained citizenship in 1942 but was denaturalized in 1953—the statute under which he was naturalized provided that persons who in the preceding ten years were members of a group advocating forcible overthrow were ineligible for naturalization. Polites sought to have the denaturalization decree set aside in light of the Court's subsequent decisions in *Nowak* and *Maisenberg*. Those decisions, he argued, required the government to prove not only that he was a CPUSA member but also that he was aware of the Party's "illegal advocacy."[24]

The Court, in its usual 5–4 alignment, rejected Polites' claim. *Nowak* and *Maisenberg*, it said, interpreted a 1906 law that required applicants to be "attached to the principles of the Constitution" and thus placed the applicant's "state of mind" in issue. Polites, by contrast, was naturalized under a 1940 statute that disqualified members of "a particular kind of organization," and his denaturalization was properly based on "objective facts."[25]

Brennan, joined by Warren, Black, and Douglas, dissented.[26]

In *Chaunt v. United States*, a 6–3 decision against the government (Frankfurter and Harlan were the swing votes), the Court considered Peter Chaunt's failure to disclose, when naturalized in 1940, three arrests on minor charges years earlier. A native of Hungary who came to the United States in 1921, Chaunt had been arrested in New Haven in 1929–30 for distributing handbills in violation of a city ordinance—he was discharged; for making a speech outside a church in violation of an ordinance—he pleaded not guilty and the outcome was unclear; and for breach of the peace—on appeal the case was "nolled" (dismissed) by the court. The government charged that his failure to disclose these arrests in response to a question on a naturalization form was fraud, justifying cancellation of his citizenship.[27]

The Court, however, in an opinion by Douglas, cited the applicable statutory criteria for naturalization—good moral character and attachment to the principles of the Constitution during the previous five years—and found that Chaunt's arrests neither took place in "the critical five-year period" nor "involve[d] moral turpitude." The government, it held, failed to justify denaturalization by "clear, unequivocal, and convincing" evidence.[28]

Clark, joined by Whittaker and Stewart, dissenting, argued that the "clear, unequivocal, and convincing" standard was inapplicable "where one has deliberately falsified his papers and thus foreclosed further investigation."[29]

Smith Act "Membership" Clause—*Scales, Noto*

When conspiracy prosecutions, its preferred avenue under the Smith Act, foundered on *Yates*'s proof requirements, the government's recourse was to the Act's "membership" clause, which had been used only sparingly. The clause made it a felony if a person "becomes or is a member" of a "society, group, or assembly of persons who teach, advocate, or encourage" violent overthrow of the government "knowing the purposes thereof." Membership-clause prosecutions raised not only First Amendment issues, but also a knotty statutory issue created by an Internal Security Act section intended to deal with the self-incrimination problem posed when one statute (the ISA) required registration of CPUSA members and another (the Smith Act) made CPUSA membership a crime.[30]

The Court granted review in *Scales*, the first membership-clause case to reach it, in the 1955 term. But, less than eager to decide, it ordered reargument and then remanded the case on *Jencks* grounds after the solicitor general confessed error. When *Scales* returned following a second trial, the Court twice ordered postponements, ultimately directing that the case be heard in the 1960 term, together with *CPUSA v. SACB*, the Party's challenge to the SACB's registration order. The government benefited from the delay: when it tried Scales a second time (in 1958) it knew *Yates*'s proof requirements and called "far more witnesses" than before. Scales's lawyer, Telford Taylor, believed the solicitor general's confession of error was strategic, aimed at obtaining a second trial and the opportunity to compile an improved record.[31]

Junius Irving Scales was born in 1920 to a wealthy and prominent North Carolina family—as a child he lived in a thirty-six-room mansion. On his nineteenth birthday, a student at the University of North Carolina, he joined the CPUSA and began working in mill towns to unionize textile workers. After serving in the Army during World War II, he returned home and became party chief for the Carolinas. His arrest in 1954 on the Smith Act charge was the start of a seven-year court battle during which he was tried, in Greensboro, North Carolina, and convicted twice, receiving a six-year prison sentence. By the time of his second trial, he had quit the party.[32]

The Court affirmed Scales's conviction and sentence, by the usual 5–4 vote, in a dense fifty-five-page opinion by Harlan. The statutory issue, discussed first, turned on the meaning of section 4(f) of the Internal Security Act: "Neither the holding of office *nor membership* in any Communist organization by any person shall constitute per se a violation of subsection (a) or subsection (c) of this section *or any other criminal statute.*" This provision, Scales contended, solved Congress's self-incrimination dilemma by nullifying the Smith Act's "membership" clause as applied to Communist organizations. The Court disagreed. The Smith Act, it said, did not make "membership *per se*" a criminal violation, for it criminalized only "knowing" membership and (as the Court would now construe it) "active and purposive membership, purposive that is as to the organization's criminal ends."[33]

Addressing Scales's constitutional challenge, the Court cited a jury instruction that, it said, "correctly interpreted" the "membership" clause. The trial judge had instructed the Greensboro jury that to convict it "must find," first, that the CPUSA advocated violent overthrow "in the sense of present 'advocacy of action' to accomplish that end as soon as circumstances were propitious" (in other words, advocacy illegal under *Yates*) and, second, that Scales was an "'active'" not merely a "nominal" member, with knowledge of the party's illegal advocacy and a specific intent to accomplish violent overthrow. A statute with these requirements of proof, the Court held, did not violate either the First or Fifth Amendment.[34]

Much of the Court's opinion was directed to the sufficiency of the evidence. It confirmed that *Yates* required proof that the party's advocacy "constituted 'a call to forcible action'" to accomplish overthrow rather than "the teaching of mere 'abstract doctrine' favoring that end"; but it now deemed "not irrelevant" evidence that the party taught Marxism-Leninism and used "Marxist 'classics' as textbooks." The Court, however, relied primarily on testimony by ex-Communist witnesses that "descended to a lower level of generality," including testimony that an instructor at a party training school "gave a demonstration of jujitsu" and explained "how to kill a person with a pencil." The prosecution's evidence, it held, "sufficed to make a case for the jury on the issue of illegal Party advocacy."[35]

Black and Douglas dissented on First Amendment grounds. "Not one single illegal act is charged to" Scales, Douglas wrote; "[n]othing but beliefs is on trial in this case." "Belief in the principle of revolution," he said, invoking Jefferson, Madison, Lincoln, and fifteen state constitutions, "is deep in our traditions." Brennan, joined by Warren, dissented on the statutory ground. Section 4(f), he found, represented "a congressional decision to extend immunity from prosecution for any membership in a Communist organization in order to safeguard" the ISA's registration provisions "against constitutional frustration."[36]

Stewart had been unconvinced after the argument, informing his colleagues at an October 1960 conference that he was "inclined to reverse on the evidence." In February, he told Harlan, "[I] cannot agree that the evidence of Party activity in this case was sufficient to meet the high standard erected in *Yates* . . . of 'advocacy of action.'" Harlan argued his position in a responsive letter, finally pleading that "[i]f you still remain unsatisfied, I do hope you will give me a further chance to thrash this thing out with you in face to face discussion, as yours is the deciding vote." In April, after extensive changes in Harlan's draft opinion, Stewart advised him that "the revisions you have so accommodatingly made enable me to concur in this opinion."[37]

The companion case to *Scales* was the membership-clause prosecution of John Francis Noto, a CPUSA official in Buffalo. Noto's trial took place prior to *Yates*, and the Court, without dissent, found the evidence against him insufficient.[38]

In an opinion by Harlan on behalf of the five-justice bloc, the Court, again reaffirming *Yates*, stated that "the mere abstract teaching of Communist theory . . . is not the same as preparing a group for violent action" and there must be substantial evidence "of a call to violence now or in the future which is both sufficiently strong and sufficiently pervasive . . . to justify the inference that such a call to violence may fairly be imputed to the Party as a whole, and not merely to some narrow segment of it." The "kind of evidence" found in *Scales* "to support the jury's verdict of present illegal Party advocacy," the Court held, "is lacking here in any adequately substantial degree."[39]

The *Scales* dissenters concurred in *Noto*'s result, Black and Douglas on First Amendment grounds, Brennan and Warren on the section 4(f) ground.[40]

The opinion in *Noto* did not foreclose a retrial. But the Justice Department, the *Times* reported, "indicated that chances of any further effort to convict [Noto] under the membership clause were exceedingly slim." Indeed, the Department reviewed all of its pending membership-clause prosecutions in the light of *Scales* and *Noto* and in succeeding months abandoned every one. Nor did it undertake new prosecutions.[41]

"*Yates* had made conspiracy prosecutions impossible," Michal Belknap wrote, "and now the membership clause too was a spent bullet." Belknap attributed this outcome to Harlan, "the crafty conservative" who "made his bow to the legislature by validating the statute." But, as a result of Harlan's "bow," Scales's conviction and six-year prison sentence were upheld. Imprisoned at Lewisburg, he was the only person ever to serve a prison sentence for violating the Smith Act's "membership" clause. On Christmas Eve 1962, however, President Kennedy, responding to requests, commuted Scales's sentence to the fifteen months he had already served.[42]

Registering the Party—*CPUSA v. SACB*

Like *Scales, CPUSA v. SACB* had a long history. The case began in 1950 at the SACB, the agency created by the Internal Security Act. After fourteen months of hearings, the board ordered the CPUSA to register as a "Communist-action organization." This order was set aside and the case remanded by the Court in 1956 because of perjuries by government witnesses. The board's second order was also remanded, by a court of appeals essentially on *Jencks* grounds. Its third order, again directing the party to register, was now before the Court.[43]

The ISA, a complex statute, made lengthy legislative findings concerning the "world Communist movement." The "movement," it found, sought "by treachery, deceit, infiltration . . . espionage, sabotage, [and] terrorism . . . to establish a Communist totalitarian dictatorship in countries throughout the world." In the United States, it found, the "Communist movement" was "an organization numbering thousands of adherents, rigidly and ruthlessly disciplined," awaiting "a moment when . . . overthrow of the Government . . . may seem possible of achievement." It defined "Communist-action organization" (the category created for the party) as an organization "substantially directed, dominated, or controlled" by the Soviet government and which "operates primarily to advance the objectives" of the "world Communist movement."[44]

Registration under the act entailed submitting a form, prescribed by the attorney general in a regulation and required to be signed by an officer of the organization, that disclosed comprehensive information, including the names and addresses of all officers and members. Members not listed by the organization were required to register themselves. Failure to register was a crime.[45]

Registration triggered a range of sanctions. The organization was barred from mailing publications or making radio or TV broadcasts unless it prominently disclosed its status as a "Communist organization"; it was denied tax exemption. Members were barred from employment by the federal government, any defense facility, or any labor union, and prohibited from obtaining or using a passport. Alien members were barred from becoming naturalized citizens, and members naturalized in the preceding five years became subject to denaturalization.[46]

The Court, in a 112-page opinion by Frankfurter for the five-justice majority, upheld the SACB's registration order, rejecting claims of both constitutional invalidity and procedural error.[47]

As to the constitutional claims, the Court held that the act's registration scheme did not violate the First Amendment. While forced registration "may in some circumstances affront the constitutional guarantee of free expression" and forced disclosure of members' names "may in certain instances infringe constitutionally protected rights of association," it said, "there must be weighed" against such infringements "the value to the public of the ends which the regulation may achieve." The act's goal, it stated, "is said to be to prevent the worldwide Communist conspiracy from accomplishing its purpose in this country," and "[i]t is not for the courts to re-examine the validity of these legislative findings and reject them." Nor was the act a bill of attainder, for "[i]t attaches not to specified organizations but to described activities in which an organization may or may not engage."[48]

The Court dismissed as "premature at this time" the party's claim that since the registration form must be signed by one of its officers, "the very act of filing" would compel the officer to incriminate himself. The Fifth Amendment privilege, it said, "must be claimed by the individual," and "[w]e cannot know now that the Party's officers will ever claim the privilege."[49]

The Court likewise refused to decide constitutional issues raised by the act's post-registration sanctions. As to the restrictions on the party's mailing of published materials, it said, "[w]e do not know ... the Party will wish to utilize the mails ... for the circulation of its publications." As to the sanctions against individual party members, the Court considered it "wholly speculative now to foreshadow whether, or under what conditions, a member of the Party may in the future apply for a passport, or seek government or defense-facility or labor-union employment, or being an alien, become a party to a naturalization or denaturalization proceeding. None of these things may happen."[50]

The dissents were based on a variety of grounds. Douglas contended that the registration requirement violated the Fifth Amendment's self-incrimination clause, both by requiring party officers to sign the form and by compelling disclosure of members' names. But he eschewed a First Amendment ground: the requirement that the party register, he said, was "in line with the most exacting adjudications touching First Amendment activities"—"[i]f lobbyists can be required to register ... so may a group operating under the control of a foreign power." Brennan relied on the Fifth Amendment, and Warren agreed with the party's claims of procedural error.[51]

Only Black dissented on First Amendment grounds. "Talk about the desirability of revolution," he said, "has a long and honorable history" in this country. And, as to the party's asserted domination by the Soviet Union, he compared the period of the Sedition Act of 1798: "The same arguments were made then about the 'Jacobins,' meaning the Jeffersonians, with regard to their alleged subservience to France, that are made today about the Communists with regard to their subservience to Russia." He also found the act a "classical bill of attainder."[52]

Despite the Court's decision, the CPUSA refused to register. It did not register even after the attorney general amended his regulation to allow not only officers but any volunteer authorized by the party to sign the registration form. The government prosecuted the party for failing to register and, in 1962, obtained a conviction. But a court of appeals reversed, holding the government was obligated to prove a signer was available. At a second trial in 1965, the government presented the testimony of two paid FBI informants that each had offered to register the party, obtaining a new conviction. But in March 1967 the court of appeals again reversed, this time on Fifth Amendment grounds. In the interim, in 1965, the Court had ruled unanimously that two party members, ordered to register by the SACB, were entitled to invoke the Fifth Amendment because the "risks of incrimination" in registering as a party member "are obvious."[53]

In April 1967, the government threw in the towel, abandoning its effort of more than sixteen years to compel the CPUSA to register. "The case is dead," a Justice Department official said. "[N]ot a single individual or group," the *Times* reported, "ever registered with the Attorney General, as required by the act."[54]

When *CPUSA v. SACB* and *Scales* were decided in 1961, however, these later defeats, and the government's inability to prosecute membership-clause cases, were not readily foreseeable. At the time, Attorney General Kennedy hailed *CPUSA v. SACB* as "momentous." The *Times*'s Arthur Krock termed it "of transcendent importance to national defense." The two decisions, Anthony Lewis predicted, "should open the way for renewed enforcement by the Government of long-dormant internal security measures."[55]

Communist Control Act—*CPUSA v. Catherwood*

While the Internal Security Act's registration-and-sanctions scheme was a serious attempt by Congress to destroy the CPUSA, no such claim could be made for the Communist Control Act of 1954, even though it expressly "outlawed" the party and stripped it of all "rights, privileges and immunities."[56]

Introduced by Hubert Humphrey to shield himself and other liberal Democrats from GOP "soft on Communism" charges in the 1954 election, the act was opposed by the Eisenhower administration and afterward was not utilized by the executive branch. "Government lawyers," Anthony Lewis observed, "do not seem to know what, if anything, it means." However, New York state terminated the CPUSA's participation in its unemployment-insurance system under "what was conceived to be the compulsion of" the Act. The state read the statute to mean that "whenever a situation advantageous to [the CPUSA] occurs" under any law, "this is to be considered a 'right,' 'privilege,' or 'immunity,' and must be deemed to be withheld by the Act."[57]

A unanimous Court, in an opinion by Harlan, held that New York was mistaken. The act's language, it said, "fell far short of compelling" the state's interpretation, and "there are good indications that the particular result of barring [the CPUSA] as employers under state and federal unemployment insurance systems was not within the contemplation of this Act." The Court failed to say what the act *did* contemplate, but it held unequivocally that the statute "does not require exclusion of [the CPUSA] from New York's unemployment compensation system."[58]

Taft-Hartley Affidavits—*Travis*

Travis v. United States, which reviewed the conviction and eight-year prison sentence of a Mine, Mill & Smelter Workers official for filing a false Taft-Hartley affidavit, turned on the issue of venue—the proper court for prosecuting the case.

The Sixth Amendment requires criminal cases to be tried before an impartial jury of "the State and district wherein the crime shall have been committed." Maurice Travis's affidavit was signed and mailed in Denver but received and filed by the NLRB in Washington, D.C. The government chose to prosecute him in Colorado.[59]

Federal statutes were ambiguous as to where the crime charged to Travis was "committed." The criminal statute under which he was charged prohibited the making of false statements "in any matter within the jurisdiction of" a federal department or agency. The Taft-Hartley provision denied statutory remedies to a union "unless there is on file with the Board" the required affidavit. A third statute stated that a crime "begun in one district and completed in another" could be prosecuted in either one.[60]

The Court, by 6–3 vote in an opinion by Douglas, held that the crime charged to Travis was committed (if at all) in the District of Columbia and could only be prosecuted there. "There would seem to be no offense," it said, "unless [Travis] completed the filing in the District of Columbia." Nor was the crime "begun" in Colorado and "completed" in Washington. "Venue should not be made to depend on the chance use of the mails," the Court argued, for the affidavit "might have been lost" in the mail or Travis "might have recalled it," in which case there would have been no crime. Harlan, joined by Frankfurter and Clark, dissented, contending that the crime charged was indeed "begun" in Colorado and "completed" in Washington, D.C., and could properly be prosecuted in either venue.[61]

Bar Admission—*Konigsberg II* and *Anastaplo*

The Court's decisions in the 1956 term setting aside rulings in two states that denied former Communists admission to the bar generated sharp criticism and fueled court-curbing efforts in the Congress. In two decisions in the 1960 term, the Court did an about-face.[62]

One decision reviewed the California bar's second rejection of Raphael Konigsberg. The first time, the state rejected him for failing to prove he was of good character and did not advocate violent overthrow of the government; the Court reversed, finding this determination without rational support in the evidence. But Harlan in dissent argued that the state's "reason for exclusion" was instead Konigsberg's refusal to answer when asked whether he was ever a CPUSA member. On remand, when he again refused to answer questions about CPUSA membership, invoking the First Amendment, the state, taking Harlan's hint, excluded him "on the ground that his refusals to answer had obstructed a full investigation into his qualifications."[63]

The five-justice majority, in an opinion by Harlan, upheld the state's action. A state is not forbidden, the Court said, "from denying admission to a bar applicant so long as he refuses to provide unprivileged answers to questions having a substantial relevance to his qualifications." As to Konigsberg's First Amendment claim, it found that his case fell within the class of cases where government action was "not intended to control the content of speech but incidentally limit[s] its unfettered exercise"—cases, it said, that call for "an appropriate weighing of the respective interests involved." The government again won the "balancing" test: "[W]e regard the State's interest in having lawyers who are devoted to the law in its broadest sense, including . . . its procedures for orderly change, as clearly sufficient to outweigh the minimal effect upon free association occasioned by compulsory disclosure in the circumstances here presented." The Court added, in a comment surely directed at Black, that First Amendment freedoms are not "'absolutes'" whose scope "must be gathered solely from a literal reading of the First Amendment."[64]

In dissent, Black, joined by Warren and Douglas, responded that "the very object of adopting the First Amendment . . . was to put the freedoms protected there completely out of the area of any congressional control that may be attempted." He again condemned the Court's "balancing test," offering an alternative description of the competing interests:

> The interest of the [state bar] in satisfying its curiosity with respect to Konigsberg's "possible" membership in the Communist Party two decades ago has been inflated out of all proportion to its real value—the vast interest of the public in maintaining unabridged the basic freedoms of speech, press and assembly has been paid little if anything more than lip service—and important constitutional rights have once again been "balanced" away.

"[T]he men who drafted our Bill of Rights," he said, "did all the 'balancing' that was to be done"[65]

In 1978, "[a] different Committee of Bar Examiners [and] a different Board of Bar Governors . . . saw fit to reverse the judgment of an earlier generation, and Konigsberg was finally admitted to the Bar."[66]

In *Anastaplo,* there was no allegation, not a whisper, that the bar applicant,

George Anastaplo, had ever been a member of the CPUSA or any other "subversive" organization. Raised in a small town in southern Illinois, he served in the Air Force during World War II and graduated near the top of his class at the University of Chicago Law School. In November 1950, having passed the Illinois bar exam, Anastaplo appeared for a routine Character and Fitness Committee interview. He had submitted a personal history form on which, in response to a question about the Constitution, he wrote, using words borrowed from the Declaration of Independence, that he believed in the people's right to "abolish" a government "destructive" of the "rights to Life, Liberty and the Pursuit of Happiness." His answer led to a discussion with the committee, which asked whether he was a member of the CPUSA or any organization on the attorney general's list. He refused to answer, contending the First Amendment "gave him a right not to disclose" his political associations.[67]

The state denied Anastaplo admission to the bar on the ground that his refusals to answer prevented the committee from "inquiring fully into his general fitness and good citizenship." His case first reached the Court in 1955, but it denied review. In 1957, after *Schware* and *Konigsberg I*, the state supreme court ordered a rehearing; new proceedings were held, but with the same outcome.[68]

The five-justice majority, again in an opinion by Harlan, upheld the state's action. The First Amendment issue, it found, was settled by *Konigsberg II*, which held that the state's interest in requiring answers to questions about CPUSA membership "outweighs any deterrent effect upon freedom of speech and association." Nor was there a "valid constitutional distinction" in that "there was some, though weak, independent evidence that [Konigsberg] had once been connected with the Communist Party, while here there was no such evidence as to Anastaplo." Still, the Court seemed almost to plead with Anastaplo to answer the committee's questions. "We find nothing to suggest that he would not be admitted now if he decides to answer," it said; he "holds the key to admission in his own hands."[69]

Black, dissenting, joined by Warren, Douglas, and Brennan, described Anastaplo's "unblemished" record and "the mountain of evidence so favorable to [him] that the word 'overwhelming' seems inadequate to describe it." The result of the Court's "balancing," he said, is that states may refuse to admit a bar applicant "if he believes in the Declaration of Independence as strongly as Anastaplo and if he is willing to sacrifice his career and his means of livelihood in defense of" First Amendment freedom. Black added: "The very most that can fairly be said against Anastaplo's position in this entire matter is that he took too much of the responsibility of preserving that freedom upon himself."[70]

In later years, Anastaplo fashioned a productive career as an academic. But shortly after his rejection, he drove a taxicab. One of his fares happened to be the state supreme court justice who had written that court's opinion against him;

the justice, Joseph E. Daily, told him, "It's all right; you'll be admitted someday." However, in 1979, after the Character and Fitness Committee reconsidered his case and certified him to the state supreme court as qualified, the state's chief justice rebuffed the move because Anastaplo had not himself initiated it, suggesting he reapply for admission. Anastaplo declined to do so.[71]

Loyalty-Security Discharge—*Cafeteria Workers*

Rachel Brawner's case showed that adverse government action without charges or a hearing was not a practice reserved for excluded aliens. Brawner was a short-order cook at a cafeteria operated by M & M Restaurants at the Naval Gun Factory, a Navy weapons facility in Washington, D.C. Her duties were "to prepare breakfast and lunch, attend the steam table, and wash dishes." M & M, the private company that employed her, operated the cafeteria under a contract with the gun factory, and Brawner had worked there for six years. In November 1956, however, she was directed "to turn in her identification badge" because the gun factory's security officer determined that she did not "meet the security requirements of the installation." Officials would give no further reason and refused to meet with her union representative because "it would serve no useful purpose." Without a badge, Brawner could no longer enter the facility to work; she sued to regain her badge and job.[72]

The five-justice majority, in an opinion by Stewart, sustained the gun factory's action. Brawner had relied on *Greene v. McElroy*, which emphasized the importance of an employee's ability to confront accusers before being stripped of security clearance. But the Court said that *Greene* held only that the military departments had not been authorized to revoke Greene's clearance and that in Brawner's case authorization existed—a Navy regulation, approved by President Truman, stating that "dealers or tradesmen or their agents shall not be admitted within a command, except as authorized by the commanding officer."[73]

Nor, the Court held, did Brawner's exclusion from the gun factory without charges or a hearing deny her due process. She was not denied "the right to follow a chosen trade or profession," it said, for she "remained entirely free to obtain employment as a short-order cook or to get any other job, either with M & M or with any other employer." While the Court recognized she could not be excluded for reasons "patently arbitrary or discriminatory—that she could not have been kept out because she was a Democrat or a Methodist"—the reason given for Brawner's exclusion, it found, was "entirely rational." And it denied she was stigmatized as disloyal: the government found only that she "failed to meet the particular security requirements of that specific military installation" and "[f]or all that appears ... may have simply thought that Rachel Brawner was garrulous, or careless with her identification badge."[74]

In dissent Brennan, joined by Warren, Black, and Douglas, argued that the Court's decision "nullifies" the right "not to be arbitrarily injured by Government," which it "purports to recognize." Under its ruling, he wrote, "[Brawner] is entitled to no process at all. She is not told what whe did wrong; she is not given a chance to defend herself. She may be the victim of the basest calumny, perhaps even the caprice of the government officials in whose power her status rested completely." Procedural fairness was "particularly" required, he added, because Brawner "was excluded as a 'security risk,' that designation most odious in our times."[75]

◇ ◇ ◇

The Court's continued—even accelerated—retreat from the decisions of the 1955 and 1956 terms was again accompanied by a diminished threat of court-curbing legislation. In the 87th Congress, which began in January 1961, none of the anti-Court bills came close to enactment. Smith's anti-preemption bill, still numbered HR 3, was approved by the House Judiciary Committee but failed to pass either house. A *Yates*-"organize" bill passed the House but died in the Senate. A *Mallory* bill was passed by the House; but it was limited to the District of Columbia, and it too died in the Senate.[76]

While the congressional threat evaporated, the Court's turnabout was now almost complete. *Watkins'* discussion of First Amendment limitations on compelled disclosure of "Communist" affiliations, its admonitions against exposure for exposure's sake, and its insistence upon clarity in authorizing resolutions for committees had come to naught. *Slochower* was a nullity—any public employee could be fired for pleading the Fifth Amendment as long as the proper words were used. So also *Konigsberg I*—any bar applicant could be denied admission if he refused to disclose political associations. The extreme care taken in past cases to avoid broad constitutional decisions and to craft narrow rationales was seemingly discarded when the constitutional rulings sustained government action.

Yet, as Lucas Powe observed, the Court had not "fully turn[ed] the clock back to 1951," and "*Yates, Scales,* and *Noto* were not *Dennis*." The Court had retained proof requirements that would soon cause the government to abandon Smith Act prosecutions. And *CPUSA v. SACB*'s evasion of the Fifth Amendment self-incrimination issues, it turned out, left the way clear for post-1962 decisions that brought about the collapse of the Internal Security Act's registration scheme.[77]

11

Frankfurter's Departure, a Near-Decision in *Gibson*, and the Era's End

(OCTOBER TERM 1961)

Flux characterized the 1961 term. Two justices left the Court, both unexpectedly for health reasons. Whittaker retired on March 29, 1962, at age sixty-one, after suffering a nervous breakdown. Only a week later, Frankfurter, seventy-nine years old, collapsed at his desk from a stroke and, following a three-month hospital stay and a period of convalescence at home, reluctantly retired—in August after the term had ended. The absence of the two justices had an immediate impact upon the Court's work. On April 25, Warren advised his colleagues of "the critical condition of our docket." He expressed concern that "we will end the Term in a state of confusion or be under the necessity of setting more cases over for reargument. The calendar for the next Term will hardly support such action."[1]

The number of decisions in "Communist" cases dropped sharply—only three signed decisions compared to fifteen in the preceding term. The signed decisions (there were also a few per curiam rulings) were in routine cases—another prosecution for filing a false Taft-Hartley affidavit, a challenge to Florida's loyalty oath for public employees, and a group of contempt-of-Congress cases collected in a single decision. The first two, decided by a nine-justice Court prior to Whittaker's and Frankfurter's illnesses, were consistent with the pattern of the preceding terms. The government won the false-affidavit case by the usual 5–4 vote, and in the loyalty-oath case, the words of the oath were so obviously unclear in application that the justices voted unanimously to invalidate it. The third decision, issued late in the term by a seven-justice Court, reversed six contempt-of-Congress convictions, by a 5–2 vote, on a narrow procedural ground.[2]

The most significant "Communist" case considered during the term, *Gibson v. Florida Legislative Investigation Committee*, was not decided, because the justices, divided 4–4 following Whittaker's retirement, ordered reargument.

The case marked a convergence of the Court's lines of decision in NAACP and "Communist" cases. Gibson, a local NAACP official, was convicted of contempt after refusing a Florida committee's demand to produce an NAACP membership list in order to identify persons who were also CPUSA members. At conference, in December 1961, the five-justice majority voted to sustain his conviction, and in March Harlan circulated a draft opinion of the Court. But with Whittaker's departure, a necessary fifth vote was lost, and Harlan's opinion was not issued.[3]

Congress was no longer an imminent threat. Mississippi's Eastland, to be sure, persisted in his effort, like that of the Florida committee in *Gibson*, to link the Court's desegregation rulings to "Communist" subversion. In May 1962, he placed in the Senate record, a tabulation he had prepared—a "box score," he called it—of each justice's votes for or against positions "advocated by Communists" in "cases involving subversive activities." Black, he said, had cast 102 votes for the "Communist" position and none against it; Clark, on the other hand, had voted 21 times for the "Communist" position and 61 times against it. Eastland reserved his harshest criticism for the author of *Brown*: "[W]hen there is a clear-cut decision between the Communist party and the security of the country," he told the Senate, "[Earl Warren] decides for the Communists." Eastland's remarks were condemned the next day by senators of both parties, and "[n]o one," the AP reported, "defended the Mississippi Democrat."[4]

False Taft-Hartley Affidavit—*Killian*

A nine-justice Court reviewed the conviction and five-year prison sentence of John J. Killian, an officer of a United Electrical, Radio, and Machine Workers (UE) local, for filing a false non-Communist affidavit.[5]

The principal issue was whether the trial judge correctly instructed the jury how to determine if an individual was a party member when he filed his affidavit. The defense argued that to convict, the jury must find objective indicia of membership, such as a "'specific formal act of joining'" and actions amounting to more than "mere cooperation with [the party] in lawful activities." But the judge's instruction—"[T]here must be present the desire on the part of the individual to belong to the Communist Party and a recognition by that Party that it considers him as a member"—focused instead on Killian's and the party's state of mind, and he refused to instruct that the jury must find that Killian's relationship with the party extended to its illegal objectives.[6]

The five-justice majority, in an opinion by Whittaker, sustained the trial judge's jury instructions. "Membership in such a secretly operating organization," it said, "is, to all but the organization and its member or members, necessarily subjective." The judge, moreover, had instructed the jury to consider objective facts in determining Killian's state of mind.[7]

Two of the three dissents were directed to the jury-instruction issue. In Brennan's view, *Douds* (the 1950 decision that upheld Taft-Hartley's affidavit requirement) required that membership be proved by "evidence from which could be inferred the existence, beyond a reasonable doubt, of an 'objective fact'—'the act of joining the Party.'" Douglas, joined by Warren, contended *Douds* required that "[m]embership . . . be proved by facts which tie the accused to the illegal aims of the party." Black, however, wanted to overrule *Douds*: "I think the Constitution absolutely prohibits the Government from sending people to jail for 'crimes' that arise out of, and indeed are manufactured out of, the imposition of test oaths that invade the freedoms of belief and political association."[8]

State Loyalty Oaths—*Cramp*

In *Cramp v. Board of Public Instruction*, the Court reviewed a loyalty oath, prescribed in a state statute, required of Florida's public employees. The oath required the oathtaker not only to deny CPUSA membership but also to swear that "I have not and will not lend my aid, support, advice, counsel or influence to the Communist Party." Failure to sign the oath resulted in "immediate discharge." David Walton Cramp Jr., who had taught in the Orange County public schools for nine years, refused to sign the oath and sued challenging its constitutionality.[9]

A unanimous Court, in an opinion by Stewart, ruled that the portion of the oath requiring the oathtaker to deny lending "aid, support, advice, counsel or influence" to the CPUSA was unduly vague and thus denied due process. These terms, it said, were not "susceptible of objective measurement":

> Could one who had ever cast his vote for [a CPUSA] candidate safely subscribe to this legislative oath? Could a lawyer who had ever represented the Communist Party or its members swear . . . that he had never knowingly lent his "counsel" to the Party? . . . Indeed, could anyone honestly subscribe to this oath who had ever supported any cause with contemporaneous knowledge that the Communist Party also supported it?

"The very absurdity of these possibilities," the Court said, "brings into focus the extraordinary ambiguity of the statutory language."[10]

Another loyalty-oath case, *Nostrand v. Little*, which the Court in 1960 sent back to Washington state courts for consideration of an issue not addressed, returned and was disposed of in a per curiam ruling. The issue was whether a public employee who refused to take the oath would be given a hearing to explain his refusal. After the state court answered in the affirmative, the Court, by 7–2 vote, dismissed the appeal "for want of a substantial federal question." Douglas, joined by Black, dissented.[11]

Nostrand, decided on January 22, was the term's last decision in a "Communist" case by a nine-justice Court.

Whittaker's Retirement, White's Appointment

Whittaker's inability to deal with stress was manifest long before 1962. A researcher found evidence of "numerous incidents throughout his life when he suffered from anxiety and depression to the extent that it impaired his ability to work." His longtime secretary said he had suffered "breakdowns" while in private practice in Kansas City. He likely would not have survived today's stringent vetting process for Supreme Court nominees.[12]

As a justice, Whittaker complained of the workload and pressure, and in early 1962 the burden became too great for him. He reportedly contemplated suicide but was dissuaded by his son. He performed no work at the Court after February 1 and, on March 6, was admitted to Walter Reed Hospital, physically and mentally exhausted. Warren, visiting him on March 15, "knew immediately that Whittaker was incapacitated and began steps to accomplish his formal retirement on grounds of disability." The following day, Warren received the certification of a three-physician board at Walter Reed that Whittaker had a "permanent" medical disability and obtained from Whittaker a letter certifying he was "permanently disabled" and "elect[ed] to retire." The chief justice sent Whittaker's letter, along with his own statutory certification, to President Kennedy. However, Whittaker, after returning to his home on March 23, may have changed his mind. On March 28, a family member told the press that while he needed rest, he "does not intend to resign as a result of the illness and medical advice" and "intends to carry on at the court with a reduced work-load."[13]

The next day, however, Whittaker unequivocally retired, and the president announced his retirement at a press conference. In a prepared statement, Whittaker cited the "continuous stresses of the court's work," which brought him to the "point of physical exhaustion." Kennedy, in his brief announcement, said that Whittaker "is retiring at the direction of his physicians for reasons of disability."[14]

On March 30, the president nominated a successor, Byron R. White, forty-four years old and the deputy attorney general. JFK and White had been friends since they served in the Navy together in the Pacific during World War II. A world-class football player, earning the nickname "Whizzer," White was an all-American at the University of Colorado in 1937 and used his pro-football earnings to finance his education at the Yale Law School. He was a law clerk to Vinson during the 1946 term and then returned to Colorado to pursue a corporate law practice. In 1960 he played a leading role in Kennedy's presidential campaign.[15]

As a justice, White resisted being categorized as liberal or conservative. But in the "Communist" cases in which he participated, he regularly voted with the government, a more consistent vote even than Whittaker's. White, in one observer's opinion, "took an extremely narrow view of First Amendment protections."[16]

Easily confirmed by the Senate, White joined the Court on April 16, but he was able to hear only the final two weeks of oral argument and did not participate in any of the term's "Communist" decisions.[17]

Frankfurter's Retirement, Goldberg's Apppointment

Frankfurter's stroke occurred as he worked in his chambers late in the day on April 5. He was taken in an ambulance to George Washington University hospital. He had seemed in satisfactory health following a heart attack in 1958, and his physician and the hospital initially issued optimistic reports. The justice's "cardiovascular insufficiency," Dr. Gregory A. Kelser said the next day, had "cleared spontaneously and left no residual after effect." On April 23, the hospital reported "continued improvement" and termed his condition "most satisfactory." But it did not disclose that he had suffered a second stroke that "left him with his speech slightly impaired and with difficulty in the use of an arm and leg." On April 30, the hospital announced that Frankfurter would not return to the Court for the remainder of the term.[18]

By July, Frankfurter was well enough to return home and to receive a forty-minute visit from the president. But on August 16 Warren was informed he would retire. His resignation letter to JFK on August 28 stated that although doctors had earlier expressed "[h]igh expectations" that "I would be able to resume my judicial duties with the beginning of the next term of the court . . . they now advise me that the stepped-up therapy essential to that end involves hazards which might jeopardize the useful years they anticipate still lie ahead for me."[19]

Frankfurter's last major opinion, issued on March 26, was his dissent to a landmark decision, *Baker v. Carr*, in which the Court, reversing a longstanding position, held that federal courts may review the apportionment of seats in state legislatures. The issue went to the heart of Frankfurter's judicial philosophy, and his dissent, Anthony Lewis said in the *Times*, was "a final, great expression" of his views. He wrote: "The Court's authority—possessed of neither the purse nor the sword—ultimately rests on sustained public confidence in its moral sanction. Such feeling must be nourished by the Court's complete detachment, in fact and in appearance, from political entanglements and by abstention from injecting itself into the clash of political forces in political settlements."[20]

On August 29, the day he announced Frankfurter's resignation, the president named a successor, Arthur J. Goldberg, his secretary of labor. The fifty-four-year-old Goldberg, the son of Russian-Jewish immigrants, was raised in Chicago in circumstances close to poverty. He attended Northwestern University and its law school, represented labor unions in private practice in Chicago, and served in the Office of Strategic Services during World War II. After the war, Goldberg, a superb labor lawyer, liberal and anti-Communist in his politics, became general counsel to both the CIO (until its 1955 merger with the AFL) and the United Steelworkers of America. In 1960, he was an early JFK supporter and his "principal liaison to the labor movement" during the election campaign. As labor secretary, Goldberg was JFK's close advisor and troubleshooter. When the vacancy arose, Kennedy, who wanted a Jew to succeed Frankfurter, chose him for the Court.[21]

Goldberg did not join the Court until the 1962 term and resigned less than three years later—persuaded by President Johnson to become U.S. ambassador to the United Nations. But during his brief tenure, "he brought to the Court," Belknap wrote, "substantial skepticism about McCarthyism's methods" and "a proclivity for activism." Goldberg did not share Frankfurter's concern for protecting the Court, believing that "it's not the function of a Supreme Court justice to worry about the Court injuring itself." He allied himself with Warren, Black, Douglas, and Brennan. Angered, Frankfurter in retirement harshly criticized his successor in private communications.[22]

More Committee-Contempt Cases—*Russell* and Others

Committee-contempt cases continued to fill the Court's docket. At the time Whittaker retired, six "Communist" contempt-of-Congress cases, argued in December, had not yet been decided. Three more were argued on April 18 and 19. In May, a seven-justice Court decided six of the cases in a single decision, *Russell v. United States*, ruling on a procedural issue common to all of them.[23]

Two of the six *Russell* defendants, Norton Anthony Russell and John T. Gojack, were HUAC witnesses. The other four were witnesses at hearings in which Eastland's SISS, ostensibly investigating Communist infiltration of the press, subpoenaed and questioned dozens of journalists. One of the four, Herman Liveright, worked at a New Orleans television station; the others were newspapermen—William A. Price, a *New York Daily News* reporter, and Robert Shelton and Alden Whitman, copyeditors at the *New York Times*. Price and Shelton relied on the First Amendment in refusing to answer; Whitman admitted he was a CPUSA member from 1935 to 1948 but refused to name individuals he knew in the Party. During the three days of hearings at which the newspapermen appeared, fourteen of the eighteen witnesses questioned were past or present *Times* employees, leading the *Times* to charge that it was "singled out for this attack" by Eastland because "we condemned segregation in the Southern schools ... [and] denounced McCarthyism and all its works."[24]

Although the six cases presented myriad issues, the only issue decided by the Court was whether grand-jury indictments in contempt-of-Congress cases "must identify the subject which was under inquiry at the time of the defendant's ... refusal to answer." The six *Russell* indictments merely charged that the questions the defendant refused to answer "were pertinent to the question then under inquiry" by the committee. This form of indictment, the Court held, by 5–2 vote in an opinion by Stewart, was inadequate.[25]

Failure to identify the subject under inquiry, the Court found, violates "the basic principle 'that the accused must be apprised by the indictment, with reasonable certainty, of the nature of the accusation against him.'" "A cryptic form of indictment," it said, "requires the defendant to go to trial with the chief issue undefined." It cited Price's prosecution: "At every stage ... Price was met with a different theory, or by no theory at all, as to what the topic had been." The Court added: "To allow the prosecutor, or the court, to make a subsequent guess as to what was in the minds of the grand jury at the time they returned the indictment would deprive the defendant of a basic protection which the guaranty of the intervention of a grand jury was designed to secure."[26]

Clark and Harlan dissented. The Court, Clark charged, "has concocted a new and novel doctrine to upset congressional contempt convictions."[27]

Three other contempt-of Congress convictions, involving HUAC witnesses Bernard Silber, Frank Grumman, and Louis Hartman, were soon reversed by per curiam order, written by Stewart, on the same faulty-indictment ground, by the same 5–2 vote. The Court shrugged off Silber's failure to raise the issue either in the court of appeals or the Supreme Court, stating it "has 'the power to notice a "plain error" though it is not assigned or specified.'"[28]

Russell, however, did not preclude the government from obtaining new indictments that complied with its requirements, and Robert Kennedy's Justice Department proceeded to do so. All six *Russell* defendants were again indicted, as were Silber and Grumman. A new indictment against Hartman, the department told the press, "will probably be sought later."[29]

But the federal courts proved inhospitable to the renewed prosecutions. Shelton's conviction on the new indictment was overturned on the ground that SISS had violated its own procedural rule requiring that subcommittee members select the witnesses to be called—this function had been "de facto delegated to the Subcommittee counsel." The decision in Shelton's case benefited the three other SISS witnesses, Whitman, Price, and Liveright. Two of the HUAC witnesses, Silber and Grumman, were acquitted by a district judge who found that HUAC failed to comply with its own rule concerning closed hearings. Another district judge directed Russell's acquittal because the pertinency of the questions had not been made clear to him. And Gojack's new conviction was reversed unanimously by the Court in 1966—eleven years after his refusal to answer—again due to the committee's failure to observe its own procedural rules.³⁰

Convergence of "Communist" and NAACP Decisions—*Gibson*

After *Brown*, Belknap wrote, the justices "allied themselves with the NAACP, accepting the organization's arguments and shielding it from attack by southern authorities." In a string of cases (*NAACP v. Alabama*, *Bates v. Little Rock*, *Shelton v. Tucker*), the Court, invoking a First Amendment "freedom of association," protected the names of NAACP members from disclosure to southern jurisdictions. These decisions stood in stark contrast to its decisions in "Communist" cases. In the case of Willard Uphaus, imprisoned for refusing to disclose the names of guests at his adult summer camp, Douglas, joined by Warren and Black, had pleaded in vain that "[a]ll groups—white or colored" should receive "the same protection against harassment as the N.A.A.C.P. enjoys."³¹

Gibson required the Court to decide whether its practice of shielding NAACP membership lists from disclosure to southern states was trumped by a state's claim that it needed the list to hunt Communists. The Florida committee contended that it wanted the list not to identify NAACP members but to determine which ones were Communists. Its chairman, describing the purpose of the hearings, said they were directed to determining the extent to which "Communists and Communist influence has been successful in penetrating, infiltrating, and influencing" organizations such as the NAACP. The committee's investigator testified he had discovered fifty-two past or present residents of Dade County (Miami) who "at one time or another" were CPUSA members, of whom fourteen "were or had been" NAACP members.³²

Theodore R. Gibson, president of the NAACP's Miami branch, was ordered to bring the branch's membership list to the hearing solely, the committee said, to enable him to "refer to it himself" in answering questions to determine if any of the fifty-two "Communists" found by the investigator were NAACP members. Gibson responded that he was willing to advise the committee based on his own personal knowledge whether persons named by it as Communists were NAACP members "but only to the extent of his own knowledge, unaided by reference to" the membership list. When Gibson refused "to resort to the membership list," he was convicted of criminal contempt and sentenced to six months' imprisonment.³³

A conference in *Gibson* on December 8, 1961, was attended by all nine justices. The "question," Frankfurter commented, only half-jokingly, "is whether the NAACP is incorporated in the First Amendment." Four justices (Harlan,

Clark, Whittaker, and Stewart) agreed with him that it was not and voted with him to affirm Gibson's conviction. Harlan thought the case was "controlled by *Uphaus.*" Warren argued unsuccessfully that "if this stands, *NAACP v. Alabama* is thwarted" and "all legislatures will let loose on" the NAACP.³⁴

Frankfurter assigned the opinion to Harlan, who circulated a draft opinion on March 13—one week after Whittaker entered the hospital but sixteen days before he resigned and three weeks prior to Frankfurter's stroke. The case, Harlan wrote, "bears no resemblance" to *NAACP v. Alabama* or *Bates v. Little Rock*, where a "compelling paramount state interest" was absent. Here, he said, the state's interest is "manifest" and "must be held to prevail over [Gibson's] objections to production of the list for the purpose for which it was sought."³⁵

With Whittaker's retirement, however, the Court, now equally divided, ordered the case reargued in the succeeding term. At the start of the 1962 term, Harlan circulated an opinion "which" he said, "I had prepared for the then majority." But his majority was irrevocably lost, and when the case was decided, the Court, by 5–4 vote in an opinion by Goldberg, reversed Gibson's conviction. The record, it said, disclosed an "utter failure to demonstrate the existence of any substantial relationship between the N.A.A.C.P. and subversive or Communist activities." It distinguished *Uphaus* and *Barenblatt* as cases decided on the basis of the CPUSA's "particular character." Black and Douglas, while joining the Court's opinion, wrote concurring opinions stating their preference for a "different approach." "[T]he constitutional right of association," Black said, "includes the privilege of any person to associate with Communists or anti-Communists."³⁶

The 1961 term was Black's twenty-fifth, and on its final day, June 25, 1962, Solicitor General Archibald Cox and Warren as chief justice, in open court, each took note of the occasion with graceful remarks. "The tributes evidently came as a surprise to Justice Black," the *Times* reported, for he "sank back into his chair."³⁷

When the Court reconvened in October, its McCarthy era had ended. Black's longtime adversary, Frankfurter, was gone, replaced by Goldberg, a substitution that marked a sea change in the Court's rulings in "Communist" cases. As the flow of "Communist" cases slowed to a trickle, a new majority ruled repeatedly against the government—and not only, as in prior years, on narrow rationales.

In the 1963 term, the Court held unconstitutional on due process grounds the Internal Security Act section that made it a felony for members of a "Communist organization" to apply for a passport. In the 1964 term, it invalidated on bill-of-attainder grounds the statute, added in 1959, making it a crime for a CPUSA member to serve as an officer or employee of a labor union. In the 1965 term, it held that CPUSA members may invoke the Fifth Amendment and refuse to comply with SACB registration orders. And in the 1967 term, it held unconstitutional on First Amendment grounds the Internal Security Act provision that made it a crime for a CPUSA member to be employed at a defense facility. The provision was overbroad, the Court said, because it applied to "a passive or inactive member" and those "unaware of" or who "may disagree with" the party's unlawful aims.[38]

By 1967, when the last of these decisions was issued, Frankfurter had died in retirement—in 1965, at age eighty-two. Goldberg had been replaced by Abe Fortas, a close advisor to President Johnson and, like Goldberg, the son of immigrant Jews and a liberal. And the Court had handed down the first of its major Vietnam War decisions, overturning on First Amendment grounds the Georgia House of Representatives' refusal to seat Julian Bond, an elected candidate who had made public statements opposing the war.[39]

EPILOGUE

Vietnam War Decisions and Some Observations

The Court's decisions during the Vietnam War represent a high-water mark in the protection of First Amendment freedoms in wartime—and, quite arguably, any other time. The cases showed graphically the changes in the mode of dissent that occurred in the 1960s.

In one group of decisions, the Court reviewed the criminal convictions of three individuals who mocked sacrosanct patriotic symbols—the flag, the military uniform—in conveying their antiwar message. One case involved a "guerilla theater" skit, performed at a Houston induction center, in which actors wearing Army uniforms shot a "Viet Cong" (with a water pistol). The Court reversed all three convictions. Two other decisions reviewed disorderly-conduct convictions based on the speaker's communication of his antiwar message using crude four-letter words in a public place. These convictions too were reversed.[1]

The "Pentagon Papers" case presented more serious circumstances. A seven-thousand-page study of America's involvement in the Vietnam conflict, ordered by the Secretary of Defense and highly classified, was copied by a former Defense Department consultant turned antiwar activist and leaked to the *New York Times* and the *Washington Post*. The newspapers began, in June 1971, to publish portions of the study, which showed that the executive branch had misled the Congress and the public about the conflict. The government sued to enjoin publication by the newspapers which, it said, "would endanger the national security." The Solicitor General told the Court in oral argument that publication will affect "lives," "the process of the termination of the war" and "the process of recovering prisoners of war."[2]

The government's lawsuit, however, sought imposition of a prior restraint on speech—in other words, to prevent publication rather than to punish it afterward—a type of restraint which, under the Court's precedent, bore "a heavy presumption against its constitutional validity." The Court, by 6–3 vote, denied the government's request for an injunction, allowing publication of the study to continue.[3]

The icing on the cake for supporters of a robust First Amendment was the adoption in 1969 of a new formula to replace the altered clear-and-present-danger standard announced by the Court in *Dennis* nearly two decades earlier. The speech at issue was not an antiwar protest but rather a hooded Klansman's statement at a KKK gathering in Ohio: "We're not a revengent [sic] organization, but if our President, our Congress, our Supreme Court, continues to suppress the white, Caucasian race, it's possible that there might have to be some revengeance [sic] taken." The Klansman, Clarence Brandenburg, was convicted under Ohio's Criminal Syndicalism Statute—a law "quite similar" to the California statute upheld by the Court in its 1927 *Whitney* decision (in which Brandeis's concurring opinion, joined by Holmes, provided a classic articulation of the clear-and-present-danger doctrine).[4]

The Court struck down the Ohio statute, overruling *Whitney*. In a unanimous per curiam opinion, it stated "the principle" that "the constitutional guarantees of free speech and free press do not permit a State to forbid or proscribe advocacy of the use of force or of law violation except where such advocacy is directed to inciting and producing imminent lawless action and is likely to incite or produce such action." The decision cited McCarthy-era precedent, *Yates* and *Noto*. The words "clear and present danger" were omitted from the new test, but the element of imminence, removed in *Dennis,* was restored.[5]

These decisions, broadly enforcing First Amendment rights during the Vietnam War, likely would not have been written if the Court, as in the McCarthy era, had been under sustained attack in the Congress, the press, and public opinion. But the Vietnam War had become unpopular, and the Court was not attacked.

The Court's McCarthy-era decisions, *Yates* in particular, Geoffrey Stone wrote, "laid the foundation" for its Vietnam War jurisprudence. *Yates*'s distinction between abstract advocacy of revolution and incitement to action undoubtedly informed the new *Brandenburg* formula. But McCarthy-era decisions may also have "laid the foundation" in another sense: as a sort of object lesson. Amid severe political repression and under harsh attack itself, the Court, despite its retreat, gave valuable protection to the rights of highly unpopular dissenters. Many of its decisions may well have been, as Gerald Gunther said, "temporary avoidance devices empty of serious doctrinal content." Yet the decisions had real consequences.[6]

Largely as a result of McCarthy-era rulings by the Court, the two most repressive laws in the government's arsenal—the Smith Act and the Internal Security

Act's registration provisions—were ultimately rendered useless. The constitutionality of the Smith Act, to be sure, was upheld in *Dennis* and *Scales*; but after *Yates* and *Noto*, the government could not prove a violation. Similarly, *CPUSA v. SACB* upheld the Internal Security Act's registration scheme; but the Court managed to consume a full decade before issuing that decision, and when no one registered, the government, now in a changed political climate, was unable to do anything about it.

Nelson blocked prosecutions under state sedition statutes that held a serious potential for abuse. At the time *Nelson* was decided, Carl Braden was already serving a fifteen-year prison sentence for sedition stemming from his attempt to desegregate a whites-only Louisville neighborhood. Nelson himself had received a twenty-year sentence in a bizarre prosecution triggered by Michael Musmanno's zeal for statewide elective office.

There was more. When the Eisenhower administration authorized summary dismissal of any federal employee on loyalty grounds, *Cole v. Young* ruled that the statute in question authorized summary dismissals only for the minority of employees holding sensitive positions. *Greene v. McElroy* (albeit taking an "escape route") led to an executive order that afforded significant confrontation rights to defense-industry employees denied security clearance. *Jencks,* even after Congress's limiting statute, may have improved the ability of criminal defendants to obtain the prior statements of government witnesses for impeachment purposes by eliminating any need to show conflict with the witnesses' trial testimony.

Still, as a reading of the Court's decisions makes plain, McCarthy-era repression took a fearsome toll in lives disrupted by lost jobs, ostracism, prison sentences, and exile. Brennan believed these hardships to have been wholly unnecessary. "[T]he paranoid fear that the American Communist Party stood ready to overthrow the government," he said a quarter-century later, was "so baseless" as to "be comical were it not for the serious hardship" inflicted at the time. The individuals whose cases the Court decided were sometimes CPUSA officials; more often they were ordinary but hapless people—Mezei a cabinet-maker, Brawner a short-order cook, Niukkanen a house painter, Lerner a subway conductor, Nelson and Globe social workers, Beilan and Adler schoolteachers.[7]

In many of the Court's decisions sustaining repressive government action, a shift of only one vote among the justices would have changed the outcome. The Court's retreat during the 1957–60 terms consisted almost exclusively of 5–4 decisions. One changed vote seemingly would have barred the firing of public employees merely for pleading the Fifth Amendment; ended the practice of deporting aliens, long resident in this country, because of CPUSA memberships many years earlier; required admission to the bar of attorney-applicants who proved good character but would not reveal political affiliations; and allowed HUAC witnesses to invoke the First Amendment in refusing to disclose political associations.

Frankfurter, an intellectual force positioned at the Court's center, more than any other justice determined its direction and led its retreat. Widely viewed as an apostle of judicial restraint, he was (at least in this reading) guided by a slightly different consideration—protecting the Court. He "always was fearful that the Court would injure itself," Arthur Goldberg observed, and "[t]his was his principal concern, always." Fred Rodell wrote that in "Frankfurter's scale of values . . . keeping the court out of trouble rates near the top." Protecting the Court usually translated into decisions deferring to the elective branches and to state governments—the same outcomes dictated by a policy of judicial restraint—but not invariably.[8]

When he perceived a diminished or acceptable political risk to the Court, Frankfurter was often willing to overturn government action and to uphold dissenters' rights. Thus, in the 1955 term he joined in *Nelson*, *Cole v. Young*, and *Slochower*; in the 1956 term, in *Yates*, *Watkins*, *Sweezy*, *Jencks*, and *Witkovich*; and in the 1957 term, in the passport decisions (*Kent* and *Dayton*) and *Rowoldt*. When, however, these decisions were sharply criticized in the press and in the Congress—most became subjects of court-curbing bills—Frankfurter retreated. He joined in decisions, assigning the opinions, which effectively nullified rulings he had joined only a short time before: *Slochower* nullified by *Beilan*, *Lerner*, and *Nelson/Globe*; *Sweezy* by *Uphaus*; *Watkins* (only its narrow holding on pertinency survived) by *Barenblatt*, *Wilkinson*, and *Braden*; and *Rowoldt* by *Niukkanen*. His votes can best be explained not by a policy of judicial restraint—his earlier votes did not reflect judicial restraint—but by a determination that retreat was necessary to shield the Court from injury.[9]

Protecting the Court, of course, is not an improper consideration for a justice, but it is one that creates its own set of problems. Political assessments are often inaccurate. Here, Frankfurter apparently failed to anticipate the extent of the hostile reaction to the decisions in favor of accused Communists during the 1955 and 1956 terms. The Court, as Barry Friedman put it, "climbed out of its foxhole before the danger had truly passed." Later, he may have misread the results of the 1958 election, in which Democrats gained sixteen Senate seats and the anti-Court ranks were diminished. Following this election, every court-curbing bill, even those that passed the House, died in the Senate. The Court's retreat may thus have continued when it was no longer politically necessary.[10]

There is an even more fundamental problem with a protecting-the-Court criterion: in a period of political repression the Court is likely to withhold a defense of dissenters' constitutional rights when it is most needed.

Black, the leader of the Court's other bloc, was untroubled by these kinds of considerations. He wrote to Fred Rodell in 1962:

> [I]f, as I strongly believe, the Supreme Court is vested with the constitutional power to interpret and determine the constitutional validity of laws, it cannot "defer" to a legislative belief or declaration of constitutionality without judicially "abdicating its own responsibility. . . ." In the performance of its high responsibility to pass upon the constitutionality of laws I believe, as you say, that it is the Court's duty to "defer" only to the Constitution itself.

Black's views were reflected in votes and opinions oblivious to political consequences—in Eastland's "box score," 102 to 0 for the "Communist" position. His opinions (and usually Douglas's), most of them dissents and concurrences, were constant reminders that the apparatus of the McCarthy era was directed at beliefs, associations, and speech, from start to finish an assault on First Amendment values, and did not differentiate among its targets, imposing a collective guilt.[11]

Other justices played outsized roles as well. Harlan's *Yates* opinion was not only important at the time but also one of the few McCarthy-era "Communist" decisions with a continuing influence on First Amendment doctrine. Douglas was an independent voice on the dissenters' side; he issued his stay of execution in *Rosenberg*, to allow exploration of a substantial death-penalty issue, although he surely knew he would receive a torrent of personal abuse. Warren, who received more abuse than any other justice, not only figured significantly in the Court's "Communist" decisions but also his contemporaneous role in *Brown* stands, more than a half century later, as a crowning achievement for any chief justice.

McCarthy-era justices, it is true, did not simply or mechanically "apply the law," but the inquiry is sterile. A direction to the justices in a constitutional case simply to "apply the law," Justice David Souter recently observed, has "only a tenuous connection to reality." He cited the Constitution's "deliberately open-ended guarantees" and constitutional values "that may well exist in tension with each other, not in harmony." In the McCarthy era, the political consequences of a decision, in the view of most of the justices, were an essential part of the calculus.[12]

"Judicial supremacy" is one of today's buzzwords. But the story of the Court in the McCarthy era was instead one of "judicial vulnerability." Not only was the Court broadly assaulted and forced to retreat, its independence at risk, but also its justices suffered personal attacks, their patriotism and competence questioned. The era's justices, some of them towering figures in Supreme Court history, were compelled to display "an uncommon portion of fortitude," as Alexander Hamilton had long ago foreseen.

Notes

Introduction

1. William J. Brennan Jr., "The Quest to Develop a Jurisprudence of Civil Liberties in Times of Security Crises," Address, Law School of Hebrew University, Jerusalem, Israel, December 22, 1987 (quote, 1) (available at http://www.hofstra. edu/PDF/law_civil_hafetz_article1.pdf). A commission created by Congress concluded in 1983 "that the factors that shaped the internment decision 'were race prejudice, war hysteria, and a failure of political leadership,' *not* military necessity." Geoffrey R. Stone, *Perilous Times: Free Speech in Wartime from the Sedition Act of 1798 to the War on Terrorism* (New York: Norton, 2004), 306, quoting Commission on Wartime Relocation and Internment of Civilians, *Personal Justice Denied*, 5. See Peter Irons, *Justice at War: The Story of the Japanese American Internment Cases* (Berkeley: University of California Press, 1983); *Hirabayashi v. United States*, 828 F. 2d 591, 598 (9th Cir. 1987). A 1988 statute, signed by President Ronald Reagan, offered an official apology and reparations to each surviving internee (Pub. L. 100-383, 102 Stat. 903). Roosevelt pardon: Proclamation No. 2068, December 23, 1933. Jefferson, following his election in 1800, pardoned those convicted under the 1798 Sedition Act, and Congress repaid the fines. Brennan, 3; Michael Linfield, *Freedom Under Fire: U.S. Civil Liberties in Times of War* (Boston: South End, 1990), 20.

2. See Stone, *Perilous Times*; Linfield, *Freedom Under Fire*; Robert Justin Goldstein, *Political Repression in Modern America: From 1870 to 1976* (Urbana: University of Illinois Press, 2001); Anthony Lewis, *Freedom for the Thought That We Hate: A Biography of the First Amendment* (New York: Basic, 2007), 11-38, 101-32.

3. Detainee Treatment Act of 2005, § 1005(e), 119 Stat. 2741-43 (December 30, 2005); Military Commission Act of 2006, § 7, 120 Stat. 2635-36 (October 17, 2006). Wiretapping: see, for example, *NY Times*, April 7, 2006, "Gonzales Suggests Legal Basis for Domestic Wiretapping."

4. William O. Douglas, *The Court Years, 1939-1975: The Autobiography of William O. Douglas* (New York: Random House, 1980), 38; *Dennis v. United States*, 341 U.S.

494, 556 (1951) (Frankfurter, J., concurring); Earl Warren, *The Memoirs of Chief Justice Earl Warren* (Garden City, N.Y.: Doubleday, 1977), 332. Similar sentiments have been voiced by lower-court judges. *An Independent Judiciary,* Report of the Commission on Separation of Powers and Judicial Independence, American Bar Association (1997), 19, 19n43.

5. Decl. of Indep., 9th "injury and usurpation"; Garry Wills, *Inventing America: Jefferson's Declaration of Independence* (New York: Vintage, 1978), 65–90, 374–79; Joseph J. Ellis, *American Sphinx: The Character of Thomas Jefferson* (New York: Vintage, 1996), 54–63.

6. William S. Carpenter, *Judicial Tenure in the United States* (New Haven: Yale University Press, 1918), 2–3; *United States v. Will,* 449 U.S. 200, 218–19 (1980); Charles Gardner Geyh, *The Origins and History of Federal Judicial Independence,* Appendix A to ABA, *An Independent Judiciary,* 68.

7. U.S. Const., Art. III, §1, cl. 1 ("The Judges, both of the supreme and inferior Courts, shall hold their Offices during good Behaviour, and shall, at stated Times, receive for their Services, a Compensation, which shall not be diminished during their Continuance in Office"). See, for example, *United States ex rel. Toth v. Quarles,* 350 U.S. 11, 16 (1955) ("The provisions of Article III were designed to give judges maximum freedom from possible coercion or influence by the executive or legislative branches of the Government").

8. James Madison, Alexander Hamilton, and John Jay, *The Federalist Papers* (London: Penguin, 1987), Isaac Kramnick ed., 436–42 [hereinafter *Federalist Papers*]. Fifty-one of the eighty-five essays in *The Federalist Papers,* all written under the pen name "Publius," are attributed to Hamilton, twenty-nine to Madison, and five to Jay. Ron Chernow, *Alexander Hamilton* (New York: Penguin, 2004), 248.

9. *Federalist Papers,* 438, 440.

10. *Id.,* 440–41.

11. *Id.,* 444; U.S. Const. Art. II, §4. Hamilton thus conflated the "good Behaviour" standard in Article III with the "high Crimes and Misdemeanors" standard in Article II, governing removal of "[t]he President, Vice President and all civil officers of the United States."

12. *Marbury v. Madison,* 5 U.S. (1 Cranch.) 137, 177 (1803). *Marbury* "adopted Hamilton's argument in the 78th number of the *Federalist.*" Robert H. Jackson, *The Struggle for Judicial Supremacy: A Study of a Crisis in American Power Politics* (New York: Vintage [paperbound], 1941), 27.

13. William H. Rehnquist, *Grand Inquests: The Historic Impeachments of Justice Samuel Chase and President Andrew Johnson* (New York: Morrow, 1992), 15–134; Richard E. Ellis, *The Jeffersonian Crisis: Courts and Politics in the Young Republic* (New York: Oxford University Press, 1971), 76–82; Barry Friedman, "The History of the Countermajoritarian Difficulty, Part One: The Road to Judicial Supremacy," 73 *N.Y.U. L. Rev.* 333, 364–68 (1998) [hereinafter Friedman, "Part One").

14. Rehnquist, *Grand Inquests,* 114 (quote); Ellis, *Jeffersonian Crisis,* 96–107; Charles Gardner Geyh, *When Congress and the Courts Collide: The Struggle for Control of America's Judicial System* (Ann Arbor: University of Michigan Press, 2006), 131–42.

15. In 1803, prior to Chase's impeachment, a lower-court judge, John Pickering, who had become mentally ill and alcoholic, was impeached and removed. Ellis, *Jeffersonian Crisis*, 69–75; Rehnquist, *Grand Inquests*, 127–128. West H. Humphreys, a district judge, was removed in 1862 for supporting the secession of Tennessee and becoming a judge in the Confederacy. Other lower-court judges impeached and convicted were Robert W. Archbald (1913), Halstead L. Ritter (1936), Harry E. Claiborne (1986), Alcee L. Hastings (1988), Walter L. Nixon (1989), and G. Thomas Porteous Jr. (2010). Mark Delahay in 1873 and George English in 1926 resigned following impeachment. Three judges were impeached but then acquitted: James H. Peck (1830), Charles H. Swayne (1903), and Harold Lauderback (1932). Geyh, *When Congress and the Courts Collide*, 120–30, 142–51; *NY Times*, December 8, 2010, "Senate, for Just the 8th Time, Votes to Oust a Federal Judge"; http://www.miketodd.net/encyc/impeach2.htm (accessed November 28, 2011).

16. Michal R. Belknap, *The Supreme Court under Earl Warren, 1953–1969* (Columbia, S.C.: University of South Carolina Press, 2005), 65 (quote); Bernard Schwartz, *Super Chief: Earl Warren and His Supreme Court: A Judicial Biography* (New York: New York University Press, 1983), 280–82 ("The American landscape soon blossomed with 'Impeach Earl Warren' billboards, and Congressmen were deluged with letters urging impeachment"); Chief Justice's *2004 Year-End Report on the Federal Judiciary*, released January 1, 2005, 5 (second quote).

17. U.S. Const. Art III, §2, cl. 1 and 2 (emphasis added). The use of the term "exceptions" suggests that "Congress could not abrogate totally the Court's appellate jurisdiction" or that it "may not remove the major portion ... since an 'exception' must by definition be less expansive than the 'rule' to which it is an exception." Martin E. Redish, "Congressional Power to Regulate Supreme Court Appellate Jurisdiction under the Exceptions Clause: An Internal and External Examination," 27 *Villanova L. Rev.* 900, 901–2 (1982). Other legal scholars dispute the existence of a congressional power to strip the Court of jurisdiction to decide a constitutional issue. See Raoul Berger, *Congress v. The Supreme Court* (Cambridge, Mass.: Harvard University Press, 1969), 285–96; Henry M. Hart Jr., "The Power of Congress to Limit the Jurisdiction of the Federal Courts: An Exercise in Dialectic," 66 *Harv. L. Rev.* 1362, 1365 (1953).

18. *Ex parte McCardle*, 74 U.S. (7 Wall) 506 (1868). The earlier case was *Ex parte Milligan*, 71 U.S. (7 Wall.) 2 (1866). See Charles Fairman, *History of the Supreme Court of the United States, Vol. VI: Reconstruction and Reunion, 1864–88, Part One* (New York: Macmillan, 1971) [hereinafter Fairman, *History, Vol. VI*], 415–29, 437–40, 449–78, 485–514; Walter F. Murphy, *Congress and the Court: A Case Study in the American Political Process* (Chicago: University of Chicago Press, 1962), 38–40; Barry Friedman, "The History of the Countermajoritarian Difficulty, Part II: Reconstruction's Political Court," 91 *Georgetown L. J.* 1, 25–38 (2002) [hereinafter Friedman, "Part Two"]; Maurice S. Culp, "A Survey of the Proposals to Limit or Deny the Power of Judicial Review by the Supreme Court of the United States—II," 4 *Indiana L. J.* 474, 484–85 (1929).

19. McCarthy-era bill: see chap. 8 herewith. 2004 bills: HR 3313, passed by the House on July 22, 2004 (same-sex marriage); HR 2028, passed by the House on September 23,

2004 (Pledge); *NY Times,* July 23, 2004, "House Backs Bill to Limit Power of Judges," and September 24, 2004, "House Passes Court Limits on Pledge."

20. *Hamdan v. Rumsfeld, cert. granted,* 546 U.S. 1002 (November 7, 2005); Detainee Treatment Act of 2005, Pub. L. 109-148, §1005(e), 119 Stat. 2680, 2741 (December 30, 2005); *Rasul v. Bush,* 542 U.S. 466 (2004); *Hamdan v. Rumsfeld,* 548 U.S. 557 (2006); Military Commissions Act of 2006, §7, Pub. L. 109-366, 120 Stat. 2600, 2635 (October 17, 2006), §7; *Boumediene v. Bush,* 553 U.S. 723 (2008); U.S. Const., Art. I, §9, cl. 2 (habeas corpus guarantee).

21. "The authorized membership of the Court, originally fixed at five, had been increased to seven in 1807, to nine in 1837, and to ten by a statute of 1863"; the number was reduced to seven in 1866 and increased to nine in 1869. Fairman, *History Vol. VI,* 161-62 (quote), 169, 487, 559-60.

22. William E. Leuchtenburg, *The Supreme Court Reborn: The Constitutional Revolution in the Age of Roosevelt* (New York: Oxford University Press, 1995), 82-162, 216-19; Noah Feldman, *Scorpions: The Battles and Triumphs of FDR's Great Supreme Court Justices* (New York: Twelve, 2010), 115-21; Robert G. McCloskey, *The American Supreme Court* (Chicago: University of Chicago Press, 2005), 4th ed., rev. by Sanford Levenson, 108-13, 117-20. A single justice, Owen J. Roberts, a Hoover appointee, switched sides on the closely divided Court. "Some believed," Leuchtenburg wrote, "that he had been brought into line by" Chief Justice Charles Evans Hughes, a Republican, "with the deliberate intent of defeating the President's plan by removing its main justification.... Others thought that Roberts had merely followed the [1936] election returns." Leuchtenburg, 143.

23. See Maurice S. Culp, "A Survey of the Proposals to Limit or Deny the Power of Judicial Review by the Supreme Court of the United States," 4 *Indiana L. J.* 386, 392-96 (1929); Friedman, "Part Two," 28-29; Stanley I. Kutler, *Judicial Power and Reconstruction Politics* (University of Chicago Press, 1968), 74-77; Thomas C. Hennings Jr., "'Equal Justice under Law,'" 47 *Georgetown L. J.* 1, 17-19 (1957); Robert J. Steamer, "Statesmanship or Craftsmanship: Current Conflict Over the Supreme Court," 11 *Western Pol. Quar.* 265, 270-71 (1958).

24. *Ex parte Merryman,* 17 Fed. Cas. 144 (C.C.D. Md. 1861). William H. Rehnquist, *All the Laws but One: Civil Liberties in Wartime* (New York: Vantage, 1998), 26-39; Bernard Schwartz, *A History of the Supreme Court* (New York: Oxford University Press, 1993), 127-28; Barry Friedman, "The History of the Countermajoritarian Difficulty, Part Four: Law's Politics," 148 *U. Pa. L. Rev.* 971, 1032-33n275 (2000) [hereinafter Friedman, "Part Four"]; Friedman, "Part Two," 21. A later Supreme Court justice termed the incident "[t]he lowest point in the history of the federal judiciary." Jackson, *Struggle for Judicial Supremacy,* 324-27.

25. *Cherokee Nation v. Georgia,* 30 U.S. (5 Pet.) 1 (1831); *Worcester v. Georgia,* 31 U.S. (6 Pet.) 515 (1832); Friedman, "Part One," 393-404 (Jackson quote, 399); Barry Friedman, *The Will of the People: How Public Opinion Has Influenced the Supreme Court and Shaped the Meaning of the Constitution* (New York: Farrar, Straus, and Giroux, 2009), 88-93.

26. *Id.,* 12-13 (first quote), 99-104; *NY Times,* October 4, 1957, "Eisenhower Calls Courts' Sanctity Little Rock Issue" (quote); Barry Friedman, "The Birth of An Academic

Obsession: The History of the Countermajoritarian Difficulty, Part Five," 112 *Yale L. J.* 153, 170–71 and n51–53 (2002) [hereinafter Friedman, "Part Five"].

27. Robert H. Jackson, *The Supreme Court in the American System of Government* (New York: Harper & Row, 1955), 25.

28. *Schenck v. United States,* 249 U.S. 47 (1919); *Frohwerk v. United States,* 249 U.S. 204 (1919); *Debs v. United States,* 249 U.S. 211 (1919); *Abrams v. United States,* 250 U.S. 616 (1919); *Schaefer v. United States,* 251 U.S. 466 (1920); *Pierce v. United States,* 252 U.S. 239 (1920); *Gilbert v. Minnesota,* 254 U.S. 325 (1920); *United States ex rel. Milwaukee Social Democratic Pub. Co. v. Burleson,* 255 U.S. 407 (1921). In *Schaefer,* the Court reversed the convictions of two (of five) defendants on grounds of insufficient evidence. 251 U.S. 471. Stone, *Perilous Times,* 192–211. Espionage and Sedition Acts: see *id.,* 146–53, 184–87.

29. *Debs,* 249 U.S. at 212–15; Brennan, "Quest to Develop," 5 (quote); Stone, *Perilous Times,* 196–98. In *Berger v. United States,* 255 U.S. 22 (1921), the Court reversed the convictions of Victor L. Berger, the *Milwaukee Leader*'s editor and formerly (also subsequently) a member of Congress, and four other Socialists for antiwar speech because of the trial judge's refusal to recuse himself despite manifest personal bias. Debs, while in prison in 1920, was again the Socialist Party's presidential candidate, receiving nearly a million votes. He was released from prison on Christmas Day 1921 by President Warren G. Harding, who commuted his sentence to time already served. *NY Times,* December 26, 1921, "Debs Is Released, Prisoners Joining Crowd in Ovation." Harry Kalven, in a 1973 article, commented that "[t]o put the case in modern context, it is somewhat as though George McGovern [the 1972 Democratic presidential nominee] had been sent to prison for his criticism of the [Vietnam] war." Kalven, "Professor Ernst Freund and *Debs v. United States,*" 40 *U. Chi. L. Rev.* 235, 237 (1973).

30. *Abrams,* 250 U.S. at 617–24; Stone, *Perilous Journey,* 203–6.

31. *Abrams,* 250 U.S. at 624–31 (Holmes, J., dissenting). Holmes drew on his opinion for a unanimous Court in *Schenck,* 249 U.S. 47, upholding the convictions of defendants who published a leaflet urging men awaiting induction to write their congressmen and to petition the government to end the draft. He wrote there that "[t]he question in every case is whether the words used . . . are of such a nature as to create a clear and present danger that they will bring about the substantive evils that Congress has a right to prevent." (*Id.*, 52.)

32. Harry Kalven Jr., *A Worthy Tradition: Freedom of Speech in America* (New York: Harper & Row, 1988), 147.

33. For the government: *Ex parte Quirin,* 317 U.S. 1 (1942); *United States v. Pelley,* 132 F. 2d 170 (7th Cir. 1942), cert. denied, 318 U.S. 764 (1943); *Hirabayashi v. United States,* 320 U.S. 81 (1943); *Yasui v. United States,* 320 U.S. 115 (1943). See Irons, *Justice at War,* 81–93. On the other hand, the Court reversed the convictions under a Mississippi sedition statute of Jehovah's Witnesses opposed to the war on religious grounds and the federal sedition conviction of an American Nazi who published pro-German articles opposing the war. *Taylor v. State of Mississippi,* 319 U.S. 584 (1943); *Hartzell v. United States,* 322 U.S. 680 (1944). In two cases seeking to denaturalize pro-Nazi German-Americans on the ground that, when obtaining citizenship, they fraudulently concealed their continued allegiance to Germany, the Court ruled against the govern-

ment in one case, imposing a standard of proof not satisfied by the evidence, but upheld a judgment of denaturalization in the other. *Baumgartner v. United States*, 322 U.S. 665 (1944); *Knauer v. United States*, 328 U.S. 654 (1946).

34. Irons, *Justice at War*, 93–103, 345–46 (first quote); *Korematsu v. United States*, 323 U.S. 214 (1944); *Ex parte Endo*, 323 U.S. 283, 294 (second quote) (1944); Stone, *Perilous Times*, 302 (final quote).

35. Kutler, *Judicial Power*, 77–82, 161–64; Fairman, *History Vol. VI*, 459–69. McCarthy-era bills: see chap. 7, 8, and 9 herewith.

36. See David H. Souter, Commencement Address, Harvard University, May 27, 2010, reprinted at http://news.harvard.edu/gazette (" . . . criticism that is frequently aimed at the more controversial Supreme Court decisions: criticism that the court is making up the law, that the court is announcing constitutional rules that cannot be found in the Constitution, and that the court is engaging in activism to extend civil liberties").

37. In 1935 and 1936, the Court struck down the Railroad Retirement Act (*Retirement Board v. Alton R. Co.*, 295 U.S. 330 [1935]); National Recovery Act (*Schechter Corp. v. United States*, 295 U.S. 495 [1935]); Frazier-Lemke Act (mortgage moratorium) (*Louisville Bank v. Radford*, 295 U.S. 555 [1935]); Agricultural Adjustment Act (*United States v. Butler*, 297 U.S. 1 [1936]); Guffey Coal Act (*Carter v. Carter Coal Co.*, 298 U.S. 238 [1936]); Municipal Bankruptcy Act (*Ashton v. Cameron County Water Improvement Dist. No. 1*, 298 U.S. 513 [1936]); and a New York state minimum-wage law (*Morehead v. New York ex rel. Tipaldo*, 298 U.S. 587 [1936]). The Warren court decisions are *Brown v. Board of Education*, 347 U.S. 483 (1954) (school desegregation); *Wesberry v. Sanders*, 376 U.S. 1 (1964) and *Reynolds v. Sims*, 377 U.S. 533 (1964) (one man, one vote); *Miranda v. Arizona*, 384 U.S. 436 (1966) (in-custody interrogation). The terms "liberal" and "conservative," however imprecise, are widely understood and are used here without quotation marks. Conservatives are more likely to take the government's side against individuals on civil-liberties issues and business's side against government on issues of economic regulation, and liberals vice versa.

38. *NY Times*, May 22, 1969, "Burger Nomination Is Lauded by Conservative Members" (first quote); Vincent Blasi, "The Rootless Activism of the Burger Court" in Blasi, ed., *The Burger Court: The Counter-Revolution That Wasn't* (New Haven, Conn.: Yale University Press, 1983), 198–217 (quotes, 198, 200); Thomas M. Keck, *The Most Activist Supreme Court in History: The Road to Modern Judicial Conservatism* (Chicago: University of Chicago Press, 2004), 40–41. The three subsequent Nixon appointees were Harry Blackmun, Lewis Powell, and William Rehnquist. The Ford appointee was John Paul Stevens. *Buckley*, 424 U.S. 1 (1976); *Roe*, 410 U.S. 113 (1973).

39. *NY Times*, June 18, 1986, "Burger Retiring, Rehnquist Named Chief," and June 22, 1986, "Has Reagan Got the Court He Wants?"; Anthony Lewis, "The Woman in the Middle" (book review), *NY Review of Books*, April 6, 2006, 37–41 (quotes). See Keck, *Most Activist Supreme Court*, 1–2, 40. *Bush v. Gore*, 531 U.S. 98 (2000): see Jack M. Balkin, "*Bush v. Gore* and the Boundary Between Law and Politics," 110 *Yale L.J.* 1407 (2001).

40. Anthony Lewis in foreword to Blasi, ed., *Burger Court*, ix (quotes). The current Court, headed by Chief Justice John G. Roberts Jr., who took office in 2005, has already shown signs of activism, notably its decision in *Citizens United v. Federal Election Com-*

mission, 558 U.S. 50 (2010), invalidating key sections of a major federal campaign-reform statute and overruling precedent. See J. Toobin, "Annals of Law" ("Without a Paddle"), *The New Yorker*, September 27, 2010, 40 ("Roberts and his fellow conservatives . . . have revived their own brand of judicial activism").

41. *Trop v. Dulles,* 356 U.S. 86, 103–4 (1958) (plurality opin.). Warren, close to retirement, told the press that "every man I have been associated with . . . basically practices judicial restraint." CQ Weekly 26 (July 19, 1968), "Warren Press Conference," 1836, 1838.

42. *Ex parte Yerger,* 75 U.S. (8 Wall.) 85 (1869). Kutler, *Judicial Power*, 89–113 (quote, 108); Stanley I. Kutler, "*Ex parte McCardle*: Judicial Impotency? The Supreme Court and Reconstruction Reconsidered," 72 *American Hist. Rev.* 835, 848 (1967).

43. In Gerald Gunther's view, the McCarthy-era court utilized "temporary avoidance devices empty of serious doctrinal content" resting its rulings "not on the broad issues tendered to it but on narrow, often tenuous, escape routes." Gunther, "Reflections on *Robel*: It's Not What the Court Did but the Way It Did It," 20 *Stanford L. Rev.* 1140, 1141, 1149 (1968).

44. Richard M. Fried, *Nightmare in Red: The McCarthy Era in Perspective* (New York: Oxford University Press, 1990), 184.

45. By the author's count, the Court issued ninety-five signed decisions in "Communist" cases and six decisions, on the merits after argument and over dissents, in per curiam opinions; it affirmed by an equally divided court without opinion in two cases. The term "'Communist' cases" is used here to mean the entire array of cases dealing with the prosecution, firing, exposure, and deportation of, or denial of government benefits to, real, suspected or former Communists or "subversives." Vietnam War decisions: see Epilogue, herewith.

Chapter 1. Defining the McCarthy Era

1. The interval between the end of the war in the Pacific and Churchill's "Iron Curtain" speech, marking the start of the Cold War, was less than seven months. Winston S. Churchill, "The Sinews of Peace," Westminster College, Fulton, Missouri, March 5, 1946.

2. See, for example, William M. Wiecek, "The Legal Foundations of Domestic Anticommunism: The Background of Dennis v. United States," 2001 *Sup. Ct. Rev.* 375, 381 ("anticommunism or its ideological predecessors seem to have been endemic in American society" since the Jackson era); Harvey Klehr, John Earl Haynes, and Kyrill M. Anderson, *The Soviet World of American Communism* (New Haven, Conn.: Yale University Press, 1998), 4–5 ("[Recently-opened Comintern archives] demonstrate that at every period of the CPUSA's history, the American Communists looked to their Soviet counterparts for advice on how to conduct their own party business").

3. *NY Times,* July 31, 1948, "Woman Links Spies to U.S. War Offices"; August 1, 1948, "Currie Accused of Helping Spies"; August 4, 1948, "Red 'Underground' in Federal Posts Alleged by Editor." See Kathryn S. Olmsted, *Red Spy Queen: A Biography of Elizabeth Bentley* (Chapel Hill: University of North Carolina Press, 2002); Sam Tanenhaus, *Whittaker Chambers: A Biography* (New York: Random House, 1997). An earlier case of possible espionage surfaced in June 1945 when hundreds of classified documents were

found in a search of the offices of *Amerasia*, a tiny pro-Communist magazine dealing with Asian affairs. See Harvey Klehr and Ronald Radosh, *The Amerasia Spy Case: Prelude to McCarthyism* (Chapel Hill: University of North Carolina Press, 1996).

4. *NY Times*, August 7, 1949, "China Lost" ("Chiang Kai-shek and many other Kuomintang leaders were on the island of Formosa"), and October 22, 1949, "Soviets Said to Plan Treaty with Mao" ("China would be brought into the Soviet military network").

5. *NY Times*, September 24, 1949, "U.S. Reaction Firm" ("President Truman announced this morning that an atomic explosion had occurred in Russia within recent weeks."); John Earl Haynes, Harvey Klehr, and Alexander Vassiliev, *Spies: The Rise and Fall of the KGB in America* (New Haven, Conn.: Yale University Press, 2009), 33–143 ("The Red bomb was a copy of the American 'Fat Man,' the plutonium implosion bomb dropped on Nagasaki on 9 August 1945, and a dramatic demonstration of the greatest triumph of Soviet intelligence" [59]).

6. *NY Times*, June 25, 1950, "War Is Declared by North Koreans"; November 1, 1950, "Korean Reds Press Attacks in Center with Fresh Help"; November 3, 1950, "U.N. Troops Slaughtered at Unsan by Chinese Reds."

7. Harvey Klehr and John Earl Haynes, *The American Communist Movement: Storming Heaven Itself* (New York: Twayne, 1992), 108 (first quote); John Earl Haynes and Harvey Klehr, *Venona: Decoding Soviet Espionage in America* (New Haven, Conn.: Yale University Press, 1999), 7 (second quote). Other histories also make clear the party's primary reliance on political means. See Maurice Isserman, *Which Side Were You On? The American Communist Party during the Second World War* (Urbana: University of Illinois Press, 1993); Ellen Schrecker, *Many Are the Crimes: McCarthyism in America* (Boston: Little, Brown, 1998), 3–41. Wallace vote: *The World Almanac and Book of Facts 2009* (Pleasantville, N.Y.: World Almanac), 545.

8. Morris L. Ernst and David Loth, *Report on the American Communist* (New York: Holt, 1952), 14, 33; Ralph S. Brown Jr., *Loyalty and Security: Employment Tests in the United States* (New Haven, Conn.: Yale University Press, 1958), 314 ("[T]his army of ex-Communists is evidence of weakness. . . . It suggests that the hold of the party on its rank-and-file has been tenuous, and the period of commitment transitory"). By 1955, according to the FBI, party membership had declined to about 23,000 and by 1958, after Khrushchev's disclosures of Stalin's crimes, to "a nearly dead Party of only 3,000 to 6,000 members" Belknap, *Cold War Political Justice: The Smith Act, the Communist Party, and American Civil Liberties* (Westport, Conn.: Greenwood, 1977), 205. Haynes and Klehr counted in the deciphered VENONA messages "349 citizens, immigrants, and permanent residents of the United States" who had a covert relationship with Soviet intelligence, "many of whom were members of" the CPUSA (*Venona*, 9).

9. Geoffrey R. Stone, "Free Speech in the Age of McCarthy: A Cautionary Tale," 93 *Calif. L. Rev.* 1387, 1390–91 (2005) (quote). Harry P. Cain, a member of the Subversive Activities Control Board, stated in 1955 that "'not more than thirty'" of the 275 organizations on the attorney general's list of "subversive" groups were Communist "fronts" and that "about 150 of those groups now are defunct." *NY Times*, May 24, 1955, "Cain Denounces Subversive List."

10. Jeff Broadwater, *Eisenhower and the Anti-Communist Crusade* (Chapel Hill: University of North Carolina Press, 1992), 208 (quote); Michal R. Belknap, *The Vinson Court:*

Justices, Rulings, and Legacy (Santa Barbara, Calif.: ABC-CLIO, 2004), 22 ("McCarthy appealed to a deep-seated distrust of political liberals"); Fred J. Cook, *The Nightmare Decade: The Life and Times of Senator Joe McCarthy* (New York: Random House, 1971), 570 ("The real foe was always the American liberal"). The term "McCarthyism" was coined in a March 1950 editorial cartoon by Herblock of the *Washington Post*.

11. HUAC: see Walter Goodman, *The Committee: The Extraordinary Career of the House Committee on Un-American Activities* (New York: Farrar, Straus, 1968).

12. A 1950 speech by GOP Senate leader Robert A. Taft to an audience of Republicans is illustrative: "[T]he greatest Kremlin asset in our history has been the pro-Communist group in the State Department who surrendered to every demand of Russia at Yalta and Potsdam. . . . [This same group] promoted at every opportunity the Communist cause in China until today communism threatens to take over all of Asia." *NY Times*, April 1, 1950, "Taft Calls Attack by Truman Biased."

13. David McCullough, *Truman* (New York: Simon & Schuster, 1992), 520.

14. *NY Times*, November 7, 1946, "Landslide Result"; Jerrold G. Rusk, *A Statistical History of the American Electorate* (Washington: CQ, 2001), 216, 377; McCullough, *Truman*, 520–23; Ted Morgan, *Reds: McCarthyism in Twentieth-Century America* (New York: Random House, 2003), 301 ("Republican candidates ran on their unvarying opposition to the New Deal . . . The next step was to link the New Deal with Communism").

15. Taft-Hartley: McCullough, *Truman*, 565–66. Mundt-Nixon: Roger Morris, *Richard Milhous Nixon: The Rise of an American Politician* (New York: Holt, 1990), 376–77; Tom Wicker, *One of Us: Richard Nixon and the American Dream* (New York: Random House, 1991), 50. HUAC: Goodman, *The Committee*, 207–25.

16. The Truman loyalty program was instituted by Executive Order 9835, 12 Fed. Reg. 1935 (March 21, 1947) (quotes). See Eleanor Bontecou, *The Federal Loyalty-Security Program* (Ithaca, N.Y.: Cornell University Press, 1953); Brown, *Loyalty and Security*, 21–61; Robert Justin Goldstein, *American Blacklist: The Attorney General's List of Subversive Organizations* (Lawrence: University Press of Kansas, 2008), 43–61, 139–45. Political motivation: John Kenneth White, *Still Seeing Red: How the Cold War Shapes the New American Politics* (Boulder, Colo.: Westview, 1997), 60; Belknap, *Cold War Political Justice*, 45–53.

17. Curt Gentry, *J. Edgar Hoover: The Man and the Secrets* (New York: Norton, 1991), 242 (HUAC "became . . . almost an adjunct of the FBI. J. Edgar Hoover dominated it, and used it, for his own purposes"), 357–58; Hearings, Export Policy and Loyalty, Before the Investigations Subcommittee of the Senate Committee on Expenditures in Government Departments, 80th Cong., 2d Sess. (1948), 1–47 (Bentley); Hearings Regarding Communist Espionage in the United States Government, Before the House Committee on Un-American Activities, 80th Cong., 2d Sess. (1948), 503–62 (Bentley), 563–84 (Chambers).

18. Tanenhaus, *Whittaker Chambers*, 212–335; Earl Latham, *The Communist Controversy in Washington: From the New Deal to McCarthy* (Cambridge: Harvard University Press, 1966), 159–83; Allen Weinstein, *Perjury: The Hiss-Chambers Case* (New York: Knopf, 1978), 3–69. FBI and Nixon: Athan G. Theoharis and John Stuart Cox, *The Boss: J. Edgar Hoover and the Great American Inquisition* (Philadelphia: Temple University Press, 1988), 250–53; Tanenhaus, 231, 245.

19. White, *Still Seeing Red*, 58–60 (Dewey quotes); Zachary Karabell, *The Last Campaign: How Harry Truman Won the 1948 Election* (New York: Vintage, 2000), 104–5; Richard Norton Smith, *Thomas E. Dewey and His Times* (New York: Simon & Schuster, 1982), 508; *NY Times*, May 18, 1948, "U.S. Hears Stassen and Dewey Debate." The Dewey campaign, however, was not silent on the issue. McCullough, *Truman*, 674 ("[T]he charge that the government was 'coddling' Communists . . . would be made again and again at nearly every stop"); Richard M. Fried, "Electoral Politics and McCarthyism: The 1950 Campaign," in Robert Griffith and Athan Theoharis, eds., *The Specter: Original Essays on the Cold War and the Origins of McCarthyism* (New York: New Viewpoints, 1974), 193–94 ("Dewey made only passing reference to the Communist issue during the autumn" but "Earl Warren, Dewey's running mate, accused the Administration of having 'coddled' and 'courted' the Communists").

20. Latham, *Communist Controversy in Washington*, 398 (quote); Smith, *Thomas E. Dewey*, 507 (quote). Smith attributed Dewey's reluctance to seize the issue to "the painful memory" of his "ill-considered attempt" in his 1944 presidential campaign "to link FDR and [Communist Party chief] Earl Browder." *Id*.

21. Wiecek, "Legal Foundations," 414 (quote); Joe Martin as told to Robert J. Donovan, *My First Fifty Years in Politics* (New York: McGraw Hill, 1960), 197–98 (quotes); Fried, "Electoral Politics and McCarthyism," in Griffith and Theoharis, eds., *The Specter*, 194 ("Republican partisans balked at Dewey's moderation and turned to the Communist issue as an inviting expedient for recouping their party's losses"). Taft: Thomas C. Reeves, *The Life and Times of Joe McCarthy: A Biography* (New York: Stein & Day, 1982), 263 (Taft quote); David M. Oshinsky, *A Conspiracy So Immense: The World of Joe McCarthy* (New York: Free Press, 1983), 133; *NY Times*, March 23, 1950, "Acheson 'Welcomes' Inquiry" (Taft "personally urged the Wisconsin Senator to press his charges").

22. Hoover, HUAC, and McCarthy: Theoharis and Cox, *The Boss*, 215, 253–56, 280–300; Gentry, *J. Edgar Hoover*, 352–55, 378–80; Richard Gid Powers, *Secrecy and Power: The Life of J. Edgar Hoover* (New York: Free Press, 1987), 320–21; Oshinsky, *A Conspiracy So Immense*, 257–58. Leaks to reporters: Theoharis and Cox, *The Boss*, 310; Broadwater, *Eisenhower*, 185; see Gentry, *J. Edgar Hoover*, 553+ note. Counter-subversives: Richard Gid Powers, *Not Without Honor: The History of American Anticommunism* (New York: Free Press, 1995), 213–14; Schrecker, *Many Are the Crimes*, 42–85; see Robert M. Lichtman, "J. B. Matthews and the 'Counter-subversives': Names as a Political and Financial Resource in the McCarthy Era," 5 *Amer. Comm. Hist.* 1 (2006).

23. Wiecek, "Legal Foundations," 415 (quote); Broadwater, *Eisenhower*, 11–12. Coplon case: Theoharis and Cox, *The Boss*, 256–61; Gentry, *J. Edgar Hoover*, 367–73; *United States v. Coplon*, 185 F. 2d 629 (2d Cir. 1950). Hiss verdict: Weinstein, *Perjury*, 497–98; Gentry, *J. Edgar Hoover*, 365–66. Rosenberg case: Ronald Radosh and Joyce Milton, *The Rosenberg File: Second Edition* (New Haven, Conn.: Yale University Press, 1997), 96–101; Powers, *Secrecy and Power*, 301–5; Gentry, *J. Edgar Hoover*, 419–22.

24. Theoharis and Cox, *The Boss*, 282.

25. Richard H. Rovere, *Senator Joe McCarthy* (New York: Harcourt, Brace, 1959), 8.

26. *Id.*, 10–11; Robert Griffith, *The Politics of Fear: Joseph R. McCarthy and the Senate*, 2nd ed. (Amherst: University of Massachusetts Press, 1987), 102; Wiecek, "Legal Foun-

dations," 375n3. See Tom Wicker, *Shooting Star: The Brief Arc of Joe McCarthy* (Orlando: Harcourt, 2006), 191 ("He played the press as if it were his personal chessboard").

27. Oshinsky, *A Conspiracy So Immense*, 3, 36–71, 107 (quote); Reeves, *Life and Times of Joe McCarthy*, 2–3, 106–7, 120–21 (Pepsi-Cola quote), 202–3, 675 ("above all a reckless adventurer, an improviser, a bluffer"); Griffith, *Politics of Fear*, 2–3, 7–12, 28–30; Wicker, *Shooting Star*, 8.

28. Wheeling speech and changes in numbers: Report of the Senate Committee on Foreign Relations Pursuant to S. Res. 231, S. Rept. No. 2108, 81st Cong., 2d Sess. (July 20, 1950) [hereinafter "Tydings Report"), 2–3 (first two quotes); Oshinsky, *A Conspiracy So Immense*, 108–14 ("81" quote, 112); Reeves, *Life and Times of Joe McCarthy*, 223–33; Cook, *Nightmare Decade*, 148–54; Wicker, *Shooting Star*, 6–7 ("one of the most consequential [speeches] in U.S. history without a recorded or an agreed-upon text"), 10–12; Lattimore: Tydings Report, 48–60, 72–74; Oshinsky, *A Conspiracy So Immense*, 136–38, 144–49; Reeves, *Life and Times of Joe McCarthy*, 261–68 (final quote, 261).

29. Hearings, State Department Employee Loyalty Investigation, Before a Subcommittee of the Senate Foreign Relations Committee, 81st Cong., 2d Sess. (1950) [hereinafter "Tydings Hearings"]; Tydings Report, 151–67 (quote, 151).

30. Tydings Hearings, 487–557 (Budenz); Oshinsky, *A Conspiracy So Immense*, 149–53; Griffith, *Politics of Fear*, 81–84; Robert M. Lichtman, "Louis Budenz, the FBI, and the 'List of 400 Concealed Communists': An Extended Tale of McCarthy-Era Informing," 3 *Amer. Communist Hist.* 25, 33–34 (2004).

31. Tydings Report, 54–60, 72–74; Lodge statement, S. Rept. No. 2108, Part 2; Griffith, *Politics of Fear*, 83, 87 (quote); Joseph Alsop, "The Strange Case of Louis Budenz," *The Atlantic Monthly*, April 1952, 30 (quote); *NY Times*, April 30, 1950, "Partisan Fires Fanned by 'Communist' Charges"; Lichtman, "Louis Budenz," 31–33.

32. Fried, "Electoral Politics and McCarthyism," in Griffith and Theoharis, eds., *The Specter*, 211–13, 216 (quote); Griffith, *Politics of Fear*, 125–26; Cook, *Nightmare Decade*, 304–12; Reeves, *Life and Times of Joe McCarthy*, 334–45; Wicker, *Shooting Star*, 86–88. See *Chicago Tribune*, July 13, 1950, "How Mr. Lucas Helps the Reds." In California, Richard Nixon won a Senate seat, defeating Rep. Helen Gahagan Douglas, a liberal Democrat, branding her the "pink lady." Morris, *Richard Milhous Nixon*, 566–621; see Greg Mitchell, *Tricky Dick and the Pink Lady: Richard Nixon vs. Helen Gahagan Douglas-Sexual Politics and the Red Scare, 1950* (New York: Random House, 1998).

33. *NY Times*, October 28, 1952, "Text of Address by McCarthy" and "M'Carthy Terms Stevenson Unfit"; November 1, 1952, "M'Carthy Slates 2d Talk"; and November 4, 1952, "McCarthy Repeats Charges" (second quote); Reeves, *Life and Times of Joe McCarthy*, 444–47 (a "planned slip of the tongue"). Stevenson, a former State Department employee, had given a deposition, read at Hiss's trial, stating that at the time he knew him Hiss's reputation for loyalty was good. Jeff Broadwater, *Adlai Stevenson and American Politics: The Odyssey of a Cold War Liberal* (New York: Twayne Publishers, 1994), 41; *NY Times*, June 3, 1949, "Stevenson Makes Deposition." The 1950 election: Rusk, *Statistical History*, 216, 377.

34. *NY Times*, November 5, 1952, "Race Is Conceded" (quote); November 6, 1952, "G.O.P. Has 48 Senate Seats." Although Eisenhower won in a landslide, the GOP's mar-

gin was only eight votes in the House and two in the Senate. Rusk, *Statistical History*, 216, 377.

35. Oshinsky, *A Conspiracy So Immense*, 258. Army-McCarthy: Reeves, *Life and Times of Joe McCarthy*, 566–637; Cook, *Nightmare Decade*, 479–519; Oshinsky, *A Conspiracy So Immense*, 403–71. During a six-month period in 1954, which encompassed the Army-McCarthy hearings, the senator's "unfavorable" rating in the polls increased from 29 percent to 45 percent and his "favorable" rating declined from 50 percent to 34 percent. Oshinsky, *A Conspiracy So Immense*, 464–65.

36. Oshinsky, *A Conspiracy So Immense*, 473–506; Reeves, *Life and Times of Joe McCarthy*, 639–75.

37. Samuel A. Stouffer, *Communism, Conformity, and Civil Liberties* (New York: Doubleday, 1955), 13–25, 41–45. The study, directed by a committee chaired by Stouffer, a Harvard sociologist, was conducted jointly by the Gallup organization and the National Opinion Research Center of the University of Chicago and polled 4,933 persons.

38. Smith Act: 54 Stat. 670, 671 (June 28, 1940); Belknap, *Cold War Political Justice*, 22–27; Wiecek, "Legal Foundations," 424. McCarran: see Michael J. Ybarra, *Washington Gone Crazy: Senator Pat McCarran and the Great American Communist Hunt* (Hanover, N.H.: Steerforth, 2004). Decisions: *Dennis*, 341 U.S. 494 (1951); *Yates*, 354 U.S. 298 (1957); *Scales*, 367 U.S. 203 (1961); *Noto*, 367 U.S. 291 (1961).

39. Internal Security Act of 1950, 64 Stat. 987 (September 23, 1950); Ybarra, *Washington Gone Crazy*, 485–87 ("What McCarran had actually done in a few minutes was hijack the anti-Communist legislation that HUAC had been pushing for three years . . . attach a train of similar bills . . . and steer the whole unwieldy thing onto the legislative fast track"); Wiecek, "Legal Foundations," 424–27; William R. Tanner and Robert Griffith, "Legislative Politics and McCarthyism: The Internal Security Act of 1950," in Griffith and Theoharis, eds., *The Specter*, 173–89; Stone, *Perilous Times*, 334–36. The preventive-detention provisions were proposed by liberal Democrats in an inept and failed attempt to substitute narrow legislation for McCarran's omnibus bill. Ybarra, *Washington Gone Crazy*, 518–25. Decision: *Communist Party*, 367 U. S. 1 (1961).

40. Truman program: Brown, *Loyalty and Security*, 54–55 (quoting Civil Service Commission, *1953 Annual Report* [1954], 32). Decisions: *Peters*, 349 U.S. 331 (1955); *Bailey*, 341 U.S. 918 (1951).

41. Exec. Order 10450, 18 Fed. Reg. 2489 (April 27, 1953). The Civil Service Commission, responsible for federal-employee hiring, disclosed in 1955 that it maintained a "reference file" containing "about 2 million names" of persons "allegedly affiliated with some sort of subversive organization or activity" and that it referred to the file as many "as 5,000 times a day in connection with Government security investigations." *NY Times*, November 29, 1955, "'Subversive' File Names 2,000,000." Decision: *Cole v. Young*, 351 U.S. 536 (1956).

42. Hearings, Security and Constitutional Rights, Before the Subcommittee on Constitutional Rights of the Senate Judiciary Committee ("Hennings Hearings"), 599–652; Brown, *Loyalty and Security*, 64–68, 488. Decisions: *Greene*, 360 U.S. 474 (1959); *Taylor*, 360 U.S. 709 (1959). Maritime-industry employees were subjected to screening under the Port Security Program; the U.S. Coast Guard by the end of 1952 had screened nearly

six hundred thousand maritime workers. Brown, 71–73, 488; Schrecker, *Many Are the Crimes*, 266–70; David Caute, *The Great Fear: The Anti-Communist Purge under Truman and Eisenhower* (New York: Simon & Schuster, 1978), 364, 605n10; *Parker v. Lester*, 227 F. 2d 708 (9th Cir. 1955).

43. Hennings Hearings, 227, 508, 532. Decision: *Harmon*, 355 U.S. 579 (1958).

44. Alien Registration Act of 1940, 54 Stat. 670, 671, 673 (June 28, 1940); *Harisiades*, 342 U.S. 580 (1952). Internal Security Act, §22, 64 Stat. 987, 1006, 1008 (September 23, 1950); *Galvan*, 347 U.S. 522 (1954). A study of 307 political deportation cases showed that 60 percent of the aliens sought to be deported had lived in the United States more than forty years and 81 percent more than thirty years. Caute, *Great Fear*, 226–30; I. F. Stone, *The Haunted Fifties 1953–1963* (Boston: Little, Brown, 1963), 32.

45. Hennings Hearings, 86–216; Stanley I. Kutler, *The American Inquisition: Justice and Injustice in the Cold War* (New York: Hill and Wang, 1982), 89–117; Caute, *Great Fear*, 245–51. Decisions: *Kent*, 357 U.S. 116 (1958); *Dayton*, 357 U.S. 144 (1958).

46. Hennings Hearings, 249–329; Caute, *Great Fear*, 70–74, 568 n4. Decision: *Pennsylvania v. Nelson*, 350 U.S. 497 (1956).

47. Brown, *Loyalty and Security*, 92–109, 166–76, 178, 181. Loyalty-oath decisions include *Garner*, 341 U.S. 716 (1951), *Wieman*, 344 U.S. 183 (1952), and *Cramp*, 368 U.S. 278 (1961); decisions involving public-employee discharges for refusal to disclose political associations include *Slochower*, 350 U.S. 551 (1956), *Beilan*, 357 U.S. 399 (1958), and *Lerner*, 357 U.S. 468 (1958).

48. Brown, *Loyalty and Security*, 109–16; see Ralph S. Brown Jr. and John D. Fassett, "Loyalty Tests for Admission to the Bar," 20 *Univ. of Chicago L. Rev.* 480 (1953). Decisions: *Schware*, 353 U.S. 232 (1957); *Konigsberg I*, 353 U.S. 252 (1957); *Konigsberg II*, 366 U.S. 36 (1961); *Anastaplo*, 366 U.S. 82 (1961).

49. Committee-contempt decisions include *Quinn*, 349 U.S. 155 (1955); *Emspak*, 349 U.S. 190 (1955); *Watkins*, 354 U.S. 178 (1957); *Sweezy*, 354 U.S. 234 (1957); *Uphaus*, 360 U.S. 72 (1959), and *Barenblatt*, 360 U.S. 109 (1959). See Goldstein, *Political Repression*, 345 ("HUAC's hearings left behind a trail of ruined reputations and wrecked careers. One study of sixty-four 'unfriendly' witnesses appearing before the committee found that fifty lost their jobs"); Kalven, *A Worthy Tradition*, 480–81 ("to refuse to answer on self-incrimination grounds tends to boomerang. It invokes in the popular mind a suspicion that the reason the witness claims the privilege is because he is a Communist"); address by SACB member Harry P. Cain, "Strong in Their Pride and Free," March 18, 1955, 7, in Box 353, Frankfurter 1955 file, Earl Warren Papers, Library of Congress, Washington, D. C. ("Warren Papers").

50. 1949 term: see Chap. 2 herewith. The October 1949 term is used here as the era's starting point. In the 1948 term, only one signed decision, *Christoffel v. United States*, 338 U.S. 84 (1949), a perjury prosecution arising from a witness's denial of Communist affiliation at a House committee hearing, fit the mold of a McCarthy-era "Communist" case. An "October Term" begins on the first Monday of October and continues until the Court has ruled on all of the argued cases, normally in June of the following year.

51. 1960 term: see chap. 10 herewith.

52. October 1961 term and subsequent years: see chap. 11 herewith.

Chapter 2. The Justices of the Vinson Court, *Douds*, and the Start of the Court's McCarthy Era

1. *NY Times*, October 3, 1949, "High Court Begins Heavy Term Today," "Douglas Injured in Fall Off Horse"; October 4, 1949, "Senate Unit Backs Minton for Court," "The Court Reconvenes." Douglas suffered thirty-six rib fractures and did not rejoin the Court until March 27, 1950. *NY Times*, March 28, 1950, "Dennis Contempt Held Tried Fairly," and June 14, 1950, "Intrepid Douglas Will Take It Easy"; see Bruce Allen Murphy, *Wild Bill: The Legend and Life of William O. Douglas* (New York: Random House, 2003), 271–80. Murphy was, in Michal Belknap's view, "the most liberal justice ever to serve on the Supreme Court," and Rutledge, "[n]ext to Murphy, was the Court's most consistent supporter of individual rights claims." Belknap, *Vinson Court*, 64–65, 75. A tabulation of Vinson-court votes in 113 "Nonunanimous Civil Liberties Cases" showed that Murphy voted 100 percent of the time, and Rutledge 96 percent, in favor of free-speech claims and claims by aliens, Negroes, and criminal defendants. C. Herman Pritchett, *Civil Liberties and the Vinson Court* (Chicago: University of Chicago Press, 1966 printing), 190.

2. *NY Times*, October 11, 1949, "High Court Hears Oath Law Pleas"; October 15, 1949, "11 Communists Convicted of Plot"; and October 16, 1949, "Communist Case to Provide Test of Smith Act" (quote). Taft-Hartley oath case: *American Communications Ass'n v. Douds*, 339 U.S. 382 (1950).

3. *NY Times*, October 18, 1949, "Medina Upheld by Supreme Court"; *Hall, Winston, Green v. United States and Hall, Winston v. Mulcahy*, 338 U.S. 851 (1949). Contempt-of-Congress: *Dennis v. United States*, 339 U.S. 162 (1950).

4. Other contempt cases: *United States v. Bryan*, 339 U.S. 323 (1950); *United States v. Fleischman*, 339 U.S. 349 (1950). Deportation: *United States ex rel. Knauff v. Shaughnessy*, 338 U.S. 537 (1950).

5. Roosevelt had long ago triumphed in the battle that precipitated his "court-packing" proposal. The Vinson court virtually always gave deference to congressional action in the economic sphere. See Pritchett, *Civil Liberties*, vii. Liberal bloc: see John P. Frank, *Mr. Justice Black: The Man and His Opinions* (New York: Knopf, 1949), 123–24 ("the four a fairly cohesive bloc"). New majority: see Belknap, *Vinson Court*, 41 ("The four Truman justices joined Reed to form a voting bloc that controlled the Court").

6. Belknap, *Vinson Court*, xii (quote); Schwartz, *Super Chief*, 32 ("four of the greatest judges ever to serve on the highest bench, brilliant jurists"); Feldman, *Scorpions*, 432 (the four were "among the most important and influential justices ever to have sat on the Court"). Owen Roberts, a Hoover appointee, was still on the Court when FDR died; he resigned in July 1945. *NY Times*, July 6, 1945 ("Roberts to Retire from High Court").

7. Roger K. Newman, *Hugo Black: A Biography*, 2nd ed. (New York: Fordham University Press, 1997), 17–20, 209–19, 226–30, 233–43; Frank, *Mr. Justice Black*, 3–31; James F. Simon, *The Antagonists: Hugo Black, Felix Frankfurter and Civil Liberties in Modern America* (New York: Simon & Schuster, 1989), 96–97; Joseph Alsop and Turner Catledge, *The 168 Days* (Garden City, N.Y.: Doubleday, 1938), 300 (quote), 301 ("entirely self-educated, he had acquired a remarkable intellectual background in economics and history"); *NY Times*, August 22, 1937, "Justice Black: A Man of Two Personalities." Black was appointed

to the Court after Senator Joseph T. Robinson of Arkansas, the majority leader who led the "court-packing" fight and as a result was FDR's almost obligatory first choice, died in July 1937. *NY Times*, October 3, 1937, "Mr. Black Explains"; Newman, *Hugo Black*, 233.

8. Newman, *Hugo Black*, 247-61; Frank, *Mr. Justice Black*, 43-45, 102-7 (quotes, 105); Simon, *The Antagonists*, 98; *NY Times*, October 2, 1937, "Radio Talk Is Brief" ("Throughout his speech, he stressed his utter divorcement from any prejudice toward Jews, Catholics or Negroes"), and October 3, 1937, "Mr. Black Explains." An exception to Black's record as a defender of civil liberties was his approval of the summary internment of Japanese-Americans during World War II. Simon, *The Antagonists*, 146-56.

9. Pritchett, *Civil Liberties*, 17 (quote); Schwartz, *Super Chief*, 49 (quote); Anthony Lewis, "Justice Black and the First Amendment" in Tony Freyer, ed., *Justice Hugo Black and Modern America* (Tuscaloosa: Univ. of Alabama Press, 1990), 249 (quote); Anthony Lewis, "Justice Black and First Amendment 'Absolutes': A Public Interview," 37 *N.Y.U. Law Review* 549, 552, 558 (1962) (quotes [orig. emphasis]); Hugo L. Black, "The Bill of Rights," 35 *N.Y.U. Law Review* 865, 867 (1960) ("It is my belief that there *are* 'absolutes' in our Bill of Rights, and that they were put there on purpose by men who knew what words meant, and meant their prohibitions to be 'absolutes'"). Never adopted: for example, *Konigsberg v. State Bar of California*, 366 U.S. 36, 49 (1961). Black also believed that the entire Bill of Rights was made applicable to the states by the Due Process Clause of the Fourteenth Amendment, a view never in those terms adopted by the Court. See *Adamson v. People of State of California*, 332 U.S. 46, 68 (1947) (Black, J., dissenting).

10. Melvin I. Urofsky, *Felix Frankfurter: Judicial Restraint and Civil Liberties* (Boston: Twayne, 1991), 27, 62 (quotes); Fred Rodell, *Nine Men: A Political History of the Supreme Court from 1790 to 1955* (New York: Random House, 1955), 270 (quote); Simon, *The Antagonists*, 109. FDR friendship: *id.*, 59-61 ("Frankfurter offered [FDR] effusive encouragement and sophisticated advice on political tactics and legislation"). Frankfurter was also a talent scout for the New Deal, sending a stream of young Harvard-trained lawyers to work at New Deal agencies. *Id.*, 62 ("They were called Felix's 'happy hot dogs' and appeared to have gotten their jobs after the professor had put in a good word for them"). Holmes and Brandeis: Urofsky, *Felix Frankfurter*, 5; Lash, "A Brahmin of the Law" in *Diaries of Felix Frankfurter*, 25-27, 36; Melvin I. Urofsky, *Louis D. Brandeis: A Life* (New York: Pantheon, 2009), 336-39, 414, 464-65, 642-45 (final quote, 337); see Bruce Allen Murphy, *The Brandeis/Frankfurter Connection: The Secret Political Activities of Two Supreme Court Justices* (New York: Oxford Univ. Press, 1982).

11. Belknap, *Vinson Court*, 52 (first quote); *West Virginia Board of Education v. Barnette*, 319 U.S. 624, 647 (1943) (Frankfurter, J., dissenting) (second quote); Vincent Blasi, "The Rootless Activism of the Burger Court" in Blasi, ed., *Burger Court*, 205 (quote). Liberal causes: Urofsky, *Felix Frankfurter*, 20-25; Felix Frankfurter, *The Case of Sacco and Vanzetti* (New York: Universal Library, 1962), Note on Republication; *NY Times*, February 23, 1965, "His Criticism of Sacco-Vanzetti Case Stirred Furor." In Urofsky's view, "[t]he judicial activism of the conservative bloc" during the New Deal and earlier years "drove Frankfurter to develop his philosophy of judicial restraint" Urofsky, *Felix Frankfurter*, 32.

12. Belknap, *Vinson Court*, 58 (quote); Melvin I. Urofsky, "Conflict among the Brethren: Felix Frankfurter, William O. Douglas and the Clash of Personalities and Philoso-

phies on the United States Supreme Court," 1988 *Duke L. J.* 71, 77. Stone, the chief justice, recruited Frankfurter to tutor Black in late 1938. Wallace Mendelson, *Justices Black and Frankfurter: Conflict in the Court* (Chicago: University of Chicago Press, 1961), 115. Justices' reactions: Belknap, *Vinson Court,* 57 ("When Black first joined the Court, Frankfurter offered him guidance . . . but during the 1940s, the relationship between them deteriorated badly"); *id.*, 58 (after "being courted by him, Vinson began to go his own way . . . the relationship between him and Vinson became extremely strained"); Bernard Schwartz, "Felix Frankfurter and Earl Warren: A Study of a Deteriorating Relationship," *Sup. Ct. Rev.* [2000], 115-42. Several justices, on the other hand—Burton, Jackson, and later John M. Harlan are examples—seemed to welcome Frankfurter's guidance. Frankfurter's response: Urofsky, "Conflict among the Brethren," 78 ("Frankfurter . . . took the refusal of the brethren to follow his lead as a personal affront, and unfortunately allowed full play to his considerable talent for invective"). Among many examples, he wrote Judge Learned Hand in 1954 that Black "'is a self-righteous, self-deluded part fanatic, part demagogue, who really disbelieves in Law" (*id.*, 80-81). He told Philip Elman, his former law clerk, that Douglas was "an absolute cynic who didn't believe in anything"; he termed Douglas one of the "two completely evil men I have ever met" (*id.*, 90).

13. James F. Simon, *Independent Journey: The Life of William O. Douglas* (New York: Harper & Row, 1980), 26-75, 92-168, 189-94, 262-66; William O. Douglas, *Go East, Young Man, The Early Years: The Autobiography of William O. Douglas* (New York: Random House, 1974), 17-40, 127-75, 257-96, 317-42, 459-65; Douglas, *Court Years,* 281-84. Douglas was reportedly FDR's preferred choice for vice president. Feldman, *Scorpions,* 174, 257-64. In 1946 Truman offered to name Douglas, an outdoorsman and conservationist, as secretary of the interior; Douglas declined the offer but expressed a willingness to serve as secretary of state. Douglas, *Court Years,* 288; Douglas to Truman, February 23, 1946, in Melvin I. Urofsky, ed., *The Douglas Letters: Selections from the Private Papers of Justice William O. Douglas,* 216-17 (Bethesda, Md.: Adler & Adler, 1987). Two years later, Douglas refused Truman's invitation to be his running mate in the 1948 presidential election. Murphy, *Wild Bill,* 251-65; Feldman, *Scorpions,* 318-20; Crusading SEC chairman: *id.*, 164-69.

14. L. A. Powe Jr., "Justice Douglas after Fifty Years: The First Amendment, McCarthyism and Rights," 6 *Const. Comm.* 267, 269-71 (1989) (quote); A. Lewis, *NY Times,* November 16, 1975, "The Opening on the United States Supreme Court, Mr. Douglas: 36 Years Out on the Frontier" (quote). A legal realist since his days as an academic, Douglas, in Powe's view, viewed doctrine as merely "the explanatory cloak for decisions reached on more significant grounds" Powe, "Justice Douglas," 6 *Const. Comm.,* 270. Personal behavior: Murphy, *Wild Bill,* 287-99, 369-77, 400.

15. Eugene C. Gerhart, *America's Advocate: Robert H. Jackson* (Indianapolis: Bobbs-Merrill, 1958), 33-35, 64, 142, 187, 229-31; Felix Frankfurter, "Mr. Justice Jackson," 68 *Harv. L. Rev.* 937, 939 (1955) (Brandeis quote); Belknap, *Vinson Court,* 68-69 (quote).

16. Dennis J. Hutchinson, "The Black-Jackson Feud," 1988 *Sup. Ct. Rev.,* 203 ("the only enduring damage was to Jackson's reputation"); 205 ("Roosevelt had all but promised him the [chief justice] job in 1941"); 215 (Jackson was "isolated and poorly informed

overseas"); 219 ("'consulted nobody'"); Clifford to Vinson, June 11, 1946, and enclosed Jackson-Truman telegrams, Box 216, Jackson file, Frederick Moore Vinson Collection, University of Kentucky, Lexington ("Vinson Papers"); Gerhart, *America's Advocate*, 258–73, 308–11; James E. St. Clair and Linda C. Gugin, *Chief Justice Fred M. Vinson of Kentucky: A Political Biography* (Lexington: University Press of Kentucky, 2002), 156–63; Feldman, *Scorpions*, 293–302. *NY Times*, June 3, 1941, "Jackson Rumored as Possibility"; June 9, 1946, "Vinson Expected to Bring Supreme Court Harmony"; June 11, 1946, "Jackson Attacks Black for Judging Ex-Partner's Case"; and June 15, 1946, "President Asked Jackson Silence." The 1945 case, *Jewell Ridge Coal Corp. v. Local No. 6167, United Mine Workers*, 325 U.S. 161, held that coal miners were entitled under the Fair Labor Standards Act to so-called portal-to-portal pay. See 325 U.S. 897 (Jackson, J., concurring in denial of rehearing); Feldman, *Scorpions*, 266–72.

17. Hutchinson, "Black-Jackson Feud," 221, 223; Belknap, *Vinson Court*, 71; John P. Frank, "Fred Vinson and the Chief Justiceship," 21 *U. Chi. L. Rev.* 212, 241 (1954) ("Justice Black bore the attack in total silence, and Justice Jackson never repeated it after his return from Nuremberg"). Douglas: William Cohen, "Douglas and the *Rosenberg* Case: Setting the Record Straight," 70 *Cornell L. Rev.* 211, 232n120 ("Jackson's feelings toward Douglas were even more extreme than Frankfurter's"). Different rules: *Dennis*, 341 U.S. 494, 561 (Jackson, J., concurring); *Douds*, 339 U.S. 382, 422 (Jackson, J., concurring and dissenting). Powerless individuals: *Knauff*, 338 U.S. 537, 550 (Jackson, J., dissenting); *Mezei*, 345 U.S. 206, 218 (Jackson, J., dissenting); *Isserman*, 345 U.S. 286, 290 (Jackson, J., dissenting).

18. Schwartz, *Super Chief*, 56 (first quote); Rodell, *Nine Men*, 266 (second quote).

19. John D. Fassett, *New Deal Justice: The Life of Stanley Reed of Kentucky* (New York: Vantage Press, 1994) 7–15, 31–206; Belknap, *Vinson Court*, 48–49; Douglas, *The Court Years*, 121 (Reed was "one of the most reactionary judges to occupy the Bench in my time" but also "the most gentle, the friendliest, the most warm-hearted individual one could meet"); Douglas, *Go East*, 458–59 ("Hugo Black also loved Stanley, though he seldom agreed with him in Conference").

20. Rodell, *Nine Men*, 268 (quote); Belknap, *Vinson Court*, 50 (quote); Daniel L. Breen, "Stanley Forman Reed," in Melvin I. Urofsky, ed., *The Supreme Court Justices: A Biographical Dictionary*, 367–72 (New York: Garland, 1994); Frank, "Fred Vinson," 243; Interview #10, November 14, 1958, Box 282, Reed Oral History Project (Columbia University) file, 17 (quotes), Stanley Forman Reed Collection, University of Kentucky, Lexington ("Reed Papers"). Reed testified briefly as a character witness for Alger Hiss at his first perjury trial in 1949, as did Frankfurter; Hiss had worked for Reed in the solicitor general's office in 1935–36 and was Frankfurter's student at Harvard. Both justices were sharply criticized in the press and in the Congress. Fassett, *New Deal Justice*, 451–57; *NY Times*, June 23, 1949 ("Frankfurter, Reed Testify to Loyalty, Integrity of Hiss").

21. Melvin I. Urofsky, *Division and Discord The Supreme Court under Stone and Vinson, 1941–1953* (Columbia: University of South Carolina Press, 1997), 151 (quote); Douglas, *The Court Years*, 245 (quote); William M. Wiecek, *The Birth of the Modern Constitution: The United States Supreme Court, 1941–1953*, vol. XII, History of the Supreme Court (Cambridge: Cambridge University Press, 2006), 403 (quote).

22. St. Clair and Gugin, *Chief Justice Fred M. Vinson*, 162 (quotes); Belknap, *Vinson Court*, 37–39; *NY Times*, September 9, 1953, "Chief Justice Vinson Dies of Heart Attack"); Richard Kirkendall, "Fred Vinson" in Leon Friedman and Fred L. Israel, eds., *The Justices of the United States Supreme Court: Their Lives and Major Opinions* (New York: Bowker/Chelsea House, 1969), vol. IV, 2639–49.

23. Bernard Schwartz, *A History of the Supreme Court* (New York: Oxford University Press, 1993), 253 (quote); Howard J. Trienens interview, February 27, 1975, Fred M. Vinson Oral History Project, University of Kentucky Library (law-clerk quote); Belknap, *Vinson Court*, 40 (quote) (he was "align[ed] with the winning side 86 percent of the time"); 42 ("a well-deserved reputation as a menace to civil liberties"); Frank, "Fred Vinson," 226 ("whenever the government sent out the fire engines, Vinson saw a fire"); St. Clair and Gugin, *Chief Justice Fred M. Vinson*, 179.

24. Mary Frances Berry, *Stability, Security and Continuity: Mr. Justice Burton and Decision-Making in the Supreme Court 1945–1958* (Westport, Conn.: Greenwood, 1978), 3–26. Truman's committee was the Special Committee to Investigate the National Defense.

25. Douglas, *The Court Years*, 247–48 (quote); Eric W. Rise, "Harold Hitz Burton," in Urofsky, ed., *Supreme Court Justices*, 77 (observer quote); Belknap, *Vinson Court*, 79 (quote); Urofsky, *Division and Discord*, 154 (quote). See Richard Kirkendall, "Harold Burton," in Friedman and Israel, eds., *Justices*, 2617 ("He did not differ significantly from the three Democrats that Truman appointed; all of them tended to uphold government power"). Exceptions: *Joint Anti-Fascist*, 341 U.S. 123, 124 (opinion of Burton, J.); *Konigsberg*, 353 U.S. 252; *Schware*, 353 U.S. 232.

26. Richard Kirkendall, "Tom C. Clark," in Friedman and Israel, eds., *Justices*, 2665–77; Frank, *Warren Court*, 77–96; Evan A. Young, *Lone Star Justice: A Biography of Justice Tom C. Clark* (Dallas: Hendrick-Long, 1998), 1–27.

27. Richard Kirkendall, "Tom C. Clark" in Friedman and Israel, eds., *Justices*, 2665 (quote); Michal R. Belknap, "Tom Campbell Clark," in Urofsky, ed., *Supreme Court Justices*, 114–15; Merle Miller, *Plain Speaking: An Oral History of Harry S. Truman* (New York: Berkley, 1974), 225–26 (quote); Douglas, *The Court Years*, 245 (quote). Overwrought dissents: for example, *Jencks*, 353 U.S. 657, 680; *Greene*, 360 U.S. 474, 510. Exceptions: *Wieman*, 344 U.S. 183; *Slochower*, 350 U.S. 551. In 1961 Clark wrote the Court's opinion in *Mapp v. Ohio*, 367 U.S. 643, a landmark decision requiring state courts to exclude, as federal courts did, unlawfully obtained evidence in criminal trials.

28. Pre-Court years: Linda C. Gugin and James E. St. Clair, *Sherman Minton: New Deal Senator, Cold War Justice* (Indianapolis: Indiana Historical Society, 1997), 33–210; Richard Kirkendall, "Sherman Minton," in in Friedman and Israel, eds., *Justices*, 2699–2703. The report that Minton directly asked Truman to be appointed is found in Douglas, *The Court Years*, 247. In the summer of 1945, when Roberts's retirement created a vacancy, Minton asked Black to speak to Truman on his behalf. Minton to Black, September 15, 1945, and Black to Minton, September 17, 1945, Box 61, Minton correspondence 1942–68 file, Hugo L. Black Papers, Library of Congress, Washington, D.C. ("Black Papers"). Press predictions as to how Minton would vote on the Court proved

grossly inaccurate. *NY Times*, September 16, 1949, "Minton Named to High Court" ("It was believed that Judge Minton would join the 'liberal' wing of the Supreme Court.... Judge Minton is expected to share the views of Justices Hugo L. Black and William O. Douglas in their decisions").

29. Gugin and St. Clair, *Sherman Minton*, 211–39 (quotes, 215); Urofsky, *Division and Discord*, 156–57 (quote); Belknap, *Vinson Court*, 86 ("Minton did not believe that judges had any special responsibility to preserve liberty"). "[F]olksy and unpretentious," Minton had cordial relations with all of the other justices. David N. Atkinson, "Justice Sherman Minton and Behavior Patterns Inside the Supreme Court," 69 *Nw. U. L. Rev.* 716, 717 (1974).

30. *Dennis*, 339 U.S. 162, 164; *NY Times*, March 28, 1950, "Dennis Contempt Held Tried Fairly"; April 10, 1947, "Dennis Is Cited, Contempt Charged"; and March 31, 1947, "Dennis Concedes He Changed Name." Dennis publicly announced that he was of Irish and Norwegian extraction and was born with the name "Francis Waldron"; a HUAC investigator testified he had used half a dozen names.

31. *Dennis*, 339 U.S. at 164–65.

32. *Id.*, 164–72 (quote, 168). Clark, who was attorney general at the time of Dennis's indictment and trial, and Douglas, still recuperating from his injuries, did not participate. The previous year's decision was *Frazier v. United States*, 335 U.S. 497 (1949). In another HUAC contempt case, *Morford v. United States*, 339 U.S. 258 (1950), where the trial judge refused to allow the defense to question prospective federal-employee jurors in order to show "actual bias," a unanimous Court in a per curiam ruling, written by Vinson (see Box 263, Marshall & Morford file, Vinson Papers), reversed on the authority of *Dennis*.

33. *Dennis*, 339 U.S. at 173–75 (Jackson, J., concurring in the result) (quotes). See *Frazier*, 335 U.S. 514–15 (Jackson, J., dissenting). At the justices' conference, Jackson, according to Burton's notes, "(1) Lambastes the rule in *Frazier* and is ready to overrule it. (2) Lambastes anybody that accepts that remedy for a Communist." Del Dickson, ed., *The Supreme Court in Conference (1940–1985): The Private Discussions Behind Nearly 300 Supreme Court Decisions* (New York: Oxford University Press, 2001), 276–77.

34. *Dennis*, 339 U.S. at 175, 180 (quote) (Black, J., dissenting); *id.*, 181, 182 (quote). (Frankfurter, J., dissenting) (quoting *The Federalist No. 78*).

35. *Bryan*, 339 U.S. 323; *Fleischman*, 339 U.S. 349. Vinson's opinions were joined by Reed, Burton, Minton, and in *Fleischman* by Jackson. In *Bryan*, Jackson concurred separately in the result. Douglas and Clark did not participate in either case. All of JAFRC's sixteen executive-board members were prosecuted for contempt of Congress and convicted. Five, who recanted and resigned, received suspended sentences; the others went to prison. Phillip Deery, "'A Blot upon Liberty': McCarthyism, Dr. Barsky and the Joint Anti-Fascist Refugee Committee," 8 *Amer. Comm. Hist.* 167, 181–87 (2009). JAFRC disbanded in 1955 (*id.*, 192). Its listing by the attorney general was reviewed by the Court in 1951 (see chap. 3, herewith).

36. *Bryan*, 339 U.S. at 335 (quote), 338 (quotes); R.S. § 859 (quote). Black's dissent: 339 U.S. at 346 (quote).

37. *Fleischman*, 339 U.S. at 357 (quote), 363 (quote); *id.*, 366 (quote) (Black, J., dissenting).

38. *Lawson* and *Trumbo v. United States*, 339 U.S. 934 (1950); Frankfurter to Jackson, May 13, 1950, Box 166, Folder 7, Robert H. Jackson Papers, Library of Congress, Washington, D.C. ("Jackson Papers") (quote); Jan Palmer, *The Vinson Court Era: The Supreme Court's Conference Votes: Data and Analysis* (New York: AMS, 1990), 273. See Fowler V. Harper and Alan S. Rosenthal, "What the Supreme Court Did Not Do in the 1949 Term: An Appraisal of Certiorari," 99 *U. Pa. L. Rev.*, 293, 307–8 (1950) (Trumbo and Lawson "contend[ed] that the First Amendment . . . guaranteed them freedom of silence"). 1959 decision: *Barenblatt v. United States*, 360 U.S. 109 (1959).

39. *Knauff*, 338 U.S. 537.

40. *Id.*, 539; Hearings on HR 7614, 81st Cong., 2d Sess., Exclusion of Ellen Knauff, Before Subcommittee No. 1 of the House Judiciary Committee, March 27, 1950, 5–17; *NY Times*, April 4, 1950, "Mrs. Knauff Wins U.S. Entrance Vote"; Ellen Raphael Knauff, *The Ellen Knauff Story* (New York: Norton, 1952). Loss of Czech citizenship: *id.*, 70–71. Upon returning to Germany when the war ended, Knauff learned that her entire family had been exterminated by the Nazis. Order granting review: 336 U.S. 966 (1949). Bail order: Knauff, *Ellen Knauff Story*, 82, 235. Each Supreme Court justice serves as "circuit justice" for one or more federal judicial circuits, primarily to decide stay motions and bail applications arising from the circuit. 28 U.S.C. § 42.

41. *Knauff*, 338 U.S. at 539–42 and n2, n3 (quotes). Wartime regulations: Proclamation 2523, 55 Stat. 1696 (November 14, 1941), authorized by Pub. L. 114, 55 Stat. 252 (June 21, 1941). War Brides Act: Pub. L. 271, 59 Stat. 659 (December 28, 1945).

42. *Knauff*, 339 U.S. at 542–47 (quotes, 543). Minton's opinion was joined by Vinson, Reed, and Burton. Douglas and Clark did not participate.

43. *Id.*, 547–50 (Frankfurter, J., dissenting); *id.*, 550–52 (Jackson, J., dissenting) (quotes).

44. *NY Times*, March 7, 1950, "Deportation Case in Hands of Court"; May 17, 1950, "German War Bride Loses Court Fight"; and May 18, 1950, "Mrs. Knauff Gets Deportation Stay"; *United States ex rel. Knauff v. McGrath*, 181 F. 2d 839 (2d Cir. 1950), 182 F. 2d 1020 (2d Cir. 1950); Frank, "The United States Supreme Court: 1949–50," 18 *U. Chi. L. Rev.*, 21–23 ("the final appeal turned out to be not to the Supreme Court but to the *St. Louis Post-Dispatch*. . . . In a series of editorials it demanded that Mrs. Knauff be given a hearing. It placed full-page ads in the Washington papers stating the case"). See *St. Louis Post-Dispatch*, January 18, 1950, editorial, "The Case of Ellen Knauff"; *NY Post*, February 14, 1950, editorial, "The Banished War Bride"; and *NY Times*, March 30, 1950, editorial, "The Knauff Affair," in Box 161, Folder 5, Jackson Papers. The private bill passed the House over the Justice Department's opposition (see H. Rept. No. 1940, 81st Cong., 2d Sess., April 24, 1950), but Pat McCarran succeeded in blocking action in the Senate. *NY Times*, July 13, 1950, "McCarran Unit Acts against Mrs. Knauff." Jackson stay: Typed copy, May 17, 1950, Box 164, Folder 5, Jackson Papers (quote, 4). Nearly ten months later, the Court dismissed the case as moot. 340 U.S. 940 (1951).

45. *NY Times*, February 21, 1951, "Parole Is Granted to War Bride Here"; March 27, 1951, "Mrs. Knauff Is Called a Spy" (quote); March 28, 1951, "Mrs. Knauff Held on Ellis Island"; May 19, 1951, "Immigration Head Bars Mrs. Knauff"; November 2, 1951, "Board Reverses War Bride's Case"; November 3, 1951, "Mrs. Knauff Leaves Ellis Island

after Winning Fight to Enter U.S." (quote). Clark letter: *NY Times*, January 17, 1950, "U.S. Upheld on Bar to Alien Suspects"; the letter, dated October 4, 1948, was directed to another government official. Law clerk mem., Box 161, Folder 5, Jackson Papers. Appeal: Bd. of Immigration Appeals, *In re: Ellen Raphael Knauff*, August 29, 1951, 1–18 (quote, 16), reprinted in Knauff, *Ellen Knauff Story*, appendix. McGrath approval: Office of the Attorney General, November 2, 1951, reprinted in Knauff, appendix.

46. *Mezei*, 345 U.S. 206, 218 (1953) (Jackson, J., dissenting).

47. *Douds*, 339 U.S. 382.

48. Section 9(h), 61 Stat. 136, 146 (June 23, 1947). Political strikes: the Court cited a strike at the Allis-Chalmers plant in Milwaukee in 1941 and testimony before Congress "that the strike had been called solely in obedience to Party orders for the purpose of starting the 'snowballing of strikes' in defense plants." *Douds*, 339 U.S. 388. But see Harvey Klehr, *The Heyday of American Communism: The Depression Decade* (New York: Basic, 1984), 404–5 ("The number of strikes led by Communist unionists was small. . . . [I]n virtually all instances there were good and sufficient trade union reasons for striking").

49. *Douds*, 339 U.S. at 387–412 (quotes, 390, 391). Reed and Burton joined Vinson's opinion and Jackson and Frankfurter joined in part. Douglas and Clark did not participate; nor did Minton, who sat on the court-of-appeals panel that decided one of the two cases affirmed in *Douds* (*Inland Steel Co. v. NLRB*, 170 F. 2d 247 (7th Cir. 1948) *aff'd sub nom. United Steelworkers of America v. NLRB*, 339 U.S. 382 (1950)). Black dissented.

50. *Douds*, 339 U.S. at 393–406 (quotes, 393, 396, 397, 399). See Kalven, *A Worthy Tradition*, 335 (while the Court did not "challenge the thesis that clear and present danger is the test for direct sanctions," it "reject[ed] the notion that partial sanctions are governed by the same criteria").

51. *Douds*, 339 U.S. at 422–35 (quotes, 422, 423, 424, 425, 427, 431) (Jackson, J., concurring and dissenting).

52. *Id.*, 435–45 (quote, 442); *id.*, 419–22 (Frankfurter, J., concurring in part) (quote, 421). Although Vinson's opinion sustained the "beliefs" portion of the oath (*id.*, 407–12), the six-justice Court was equally divided on this issue. Four weeks later, the Court decided *Osman v. Douds*, 339 U.S. 846 (1950), raising identical issues but in which Douglas and Minton were able to participate. In a per curiam ruling, written by Vinson, the eight-justice Court voted 6–1 to uphold the "membership" and "affiliation" portions of the oath (with Douglas evidently not reaching the issue) and divided 4–4 on the "beliefs" portion. Per curiam author: see Vinson draft, recirculated May 29, 1950, Box 263, Osman file, Vinson Papers. The tie vote resulted in the affirmance of lower-court decisions upholding the entire oath.

53. 339 U.S. at 445–53 (quotes, 450–51) (Black, J., dissenting).

54. 64 Stat. 987 (Sept. 23, 1950); Veto of Internal Security Bill, September 22, 1950, *Public Papers of the Presidents: Harry S. Truman 1950*, 645–53 (quotes, 646, 647); Tanner and Griffith, "Legislative Politics and 'McCarthyism,'" in Griffith and Theoharis, eds., *The Specter*, 187; *NY Times*, Sept. 24, 1950, "Red Bill Veto Beaten, 57–10, By Senators," and October 29, 1950, "Subversive Control Board Ready for Its First Case."

Chapter 3. *Dennis,* **the Attorney General's List, Loyalty Programs, Contempts, and More**

1. *Joint Anti-Fascist Refugee Committee v. McGrath,* 341 U.S. 123 (1951) (attorney general's list); *Bailey v. Richardson,* 341 U.S. 918 (1951) (federal loyalty program); *Blau (Patricia) v. United States,* 340 U.S. 159 (1950) (contempt); *Blau (Irving) v. United States,* 340 U.S. 332 (1951) (same); *Rogers v. United States,* 340 U.S. 367 (1951) (same); *Garner v. Board of Public Works,* 341 U.S. 716 (1951) (state loyalty program); *Feiner v. New York,* 340 U.S. 315 (1951) (soap-box speaker); *Tenney v. Brandhove,* 341 U.S. 367 (1951) (1871 statute); *Collins v. Hardyman,* 341 U.S. 651 (1951) (same). The Court denied review of Alger Hiss's perjury conviction. *Hiss v. United States,* 340 U.S. 948 (1951).

2. *Dennis v. United States,* 341 U.S. 494 (1951).

3. *NY Times,* September 25, 1950, "M'Grath To Press New Curbs on Reds" (first quote), October 1, 1950, "Anti-Subversives Law Imposes Heavy Tasks" (final quote), and October 24, 1950, "U.S. Opens Round-Up of 86 As Alien Reds" (second and third quotes).

4. *Joint Anti-Fascist,* 341 U.S. 123; *Bailey,* 341 U.S. 918; *NY Times,* October 12, 1950, "High Court Hears Fealty Oath Pleas," and May 1, 1951, "Court Voids 3 Red Listings." Executive Order 9835, 12 Fed. Reg. 1935 (1947), which created the loyalty program, directed the attorney general to furnish to the Loyalty Review Board the names of the organizations listed by him for use in the program (Executive Order 9835, Part III, §3). "[T]he linkage between the List and all subsequent employee-loyalty programs was crucial." Wiecek, *Birth of the Modern Constitution,* 581. See Goldstein, *American Blacklist,* 140–43, 148–61. In their lawsuits, the three organizations denied the "Communist" label and charged they had suffered loss of membership and financial loss as a result of being listed.

5. Clark did not participate in either decision.

6. *Joint Anti-Fascist,* 341 U.S. at 124–42 (opinion of Burton, J., joined by Douglas); *id.,* 149–74 (Frankfurter, J., concurring) (quote, 161); *id.,* 174–83 (Douglas, J., concurring); *id.,* 183–87 (Jackson, J., concurring). Burton's opinion began as an "opinion of the Court." Burton draft, circulated November 20, 1950, Box 133, Joint Anti-Fascist Folder 1, Reed Papers.

7. 341 U.S. at 142–49 (Black, J., concurring) (quotes, 143–44). See U.S. Const., Art. I, §9, cl. 3 ("No Bill of Attainder . . . shall be passed"), §10 ("No state shall . . . pass any Bill of Attainder . . ."). "[L]egislative acts, no matter what their form, that apply either to named individuals or to easily ascertainable members of a group in such a way as to inflict punishment on them without a judicial trial are bills of attainder prohibited by the Constitution." *United States v. Lovett,* 328 U.S. 303, 315 (1946).

8. 341 U.S. at 197–213 (Reed, J., dissenting) (quotes, 202–3).

9. *Id.,* 177–83 (Douglas, J., concurring) (quote, 180), 209 (Reed, J., dissenting) (quote). Douglas's notes of the October 14 conference in *Bailey* indicate five votes to reverse: Black, Frankfurter, Jackson, Minton, and his own. Box 199, Argued Cases Nos. 25–49 file, William O. Douglas Collection, Library of Congress, Washington, D.C. ("Douglas Papers"). But "Minton abandoned the majority, leaving the Court split 4–4." Wiecek, *Birth of the Modern Constitution,* 586.

10. The three cases were remanded to the district court "with instructions to deny [the attorney general's] motion that the complaint be dismissed for failure to state a

claim upon which relief can be granted." *Joint Anti-Fascist*, 341 U.S. at 142 (opinion of Burton, J.). See Arthur J. Sabin, *In Calmer Times: The Supreme Court and Red Monday* (Philadelphia: University of Pennsylvania Press, 1999), 74 (the organizations' victory "was entirely pyrrhic; it changed nothing"). Almost simultaneously with the Court's decisions, the president changed the standard of proof in loyalty cases, making it easier to remove employees. The earlier standard, "reasonable grounds exist for belief that the person involved is disloyal," was changed to "there is a reasonable doubt as to the loyalty of the person involved." Exec. Order 10241, 16 Fed. Reg. 3690 (April 28, 1951); *NY Times*, April 29, 1951, "Truman Sharpens Loyalty Standard."

11. *NY Times*, May 2, 1951, "Government Firm on Loyalty Tests" (initial quotes); A. Krock, *NY Times*, May 3, 1951, "Effects of Burton Decision Are Doubtful" (final quotes); A. Krock, *NY Times*, May 6, 1951, "Whole Loyalty Issue Is Left in Uncertainty." Krock's view, citing lawyers he "consulted," was that the Court "has no control whatever of the character, procedure or method of Presidential steps leading to the discharge of executive employees [*sic*]."

12. *NY Times*, April 30, 1953, "62 Units Are Added To Subversive List" (quote), and July 25, 1955, "Attorney General's List"; Caute, *The Great Fear*, 170. See Goldstein, *American Blacklist*, 180–204. Brownell adopted regulations in May 1953 allowing a newly listed group to file a "notice of contest" and to obtain a hearing. 18 Fed. Reg. 2619, May 6, 1953. The Independent Socialist League was removed from the list in 1958. The same year, the National Lawyers Guild, which had filed a lawsuit in 1953 to forestall being listed, also won its fight. *NY Times*, September 13, 1958, "U.S. Abandons Bid To Cite Law Guild"; Ann Fagan Ginger and Eugene M. Tobin, eds., *The National Lawyers Guild: From Roosevelt through Reagan*, (Philadelphia: Temple Univ. Press, 1988), 136–37, 158–59.

13. *Blau (Patricia)*, 340 U.S. 159; *Blau (Irving)*, 340 U.S. 332; *Rogers*, 340 U.S. 367; *NY Times*, December 12, 1950, "High Court Upholds Self-Incrimination As Plea in Red Case."

14. *Blau (Patricia)*, 340 U.S. 159–60 and n1 (quotes).

15. *Id.*, 161 (quotes).

16. *NY Times*, December 17, 1950, "Incrimination Ruling May Have Wide Effect" (quotes). The day after the decision was issued, Rep. John E. Rankin (D.-Miss.), a former HUAC member, took the House floor to denounce it as "one of the most dangerous decisions I have ever read." 96 Cong. Rec. 16465 (December 12, 1950). Settled principles: for example, *Counselman v. Hitchcock*, 142 U.S. 547 (1892); *Arndstein v. McCarthy*, 254 U.S. 71 (1920); *Hoffman v. United States*, 341 U.S. 479 (1951).

17. *Blau (Irving)*, 340 U.S. at 333–34. The dissenters argued that the spousal privilege was inapplicable. *Id.*, 334–35 (Minton, J., dissenting). Clark did not participate. Jackson initially concurred in the majority's result but later elected to join Minton's dissent. Jackson Mem., December 21, 1950, Box 166, Folder 7, Jackson Papers.

18. *Rogers*, 340 U.S. at 368–75 (quotes, 368, 373, 374–75). Vinson was joined by Reed, Jackson, Burton, and Minton. Clark did not participate.

19. *Id.*, 375–81 (Black, J., dissenting) (quotes, 377, 378). The "dilemma" Black described was not fanciful. Frank, "The United States Supreme Court: 1950–51," 19 *U. Chi. L. Rev.*, 204 (dilemma "is exactly what has happened subsequent to the opinion").

20. Black draft opin. of Court, circulated December 1, 1950, Vinson draft dissent, circulated December 12, 1950, Jackson to Black, December 5, 1950, Jackson Mem., December 21, 1950, and Reed to Black undated, Box 308, Rogers file, Black Papers; Jackson conf. notes, Box 166, Folder 7, Jackson Papers (5–3 vote to reverse).

21. *Tenney*, 341 U.S. 367; *Collins*, 341 U.S. 651. The statute, Act of April 20, 1871, 17 Stat. 13, refers in part to "two or more persons" who "go in disguise on the highway or on the premises of another" for the purpose of depriving "any person or class of persons" of equal protection of the law.

22. *Tenney*, 341 U.S. at 369–79 (quote, 379); *NY Times*, May 22, 1951, "Lawmakers Held Immune to Suits." Douglas, the sole dissenter, wrote: "[W]hen a committee perverts its power, brings down on an individual the whole weight of government for an illegal or corrupt purpose, the reason for its immunity ends." 341 U.S. at 383.

23. *Collins*, 341 U.S. at 652–63 (quotes, 654, 662); *NY Times*, June 5, 1951 ("High Court Upholds Meeting Disrupters"). Burton, joined by Black and Douglas, dissented. 341 U.S. 663–64. The Soviet Union and the CPUSA opposed the Marshall Plan.

24. *Feiner*, 340 U.S. 315; *id.*, 321 (Black, J., dissenting) (final quote); *id.*, 330 (Douglas, J., dissenting) (quotes from speech); *NY Times*, February 3, 2009, "Irving Feiner, 84, Central Figure in Constitutional Free Speech Case, Is Dead."

25. *Feiner*, 340 U.S. at 316–21 (quotes, 319, 321); *id.*, 326 (Black, J., dissenting) (final quote); *id.*, 331 (Douglas, J., dissenting) (quotes). Frankfurter concurred in the result in an opinion filed jointly in *Feiner* and two other First Amendment cases (not "Communist" cases) decided the same day (see 340 U.S. 273).

26. Urofsky, *Division and Discord*, 168 (quote). See Harry Kalven Jr., *The Negro and the First Amendment* (Chicago: University of Chicago Press, 1965), 140 ("If the police can silence the speaker, the law in effect acknowledges a veto power in hecklers who can, by being hostile enough, get the law to silence any speaker of whom they do not approve").

27. *Garner*, 341 U.S. 716. Clark's opinion was joined by Vinson, Reed, Jackson, and Minton; Frankfurter and Burton filed opinions concurring in part and dissenting in part. Justices' votes and opinions: Box 193, Folder 15, and Box 207, Folders 12–13, Harold H. Burton Collection, Library of Congress, Washington, D.C. ("Burton Papers"); Box 209, Garner files, Douglas Papers; Box 308, Garner file, Black Papers; Jackson mem. for the conf., May 29, 1951, Box 175, Office Memos OT 1950 file, Reed Papers; Palmer, *Vinson Court Era*, 309. The five who voted to reverse at the conference were Black, Douglas, Frankfurter, Jackson, and Burton.

28. *Garner*, 341 U.S. at 717–20 (quotes).

29. *Id.*, 720 (quote).

30. *Id.*, 725–26 (Frankfurter, J., concurring and dissenting) (quote); *id.*, 729–30 (Burton, J., concurring and dissenting) (quote). Frankfurter urged that the fifteen employees be reinstated and allowed to take a valid oath.

31. *Id.*, 723–24 (quote). See Kalven, *A Worthy Tradition*, 347 ("The city officials are likely to accede to so explicit a message from the Court; and should they fail to do so, the Court has already informed them and the world that their oath is unconstitutional").

32. *Garner*, 341 U.S. at 730–36 (Douglas, J., dissenting) (quotes, 733, 735). The two

decisions were *Cummings v. Missouri*, 71 U.S. (4 Wall.) 277 (1866) and *Ex parte Garland*, 71 (4 Wall.) 333 (1866).

33. In another case involving the "innocent member" issue, *Gerende v. Board of Supervisors of Elections*, 341 U.S. 56 (1951), decided in a per curiam opinion written by Frankfurter, the Court, without dissent, upheld a Maryland statute that required a candidate for state office to swear "he is not *knowingly* a member of an organization" engaged in attempting violent overthrow of the government. *Id.* 57 (emphasis added). See Frankfurter draft per curiam, circulated April 11, 1951, Box 271, Gerende file, Vinson Papers. The oath was challenged by Thelma Gerende, a Progressive Party candidate for the Baltimore city council. *NY Times*, April 13, 1951, "High Court Backs Oath of Loyalty." A separate appeal by a Progressive Party candidate for governor became moot when, shortly before the election, the Court (Black, Douglas, and Vinson dissenting) declined to expedite hearing of the case. *Shub v. Simpson*, 340 U.S. 861, 340 U.S. 881 (1950).

34. Michal R. Belknap, "Cold War in the Courtroom: The Foley Square Communist Trial," in Michal R. Belknap, *American Political Trials*, 240, 245–50 (Medina description) (Westport, Conn.: Greenwood, 1981); Belknap, *Cold War Political Justice*, 77–112; *NY Times*, January 17, 1949, "400 Police on Duty as 12 Communists Go on Trial Today") (quotes), October 15, 1949, "11 Communists Convicted of Plot"; October 22, 1949, "Law Change Cited." Twelve defendants were indicted, but the case against CPUSA national chairman William Z. Foster was severed due to his ill health. *NY Times*, January 19, 1949, "Communist Trial to Continue Here with Foster Out." One defendant, Robert G. Thompson, a decorated World War II hero, was given a three-year sentence. The day after the jury verdict, President Truman announced the appointment of the chief prosecutor, John F. X. McGohey, to a federal judgeship. *NY Times*, October 16 1949, "McGohey Is Named Federal Judge." Medina received fifty thousand congratulatory letters. Belknap, *Cold War Political Justice*, 113.

35. *NY Times*, January 17, 1949, "Text of Indictment of 12 Communists" (emphasis added); Belknap, "Cold War in the Courtroom," *American Political Trials*, 238; *Dennis*, 341 U.S. at 582 (Douglas, J., dissenting) (quote). The indictment tracked the language of the Smith Act. Act of June 28, 1940, §§ 2(a), 3, 54 Stat. 671. The Court's limited grant of certiorari had removed sufficiency of the evidence from the scope of its review and left only the issue of the act's constitutionality. *Dennis*, 340 U.S. 863, 341 U.S. at 497, 516. Douglas nonetheless assigned to his law clerk "the task of reviewing the massive transcript of the trial, saying 'What I want to know from these twenty-three volumes is this: Is there any evidence in here that the Communists have advocated or privately agreed among themselves to advocate the actual use of violence against the government?'" Murphy, *Wild Bill*, 305. See Belknap, 242 ("[T]he prosecution relied mainly on articles, pamphlets, and books. . . . Much of this literary evidence was quite dated, and the government could offer no proof that American Communists were about to translate into action any of the ideas it contained").

36. Wiecek, "The Legal Foundations of Domestic Anticommunism," *Sup. Ct. Rev. [2001]*, 429 (observer quote); conf. notes, December 9, 1950, Box 207, Dennis file, Douglas Papers (Douglas quote); Dickson, *Supreme Court in Conference*, 278–79.

37. *Dennis*, 341 U.S. at 495–517 (quotes, 510) (opin. of Vinson, C.J.). Reed, Burton, and

Minton joined Vinson's opinion; Frankfurter and Jackson concurred in separate opinions; Black and Douglas dissented; Clark did not participate. As late as five days before the decision, Vinson believed he was writing an opinion of the Court. Vinson draft opin. of the Court, circulated May 31, 1951, Box 306, Dennis file, Black Papers. Holmes-Brandeis formulation: *Whitney v. California*, 274 U.S. 357, 377 (1927) (Brandeis, J., concurring) (quote). See *Bridges v. California*, 314 U.S. 252, 263 (1941) ("the degree of imminence [must be] extremely high before utterances can be punished"). Hand's view: *United States v. Dennis*, 183 F. 2d 201, 212 (2d Cir. 1950); Stone, *Perilous Times*, 398–402; Wiecek, *Birth of the Modern Constitution*, 556–63. Hand, as did the Court, compensated for the absence of evidentiary proof by taking "judicial notice of the contemporary world situation" (*id.*, 561). See Stone, 402 ("under [the Holmes-Brandeis approach] the convictions in *Dennis* would clearly have to be reversed"); Brennan, "Quest to Develop," 7 (*Dennis* "reinterpret[ed] the clear and present danger test in a way that emasculated it").

38. *Dennis*, 341 U.S. at 561–79 (Jackson, J., concurring) (quotes, 567–68). In a final section of his opinion, Jackson argued that the convictions could be sustained, wholly aside from the speech issues, on the basis of conspiracy law, under which a conspiracy may be held unlawful in itself, "independently of any other evil it seeks to accomplish," and "no overt act is or need be required." *Id.*, 572–77 (quotes, 573, 574). See Pritchett, *Civil Liberties and the Vinson Court*, 75–76. Ironically, in the flag-salute case (*West Virginia State Board of Education v. Barnette*, 319 U.S. 624 [1943]), to which Jackson referred, he had written: "[F]reedom to differ is not limited to things that do not matter much. That would be a mere shadow of freedom. The test of its substance is the right to differ as to things that touch the heart of the existing order" (*id.*, 642).

39. *Id.*, 517–61 (Frankfurter, J., concurring) (quotes, 525, 539–40). Frankfurter did not accept Vinson's "reinterpreting" of the clear-and-present-danger test, arguing that unless the defendants are to be subjected "to the risk of an *ad hoc* judgment influenced by the impregnating atmosphere of the times, the constitutionality of their conviction must be determined by principles established in cases decided in more tranquil periods." *Id.*, 527–28.

40. *Dennis*, 341 U.S. at 581–92 (Douglas, J., dissenting) (quotes, 587–89). In answer to Jackson's reliance on conspiracy law, Douglas wrote: "To make a lawful speech unlawful because two men conceive it is to raise the law of conspiracy to appalling proportions." *Id.*, 584.

41. *Id.*, 579–81 (Black, J., dissenting) (quote, 581).

42. *NY Times*, June 5, 1951, "Decision Is 6–2" (first quote), and "The Smith Act Upheld" (second quote); *Wash. Post*, June 6, 1951, "Freedom with Security" (quote); Belknap, *Cold War Political Justice*, 142 (*LA Times* and final quote). Belknap counted only five major newspapers in the entire country—most prominently, the *New York Post* and *St. Louis Post-Dispatch*—that voiced opposition to the decision. *Id.*, 141. A week after the decision, President Truman promoted Medina to the court of appeals to succeed Learned Hand who had retired and appointed Thomas F. Murphy, who had successfully prosecuted Alger Hiss, to Medina's seat on the district court. *New York Times*, June 12, 1951, "Truman Promotes Medina"; *Chicago Tribune*, June 12, 1951, "Nominates Hiss Prosecutor As Federal Judge."

43. *NY Times*, June 15, 1951, "Moves to Prosecute Reds Mapped by Federal Aides" (quote); Robert Mollan, "Smith Act Prosecutions: The Effect of the *Dennis* and *Yates* Decisions," 26 *Univ. of Pittsburgh L. Rev.* 705, 708–10, and n17–19 (1965).

44. *Sacher*, 341 U.S. 952 (1951). Frankfurter in conference voted to grant review but did not make his vote public. Palmer, *The Vinson Court Era*, 331; see chap. 4, herewith. One of the six was Eugene Dennis, not an attorney, who represented himself at the trial.

45. *NY Times*, July 3, 1951, "7 Convicted Reds Are Taken To Jail"; Belknap, *Cold War Political Justice*, 144. The flight of the four *Dennis* defendants led to contempt convictions and prison sentences for detective-story writer Dashiell Hammett and two others, trustees of a fund collected to provide bail for *Dennis* defendants. Hammett and the others were cited for contempt and imprisoned when, invoking the Fifth Amendment, they refused to answer questions and produce fund records. The Court declined review, Black and Douglas dissenting. *Hammett* and *Field v. United States*, 342 U.S. 894 (1951). *United States v. Field*, 193 F.2d 92 (2d Cir. 1951); Reed opinion denying bail, July 25, 1961, Box 216, Reed file, Vinson Papers. Additional work: *Kremen*, 353 U.S. 346 (1957); *Green*, 356 U.S. 165 (1958).

46. See chap. 1, herewith. The Rosenberg jury verdict was received on March 29 and sentencing took place on April 5, 1951. *NY Times*, April 6, 1951, "Atom Spy Couple Sentenced to Die."

Chapter 4. Deportations, Fallout from *Dennis*, and the Rosenberg Case

1. Deportation: *Harisiades v. Shaughnessy*, 342 U.S. 580 (1952); *Carlson v. Landon*, 342 U.S. 524 (1952); *United States v. Spector*, 343 U.S. 169 (1952); *Kwang Hai Chew v. Colding*, 344 U.S. 590 (1953); *Shaughnessy v. United States ex rel. Mezei*, 345 U.S. 206 (1953); *Heikkila v. Barber*, 345 U.S. 229 (1953); *Bridges v. United States*, 346 U.S. 209 (1953). *Dennis* fallout: *Stack v. Boyle*, 342 U.S. 1 (1951); *Sacher v. United States*, 343 U.S. 1 (1952); *In re Isserman*, 345 U.S. 286 (1953). State loyalty: *Adler v. Board of Education*, 342 U.S. 485 (1952); *Wieman v. Updegraff*, 344 U.S. 183 (1952). Doctor draft: *Orloff v. Willoughby*, 345 U.S. 83 (1952). The Court denied review (Black and Douglas dissenting) of a lower court's refusal to dismiss the perjury indictment against William Remington, a government employee accused by ex-Communist Elizabeth Bentley of having disclosed military information to her during World War II; the grand-jury foreman had been associated in a book-publishing venture with Bentley (the main prosecution witness), and potential success in the venture was enhanced by the grand jury's indictment of Remington. *Remington v. United States*, 343 U.S. 907 (1952); Gary May, *Un-American Activities: The Trials of William Remington* (New York: Oxford University Press, 1994), 155–58, 234–38.

2. *Rosenberg v. United States*, 346 U.S. 273 (1953); *id.* 310 (Frankfurter, J., dissenting) (quote).

3. 1952 elections: see chap. 1, herewith. "[I]n 1953, 185 members of the House applied for membership on HUAC." Goldstein, *Political Repression in Modern America*, 346.

4. *Harisiades*, 342 U.S. 580.

5. *Id.*, 581–83 (quote, 583); *NY Times*, March 11, 1952, "High Court Upholds De-

portation and Denial of Bail to Alien Reds." After a 1939 decision (*Kessler v. Strecker*, 307 U.S. 22 [1939]) held that then-existing law authorized the deportation of current but not former CPUSA members, the Party "dropp[ed] aliens from membership . . . in order to immunize them" (*Harisiades*, 342 U.S. at 593), and Congress enacted a statute to reach past members.

6. *Id.*, 584–91, 593–95 (quotes, 591, 594). Frankfurter, concurring, stated that "what classes of aliens shall be allowed to enter and what classes of aliens shall be allowed to stay, are for Congress exclusively to determine." *Id.*, 596–97. Clark did not participate. See U.S. Const., Art. I, §9, cl. 3 ("No . . . ex post facto Law shall be passed"). Drafts of Jackson's opinion had contained even more strident anti-Communist rhetoric, but Frankfurter in a letter "emphasize[d]" to him "our responsibility not to fan the flames." He cited a report from philosopher Bertrand Russell, after visiting several American universities, that "a feeling of fear and terror prevails among faculties," and from Graham Greene, "the sober, eminent English Catholic novelist," who visiting Hollywood found that "nothing short of a reign of terror prevails there." Frankfurter to Jackson, February 27, 1952, and Jackson draft opinion, reprinted February 20, 1952, Box 172, Folder 5, Jackson Papers.

7. *Harisiades*, 342 U.S. at 598–601 (Douglas, J., dissenting) (quotes, 600, 601).

8. *Carlson*, 342 U.S. 524, 528, 531.

9. *Id.*, 526–47 (quotes, 542, 546); Internal Security Act of 1950, § 23, 64 Stat. 987, 1010. The detention of one of the individuals, John Zydok, was ruled invalid on a technical ground; he was ordered released unless the government rearrested him under a new warrant. *Carlson*, 342 U.S. at 546–47; see *id.*, 532 and n17. See U.S. Const., 8th Amend. ("Excessive bail shall not be required . . ."").

10. *Carlson*, 342 U.S. at 558–68 (Frankfurter, J., dissenting) (quotes, 559, 564); *id.* 547–58 (Black, J., dissenting); *id.*, 568–69 (Douglas, J., dissenting); *id.*, 569 (Burton, J., dissenting) (quote). Black's dissent invoked the First, Fifth, and Eighth Amendments.

11. Frankfurter to Jackson, January 16, 1952; Jackson to Frankfurter, February 21, 1952; Frankfurter to Jackson, February 23, 1952 (quote); Jackson to Frankfurter, February 25, 1952, Frankfurter Papers, Pt. I, microfilm reels 55–56.

12. *Spector*, 343 U.S. 169, *rev'g* 99 F. Supp. 778 (S.D.Cal. 1951). The extended delay in deporting Spector was attributable to the refusal of the Soviet Union to accept American Communist deportees. *NY Times*, November 6, 1951, "Deportation Order Upheld." Attorney General McGrath testified during congressional hearings on the Internal Security Act that "'[a]s a result of numerous refusals on the part of Russia to issue a travel document to this alien [Spector], he is free to travel in the United States and continue his communistic activities.'" *NY Times*, April 8, 1952, "High Court Backs Alien Ouster Law." Spector was later tried and convicted under the Smith Act; but the Court ordered his acquittal in *Yates* in 1957 (see chap. 7, herewith).

13. *Spector*, 343 U.S. at 170–73 (quotes, 171, 172). Clark did not participate.

14. *Id.*, 174–80 (Jackson, J., dissenting) (quotes, 177, 180); *id.*, 173–74 (Black, J., dissenting). Jackson's rationale was sustained in later decisions of the Court. E.g., *United States v. Gaudin*, 515 U.S. 506, 510–11 (1995) ("The Constitution gives a criminal defendant the right to demand that a jury find him guilty of all the elements of the crime with which he is charged").

15. *NY Times*, April 8, 1952, "High Court Backs Alien Ouster Law."

16. *Kwong Hai Chew*, 344 U.S. 590 (quotes, 596, 600, 603). Minton dissented without opinion. Coast Guard clearance: *id.*, 594 and n3, 602. Chew was later given a hearing, at which ex-Communist seamen testified against him; when INS examiners ruled adversely to him, Chew appealed; his legal battle to remain in the United States continued at least until 1967. Ellen Schrecker, "Immigration and Internal Security: Political Deportations During the McCarthy Era," 60 *Science & Society* 393, 408–9 (1997).

17. *Mezei*, 345 U.S. 206, 209 (quote); *NY Times*, March 17, 1953, "High Court Backs U.S. on Alien Curb," and April 23, 1953, "Stateless, He Faces Life on Ellis Island."

18. *Mezei*, 345 U.S. at 207–16 (quotes, 214, 216). Clark's opinion was joined by Vinson, Reed, Burton, and Minton. Black, in a letter to Clark before the decision was issued, argued that Mezei's liberty was "taken away by an unreviewable decision of a government agent made on concealed reports supplied by secret informers." Black to Clark, March 9, 1953, Box A22, Folder 9, Tom C. Clark Papers, Tarlton Law Library, University of Texas at Austin ("Clark Papers").

19. 345 U.S. at 218–28 (Jackson, J., dissenting) (quote, 219); *id.*, 216–18 (Black, J., dissenting).

20. *NY Times*, April 23, 1953, "Stateless, He Faces Life on Ellis Island"; April 24, 1953, "Hope for Stateless Man"; January 1, 1954, "Barred Alien's Case Stated" (Mezei letter to editor); February 25, 1954, "Alien Faces 'Exile' on Ellis Island"; February 27, 1954, "2 Ex-Red Officials Identify Suspect"; April 10, 1954, "Hungarian Who Jumped His Ship in '23 To Enter U.S. Is Declared Security Risk"; August 10, 1954, "Exclusion Order Valid"; and August 12, 1954, "Alien, Long Held, Freed" (quote). IWO: Arthur J. Sabin, *Red Scare in Court: New York versus the International Workers Order* (Philadelphia: University of Pennsylvania Press, 1993), 10–24; Goldstein, *American Blacklist*, 67–69; Wiecek, *Birth of the Modern Constitution*, 589 (IWO "was a fraternal benefit society that wrote life insurance policies. Fewer than 10 percent of its policyholders in the 1930s were Communists").

21. *Heikkila*, 345 U.S. 229; Administrative Procedure Act, § 10, 60 Stat. 237, 243 (quotes).

22. *Heikkila*, 345 U.S. at 230–38. The statute relied on was Immigration Act of 1917, § 19(a), 39 Stat. 889 (February 5, 1917), as amended, 54 Stat. 671 (June 28, 1940). At the Court's conference, Douglas and Jackson joined Black and Frankfurter in voting for Heikkila, later switching sides. Palmer, *The Vinson Court Era*, 371.

23. *Heikkila*, 345 U.S. at 237–41 (quote, 239) (Frankfurter, J., dissenting).

24. *Time*, May 5, 1958, "Round Trip to Helsinki" (quote); *NY Times*, August 20, 1958, "U.S. Again Seeks to Oust Heikkila"; and September 25, 1958, "Heikkila Wins Point"; Fried, *Nightmare in Red*, 189.

25. *Bridges*, 346 U.S. 209; *Bridges v. Wixon*, 326 U.S. 135 (1945); Kutler, *American Inquisition*, 118–51; *NY Times*, June 16, 1953, "Supreme Court Frees Bridges under Statute of Limitations." Automatic revocation: 8 U.S.C. § 738(e) (quoted in *Bridges*, 199 F.2d 845, 846 [9th Cir. 1952]). Bridges readily admitted that he cooperated with the CPUSA to advance his union's interests but denied membership (see, for example, Kutler, 150; *Bridges*, 133 F. Supp. 638, 640 [N.D.Cal. 1955]). As in *Dennis*, defense attorneys at Bridges's trial, including Vincent Hallinan, his lead attorney, were cited and imprisoned

for contempt of court for alleged misbehavior at the trial. The Court refused to review their convictions, Black and Douglas dissenting. *Hallinan v. United States*, 341 U.S. 952 (1951); *MacInnis v. United States*, 342 U.S. 953 (1952). Hallinan, while in prison, was selected as the Progressive Party's presidential nominee in the 1952 election. *NY Times*, July 5, 1952, "Progressive Party Gathers in Chicago."

26. *Bridges*, 346 U.S. at 210–28 (quote) (216); *id.*, 228–34 (Reed, J., dissenting). Clark and Jackson (both ex-attorney generals) did not participate.

27. *NY Times*, June 16, 1953, "Bridges Is Jubilant" (INS quote). 1955 decision: *Bridges*, 133 F. Supp. 640–43 ("Only a weak yielding to extra-judicial clamor would excuse acceptance of the testimony of the witnesses in this case"); Kutler, *American Inquisition*, 148–49. The government sought to prove Bridges a party member using paid ex-Communist informers, including Paul Crouch and Manning Johnson. Charles P. Larrowe, *Harry Bridges: The Rise and Fall of Radical Labor in the United States* (New York: Lawrence Hill, 1972), 310–12; see Lichtman and Cohen, *Deadly Farce*, 2–3, 13, 143, 170n54; Richard H. Rovere, "The Kept Witnesses," in *The American Establishment and Other Reports, Opinions, and Speculations*, 118–20, 129–30 (New York: Harcourt, Brace, 1962); *NY Times*, April 16, 1955, "Brownell Drops Informant Plan"; August 24, 1955, "U.S. Bureau Lists Informants' Fees"; *Communist Party v. SACB*, 351 U.S. 115 (1956) (perjuries by Crouch, Johnson, and a third witness required reversal of SACB registration order).

28. *Adler*, 342 U.S. 485 (quotes, 489, 490). New York's courts construed the Feinberg Law as requiring that the teacher "knew" of the organization's unlawful purposes, obviating the innocent-member issue. *Id.*, 494 and n8. The law, enacted in 1949, was sponsored by Benjamin Feinberg, an upstate Republican and the state senate majority leader. *NY Times*, March 4, 1952, "Feinberg Act Wins."

29. *Adler*, 342 U.S. at 486–96 (quotes, 492, 493). The right-privilege distinction invoked by the Court, under which public employment is a privilege which "may be subjected to any conditions," was rejected by the Court in 1967 in another case under the Feinberg Law. *Keyishian v. Board of Regents*, 385 U.S. 589, 605–6 (1967).

30. *Adler*, 342 U.S. at 497–508 (Frankfurter, J., dissenting) (quote, 500). "Ripeness" refers to the timing of the lawsuit and fitness of the issues for judicial decision (see, for example, *Abbott Laboratories v. Gardner*, 387 U.S. 136 (1967)). During the 1952 term, the Court in a per curiam opinion (Black and Douglas dissenting) refused on ripeness grounds to adjudicate the constitutionality of a Michigan statute requiring registration of the CPUSA, "Communists," and "Communist front organizations." *Albertson v. Millard*, 345 U.S. 242 (1953). The law was challenged in a federal district court only five days after its enactment; the Court directed lower federal courts to await interpretation of the law by Michigan's courts.

31. *Adler*, 342 U.S. at 508–11 (Douglas, J., dissenting) (quote, 509); *id.*, 496–97 (Black, J., dissenting).

32. *NY Times*, June 16, 2009, "When Suspicion of Teachers Ran Unchecked," and accompanying photos and captions at NYTimes.com. Adler later admitted CPUSA membership but quit the Party in 1956.

33. *Wieman*, 344 U.S. 183 (quotes, 186).

34. *Id.*,184–92 (quotes, 190, 191). Testimony of J. Edgar Hoover, Hearings before House Committee on Un-American Activities on HR 1884 and HR 2122, 80th Cong., 1st Sess., 46 (1947) (quote). Burton concurred only in the result. Jackson did not participate.

35. *Wieman*, 344 U.S. at 194–98 (Frankfurter, J., concurring); *id.*, 192–94 (Black, J., concurring) (quote). The Sedition Act of 1798 was in effect two and one-half years, and only fourteen individuals were prosecuted under the act. Lewis, *Freedom for the Thought That We Hate*, 12,

36. Jackson Mem., circulated October 9, 1951, Box 217, Sacher file, Douglas Papers (quotes); *Sacher*, 342 U.S. 858 (1951); F. R. Crim. P. 42(a) and (b), 18 U.S.C.A. Black, Frankfurter, Douglas, Jackson, and Burton voted in favor of rehearing. Palmer, *Vinson Court Era*, 331. The day before Jackson circulated his memorandum, Frankfurter advised him of "a new bit of evidence of the fear that is at present holding our profession." "Henry Wallace [the former vice president]," he wrote, "is to appear shortly before the McCarran Committee in connection with the China post-mortem. . . . [A]t least half a dozen reputable lawyers have refused to appear with him." Frankfurter to Jackson, October 8, 1951, Box 168, Folder 1, Jackson Papers.

37. *Sacher*, 343 U.S. 1, 3–14 (quote, 7). Vinson, Reed, Burton, and Minton joined Jackson's opinion. Clark did not participate.

38. *Id.*, 9–14 (quotes 11, 13).

39. *Id.*, 23–42 (Frankfurter, J., dissenting) (quotes, 34,35); *id.*, 14–23 (Black, J., dissenting); *id.*, 89 (Douglas, J., dissenting). Frankfurter attached to his opinion extensive excerpts from the trial record, demonstrating Medina's continuous hostility to the lawyers. *Id.*, 42–89.

40. *Isserman*, 345 U.S. 286 (quote, 287).

41. *Id.*, 286–90 (opinion of Vinson, C.J.) (quotes, 289). Clark did not participate. Isserman served four months of his six-month prison sentence for the *Dennis* contempt. *NY Times*, April 7, 1953, "High Court Bars Lawyer for Reds."

42. 345 U.S. at 290–94 (Jackson, J., dissenting) (quotes, 291, 294).

43. *Isserman v. Ethics Committee*, 345 U.S. 927 (1953). The New Jersey disbarment also led to Isserman's disbarment in the federal district court in Manhattan where previously, following his *Dennis* contempt, he had received only a two-year suspension. See *Association of the Bar of the City of New York v. Isserman*, 271 F. 2d 784, 785 (2d Cir. 1959).

44. *Stack*, 342 U.S. 1 (quote, 3, 5–6); *NY Times*, November 6, 1951, "High Court Attacks $50,000 Bail."

45. 342 U.S. at 2–7 (quotes, 4, 5). Minton did not participate. Frankfurter, joined by Jackson, wrote a concurring opinion directed to procedural issues. *Id.*, 7–18.

46. *Orloff*, 345 U.S. 83 (quotes, 84, 90); *NY Times*, March 10, 1953, "Supreme Court Upholds Army in Barring Commission to Doctor." Doctor-draft statute: 64 Stat. 826 (September 9, 1950).

47. *Orloff*, 345 U.S. 84–95 (quotes, 90, 93).

48. *Id.*, 97–99 (Frankfurter, J., dissenting) (quote, 98); *id.*, 95–97 (Black, J., dissenting) (quote, 97).

49. *NY Times*, February 3, 1953, "Connecticut Doctor to Start Infantry Training as Private." Nugent did sign statements denying he had ever been a Communist.

50. The Rosenbergs were indicted with Morton Sobell, Julius's friend and college classmate, and Anatoli Yakovlev, a Soviet consular official and spy who left the country. Decrypted VENONA messages confirm Julius's involvement with Soviet intelligence. Haynes and Klehr, *Venona*, 295–311. David Greenglass received a fifteen-year prison sentence, and Ruth Greenglass, named as an unindicted co-conspirator, escaped prosecution entirely. Radosh and Milton, *Rosenberg File*, 100, 287. Ethel: *id.*, 98 (quote); *id.* ("the evidence against Ethel rested entirely on the Greenglasses' uncorroborated word and placed her in an accessory role at best"); *id.*, 99 ("Hoover wrote . . . 'if Julius Rosenberg would furnish details of his extensive espionage activities it would be possible to proceed against other individuals . . . *proceeding against his wife might serve as a lever in this matter*.'") (orig. emphasis). Ruth belatedly recalled, and both Greenglasses testified, that Ethel typed David's handwritten notes—key testimony that now appears to have been perjured. *Id.*, 164, 197; *NY Times*, September 12, 2008, "57 Years Later, Figure in Rosenberg Case Says He Spied for Soviets." *Ex parte*: Radosh and Milton, *Rosenberg File*, 275–82; Michael E. Parrish, "Cold War Justice: The Supreme Court and the Rosenbergs," 82 *Amer. Hist. Rev.* 805, 811 (1977).

51. *Rosenberg*, 344 U.S. 838, 850 (1952); Frankfurter Mem., June 4, 1953, Frankfurter Papers, Pt. 1, microfilm reel 70 ("FF June 4 Mem."), 1–3; Parrish, "Cold War Justice," 816–19. Burton explained at the conference that "this was a death case about which two Justices seemed to have strong feelings" and he "would join them." FF June 4 Mem. 2. Frankfurter's and Burton's votes were not publicly disclosed. When rehearing was denied in November, by an identical vote, Frankfurter appended a statement that "[p]etitioners are under death sentence, and it is not unreasonable to feel that before life is taken review should be open in the highest court of the society which has condemned them." 344 U.S. 89–90. See U.S. Const., Art III, §3 (treason clause).

52. Radosh and Milton, *Rosenberg File*, 51, 202–7; *Rosenberg*, 200 F. 2d 666, 670 (2d Cir. 1953) (quote) *aff'g* 108 F. Supp. 798 (S.D.N.Y. 1952); 28 U.S.C. § 2255; *NY Times*, March 15, 1951, "Columbia Teacher Arrested, Linked to 2 on Trial as Spies"; Parrish, "Cold War Justice," 820–21. Perl was an expert in aerodynamics who taught physics at Columbia. The lower courts denied the § 2255 motion on the ground that the Rosenbergs neither sought a mistrial nor showed that the jury became aware of Saypol's disclosures.

53. FF June 4 Mem., 3–5 (quote); Parrish, "Cold War Justice," 822–24. Vinson, Reed, Clark, and Minton opposed Frankfurter's requested delay.

54. Frankfurter Mem., May 20, 1953, 2, Frankfurter Papers, Pt. 1, microfilm reel 70 (quotes).

55. Douglas Mem., May 22, 1953 (quote), Frankfurter Mem., May 22, 1953 (second quote), and Frankfurter to Burton, May 23, 1953 (quotes), Frankfurter Papers, Pt. 1, microfilm reel 70; FF June 4 Mem., 6–7; Parrish, "Cold War Justice," 823–25. Frankfurter "believed it wholly unethical for Douglas to issue a statement in which he essentially prejudged the merits of the case." Urofsky, *Felix Frankfurter*, 121. Jackson told Frankfurter that Douglas's memorandum was "the dirtiest, most shameful, most cynical performance that I think I have ever heard of in matters pertaining to law." FF June 4 Mem., 6.

56. FF June 4 Mem., 7–9 (quotes); *Rosenberg*, 345 U.S. 965; Parrish, "Cold War Justice," 825–26. Afterward, Jackson told Frankfurter: "That S.O.B.'s bluff was called." In

the Court's published order, Douglas noted only that he "is of the opinion the petition for certiorari should be granted."

57. *NY Times*, May 30, 1953, "Rosenbergs' Deaths Set for Mid-June" and June 3, 1953, "Rosenbergs Deny Any Guilt As Spies"; *Rosenberg*, 345 U.S. 989; Parrish, "Cold War Justice," 831–32; Burton Mem., June 15, 1953, Frankfurter Papers, Pt. 1, microfilm reel 70.

58. *Rosenberg v. Denno*, 346 U.S. 271 (1953); Frankfurter typed "Addendum—June 19, 1953," 1, Frankfurter Papers, Pt. 1, microfilm reel 70 ("FF June 19 Addendum"); Parrish, "Cold War Justice," 832–33; *NY Times*, June 16, 1953, "High Court Denies a Rosenberg Stay." Finerty, nearly two decades earlier, had been a defense attorney in the case of Tom Mooney, a left-wing union organizer convicted of murder and sentenced to death on the basis of perjured testimony, whose habeas corpus action succeeded. *Mooney v. Holohan*, 294 U.S. 103 (1935). Frankfurter, as a law professor, had protested Mooney's conviction. Michael E. Parrish, *Felix Frankfurter and His Times: The Reform Years* (New York: Free Press, 1982), 97–101.

59. FF June 19 Addendum, 2; *NY Times*, June 16, 1953, "High Court Denies a Rosenberg Stay"; June 18, 1953, "Volunteers Cited Key Legal Points"; and June 20, 1953, "Spy Case a Story of Legal Battles" (Kaufman quote); Radosh and Milton, *Rosenberg File*, 381–82 (quotes about Edelman), 392–95, 400; Ladd to Director, June 18, 1953, FBI 65-58236-1901 (Edelman "reportedly unemployed ... expelled from the CP in 1947 for disagreeing with the National leadership of the Party ... extremely critical of the handling of the Rosenberg defense"); Parrish, "Cold War Justice," 832. "Next friend" in American and English law refers to an individual who represents in court a person not competent or otherwise unable to defend himself—for example, a parent on behalf of a minor child or "friends of prisoners who may not be able to reach a court." Douglas, *The Court Years*, 79. The Rosenbergs' lawyers wired Kaufman requesting that he give no consideration to Farmer's arguments (Radosh and Milton, *Rosenberg File*, 394). Farmer reportedly "gave up a lucrative law practice" in Nashville and "has devoted virtually all his time" to promoting world government. *Wash. Times-Herald*, June 18, 1953, clipping in Box 183, Folder 8, Jackson Papers; Radosh and Milton, *Rosenberg File*, 383.

60. Radosh and Milton, *Rosenberg File*, 400–401; *Rosenberg*, 346 U.S. 273, 314–17 (appendix to Douglas, J., dissenting); Espionage Act of 1917, 40 Stat. 217, 218 (June 15, 1917); Atomic Energy Act of 1946, 60 Stat. 755, 766–67 (August 1, 1946) (quote); *NY Times*, June 17, 1953, "Ruling By Douglas in Rosenberg Case Delayed to Today."

61. *Id.*; FF June 19 Addendum, 4–6 (first two quotes); Radosh and Milton, *Rosenberg File*, 401; Belmont to Ladd, June 17, 1953, FBI 65-58236-1823 (FBI quotes); Parrish, "Cold War Justice," 834–35. The FBI obtained its information third-hand, a Saypol assistant told Judge Kaufman who told the Bureau. FBI 65-58236-1823; Parrish, "Cold War Justice," 835n83. The FBI's report states that Vinson and Brownell met at 11:00 P.M. on June 16; but Vinson's log (kept by a secretary) states the meeting was held from 12:25 P.M. to 2:10 P.M. on June 17. Box 299, Chief Justice's Log May—September 1953, Vinson Papers.

62. *Rosenberg*, 346 U.S. at 313–21 (appendix to opinion of Douglas, J., dissenting) (quotes, 321); FF June 19 Addendum, 6; *NY Times*, June 18, 1953, "Rosenbergs Gain a

Stay." Circuit Judge Jerome Frank, who sat on the court-of-appeals panel in *Rosenberg*, later told Douglas that if the Atomic Energy Act issue had been presented, "there was no doubt that the Court of Appeals would have held that the imposition of the death sentence was improper." Douglas, *The Court Years*, 79.

63. Application to Convene Court in Special Term, June 17, 1953, 1 (quote), Box 234, Rosenberg stay/official papers file, Douglas Papers; Chief Justice's announcement, June 17, 1953, 6:00 p.m. (quotes), Box 284, Rosenberg file, Vinson Papers; *NY Times*, June 18, 1953, "Rosenbergs Gain a Stay"; Simon, *Independent Journey*, 307; Douglas, *The Court Years*, 81. While Vinson "had no authority to convene a Special Term" himself, only Black objected. *Id.*

64. *NY Times*, June 19, 1953, "Court Hears Spy Debate" (quote); Parrish, "Cold War Justice," 82 *Am. Hist. Rev.* 835; Simon, *Independent Journey*, 309. Douglas's "impression was that Bloch never raised the [Atomic Energy Act] point because the Communist consensus of that day was that it was best for the cause that the Rosenbergs pay the extreme price." Douglas, *The Court Years*, 79; see Cohen, "Douglas and the *Rosenberg* Case," 211, 245n180 (1985).

65. St. Clair and Gugin, *Chief Justice Fred M. Vinson*, 251 (quoting Vinson law clerk William Oliver); Dickson, *Supreme Court in Conference*, 608, and Clark notes, Box A26, Folder 9, Clark Papers (Black quote; orig. emphasis); FF June 19 Addendum, 6 (final quotes); Parrish, "Cold War Justice," 835–36. Burton's comment referred to a proposal that the Court shorten the stay and receive briefs and argument within three weeks. *Id.*, 836. Upholding the stay, Douglas wrote later, meant "only that the District Court would consider the question and rule on it, before fall the Court of Appeals could pass on it, and it would then be ripe for decision by us in October." Douglas, *The Court Years*, 81.

66. *NY Times*, June 20, 1953, "Six Justices Agree"; *Rosenberg*, 346 U.S. 273, 288–89 (per curiam) (quotes); *id.*, 289–93 (Jackson, J., concurring); *id.*, 293–96 (Clark, J., concurring). Black had argued vainly in conference that "[i]t is terrible to take this matter up without more information." Dickson ed., *Supreme Court in Conference*, 608.

67. *Rosenberg*, 346 U.S. at 302–3 (Frankfurter mem.); *id.*, 310–13 (Douglas, J., dissenting) (quotes); *id.*, 296–301 (Black, J., dissenting) (quote); *NY Times*, July 17, 1953, "Vinson Defends Rosenberg Order by Douglas and Action Vacating It." The Black and Douglas opinions "were read from the bench" (*id.*).

68. *NY Times*, June 19, 1953, "Court Hears Spy Debate" (third quote), and "Many Abroad Ask Mercy for Spies"; June 20, 1953, "Six Justices Agree" (Eisenhower quote), "Pair Silent to End," and "Spy Case A Story of Legal Battles"; Radosh and Milton, *Rosenberg File*, 413, 416–17 (first and second quotes); Director to Attorney General, June 16, 1953, FBI 65-58236-1782.

69. *Rosenberg*, 346 U.S. at 301–10 (Frankfurter, J., dissenting) (quotes, 302, 310); *id.*, 277–88 (opinion of the Court) (quotes, 277, 287). Vinson defended Douglas's action, stating that he "did not act to grant some form of amnesty or last-minute reprieve . . . he simply acted to protect jurisdiction over the case, to maintain the status quo until a conclusive answer could be given" (*id.*, 286). *NY Times*, July 17, 1953, "Vinson Defends Rosenberg Order by Douglas and Action Vacating It."

70. A. Krock, *NY Times*, June 21, 1953, "Case of the Rosenbergs Will Long Be Debated"

(quote); 99 *Cong. Rec.* 6888 (June 19, 1953) (Chelf quote). In Lafayette Park, across the street from the White House, a crowd estimated at seven thousand gathered "to shout and cheer approval of the execution." *Wash. Times-Herald*, June 20, 1953, clipping in Box 183, Folder 8, Jackson Papers.

71. *NY Times*, June 18, 1953, "Rosenbergs Gain a Stay" (Reed quote); June 19, 1953, "5 To Study Impeachment," and A. Krock, "Very Much Like the Queen in Wonderland" (first quotes); June 30, 1953, "Justice Douglas Accused in House"; July 1, 1953, "House Move to Impeach Douglas Bogs Down"; and July 8, 1953, "Move to Impeach Douglas Quashed"; *Louisville Courier-Journal*, June 18, 1953 (AP dispatch), "Judge Halts Rosenbergs Execution" (second sentence quote); Douglas, *The Court Years*, 85–86 (final quotes); H. Res. 290, 83rd Cong., 1st Sess. (1953) (impeachment res.).

72. Radosh and Milton, *Rosenberg File*, 451 (first quote); Frankfurter to Harlan, October 23, 1956, Box 532, Frankfurter 1956 file, John M. Harlan Papers, Seeley G. Mudd Manuscript Library, Princeton, N.J. ("Harlan Papers") (quote); Douglas, *The Court Years*, 83 (quote); Cohen, "Douglas and the *Rosenberg* Case," 214 (observer quote). See Wiecek, *Birth of the Modern Constitution*, 602–3 ("Seldom in its two centuries' experience has the Court so bungled a series of appeals and done such violence to elementary standards of fairness and deliberative judgment"); Belknap, *Vinson Court*, 101 ("[The Rosenbergs] went to their deaths without ever getting a full hearing on the merits of their case, despite the fact that at various times five different members of the Supreme Court had voted that they should have one").

Chapter 5. The Coming of the Warren Court, the *Emspak* Trilogy, and *Brown*'s Consequences

1. *NY Times*, September 9, 1953, "Chief Justice Vinson Dies of Heart Attack in Capital" (quote), "U.S. Mourns Vinson," and "Warren Advanced for Chief Justice"; St. Clair and Gugin, *Chief Justice Fred M. Vinson*, 324–26, 336–39. Frankfurter did not praise Vinson; he told Philip Elman, his former law clerk, that Vinson's death was "the first solid evidence I've ever had that there really is a God." *Id.*, 325; Norman I. Silber, *With All Deliberate Speed: The Life of Philip Elman* (Ann Arbor: University of Michigan Press, 2004), 219. "What he meant," Elman said, "was that Vinson's departure from the Court was going to remove the roadblock in the" school-desegregation cases.

2. Eisenhower, *White House Years*, 226–30 (first quote, 228); Warren, *Memoirs*, 260–61, 269–70 (second quote, 260); Newton, *Justice for All*, 2–10 (final quote, 9); Brownell, *Advising Ike*, 163–68; Schwartz, *Super Chief*, 2–7; *NY Times*, September 30, 1953, "Naming of Warren Is Possible Today," and October 1, 1953, "Eisenhower Names Warren To Be Chief Justice of U.S." Warren, a favorite-son candidate for the 1952 Republican presidential nomination, supported Eisenhower in a pivotal convention-seating contest with his main rival, Senator Robert A. Taft, and in the election directed the successful GOP campaign in California. See Brownell, *Advising Ike*, 114–18. According to Brownell, the associate justice most seriously considered for promotion to chief was Jackson, who was however not only a Democrat but also a supporter of FDR's court-packing plan. In subsequent years Eisenhower became disenchanted with Warren, reportedly calling the appointment his biggest mistake as president. Schwartz, *Super Chief*, 173–74.

3. Cray, *Chief Justice*; Newton, *Justice for All*; Warren, *Memoirs*; Schwartz, *Super Chief*, 17 (Truman quote). Hiram Johnson: Warren, *Memoirs*, 38–39, 171; Newton, *Justice for All*, 32–34; Roger K. Newman, Book Review of Powe, *Warren Court*, 18 *Const. Com.* 661 (2001) (Warren "relished telling stories about Hiram Johnson, who came as close to a political model as anybody"). Health insurance: Cray, *Chief Justice*, 161–66; Warren, *Memoirs*, 186–89; Newton, *Justice for All*, 185–92.

4. Cray, *Chief Justice*, 116–23, 157–59 (first quote [123]); John D. Weaver, *Warren: The Man, The Court, The Era* (Boston: Little, Brown, 1967), 107 (testimony quotes); Warren, *Memoirs*, 149 (quote); Schwartz, *Super Chief*, 14–17 (final quote); Newton, *Justice for All*, 123–42.

5. Schwartz, *Super Chief*, epigraph (Brennan quote), 29 (quote), 68, 204 (Stewart quote); Cray, *Chief Justice*, 255 (Warren quote); Anthony Lewis, "Earl Warren," Friedman and Israel, eds., *Justices*, 2721, 2726 (quote). See Schwartz, *Super Chief*, 134 (quoting Stewart: "[I]f the Chief Justice can see some issue that involves widows or orphans or the underprivileged . . . he's going to come down on that side").

6. G. Edward White, *Earl Warren: A Public Life* (New York: Oxford University Press, 1982), 114 (quote); Belknap, *Supreme Court under Earl Warren*, 57 (quote). See Edward R. Long, "Earl Warren and the Politics of Anti-Communism," 51 *Pacific Hist. Rev.* 51 (1982).

7. *Brown v. Board of Education*, 347 U.S. 483 (1954) (*Brown I*); *Brown v. Board of Education*, 349 U.S. 294 (1955) (*Brown II*). NAACP cases: for example, *NAACP v. State of Alabama*, 357 U.S. 449 (1958); *Shelton v. Tucker*, 364 U.S. 479 (1960). See Walter F. Murphy, "The South Counterattacks: The Anti-NAACP Laws," 12 *Western Pol. Quar.* 371 (1959); Michael J. Klarman, *From Jim Crow to Civil Rights: The Supreme Court and the Struggle for Racial Equality* (New York: Oxford University Press, 2004), 335 ("without an active NAACP to bring enforcement actions, *Brown* would have been doomed to irrelevance").

8. *Barsky v. Board of Regents*, 347 U.S. 442 (1954). The Court denied review of Barsky's contempt-of-Congress conviction. *Barsky v. United States*, 334 U.S. 843 (1948), 339 U.S. 971 (1950). In Spain, Barsky "headed seven front line, evacuation and base hospitals"; Ernest Hemingway, an observer of the war, termed him "a saint." Deery, "'A Blot upon Liberty,'" 171.

9. *Barsky*, 347 U.S. at 443–56 (quote, 452); Conf. notes, January 8, 1954, Box 1147, Nos. 26–74 Argued Cases file, Douglas Papers (quote).

10. *Barsky*, 347 U.S. at 467–72 (Frankfurter, J., dissenting) (quotes, 469, 470); *id.*, 456–67 (Black, J., dissenting); *id.*, 472–74 (Douglas, J., dissenting) (quote, 474).

11. *Galvan*, 347 U.S. 522 (1954); *id.*, 532 (Black, J., dissenting); *NY Times*, May 25, 1954, "High Court Backs McCarran Act." *Galvan*, unlike *Harisiades*, was brought under an Internal Security Act section that dispensed with the government's need to prove in each case that the CPUSA was an organization advocating forcible overthrow.

12. *Galvan*, 347 U.S. at 523–32 (quotes, 526, 528). The Court found *Harisiades* dispositive as to the constitutionality of deporting "innocent members" (the *Harisiades* opinion is silent on the issue), stating that "the same issue was before the Court with respect to at least one of the aliens in *Harisiades*." *Id.*, 530.

13. *Id.*, 532–33 (Black, J., dissenting) (quotes, 533); *id.*, 533–34 (Douglas, J., dissenting).

14. *Sacher v. Association of the Bar of City of N.Y.*, 347 U.S. 388 (1954) (quote, 389); *id.*, 389–95 (Reed, J., dissenting) (quote, 391). Clark did not participate. The Court in another per curiam ruling upheld, over the dissent of Douglas and Black, an interstate compact regulating employment of longshoremen on the New York waterfront, which gave a Waterfront Commission discretion to refuse employment if the applicant "is a Communist or teaches the Communist creed." *Linehan v. Waterfront Commission of New York Harbor*, 347 U.S. 439 (1954); *id.*, 440 (Douglas, J., dissenting) (quote).

15. Frankfurter note on draft per curiam, circulated March 19, 1954, Box 631, Sacher file, Warren Papers.

16. Schwartz, *Super Chief*, 149–55 (quote, 149); Belknap, *Supreme Court under Earl Warren*, 20, 96; Lewis, "Earl Warren" in Friedman and Israel, eds., *Justices*, 2729 (quote); Schwartz, "Felix Frankfurter and Earl Warren." As Frankfurter's relationship with Warren deteriorated, his references to him in private correspondence, particularly with Judge Learned Hand, became increasingly derogatory. *Id.*, 128–42.

17. Conf. notes, January 16, 1954, Box 1147, Nos. 26–74 Argued Cases file, Douglas Papers (quote); Schwartz, *Super Chief*, 177, quoting Burton conf. notes; *Emspak*, 349 U.S. 190, 193 (1955) (first quote).

18. Reed draft opinion and Black to Chief Justice et al., April 23, 1954 (quote), Box 419, Emspak file, Warren Papers; Schwartz, *Super Chief*, 178; Belknap, *Supreme Court Under Earl Warren*, 59. Black made his motion for reargument with Jackson's and Frankfurter's encouragement. Frankfurter to Black, May 15, 1954, Box 320, Emspak file, Black Papers.

19. *NY Times*, January 14, 1954, "Harlan Is Named to Federal Bench"; April 2, 1954, "Justice R. H. Jackson Has a Heart Attack"; October 10, 1954, "Justice Jackson Dead at 62," "Tributes for Jackson," and "Dewey and Dulles in Line For Bench"; and November 9, 1954, "Eisenhower Names U.S. Judge Harlan to Supreme Court"; Gerhart, *America's Advocate*, 467–68.

20. Tinsley E. Yarbrough, *John Marshall Harlan: Great Dissenter of the Warren Court* (New York: Oxford University Press, 1992), 9–86; *Plessy v. Ferguson*, 163 U.S. 537, 559 (1896) (Harlan, J., dissenting) (quote).

21. Norman Dorsen, "John Marshall Harlan" in Friedman and Israel, eds., *Justices*, 2803–5 (quote); Schwartz, *Super Chief*, 176 (quotes); Yarbrough, *John Marshall Harlan*, xi–xii (Lewin quote); Stewart statement to press, December 1971, Box 586, Folder 137, Potter Stewart Papers, Sterling Memorial Library, Yale University, New Haven ("Stewart Papers") (quote).

22. Schwartz, *Super Chief*, 176 ("Harlan, like Jackson, became a firm adherent of Frankfurter's judicial restraint philosophy"); Yarbrough, *John Marshall Harlan*, xii ("mustard" quote); Lucas A. Powe, *The Warren Court and American Politics* (Cambridge: Harvard University Press, 2000), 143 ("lite" quote); Belknap, *Supreme Court under Earl Warren, 1953–1969*, 59 (quote), 97 (quote). The court-of-appeals decision was *United States v. Flynn*, 216 F. 2d 354 (2d Cir. 1954), *cert. denied*, 348 U.S. 909 (1955); *NY Times*, January 11, 1955, "High Court Bars Pleas of 13 Reds." 1957 Smith Act decision: *Yates v. United States*, 354 U.S. 298, 325 (1957) (quote; orig. emphasis). 1956 decision: *Cole v. Young*, 351 U.S. 536 (1956); Schrecker, *Many Are the Crimes*, 296–97 (quote).

23. *NY Times*, November 30, 1954, "Harlan Approval Blocked until '55"; February 25, 1955, "Harlan Hearing Held by Senators"; and March 17, 1955, "Senate Confirms Harlan

to Bench." Pat McCarran, the Judiciary Committee chairman when the Democrats last controlled the Senate, died in September 1954. *NY Times*, September 29, 1954, "Senator M'Carran Is Dead in Nevada." Eastland: see Jeff Woods, *Black Struggle, Red Scare: Segregation and Anti-Communism in the South, 1948-1968* (Baton Rouge: Louisiana State University Press, 2004), 42-47.

24. Conf. notes, April 9, 1955, Box 1156, Argued Cases Nos. 1-24 file, Douglas Papers; Schwartz, *Super Chief*, 177-79, quoting Burton's notes; Fassett, *New Deal Justice*, 590-93. Emspak and Quinn were officials of the United Electrical, Radio and Machine Workers (UE), expelled from the CIO in 1949 as Communist-dominated; UE was a prime HUAC target. See Arthur J. Goldberg, *AFL-CIO: Labor United* (New York: McGraw Hill, 1956), 178-87; Steve Rosswurm, "Introduction: An Overview and Preliminary Assessment of the CIO's Expelled Unions," in *The CIO's Left-Led Unions*, Steve Rosswurm ed., 1-17 (New Brunswick, N.J.: Rutgers University Press, 1992).

25. *Quinn v. United States*, 349 U.S. 155, 158-70 (1955) (quotes, 157-58, 163, 165, 167).

26. *Emspak v. United States*, 349 U.S. at 191-202 (quotes, 193, 195). As in *Quinn*, Emspak's conviction was reversed for the additional reason that his Fifth Amendment objection was not "specifically overrule[d]" by the Committee, nor was he "specifically" directed to answer. *Id.*, 202.

27. *Bart v. United States*, 349 U.S. 219 (1955) (quotes, 221-22). Warren received effusive praise from his colleagues. Frankfurter note on draft opinion circulated April 27, 1955 ("These three opinions are very important and make me happy"); Douglas to Warren, April 25, 1955 ("I think your opinion in *Quinn* is magnificent, one of the best in all the annals of the Court"); Burton to Warren, April 28, 1955 ("an excellent way to handle the cases"); and Black to Warren, May 4, 1955 ("very fine opinions"), Box 574, Quinn file, Warren Papers.

28. *Quinn*, 349 U.S. at 171-89 (quote, 183) (Reed, J., dissenting); *id.*, 171 (Harlan, J., concurring); *Emspak*, 349 U.S. at 203-18 (Harlan, J., dissenting); *Bart*, 349 U.S. at 223-27 (Reed, J., dissenting); *id.*, 227-31 (Harlan, J., dissenting). Harlan stated in *Quinn* that he "agree[d] with the result" but dissented from the Court's "second ground."

29. *NY Times*, May 24, 1955, "High Court Clears Three of Red Inquiry Contempt" (first quote), and May 29, 1955, "Fifth Amendment Ruling Debated" (second quote); *Wash. Evening Star*, May 25, 1955, editorial, "Balky Witnesses" (quote), clipping in Box 160, Reed Papers.

30. *Peters v. Hobby*, 349 U.S. 331 (1955). *Bailey*: chap. 3, herewith.

31. 349 U.S. at 333-36.

32. *Id.*, 336-37. See U.S. Const., 6th Amend. ("In all criminal prosecutions, the accused shall enjoy the right . . . to be confronted with the witnesses against him.)

33. *NY Times*, April 20, 1955, "Federal Loyalty Program Challenged in High Court"; Schwartz, *Super Chief*, 153 (quote). Soboloff: *NY Times*, March 6, 1955, "New Controversy Shaping Up on Internal Security Question" ("It was reliably reported that . . . Mr. Sobeloff . . . was in sharp disagreement with the Government's contention that the Peters case did not involve a violation of Constitutional rights"); March 5, 1955, ("Loyalty Program's Legality Divides Justice Department"; and March 16, 1955, "U.S. Solicitor Sees Flaws in the Law."

34. Conf. notes, April 23, 1955, Box 1156, Argued Cases Nos. 350–399 file, Douglas Papers (quotes).

35. *Peters*, 349 U.S. at 333–49 (quotes, 338, 345). Minton, who voted for the government at the conference, switched sides. Black joined the Court's opinion but said he would still "prefer to decide this case on the constitutional questions." *Id.*, 349–50 (Black, J., concurring). Douglas concurred separately and reached the constitutional issue, emphasizing the unreliability of "faceless informers." *Id.*, 350–52.

36. *Peters*, 349 U.S. at 353–57 (Reed, J., dissenting).

37. The Eisenhower order, Exec. Order 10450, 18 Fed. Reg. 2489 (April 27, 1953), which became effective in May 1953, authorized the Loyalty Review Board to determine pending appeals. *Id.*, § 11; *Peters*, 349 U.S. at 346–47 and n22. Douglas to Black, undated, Box 323, Peters file, Black Papers (quote); Schwartz, *Super Chief*, 155.

38. A. Krock, *NY Times*, June 7, 1955, "Plaintiff Won on Grounds He Never Cited" (quote).

39. *In re Disbarment of Isserman*, 348 U.S. 1 (1954); *NY Times*, October 15, 1954, "High Court Upsets Its Ban on Lawyer"; per curiam author: draft order, recirculated October 8, 1954, and Black mem. to justices, Box 315, Isserman file, Black Papers. Warren and Clark did not participate. Jackson evidently did participate, although the Court's order was not released until October 14, 1954, five days after his death (see Fassett, *New Deal Justice*, 587). Reinstatements: *In re Isserman*, 35 N. J. 198, (1961); *Association of the Bar of the City of New York v. Isserman*, 271 F. 2d 784 (2d Cir. 1959).

40. *In the Matter of Application of Ben G. Levy*, 348 U.S. 978 (1955) (quote), *rev'g* 214 F. 2d 331, 332 (5th Cir. 1954) (first quote); Warren handwritten draft order, April 4, 1955, Box 631, Levy file, Warren Papers; *Houston Chronicle*, April 11, 2004, "Ben Levy, Founder of ACLU Here Made His Mark." Levy had also admitted to "efforts on behalf of the defendants in the Rosenberg case." 214 F.2d at 333.

41. Richard Kluger, *Simple Justice: The History of* Brown v. Board of Education *and Black America's Struggle for Equality* (New York: Vintage, 2004), 287–542, 590–619, 700 (quote); Schwartz, *Super Chief*, 72–82 (Frankfurter quote, 72); *Brown*, 345 U.S. 972 (1953) (reargument order).

42. Kluger, *Simple Justice*, 681–702 (Warren-to-Reed quote, 702); Schwartz, *Super Chief*, 82–101 (first quotes, 87).

43. *Brown I*, 347 U.S. at 486–96 (quotes); *Plessy*, 163 U.S. at 551 (quotes); Schwartz, *Super Chief*, 106–8. The Court decided in a separate opinion the case from the District of Columbia, which is not subject to the Equal Protection Clause, holding that public-school segregation was also violative of the Fifth Amendment's Due Process Clause. *Bolling v. Sharpe*, 347 U.S. 497 (1954) ("it would be unthinkable that the same Constitution would impose a lesser duty on the Federal Government" [*id.*, 500]). Gunnar Myrdal: *An American Dilemma: The Negro Problem and American Democracy* (New York: Harper, 1944).

44. *Brown I*, 347 U.S. at 495–96; Kluger, *Simple Justice*, 739–47; Schwartz, *Super Chief*, 111–20.

45. *Brown II*, 349 U.S. at 298–301; Kluger, *Simple Justice*, 743, 744, 747–49; Schwartz, *Super Chief*, 120–21. The cases were class actions, and Warren initially urged that relief not be limited to the named plaintiffs.

46. *NY Times*, May 18, 1954, "Editorial Excerpts from the Nation's Press on Segregation Ruling" (*Evening Star* quote) and ("Georgia") (quote); May 24, 1954, "Talmadge Defies High Court Ruling" (quote); and July 18, 1954, "Talmadge Clash on Bias Indicated." See Numan V. Bartley, *The Rise of Massive Resistance: Race and Politics in the South During the 1950s* (Baton Rouge: Louisiana State University Press, 1969), 67–81.

47. 100 *Cong. Rec.* 7251–57 (May 27, 1954) (quotes); *NY Times*, May 28, 1954, "Eastland Scores Supreme Court." See Woods, *Black Struggle, Red Scare*, 54–56; Bartley, *Rise of Massive Resistance*, 117–20 ("Within three months Eastland's office had mailed out more than 300,000 copies of the speech. . . . It was the most important speech of the resistance"); George Lewis, *The White South and the Red Menace: Segregationists, Anticommunism, and Massive Resistance, 1945–1965* (Gainesville: University Press of Florida, 2004), 51–66. The Southern Conference for Human Welfare, created in 1938 by "[m]iddle-class white New Dealers and pre-war liberal and leftist supporters of the united front against fascism," was a longstanding HUAC target. Woods, *Black Struggle, Red Scare*, 29–31. Hiss witnesses: see chap. 1, herewith.

48. 100 *Cong. Rec.* 11522–27 (July 23, 1954) (quotes); 101 *Cong. Rec.* 6963–64 (May 25, 1955) introducing S. Res. 104, 84th Cong., 1st Sess. (final quote); *NY Times*, May 26, 1955, "Inquiry on Court Asked." Eastland was also chairman of the Judiciary Committee's Internal Security Subcommittee (SISS). Institute of Pacific Relations was the subject of a prolonged investigation by SISS, under Pat McCarran's direction, in 1951–52. See Hearings, Institute of Pacific Relations, Before the Senate Subcommittee to Investigate the Administration of the Internal Security Act, 82nd Cong., 1st & 2nd Sess. (1951–52).

49. Lewis, *White South*, 53. See Woods, *Black Struggle, Red Scare*, 48 ("Certain that red-baiting was an answer to the Supreme Court's decision and the proper foundation for massive resistance, southern segregationists redoubled their search for evidence that the civil rights movement was closely allied with the Communist Party and its goals").

50. Griffith, *Politics of Fear*, 291 (quote). The legislation included the Communist Control Act of 1954, the Immunity Act of 1954, and a law stripping U.S. citizenship from individuals convicted of Smith Act violations (Pub. L. 772, 68 Stat. 1146 [September 3, 1954]). See *NY Times*, April 10, 1954, "Brownell Seeks New Laws to End Communist Party"; August 25, 1954, "Text of Eisenhower Statement on Red Control Bill"; and September 5, 1954, "Eisenhower Signs Last Bill on Reds" (citizenship-stripping bill "the last of eight 1954 enactments approved by President Eisenhower to deal with the Communist menace"). Flanders's resolution is quoted at Oshinsky, *A Conspiracy So Immense*, 474; *id.*, 482 ("transgressing" quote), 492 (Lehman quote). See Chap. 1, herewith.

51. Oshinsky, *A Conspiracy So Immense*, 482–83 (Nixon quote); Reeves, *Life and Times of Joe McCarthy*, 654.

52. Pub. L. 637, 68 Stat. 775 (August 24, 1954) (quotes, 776); 100 *Cong. Rec.* 14208–36 (August 12, 1954) (Humphrey quotes, 14210); Griffith, *Politics of Fear*, 292–94; William K. Klingaman, *Encyclopedia of the McCarthy Era* (New York: Facts on File, 1996), 82–83; *NY Times*, August 13, 1954, "Senate, By 85–0, Votes to Outlaw Communist Party." Humphrey's proposal was offered as a substitute for GOP Senator John Marshall Butler's bill to create a new category of "Communist-infiltrated" organizations under the Internal Security Act (aimed at left-wing labor unions); after Butler's provisions

were added back, the substitute was adopted without a dissenting vote. *100 Cong. Rec.* 14234. Although Humphrey's proposal was opposed by Hoover and the administration, Eisenhower signed the bill into law. *NY Times*, August 14, 1954, "Eisenhower Aides Try to Block Bill Outlawing Reds," and August 25, 1954, "Text of Eisenhower Statement on Red Control Bill."

53. *NY Times*, November 5, 1954, "Democrats Offer Harmony in Rule of 84th Congress" and November 4, 1954, "The Congressional Elections"; Oshinsky, *A Conspiracy So Immense*, 483; Griffith, *Politics of Fear*, 305–6; Rusk, *Statistical History*, 216, 377.

54. *NY Times*, January 16, 1955, "'Risk' Ouster Criticized," and January 25, 1955, "Mr. Cain Speaks Up"; Burton to Frankfurter, February 13, 1955, Frankfurter Papers, Part 2, microfilm reel 1 (quote). Frankfurter in March sent another Cain speech to Warren. Frankfurter to Warren undated, Box 353, Frankfurter 1955 file, Warren Papers. See *Jay v. Boyd*, 351 U.S. 345, 376 (1956) (Douglas, J., dissenting) (quoting still another Cain speech).

Chapter 6. *Nelson*, *Cole v. Young*, and the Beginning of the Campaign against the Court

1. *Cammer v. United States*, 350 U.S. 399 (1956) (contempt); *Ullmann v. United States*, 350 U.S. 422 (1956) (same); *Jay v. Boyd*, 351 U.S. 345 (1956) (deportation); *United States v. Zucca*, 351 U.S. 91 (1956) (denaturalization); *Communist Party v. Subversive Activities Control Board*, 351 U.S. 115 (1956) (SACB registration order); *Cole v. Young*, 351 U.S. 536 (1956) (federal loyalty); *Slochower v. Board of Higher Education*, 350 U.S. 551 (1956) (state loyalty); *Black v. Cutter Laboratories*, 351 U.S. 292 (1956) (private-employer firing); *Pennsylvania v. Nelson*, 350 U.S. 497 (1956) (state sedition). The Court denied review in two cases involving the Gwinn Amendment, a 1952 federal statute (66 Stat. 403) prohibiting the occupancy of federally financed public housing by members of "subversive" organizations on the attorney general's list; in each case, a state court had stopped a local housing authority from evicting tenants. *Housing Authority v. Lawson*, 350 U.S. 882 (1955); *Housing Authority v. Cordova*, 350 U.S. 969 (1956).

2. Murphy, *Congress and the Court*, 86–92 (quotes, 86, 91). HR 3 was introduced at the start of the 84th Congress. 101 *Cong. Rec.* 31 (January 5, 1955).

3. *Ullmann*, 350 U.S. 422 (quotes from statute, 424); Elizabeth Terrill Bentley 112-page statement to FBI, November 30, 1945, 19–25; Haynes and Klehr, *Venona*, 129–31, 136–37. Immunity Act: 68 Stat. 745 (August 20, 1954). 1896 decision: *Brown v. Walker*, 161 U.S. 591 (1896). Ullmann received a six-month prison sentence.

4. *Ullmann*, 350 U.S. at 423–39 (quotes, 431, 439).

5. *Id.*, 440–55 (Douglas, J., dissenting) (quotes, 440–41, 449, 452). See Robert G. McCloskey, "The Supreme Court Finds a Role: Civil Liberties in the 1955 Term," 42 *Virginia L. Rev.* 735, 748 (1956) ("[I]t would be idle to pretend that the witness under this law has as much immunity as he might enjoy if he kept silent").

6. *Cammer*, 350 U.S. 399 (quote, 401), rev'g 223 F. 2d 322 (D.C.Cir. 1955) and 122 F. Supp. 388 (D.D.C. 1954). 1950 case: see chap. 2, herewith. Gold's conviction for filing a false Taft-Hartley affidavit was reviewed by the Court in 1957; see chap. 7, herewith.

7. *Cammer*, 350 U.S. 399–408 (quotes, 400, 405); 18 U.S.C. § 401(2). Reed concurred only in the judgment. Harlan did not participate.

8. Immigration and Nationality Act of 1952, § 244(a)(5), 66 Stat. 215 (June 27, 1952) (quote); *Jay*, 351 U.S. 345 (quotes, 349–50).

9. *Id.*, 347–61 (quotes, 347–48, 357–58); 8 CFR, Rev. 1952, § 244.3.

10. *Jay*, 351 U.S. at 361–62 (Warren, C.J., dissenting) (quotes); *id.*, 362–70 (Black, J., dissenting) (quote, 368); *id.*, 370–74 (Frankfurter, J., dissenting); *id.*, 374–76 (Douglas, J., dissenting). Frankfurter argued that the discretion given the attorney general could not be delegated to subordinate officials.

11. *Zucca*, 351 U.S. 91; Immigration and Nationality Act of 1952, § 340(a), 66 Stat. 260 (June 27, 1952), as amended, 68 Stat. 1232 (September 3, 1954) ("It shall be the duty of the United States district attorneys . . . *upon affidavit showing good cause therefore*, to institute proceedings . . . for the purpose of revoking and setting aside the order admitting such person to citizenship") (emphasis added).

12. *Zucca*, 351 U.S. 91–100 (quotes, 95, 99). Harlan did not participate.

13. *Id.*, 100–104 (Clark, J., dissenting) (quotes, 103). While the government was obligated to prove its case at trial through witnesses, Clark argued that allowing the defendant advance discovery of a witness's testimony "clearly frustrates an important government program" (*id.*, 104).

14. *Hyun v. Landon*, 350 U.S. 590 (1956), *aff'g by an equally divided court*, 219 F. 2d 404 (9th Cir. 1955) (quotes, 406). Clark did not participate. Douglas's conference notes show that Warren, Black, Frankfurter and Douglas voted to reverse. Frankfurter stated it was "unfair to make [Hyun] pay [the] fare of guards to go to Hawaii"; Warren likewise found it "a very questionable practice" to require Hyun to "pay the transportation of guards." Conf. notes, May 9, 1956, Box 1164, Argued Cases Nos. 200–249 file, Douglas Papers. Another case involving deportation, decided by per curiam order, challenged "orders of supervision" governing the conduct of 14 "Communist" aliens (three of them Smith Act defendants) released on "supervised parole" pending deportation. A lower court dismissed the aliens' suit for declaratory relief finding "no justiciable controversy between the parties"; but the Court, after argument, unanimously reversed and remanded "for consideration on the merits." *Nukk v. Shaughnessy*, 350 U.S. 869 (1955), *rev'g* 125 F. Supp. 498 (S.D.N.Y. 1954) (three-judge district court).

15. *Communist Party*, 351 U.S. 115; Dickson, ed., *The Supreme Court in Conference*, 288 (Black quote). Black's reference was to the Third Amendment restricting the quartering of soldiers in private homes.

16. *Id.*, 288–90 (quotes); Conf. notes, November 18, 1955, Box 1164, Argued Cases Nos. 25–49 file, Douglas Papers. Earlier registration schemes: *United States v. Harriss*, 347 U.S. 612 (1954) (lobbyists); *Bryant v. Zimmerman*, 278 U.S. 63 (1928) (Ku Klux Klan).

17. Dickson, ed., *The Supreme Court in Conference*, 290–94 (Warren, Clark quotes); *Communist* Party, 351 U.S. 119–21 (quote, 120). Matusow: Lichtman and Cohen, *Deadly Farce*, 112–45. All three witnesses, whom the *Times* termed "professional informers," were part of the Justice Department's stable of informer-witnesses. See sources cited at chap. 4, herewith; *NY Times*, May 1, 1956, "High Court Sees Taint in Red Case."

18. Frankfurter "Dear Brethren" letter, April 2, 1956 (quote), Clark mem., April 4, 1956 (quote), and Clark mem., April 17, 1956, 3–4, (quote), Box A43, Folder 4, Clark Papers;

Frankfurter mem., April 4, 1956, Box 428, CPUSA v. SACB file, Warren Papers. See Belknap, *The Supreme Court under Earl Warren*, 60–61; Schwartz, *Super Chief*, 185–88.

19. *Communist Party*, 351 U.S. at 116–25 (quotes, 122–25).

20. *Id.*, 125–30 (Clark, J., dissenting) (quote, 128).

21. *Washington Post*, May 2, 1956, "'Taint' Ruling Halts 'Subversives' Cases" (quotes): 102 Cong. Rec. 7341 (May 2, 1956) (Andrews quotes).

22. *Black*, 351 U.S. 292; *Black*, 43 Cal.2d 788 (1955); *LA Times*, August 23, 2009, "Doris Brin Walker Dies at 90; Radical Lawyer Helped Acquit Angela Davis of Murder." Walker concealed her educational background when she was hired at Cutter and in subsequent years resumed law practice.

23. *Black*, 351 U.S. at 296–97; 43 Cal.2d at 806, 809 (quotes).

24. 351 U.S. at 299 (quote); *id.*, 300–304 (Douglas, J., dissenting). Douglas argued that judicial confirmation of the employer's action provided the government-action component.

25. *Slochower*, 350 U.S. 551 (quotes, 555).

26. *Id.*, 552–59 (quotes, 557, 558). The Court found that the college's faculty board "had possessed the pertinent information [about his 1940–1941 affiliations] for 12 years." *Id.*, 558. See Schwartz, *Super Chief*, 183–85. *Wieman*: see chap. 4, herewith. *Garner*: see chap. 3, herewith.

27. *Slochower*, 350 U.S. at 559–64 (Reed, J., dissenting) (quotes, 561, 562); *id.*, 565–67 (Harlan, J., dissenting).

28. *NY Times*, April 10, 1956, "Slochower to Get and Lose Old Job," "High Court Bars Ouster for Using 5th Amendment"; Biographical Note, The Papers of Harry Slochower, Brooklyn College Archives and Special Collections (2003) (quote).

29. *Cole*, 351 U.S. 536 (quotes, 538n1, 540); *NY Times*, June 12, 1956, "High Court Limits Ouster of 'Risks' to Sensitive Jobs"; Schrecker, *Many Are the Crimes*, 296; Veterans' Preference Act, § 14, 58 Stat. 390 (June 27, 1944); Act of August 26, 1950, §§ 1, 3, 64 Stat. 476.

30. *Id.*, (quote); *Cole*, 351 U.S. at 538n1, 544; Exec. Order 10450, 18 Fed. Reg. 2489, April 27, 1953, § 1.

31. *Cole*, 351 U.S. at 538–65 (quotes, 543, 544). The "general personnel laws" authorized "dismissals for 'such cause as will promote the efficiency of the service.'" *Id.*, 543.

32. *Id.*, 565–69 (Clark, J., dissenting) (quotes, 566, 569).

33. *NY Times*, June 14, 1956, "U.S. Starts Curbs on 'Risk' Program," and June 17, 1956, A. Lewis, "Security Program Setup Is Due for Some Changes" (quote); *Chicago Tribune*, June 16, 1956, "U.S. Restores Jobs to 17 Fired as Security Risks." See *NY Times*, June 16, 1956, "Sense on Security."

34. Mundt: 102 Cong. Rec. 10173–77 (June 13, 1956) (quote); S. 4047, 84th Cong., 2d Sess. McCarthy: 102 Cong. Rec. 10151–52 (June 13, 1956), 10319–21 (June 14, 1956); S. 4052, 84th Cong., 2d Sess. Eastland: *NY Times*, June 28, 1956, "2 Groups Support Court on Loyalty"; S. 4050, 84th Cong., 2d Sess. Walter's bill: H.R. 11721; *NY Times*, July 7, 1956, "Brownell Moves to Nullify Curb on 'Risk' Ousters."

35. *Nelson*, 350 U.S. 497; Daniel J. Leab, *I Was a Communist for the FBI: The Unhappy Life and Times of Matt Cvetic* (University Park: Pennsylvania State University

Press, 2000), 66–68, 75–85 (quotes, 67–68, 82); Steve Nelson, James R. Barrett, and Rob Ruck, *Steve Nelson, American Radical* (Pittsburgh: University of Pittsburgh Press, 1981), 320–40; Steve Nelson, *The 13th Juror: The Inside Story of My Trial* (New York: Masses and Mainstream, 1955), 146–86; Michael A. Musmanno, *Across the Street from the Courthouse* (Philadelphia: Dorrence, 1954), 100–102, 106, 186–99 (first quote, 101); *NY Times*, September 1, 1950, "Pennsylvania Jails Trio As Communists"; February 1, 1952, "Steve Nelson Guilty On 12 Sedition Counts"; and July 11, 1952, "Pennsylvania Red Gets 20-Year Term." Prior to and during World War II, according to Haynes and Klehr, Nelson was both "an open CPUSA official and a West Coast leader of its covert apparatus" linked to Soviet espionage. *Venona*, 229–31, 325–26; see Haynes, Klehr, and Vassiliev, *Spies*, 84, 121–22; Leab, *I Was a Communist for the FBI*, 84–85, 154n33. Cvetic in 1951 "began to show signs of that increasing exaggeration that would undermine his credibility and would cause him grief with the FBI." *Id.*, 97.

36. *Nelson*, 350 U.S. at 499, 510 (quoting statute); 377 Pa. 58, 70 (1954) (final quote). Sedition under the act extended to a range of other actions, including incitement to acts "with a view to bringing the [government] into hatred or contempt." See Nelson, Barrett, and Ruck, *Steve Nelson*, 320 ("the act had been a dead letter since the 1926 prosecution of a handful of workers from Jones & Laughlin's Aliquippa works").

37. *Nelson*, 350 U.S. at 498–512 (quotes, 502, 504, 509). Smith Act prosecution: *NY Times*, August 21, 1953, "Five Convicted as Reds in Long Trial at Pittsburgh"; *Mesarosh v. United States*, 350 U.S. 922 (1955) (granting review in Smith Act case). At their November 18, 1955, conference, the justices had split 4–4, with Clark voting with the three dissenters to uphold Nelson's conviction and Harlan "not ready to vote." Conf. notes, Box 1164, Argued Cases Nos. 1–24 file, Douglas Papers; Schwartz, *Super Chief*, 182–83. Afterward, Clark switched, and Harlan joined the majority.

38. *Nelson*, 350 U.S. at 512–20 (Reed, J., dissenting) (DOJ quote, 518); *NY Times*, November 16, 1955, "Sedition Power of States Tested" (Smith quote).

39. *NY Times*, April 27, 1956, "Appeal Sedition Ruling"; H. Alexander, *Boston Herald*, May 20, 1956, "Personalities Explain Why Revolt Rises against Bench" (quote), and *Houston Chronicle*, May 16, 1956, "Move to Curb Supreme Court Spreads in Nation, Congress" (quote); *Nelson*, 351 U.S. 934 (1956) (denying rehearing).

40. A. Krock, *NY Times*, May 20, 1956, "Supreme Court Faces New Attack on Power" (quote), and May 14, 1956, "High Court Faces Congress Attack" (quote).

41. 102 *Cong. Rec.* 6063–64 (April 11, 1956) (quotes); S. 3603 (McCarthy), S. 3617 (Bridges), 84th Cong., 2d Sess. McCarthy in his speech did not overlook *Slochower*, stating that the decision "handed another solid victory to the Communist Party" and that "a majority of the Justices have fallen hook, line, and sinker for the leftwing view of what taking the fifth amendment implies." 102 *Cong. Rec.* 6064.

42. 102 *Cong. Rec.* 6383–86 (April 16, 1956) (quotes). Smith, with his employer-supporters in mind, cautioned "it is very important that we have a general law"—that is, a law that would overturn the Court's labor-law preemption decisions, not one limited to sedition. During the term, the Court handed down another decision holding state labor law "superseded" by federal law, this one nullifying a "right to work" provision (in other words, banning union-shop agreements) in Nebraska's constitution. *Railway*

Employes' [sic] Department v. Hanson, 351 U.S. 225, 232 (1956). It also held that federal labor law precluded a state-court injunction against a union's peaceful picketing, notwithstanding that the union (John L. Lewis's United Mine Workers) had not filed Taft-Hartley non-Communist affidavits. *United Mine Workers v. Arkansas Oak Flooring Co.*, 351 U.S. 62 (1956). By May, seven bills had been introduced to strip the Court of jurisdiction over suits challenging the validity of state laws "relating to the establishment, maintenance or operation of public schools." *NY Times*, May 14, 1956, "High Court Faces Congress Attack."

43. 102 *Cong. Rec.* 7903–4, 7988–89 (quotes) (May 10, 1956); *Chicago Tribune*, May 13, 1956, "Legislation From the Bench"; S. 3143 (Byrd), 84th Cong., 2d Sess.

44. Murphy, *Congress and the Court*, 88–89 (quotes), 282n43, 44; *NY Times*, May 12, 1956, "Senators Attack Sedition Decision," and June 27, 1956, "Warren Assailed by Two Senators." Not only Warren but Reed, Frankfurter, Douglas, Burton, and Clark lacked prior judicial experience; Harlan had served less than a year, and Black only as a police court judge; Minton alone had substantial prior judicial experience.

45. 102 *Cong. Rec.* 7274–81 (April 30, 1956) (quotes, 7277); S. 3959 (Smathers), S. Res. 264 (Stennis), 84th Cong., 2d Sess. Smathers said his proposal "might be compared somewhat with the farm system in baseball." 102 *Cong. Rec.* 7276.

46. *NY Times*, May 19, 1956, "States See Peril in Sedition Edict," July 7, 1956, "Southerner Asks Court Restraint" (final quote), and September 1, 1956, "Bar Shuns Stand on Segregation"; Proceedings of the House of Delegates, 79th Annual Meeting, 42 *A.B.A Journal* 1051, 1053, 1066 (1956); Proceedings of the Assembly, 79th Annual Meeting, *id.*, 1041, 1043 (quote); 1955 Annual Meeting, Proceedings of the House of Delegates, 41 *A.B.A Journal* 1068, 1075 (1955).

47. James F. Byrnes, "'The Supreme Court Must Be Curbed,'" *U.S. News & World Report*, May 18, 1956, 50–58 (quotes, 56, 58). Frankfurter, in a note to Warren, wrote, "Jimmy saddens me." Frankfurter to Warren, undated, Box 353, Frankfurter October 1953–1954 file, Warren Papers. Byrnes served on the Court in 1941–42. See David Robertson, *Sly and Able: A Political Biography of James F. Byrnes* (New York: Norton, 1994), 297–312. One of the five cases decided in *Brown* involved public schools in a South Carolina county.

48. *NY Times*, June 28, 1956, "Governors Score High Court Stand" (quotes); Murphy, *Congress and the Court*, 95–96.

49. S. Rept. No. 2230, 84th Cong., 2d Sess. (June 14, 1956); H. Rept. No. 2576 (July 5, 1956), 84th Cong., 2d Sess.; Murphy, *Congress and the Court*, 92–95; *NY Times*, June 13, 1956, "Senate Group Votes Curb on U.S. Courts," and June 27, 1956, "Sedition Bill Gains"; Powe, *Warren Court*, 88. The companion bill reported by the Senate Judiciary Committee was S 3143. It also reported Bridges' sedition-only bill. S. Rept. No. 2117 (June 5, 1956), 84th Cong., 2d Sess.; *NY Times*, June 1, 1956, "Sedition Power for States Gains."

50. Murphy, *Congress and the Court*, 174–75; *NY Times*, June 28, 1956, "2 Groups Support Court on Loyalty"; July 7, 1956, ("Brownell Moves to Nullify Curb on 'Risk' Ousters"; July 8, 1956, "Risks and Rights"; and July 28, 1956, "Congress Quits after Approving Foreign Aid Fund."

51. Murphy, *Congress and the Court*, 96.

Chapter 7. The "Red Monday" Decisions, *Jencks*, and a Crescendo of Anti-Court Attacks

1. Robert G. McCloskey, "Useful Toil or Paths of Glory? Civil Liberties in the 1956 Term of the Supreme Court," 43 *Virginia L. Rev.* 803, 830 (1957).

2. The signed decisions were *Mesarosh v. United States*, 352 U.S. 1 (1956); *Leedom v. International Union of Mine, Mill and Smelter Workers*, 352 U.S. 145 (1956); *Amalgamated Meat Cutters v. National Labor Relations Board*, 352 U.S. 153 (1956); *United States v. Witkovich*, 353 U.S. 194 (1957); *Schware v. Board of Bar Examiners*, 353 U.S. 232 (1957); *Konigsberg v. State Bar of California*, 353 U.S. 252 (1957); *Jencks v. United States*, 353 U.S. 657 (1957); *Watkins v. United States*, 354 U.S. 178 (1957); *Sweezy v. State of New Hampshire*, 354 U.S. 234 (1957); *Yates v. United States*, 354 U.S. 298 (1957); and *Service v. Dulles*, 354 U.S. 363 (1957). The per curiam decisions were *Kremen v. United States*, 353 U.S. 346 (1957) and *Gold v. United States*, 352 U.S. 985 (1957). Powe, *Warren Court*, 93, 98 (quote). "Red Monday" was an allusion to "Black Monday," either May 27, 1935, when an earlier Court gutted the New Deal's legislative program (*id.*, 93), or (to segregationists) May 17, 1954, when *Brown I* was issued (Sabin, *In Calmer Times*, 12).

3. The state contempt case was *Sweezy*, and the bar-admission cases *Schware* and *Konigsberg*.

4. *Jencks*, 353 U.S. 657. See McCloskey, "Useful Toil or Paths of Glory?" 43 *Virginia L. Rev.* at 821–22 (*Jencks* "probably excited the greatest public furor for the smallest cause").

5. *NY Times*, September 8, 1956, "Minton Retiring from High Court"; September 30, 1956, "President Names Jersey Democrat to Supreme Court"; October 17, 1956, "Brennan Assumes High Court Duties"; February 1, 1957, "Justice Reed, 72, to Retire From the Supreme Court"; March 3, 1957, "Federal Judge in Missouri Named to Supreme Court"; and March 26, 1957, "Whittaker Takes Post as Justice of Supreme Court."

6. *NY Times*, November 8, 1956, "Democrats Retain Senate Control"; March 20, 1957, "Senate Confirms 2 for High Court"; and May 3, 1957, "M'Carthy Is Dead of Liver Ailment at the Age of 47" (quote); Rusk, *Statistical History*, 216, 377.

7. *NY Times*, September 8, 1956, "Minton Retiring from High Court; Cites Ill Health," "A Moderate at Heart" (quotes), and September 30, 1956, "President Names Jersey Democrat to Supreme Court"; Brownell, *Advising Ike*, 179–80; Eisenhower, *White House Years*, 230; Seth Stern and Stephen Wermiel, *Justice Brennan: Liberal Champion* (Boston: Houghton Mifflin Harcourt, 2010), 71–87; Stephen J. Wermiel, "The Nomination of Justice Brennan: Eisenhower's Mistake? A Look at the Historical Record," 11 *Const. Comm.* 515–37 (1995); Kim Isaac Eisler, *A Justice for All: William J. Brennan, Jr., and the Decisions That Transformed America* (New York: Simon & Schuster, 1993), 88–92; Hunter R. Clark, *Justice Brennan: The Great Conciliator* (New York: Birch Lane, 1995), 77–84. In addition to his physical ailments, Minton "[i]n his last term . . . became persuaded his mental faculties were declining." Atkinson, "Justice Sherman Minton," 69 *Nw. U. L. Rev.* at 720, 736.

8. Eisler, *A Justice for All*, 18–21, 81–82 (first quote, 21); Brownell, *Advising Ike*, 180 (quote); *NY Times*, September 30, 1956, "A Jaunty Judge"; February 27, 1957, "Brennan Favors Inquiries on Reds"; and July 22, 1990, L. Greenhouse, "An Activist's Legacy" (quote); Stern and Wermiel, *Justice Brennan*, 3–68, 114–17; Wermiel, "The Nomina-

tion of Justice Brennan," 11 *Const. Comm.* 517 (decisions "unmistakably liberal"); Stephen J. Friedman, "William J. Brennan," in Friedman and Israel, eds., *Justices* 2849, 2850–52; Clark, *Justice Brennan*, 15–19, 104–9. McCarthy, provided with copies of the two speeches, used them to harass Brennan at his confirmation hearings. Eisenhower soon regretted the appointment, as he did Warren's appointment, and famously told CBS's Fred Friendly, "I made two mistakes as President and they are both sitting on the Supreme Court." *Id.*, 79–80; Stern and Wermiel, *Justice Brennan*, 139.

9. Schwartz, *Super Chief*, 205–6 (quotes); *NY Times*, July 22, 1990, L. Greenhouse, "An Activist's Legacy"; Powe, *Warren Court*, 90 (quote); Stern and Wermiel, *Justice Brennan*, xiii, 153–54, 158–59.

10. Brownell, *Advising Ike*, 180–81 (quote); Schwartz, *Super Chief*, 215–17 (quote); *NY Times*, February 1, 1957, "Justice Reed, 72, to Retire from the Supreme Court" (Reed quote); February 7, 1957, "Eisenhower Favors a Jurist in Reed Job"; March 3, 1957, "Federal Judge in Missouri Named to Supreme Court," "Whittaker's Dream as a Youth Was to Become a Good Lawyer"; Leon Friedman, "Charles Whittaker," in Friedman and Israel, eds., *Justices*, 2893–95.

11. *Id.*, 2903 (Friedman quote); Douglas, *The Court Years*, 173 (quote); *NY Times*, March 29, 1962, "Whittaker Must Rest," and March 30, 1962, "Ailing Justice Whittaker Leaving Supreme Court"; David J. Garrow, "Mental Decrepitude on the U.S. Supreme Court: The Historical Case for a 28th Amendment," 67 *U. Chi. L. Rev.* 995, 1045–50 (2000); see chap. 11, herewith. In the 1956 term Whittaker participated only in *Service v. Dulles*, an 8-0 decision.

12. *Mesarosh*, 352 U.S. 1 (quotes, 3, 4, 7, 8). Mazzei "was a paid informer of the Government—he had been in its employ from 1942 to 1953 for the purpose of infiltrating the Communist Party and reporting the facts found." *Id.*,10.

13. *Id.*, 3–14 (quotes, 9, 14). The Court announced its ruling on October 10, minutes after hearing oral argument on the SG's motion; but the opinions were not issued until November 5. See *Mesarosh*, 352 U.S. 862; *NY Times*, October 11, 1956, "High Court Gives 5 Reds New Trial," and November 6, 1956, "Trial Taint Voids Guilt for Nelson." Brennan, who joined the Court on October 16, did not participate.

14. 352 U.S. at 15–25 (Harlan, J., dissenting); see 352 U.S. 808 (Frankfurter, J.).

15. *Yates*, 354 U.S. 298 (quote, 300). Brennan and Whittaker did not participate. The defendants received five-year prison sentences. At the October 12 conference, Reed, Burton, Minton, and Clark voted to affirm and Warren, Black, and Douglas to reverse; when Frankfurter and Harlan were not ready to vote, Warren scheduled another conference for November 2, at which the two justices voted to reverse. Dickson, ed., *Supreme Court in Conference*, 280–87; Schwartz, *Super Chief*, 232–34; Berry, *Stability, Security, and Continuity*, 203–4.

16. 354 U.S. at 304–12 (quote, 304); Belknap, *Supreme Court under Earl Warren*, 63 (quote); Kalven, *A Worthy Tradition*, 211 (quote).

17. *Yates*, 354 U.S. at 312–27 (quotes, 315–16, 318, 319). See Stone, *Perilous Times*, 414 ("Harlan interpreted the statute narrowly to avoid having to hold it unconstitutional, thus implying that a broader construction would have violated the First Amendment").

18. *Yates*, 354 U.S. at 327–34 (quotes, 327, 328, 330). See Kalven, *A Worthy Tradition*,

195 ("[T]he Court, having looked at the trial record, will announce with astonishment how little it contains"); Powe, *Warren Court*, 94 ("*Yates* was the first time the Court would evaluate the necessary proof in a Smith Act case").

19. *Yates*, 354 U.S. at 338 (Burton, J., concurring in the result), 339–44 (Black, J., concurring and dissenting) (quotes, 339), and 344–50 (Clark, J., dissenting).

20. *NY Times*, June 19, 1957, "U.S. Press Comment on Decisions in Watkins, Smith Cases," quoting newspapers. See *Gitlow v. New York*, 268 U.S. 652, 673 (1925) (Holmes, J., dissenting) ("Every idea is an incitement.... The only difference between the expression of an opinion and an incitement in the narrower sense is the speaker's enthusiasm for the result").

21. *Yates*, 354 U.S. at 325 (quote; orig. emphasis); *NY Times*, December 3, 1957, "U.S. Court Clears 9 California Reds" (quote). By per curiam order, the Court (Clark dissenting) vacated and remanded "in light of *Yates*" the Smith Act conspiracy convictions of six Michigan CPUSA officials. *Wellman v. United States*, 354 U.S. 931 (1957). Abandonment of prosecutions: Belknap, *Cold War Political Justice*, 258–61; Belknap, *Supreme Court under Earl Warren*, 64; Stone, *Perilous Times*, 415; Mollan, "Smith Act Prosecutions," 26 *Univ. of Pittsburgh L. Rev.* 729–34. The government retried only one conspiracy case after *Yates*, against a group of Colorado communists; but the conviction it obtained was reversed on *Jencks* grounds. *Bary v. United States* 292 F.2d 53, 56–58 (10th Cir. 1961). "Membership" cases: *Scales* and *Lightfoot v. United States*, 353 U.S. 979 (1957); *NY Times*, June 23, 1957, "Smith Act Convictions Will Be Hard to Obtain"; see chap. 10, herewith.

22. *Kremen*, 353 U.S. 346; *Time*, September 7, 1953, "Communists: Reds in the Sierra" (quote); *NY Times*, August 28, 1953, "2 Top Red Fugitives Captured by F.B.I. in Sierra Hide-Out" (quote). Steinberg was also charged with harboring Thompson.

23. 353 U.S. at 347 (quote), 349–59; Conf. notes, March 8, 1957, Box 1180, Kremen Conf. & Misc. Memos file, Douglas Papers (quotes); *NY Times*, May 14, 1957, "3 Win a New Trial in Harboring of Red." Whittaker did not participate.

24. Douglas draft opinion, recirculated April 18, 1957 (quotes), Box 1180, Kremen Galley Drafts file, and Frankfurter draft concurrence, recirculated April 18, 1957, first Kremen file, Douglas Papers; Harlan draft concurrence, circulated April 10, 1957, Box A55, Folder 1, Clark Papers.

25. Douglas to Harlan (quote) and Harlan to Douglas (quote), April 18, 1957, Box 1180, Kremen Galley Drafts file, Douglas Papers.

26. Harlan to Douglas, April 24, 1957 (quote) and Frankfurter to Warren, May 7, 1957, Box 1180, Kremen Conf. & Misc. Memos file, Douglas Papers; *Kremen*, 353 U.S. 346–48 (quote), 349–59 (appendix listing seized items); Frankfurter to Warren, April 19 and May 1, 1957, Pt. 2, microfilm reel 22, Frankfurter Papers. Whittaker did not participate. Frankfurter, unhappy with the compromise, wrote on a draft of the per curiam, "I shall be a good boy & a bad judge & assent to this against my intellectual guidance." Harlan draft, circulated May 10, 1957, Box 28, Kremen per curiam file, John M. Harlan Papers, Seeley G. Mudd Manuscript Library, Princeton, N.J. ("Harlan Papers").

27. 353 U.S. at 348 (Burton-Clark dissent) (quote).

28. *Watkins*, 354 U.S. 178 (quote, 200).

29. *Id.*, 182–86 (quotes). Prior to 1953 Watkins had been an official of the Farm Equip-

ment Workers International, expelled by the CIO as Communist-dominated. Goldberg, *AFL-CIO*, 181; Rosswurm, *CIO's Left-Led Unions*, 1–2.

30. 354 U.S. at 187, 195–201 (quotes, 187, 197). Burton and Whittaker did not participate.

31. *Id.*, 201–15 (quotes, 206, 208–9, 214–15). Frankfurter joined Warren's opinion but added a concurrence underscoring the narrowness of the Court's holding. *Id.*, 216–17.

32. *Id.*, 217–33 (Clark, J. dissenting) (quote, 217). A week later, the Court (again over Clark's dissent) vacated three other contempt-of-Congress convictions, remanding the cases for consideration in light of *Watkins*. *Flaxer v. United States*, 354 U.S. 929 (1957); *Sacher v. United States*, 354 U.S. 930 (1957); *Barenblatt v. United States*, 354 U.S. 930 (1957). Sacher's case returned to the Court in the 1957 term and Flaxer's and Barenblatt's cases a year after that. See chap. 8 and chap. 9, herewith.

33. *Sweezy*, 354 U.S. 234.

34. *Id.*, 235–45 (quotes, 236–37, 243, 244, 245); *NY Times*, March 2, 2004, "Paul Sweezy, 93, Marxist Publisher and Economist, Dies." Progressive Party: see chap. 1, herewith.

35. *Sweezy*, 354 U.S. at 245–55 (opinion of Warren, C.J.) (quotes, 250, 254–55).

36. *Id.*, 255–67 (Frankfurter, J., concurring) (quotes, 257, 261, 266–67).

37. *Id.*, 267–70 (Clark, J., dissenting). The state's action cannot be set aside, Clark wrote, unless "the interest in protecting [Sweezy's constitutional] rights is greater than the State's interest in uncovering subversive activities within its confines." *Id.*, 269. A week after the decision, the Court (Clark dissenting) vacated four contempt convictions arising from hearings before Ohio's "little HUAC" commission, remanding the cases for consideration in light of *Sweezy* and *Watkins*. *Morgan* and *Raley v. Ohio*, 354 U.S. 929 (1957). The cases returned in the 1958 term, see chap. 9, herewith.

38. Douglas note, June 3, 1957 (quotes), Box 1174, Argued Cases Nos. 150–199 file, Douglas Papers; Belknap, *Supreme Court under Earl Warren*, 65. Warren, Douglas added, "is pretty disturbed over Frankfurter's bad faith in the matter." Until less than two weeks before the decision was issued, Warren believed he was writing an opinion of the Court. Warren draft opin., June 5, 1957, Box 579, Sweezy file, Warren Papers.

39. *Schware*, 353 U.S. 232 (quotes, 234–35, 240). Whittaker did not participate.

40. *Id.*, 233–47 (quotes 240–41, 245–47). Frankfurter, Clark, and Harlan concurred separately. *Id.*, 247–51.

41. *Konigsberg*, 353 U.S. 252 (quotes, 259, 262). Whittaker did not participate.

42. *Id.*, 258–74 (quotes, 264–65, 267, 271). After California again rejected Konigsberg's application, the case returned to the Court in the 1960 term. See chap. 10, herewith.

43. 353 U.S. at 274–76 (Frankfurter, J., dissenting); *id.*, 276–312 (Harlan, J., dissenting) (quotes, 280, 282). Frankfurter believed the state court rejected Konigsberg's appeal for failure to comply with a local procedural rule—a view not shared by the Court (*id.*, 254–58).

44. Burton to Black, undated, Box 329, Konigsberg file I, Black Papers (orig. emphasis). See Berry, *Stability, Security, and Continuity*, 202–3.

45. *Service v. Dulles*, 354 U.S. 363; Klehr and Radosh, *Amerasia Spy Case*, 11–27.

46. *Id.*, 56–64, 109–22; see chap. 1, herewith.

47. *Service*, 354 U.S. at 365–69. Evidently because Acheson treated the Loyalty Review Board's determination as "advisory" only (*id.*, 369), the Court did not base its decision on *Peters*.

48. Id., 369–70 (quotes), 383–87. The McCarran Rider was attached to each of a series of appropriation acts between 1947 and 1953. Id., 370nn10–11. Not complied with: the department's regulations, for example, precluded dismissal unless the deputy undersecretary, acting on the departmental loyalty board's findings, recommended it—in Service's case the deputy undersecretary approved the loyalty board's decision in Service's favor. Id., 383–86.

49. Id., 373–89 (quote, 388). Clark did not participate.

50. *Witkovich*, 353 U. S, 194 (quotes 195–96) aff'g 140 F. Supp. 815, 820 (N.D. Ill. 1956); Immigration and Nationality Act of 1952, § 242(d)(3), 66 Stat. 163, 211, originally part of § 23, Internal Security Act of 1950, 64 Stat. 1010. *Carlson*: see chap. 4, herewith.

51. *Witkovich*, 353 U.S. 194–98 and n.* (quotes); *NY Times*, April 30, 1957, "Alien Is Upheld on Red Queries."

52. 353 U.S. at 199–202 (quotes, 201–2).

53. Id., 202–9 (Clark, J., dissenting) (quote, 207–8). The government told the Court that three thousand deportation cases "could be affected" by its ruling. *NY Times* April 30, 1957, "Alien Is Upheld on Red Queries."

54. *Barton v. Sentner*, 353 U.S. 963 (1957) (dissent quote) aff'g *Sentner v. Colarelli*, 145 F. Supp. 569 (E.D. Mo. 1956) (3-judge court) (order quote, 573); *NY Times*, May 21, 1957 ("Right of an Alien to Be Red Upheld"); Caute, *Great Fear*, 232, 235. Antonia's husband, William Sentner, a CPUSA official prominent in the left-wing UE, was convicted under the Smith Act in 1954. Rosemary Feurer, "William Sentner, the UE, and Civic Unionism in St. Louis," in Rosswurm, *CIO's Left-Led Unions*, 95, 117 (Antonia was "probably prosecuted under the McCarran Act because of her relationship to [her husband]").

55. *Gold v. United States*, 237 F.2d 764, 775 (D.C. Cir. 1956) (opin. of Bazelon, J.) (quotes, 775); *NY Times*, January 29, 1957, "High Court Gives Gold a New Trial"; Schrecker, *Many Are the Crimes*, 338 (first quote). Bryson, president of the National Union of Marine Cooks and Stewards, was also convicted. *Bryson v. United States*, 238 F.2d 657 (9th Cir. 1956), cert. denied, 355 U.S. 817 (1957).

56. *Gold*, 352 U.S. 985 (quote); id., 985–86 (Reed, J., dissenting) (quote); id., 986 (Clark, J., dissenting). The Court relied on *Remmer v. United States*, 350 U.S. 377 (1956), a recent decision in an income tax-evasion case, also involving an FBI juror interview. Per curiam author: see Box 633, Gold file, Warren Papers. The government did not retry Gold, deciding he "could not be prosecuted successfully." *NY Times*, May 10, 1957, "U.S. Abandons Case against Ben Gold."

57. *Mine, Mill and Smelter Workers*, 352 U.S. 145 (quote 151); *NY Times*, December 11, 1956, "Unions Absolved on Non-Red Oaths." Travis's conviction for filing a false affidavit was reviewed by the Court in the 1960 term; see chap. 10, herewith. Mine-Mill was a prime government target. Schrecker, *Many Are the Crimes*, 338–44, 355–58.

58. *Amalgamated Meat Cutters*, 352 U.S. 153–56. The Fur and Leather Workers Union was absorbed by the Amalgamated Meat Cutters & Butcher Workers in 1955. Id., 153 n.1. Frankfurter filed a concurring opinion suggesting an additional ground for reversal. Id., 156–57.

59. James J. Lorence, *The Suppression of Salt of the Earth: How Hollywood, Big Labor, and Politicians Blacklisted a Movie in Cold War America* (Albuquerque: University of

New Mexico Press, 1999), 56–62, 80–84, 87–88, 113–47; Schrecker, *Many Are the Crimes*, 314–16, 331–36 (quote, 336).

60. *Jencks*, 353 U.S. 657 (quote, 663); Lichtman and Cohen, *Deadly Farce*, 91–92, 112–45. Matusow was one of the witnesses whose perjuries led the Court in 1956 to set aside the SACB's registration order against the CPUSA; see chap. 6, herewith. Jencks received a five-year prison sentence.

61. *Jencks*, 353 U.S. at 658–72 (quotes, 668–69). Frankfurter, Black, Douglas, and Warren joined Brennan's opinion. Whittaker did not participate. 1953 precedent: *Gordon v. United States*, 344 U.S. 414.

62. 353 U.S. at 670–72 (quotes). The Court adopted the holding in a noted court-of-appeals decision written by Learned Hand. *United States v. Andolschek*, 142 F.2d 503, 506 (2d Cir. 1944).

63. *Jencks*, 353 U.S. at 672–80 (Burton, J., concurring) (quote, 676). Burton also considered an issue not addressed by the Court, finding that the trial judge's instructions "failed to give the jury sufficient guidance" as to the meaning of "member of the Communist Party" and "affiliated with such party"—terms used in Taft-Hartley. *Id.*, 678–79. Frankfurter noted his agreement with Burton's position on the jury instructions. *Id.*, 672.

64. *Id.*, 680–84 (Clark, J., dissenting) (quote, 681–82).

65. If Jencks had been retried, the defense would have learned that Matusow reported to the FBI: "I have never been told by Jencks that he is a member of the Communist Party, and I have never seen any direct evidence to prove that he is a member of the Communist Party." Lichtman and Cohen, *Deadly Farce*, 47, 179 n. 9 (quoting Boardman to Director, February 2, 1955, FBI 100-375988-425). Later: *LA Times*, December 23, 2005, "Clinton Jencks, 87; Organizer Who Led Mineworkers Strike Later Taught at San Diego State"; *The Guardian*, December 31, 2005, ("Clinton Jencks: Union organiser . . . in a legendary movie from the red-baiting 1950s."

66. Murphy, *Congress and the Court*, 120 (quote); *NY Times*, June 27, 1957, "Transcript of the President's News Conference" (quote).

67. *NY Times*, June 19, 1957, "U.S. Press Comment on Decisions in Watkins, Smith Cases" (quoting newspapers); *NY Daily News*, June 18, 1957, "Aid and Comfort to the Enemy" (quote), clipping in Clark Papers; Murphy, *Congress and the Court*, 128 (quoting *Herald-Tribune*), 128–30. The Court did have a few defenders, notably, the *Washington Post* (and cartoonist Herblock), *St. Louis Post-Dispatch*, and *New York Post*.

68. *NY Times*, July 16, 1957, "Court Criticized on Lawyer Cases" (quote).

69. Warren, *Memoirs*, 321–30 (quotes, 322, 324, 330); Schwartz, *Super Chief*, 283–86 (dues quote, 285); *NY Times*, July 26, 1957, "Bar Unit Assails High Court Trend" (quote), July 24, 1957, "London Conference of Bar Opens Today," and February 21, 1959, "U.S. Bar Accepts Warren's Action"; *Columbia (S.C) State*, July 26, 1957, "Self-Preservation," quoted at 103 Cong. Rec. 13286–87 (August 1, 1957) (Thurmond). See Powe, *Warren Court*, 100 ("Warren believed he had been sandbagged into coming to London to garner publicity for a simultaneous attack on the Court").

70. *Ny Times*, June 25, 1957, "Law Group Head Hits High Court" (quote), June 27, 1957, "Law Heads Avoid Censure of Court" (quote), and October 28, 1957, "Laws to Reverse High Court Asked."

71. *NY Times*, July 14, 1957, "Chief Justices Authorize Study of Court Role in States' Rights," and September 24, 1957, "Justices to Study U.S.-State Rights" (quotes).

72. *Mallory v. United States*, 354 U.S. 449 (1957); 103 Cong. Rec. 12808 (July 26, 1957) (Jenner), quoting Olney in *Evening Star*.

73. *NY Times*, June 5, 1957, "U.S. Aides Study F.B.I. Data Ruling," June 27, 1957, "F.B.I. Ready to Act to Shield Informers" (quote), and June 28, 1957, "President Seeks Curb on File Use" (quotes).

74. 103 Cong. Rec. 10120 (June 24, 1957) (quote), 10984-85 (July 8, 1957); *NY Times*, June 28, 1957, "President Seeks Curb on File Use," June 29, 1957, "Bill to Protect F.B.I. File Voted By Senate Group," and July 3, 1957, "House Study Set on Court Rulings"; H. Rept. No. 700, 85th Cong., 1st Sess. (July 5, 1957); S. Rept. No. 981, 85th Cong., 1st Sess. (August 15, 1957); Murphy, *Congress and the Court*, 131-35.

75. 103 Cong. Rec. 15915-36 (August 26, 1957), 16113-31 (August 27, 1957); *NY Times*, August 23, 1957, "Milder F.B.I. Bill Expected to Pass," and August 27, 1957, "Senate Approves F.B.I. Files Bill"; Murphy, *Congress and the Court*, 135-50. The principal differences between the House and Senate bills related to oral reports to government agents and to federal rules provisions, not mentioned in *Jencks*, which a lower court held authorized pretrial discovery of government records.

76. Pub. L. 85-269, 71 Stat. 595 (September 2, 1957), 18 U.S.C. § 3500.

77. Frankfurter to Brennan, August 29, 1957, Box I:3, Jencks 3 of 3 file, Brennan Papers. Brennan was "absolutely stunned by the controversy generated by his opinion in what he viewed as a straightforward criminal-procedure case." Stern and Wermiel, *Justice Brennan*, 129-30.

78. *NY Times*, July 3, 1957, "House Study Set on Court Rulings" (quote); 103 Cong. Rec. 16760-61 (August 30, 1957) (Cramer); Murphy, *Congress and the Court*, 177-79; Shelden D. Elliott, "Court-Curbing Proposals in Congress," 33 *Notre Dame Lawyer* 597-604 (1958).

79. Murphy, *Congress and the Court*, 172. Sen. Bridges' anti-preemption bill directed only to state sedition statutes was also reintroduced. S. 654, 85th Cong. 1st Sess.

80. H. Rept. No. 1201, 85th Cong., 1st Sess. (August 20, 1957); S. Rept. No. 686, 85th Cong., 1st Sess. (July 19, 1957); Murphy, *Congress and the Court*, 174-75. The *Cole* bill was S 1411; Walter's bill was HR 981.

81. 103 Cong. Rec. 12806-13 (July 26, 1957) (quotes, 12806, 12812); Murphy, *Congress and the Court*, 154-56. A companion bill, HR 9207, was introduced in the House. See Hennings, "'Equal Justice Under Law,'" 47 *Georgetown L. J.* at 18 ("The result of [the Jenner bill] would be to vitiate the effect of the fifth and fourteenth amendments in these five fields").

82. Murphy, *Congress and the Court*, 156-57; *Limitation of Appellate Jurisdiction of the United States Supreme Court*, Hearing Before the Subcommittee to Investigate the Administration of the Internal Security Act and Other Internal Security Laws, 85th Cong., 1st Sess. (August 7, 1957), 1-33 (quote, 27).

83. Stone, *Perilous Times*, 413.

84. Constitutional issues: see chaps. 9 and 10 herewith.

85. Hennings, "'Equal Justice Under Law,'" 47 *Georgetown L. J.* at 19.

Chapter 8. *Beilan, Lerner,* and the Court's Shift, Passport Cases, and Congress's Court-Curbing Climax

1. Powe, *Warren Court,* 141–42. The "again" in Powe's comment presumably referred to Frankfurter's acquiescence in *Dennis* and like decisions during the Vinson years. See Belknap, *Supreme Court Earl Warren,* 67, 69 ("[T]he furor in Congress caused the Court, led by Frankfurter, to lurch to the right.... With the Court under fire in the Congress and Frankfurter's personal relationship with the Chief deteriorating, he and Harlan deserted the liberals"); Friedman, *The Will of the People,* 255 ("From the time of the congressional fight on, Frankfurter voted with the government in virtually all domestic security cases").

2. *Brown v. United States,* 356 U.S. 148 (1958) (contempt); *Green v. United States,* 356 U.S. 165 (1958) (same); *Yates v. United States,* 355 U.S. 66 (1957) (same); *Beilan v. Board of Public Education,* 357 U.S. 399 (1958) (state public-employee loyalty); *Lerner v. Casey,* 357 U.S. 468 (1958) (same); *Rowoldt v. Perfetto,* 355 U.S. 115 (1957) (deportation); *Heikkinen v. United States,* 355 U.S. 273 (1958) (same); *Bonetti v. Rogers,* 356 U.S. 691 (1958) (same); *Nowak v. United States,* 356 U.S. 650 (1958) (denaturalization); *Maisenberg v. United States,* 356 U.S. 668 (1958) (same); *Kent v. Dulles,* 357 U.S. 116 (1958) (passport); *Dayton v. Dulles,* 357 U.S. 144 (1958) (same); *Speiser v. Randall,* 357 U.S. 513 (1958) (gov't benefits); *First Unitarian Church v. County of Los Angeles,* 357 U.S. 545 (1958) (same). Per curiam: *Harmon v. Brucker,* 355 U.S. 579 (1958) (Army discharges); *Sacher v. United States,* 356 U.S. 576 (1958) (contempt of Congress). The Court dismissed by per curiam order, after argument, a suit for monetary damages brought by twenty-three blacklisted Hollywood actors and screenwriters against major film studios. *Wilson v. Loew's Incorporated,* 355 U.S. 597 (1958).

3. Frankfurter was on the losing side only in *Bonetti.* The deportation decision was *Rowoldt. Galvan:* see chap. 5, herewith.

4. *Scales v. United States,* 355 U.S. 1 (1957); *Lightfoot v. United States,* 355 U.S. 2 (1957); Schwartz, *Super Chief,* 312–13. At conferences on October 12 and November 2, 1956, and March 22, 1957, the justices were in apparent disarray. Dickson ed., *Supreme Court in Conference,* 301–3. The Court may have been ready to reverse on *Jencks* grounds even prior to the SG's confession of error. Draft per curiam orders, recirculated May 13, 1957, and Clark draft dissents, circulated May 23, 1957, Box 633, Scales and Lightfoot files, Warren Papers.

5. *NAACP v. Alabama,* 357 U.S. 449 (1958) (quote, 462). Little Rock: *NY Times,* September 4, 1957, "Little Rock Told to Integrate Now Despite Militia" ("Text of U.S. Judge's Integration Order"); September 5, 1957, "Arkansas Troops Bar Negro Pupils"; September 25, 1957, "President Sends Troops to Little Rock." Special-term decision: *Cooper v. Aaron,* 358 U.S. 1 (1958).

6. *NY Times,* June 18, 1958, "Walter Proposes Passport Curbs," and July 8, 1958, "Eisenhower Urges Congress Adopt Passport Curbs," "Eisenhower's Message on Passports." Court-curbing bills: see Murphy, *Congress and the Court,* 157–223; also see "The Court-Curbing Bills and Lyndon's Miracle" later in chapter 8. With HR 3 pending in the Congress, the Court in two labor cases rejected federal-preemption claims, upholding state-court judgments adverse to unions. *Machinists v. Gonzales,* 356 U.S. 617 (1958); *Automobile Workers v. Russell,* 356 U.S. 634 (1958).

7. *Yates*, 355 U.S. 66, 67–70, 356 U.S. 363, 364–66; *Yates*, 227 F.2d 848 (9th Cir. 1955) (reversing three-year sentence for criminal contempt). Mathes also sought to continue Yates's imprisonment for civil contempt after the trial ended, but the court of appeals again intervened. *Yates*, 227 F.2d 844 (9th Cir. 1955).

8. *Yates*, 355 U.S. at 67–76 (quotes, 68, 73, 75). Burton concurred only in the judgment.

9. *Id.*, 76–79 (Douglas, J., dissenting). Douglas argued that Yates's refusal to answer on the second occasion was "merely a failure to purge herself of the first contempt, not a new one."

10. *Yates*, 356 U.S. 363 (1958) (quotes, 366, 367). Warren, Black, and Douglas concurred in the result, "acquiesc[ing]" in the opinion. *Id.*, 367. The dissenters argued that Yates served only fifteen days on the specific sentence at issue and that the Court should not "pass on the adequacy of time already served on other judgments." *Id.*, 367 (Clark, J., dissenting). Per curiam author: see draft circulated by Frankfurter, May 1, 1958, in Pt. 2, microfilm reel 35, Frankfurter Papers.

11. Frankfurter "Dear Brethren" letter, April 10, 1957 (quote) and Frankfurter to Reed, January 16, 1957, Pt. 2, microfilm reel 35; Frankfurter eight-page draft opinion in *Brown*, recirculated April 17, 1957, Brennan to Frankfurter, April 16, 1957, Clark to Frankfurter, April 17, 1957 ("[a] dissent will be prepared . . . by one of the four of us"), Frankfurter to Harlan, May 22, 1957, and Frankfurter-Harlan Mem. for the Conf., May 29, 1957, Pt. 2, microfilm reel 28, all in Frankfurter Papers. Burton draft opin. in *Yates*, circulated March 18, 1957, Box 1189, Conf. and Misc. Memos file, Douglas Papers.

12. *Yates* and *Brown*, 354 U.S. 907 (1957) (ordering reargument); conf. notes, October 28, 1957 ("FF-changed his mind"), Box 1185, Argued Cases Nos. 25–49 file, Douglas Papers.

13. *Brown*, 356 U.S. 148, 149–52 (quotes, 149, 152); *NY Times*, April 1, 1958, "New Curb Voted on Invoking 5th." The trial judge also held that Brown obtained citizenship by fraud, a ruling she apparently did not appeal. She received a six-month prison sentence for contempt.

14. *Brown*, 356 U.S. at 149–57 (quote, 156). 1919 precedent: *Ex parte Hudgings*, 249 U.S. 378 (1919) (quote, 383).

15. *Brown*, 356 U.S. at 157–61 (quote, 158) (Black, J., dissenting); *id.*, 161–64 (Brennan, J., dissenting).

16. *Green*, 356 U.S. 165.

17. *Id.*, 167–89 (quotes, 183–84). Frankfurter in a concurring opinion listed "at least two score" decisions of the Court upholding the power of judges to punish contempts summarily. *Id.*, 189–94. See U.S. Const., Art. III §2, cl. 3 (jury trial); 5th Amend. (indictment by grand jury); 6th Amend. (jury trial).

18. *Green*, 356 U.S. at 193–219 (quotes, 193–94) (Black, J., dissenting); *id.*, 219–23 (Brennan, J., dissenting).

19. *Sacher*, 356 U.S. 576–78; Strategy and Tactics of World Communism: The Significance of the Matusow Case, Hearing Before the Subcommittee to Investigate the Administration of the Internal Security Act and Other Internal Security Laws of the Senate Committee on the Judiciary, 84th Cong., 1st Sess. (1955), 829–44 (quote, 836). Sacher: see chap. 4, herewith, and chap. 5, herewith. Smith Act case: *United States v. Flynn*, 130

F. Supp. 412, 415 (S.D.N.Y. 1955); Lichtman and Cohen, *Deadly Farce*, 65–67, 125–27. SISS concluded that Matusow's recantation was "a collective product of the Communist conspiracy" intended "to discredit Government witnesses, the Department of Justice, the courts, the FBI, and congressional investigating committees." S. Rept. No. 2050, 84th Cong., 1st Sess. (April 6, 1955), 88–89.

20. *Sacher*, 356 U.S. 577 (quote); *id.* 578–79 (Clark, J., dissenting). Burton did not participate.

21. Douglas to Frankfurter, April 23, 1958 (quote), and Harlan to Frankfurter, April 23, 1958 (quote), Pt. 2, microfilm reel 33, Frankfurter Papers.

22. *Beilan*, 357 U.S. 399; *Lerner* 357 U.S. 468. *Slochower*, 350 U.S. 551 (quote, 558); see chap. 6, herewith.

23. *Beilan*, 357 U.S. at 400–404 and n3. Beilan's Fifth Amendment plea before HUAC was also cited by the board as a ground of "incompetency"; but the Pennsylvania Supreme Court relied only on his refusal to answer the superintendent's questions.

24. *Id.*, 400–409 (quotes, 405–6, 408).

25. *Lerner*, 357 U.S. at 470–76 (quotes, 472, 474, 476).

26. *Id.*, 470–79 (quotes, 477, 478). Frankfurter added a concurring opinion (for both cases), reiterating that the two employees were fired for refusing to answer questions relevant "to an inquiry by their supervisors into their dependability" and "were not labeled 'disloyal.'" *Id.*, 409–11. See Kalven, *A Worthy Tradition*, 540 (Frankfurter's opinion "professes to be unable to see why anyone would think a dismissal for refusal to answer about Communist affiliations had anything to do with loyalty when the state has said it did not").

27. 357 U.S. at 412–16 (Douglas, J., dissenting in both cases) (quotes, 415–16); *id.*, 411–12 (Warren, C.J., dissenting in both cases); *id.*, 417–25 (Brennan., J., dissenting in both cases).

28. *NAACP*, 357 U.S. 449 (quotes, 462); *Beilan*, 357 U.S. at 414 (Douglas, J., dissenting) (quotes). Douglas was critical of Harlan's suggestion in *NAACP* (357 U.S. at 463) that a "compelling" state interest would "justify the deterrent effect" on members' freedom of association. He wrote to Harlan, "I thought that when we dealt with these racial problems and with free speech and free assembly . . . we were dealing with something that is right close to the absolute." Douglas to Harlan, April 22, 1958, Box 1185, Douglas Memoranda file, Douglas Papers.

29. *Rowoldt*, 355 U.S. 115, 117–18 (quotes); 228 F. 2d 109, 110 (8th Cir. 1956) ("a native and citizen of Germany"); Schwartz, *Super Chief*, 266–67 (Warren thought Frankfurter's vote and opinion in *Rowoldt* "showed that [his] restraint doctrine was often a façade to mask the fact that the Justice could be as human in his decision process as any of the Brethren").

30. *Rowoldt*, 355 U.S. at 116–21 (quote, 120); *Galvan*, 347 U.S. at 528 (quote).

31. *Rowoldt*, 355 U.S. at 119–20 and n2 (quotes).

32. *Id.*, 121–29 (Harlan, J., dissenting) (quotes, 123 and n5) (orig. emphasis). Harlan's view of the case had changed dramatically. *Rowoldt* was ready for decision in the 1956 term but was reargued; at the justices' conference in 1956, Harlan deemed the Internal Security Act's deportation provision unconstitutional as applied, telling his colleagues

that "application of this Act retroactively to 1935 is irrational." Conf. notes, November 16, 1956, Box 1185, Argued Cases Nos. 1–24 file, Douglas Papers (quote); Harlan undated notes, Box 38, Rowoldt file, Harlan Papers; 354 U.S. 934 (1957) (ordering reargument).

33. *Bonetti*, 356 U.S. 691 (quote, 699). Burton voted in conference to affirm but switched sides the following month. Conf. notes, April 11, 1958, Box 1186, Argued Cases Nos. 85–99 file, Douglas Papers; Burton mem., May 21, 1958, Box 441, Bonetti file, Warren Papers.

34. *Id.*, 692–93 (quotes); Act of October 16, 1918, as amended by § 22 of the Internal Security Act of 1950, 64 Stat. 1006 (quote); *NY Times*, June 3, 1958, "U.S. Fails to Oust an Alien Ex-Red."

35. *Bonetti*, 356 U.S. at 692–700 (quotes, 697).

36. *Id.*, 700–703 (Clark, J., dissenting) (quote, 701).

37. *Heikkinen*, 355 U.S. 273, 274–75; *NY Times*, January 7, 1958, "High Court Upsets Conviction of Alien"; Immigration Act of 1917, § 20(c), 39 Stat. 890, as amended, 64 Stat. 1012 (quote). *Spector*: see chap. 4, herewith.

38. *Heikkinen*, 355 U.S. at 274–80 (quotes, 276, 277, 279).

39. *Nowak*, 356 U.S. 660 (quote, 663); *Maisenberg*, 356 U.S. 670. Earlier cases: *Schneiderman v. United States*, 320 U.S. 118 (1943); *Bridges*, see chap. 4, herewith; *Zucca*, see chap. 6, herewith.

40. *Nowak*, 356 U.S. 661–62, 667 (quotes, 662n2, 663); *Maisenberg*, 356 U.S. at 671–72; *NY Times*, May 27, 1958, "Court Reinstates Citizenship of 2"; Nationality Act of 1906, § 4, 34 Stat. 596, 598 (June 29, 1906); http://politicalgraveyard.com. Maisenberg was a candidate for Michigan presidential elector in Earl Browder's 1940 presidential bid.

41. *Nowak*, 356 U.S. at 661–68 (quotes, 663, 664, 666); *Maisenberg*, 356 U.S. at 671–73; *id.*, 669 (Burton, Clark, and Whittaker, dissenting).

42. *NY Times*, May 27, 1958, "Court Reinstates Citizenship of 2."

43. Kutler, *American Inquisition*, 89–117; Boudin, "Constitutional Right to Travel," 47, 52–72 (1956); see chap. 1, herewith. Robeson: *Robeson v. Dulles*, 235 F. 2d 810 (D.C.Cir. 1956), cert. denied, 352 U.S. 895 (1956); Duberman, *Paul Robeson*, 388–89, 424–25, 432–33, 450–53, 463–64. Miller: Miller, *Timebends*, 356–57. Pauling: Hennings Hearings, 103–40; Kutler, *American Inquisition*, 89–91. Boudin: *Boudin v. Dulles*, 235 F.2d 532 (D.C.Cir. 1956).

44. Kutler, *American Inquisition*, 95–96 (quotes); Immigration and Nationality Act of 1952, § 215, 66 Stat. 190 (quotes); State Dept. Reg. No. 108.162, effective August 28, 1952, 17 Fed. Reg. 8013 (quotes); Proclamation No. 3004, 67 Stat. C31 (January 17, 1953).

45. *Kent*, 357 U.S. 116; Kutler, *American Inquisition*, 101–14; *NY Times*, June 17, 1958, "Disputatious Artist" (quote) and Dec. 24, 1982, "Dr. Walter Briehl, a Pioneer of Group Therapy Methods." Kent's case was joined in the courts with that of Walter Briehl, a Los Angeles psychiatrist, also alleged to be a Communist, who likewise refused to sign a non-Communist affidavit.

46. *Kent*, 357 U.S. at 117–30 (quotes, 124, 127, 128): Act of August 18, 1856, 11 Stat. 52, 60, and Pub. L. 493, 44 Stat, Part 2, 887 (July 3, 1926) (quote).

47. *Kent*, 357 U.S. at 125–30 (quotes, 125–26, 129).

48. *Id.*, 130–43 (Clark, J., dissenting) (quote, 135).

49. *Dayton*, 357 U.S. 144 (quotes, 146, 149, 150). The Department based its denial on its regulation barring issuance of passports to persons "going abroad to engage in activities which will advance the Communist movement." *Id.*, 150 and n7–8.

50. *Id.*, 145–50 (quotes, 150); *id.*, 154 (Clark, J., dissenting) (quote).

51. Conf. notes, April 11, 1958, Box 1198, Dayton Cert. & Conf. Memos file (quotes) and Douglas draft opin., circulated May 9, 1958 (quote, 11) and Whittaker to Douglas, May 2, 1958, Dayton Vote of Court file, Douglas Papers; Bernard Schwartz, *The Unpublished Opinions of the Warren Court* (New York: Oxford University Press, 1985), 45–72 (reproducing both Douglas's and Clark's opinions) (Clark quote, 71); Schwartz, *Super Chief*, 310–11. Frankfurter returned Douglas's May 9 draft with the notation "Yes FF." Schwartz viewed Douglas's opinion as broad enough to have barred reliance by the government on undisclosed information in loyalty-security cases (*Unpublished Opinions*, 73–75).

52. Frankfurter draft opin., circulated May 13, 1958, and Harlan draft opin., circulated June 13, 1958, in Pt. 2, microfilm reel 29, Frankfurter Papers; Douglas mem. to conf., June 13, 1958 (quote), Box 1198, Dayton Vote of Court file, Douglas Papers; Schwartz, *Unpublished Opinions*, 73.

53. Krock, *NY Times*, June 19, 1958, "The Court on 'The Right to Travel'" (quote); Lawrence, *U.S. News & World Report*, July 18, 1958, 100, "Legalizing Treason?" (quote); 104 Cong. Rec. 11536–37 (June 17, 1958) (Walter); 104 Cong. Rec. 11558–61 (June 18, 1958) (Eastland) (quote); *NY Times*, July 8, 1958, "Eisenhower's Message on Passports" (quote). Another *U.S. News & World Report* article, by William H. Rehnquist, a former Jackson law clerk then practicing in Phoenix, added fuel to criticism of the Court's decisions, asserting that "liberal" law clerks who had "extreme solicitude for the claims of Communists" exerted a disproportionate influence. Rehnquist, "Who Writes Decisions of the Supreme Court?" *U.S. News & World Report*, December 13, 1957; *NY Times*, December 10, 1957, "'Sway' of Clerks on Court Cited" (AP dispatch).

54. *NY Times*, June 26, 1958, "Robeson to Leave for Britain Soon" (quote), and June 27, 1958, "Robeson and Lamont Passports Received."

55. *Speiser*, 357 U.S. 513 (quote, 516), *rev'g* 48 Cal.2d 472 (1957). Speiser was a lawyer associated with the ACLU. *NY Times*, September 1, 1991, "Lawrence Speiser, 68, a Civil Liberties Lawyer."

56. *Speiser*, 357 U.S. at 514–29 (quotes, 520). Burton concurred only in the result. Warren, who was governor when the statute was enacted, did not participate. *NY Times*, July 1, 1958, "California Upset on Loyalty Oath." At oral argument the state conceded that abstract advocacy lawful under *Yates* would not trigger loss of the exemption. 357 U.S. at 519 and n4.

57. *Id.*, 526–29 (quotes, 526); *id.*, 532–44 (Clark, J., dissenting) (quote, 541).

58. *First Unitarian Church*, 357 U.S. 545; *id.*, 548 (Clark, J., dissenting). Burton concurred only in the result, and Warren did not participate.

59. 357 U.S. at 529–32 (quote, 530) (Black, J., concurring).

60. Hennings Hearings, 436 (quote), 532–33; Brown, *Loyalty and Security*, 86–89, 487; *NY Times*, January 16, 1958, "U.S. Calls Army Wrong on 'Risks,'" and March 4, 1958,

"High Court Curbs Army Discharges in Security Cases" (quote). The Army's unfavorable security determinations were communicated to the FBI and "become a permanent part of the individual's file." Brown, 81–89 (quote, 89).

61. *Harmon*, 355 U.S. 579 rev'g 243 F. 2d 613 (D.C. Cir. 1957) (quote, 617); Law-clerk cert. mem. in *Abramowitz* (undated), Box 1186, Argued Cases Nos. 125–149 file, Douglas Papers; *NY Times*, January 16, 1958, "U.S. Calls Army Wrong on 'Risks.'" A general discharge under honorable conditions is "something halfway between honorable and undesirable." *Id.* The Army charged that Harmon had participated in Communist-connected activities, his father was a CPUSA member, and his stepmother associated with Communists; Abramowitz was alleged to have been a CPUSA member in 1948–49 and a subscriber to the *Daily Worker. Dallas Morning News*, March 4, 1958, "Justice Clark Questions Court," clipping in Clark Papers.

62. *NY Times*, January 16, 1958, "U.S. Calls Army Wrong on "Risks" (quotes); Excerpts from argument of Donald B. MacGuiness in *Abramowitz*, 5, 8, Box I:11, Folder 12, Brennan Papers; Servicemen's Readjustment Act, § 301, 58 Stat. 286–87 (June 22, 1944) (quote).

63. *Harmon*, 355 U.S. at 580–83; Frankfurter Mem., February 6, 1958 (quotes), and edited draft opin. (undated), Warren Mem. and Black-Frankfurter draft, January 23, 1958, and Frankfurter to Whittaker, February 26, 1958, in Pt. 2, microfilm reel 29, Frankfurter Papers; Whittaker to Conf. and draft opinion, January 31, 1958, Box 1186, Argued Cases Nos. 50–84 file, Douglas Papers; Brennan to Whittaker, February 21 and 28, 1958, Box I:11, Folder 12, Brennan Papers.

64. *Harmon*, 355 U.S. at 580–83 (quotes; orig. emphasis); 58 Stat. 286.

65. *Id.*, 583–86 (Clark, J., dissenting) (quote); *Dallas Morning News*, March 5, 1958, "The Court Protects the Dangerous," clipping in Clark Papers (quote). In *Marshall v. Brucker*, 356 U.S. 34 (1958), the Court granted review and, Clark dissenting, summarily reversed the lower court's judgment "in the light" of *Harmon*.

66. Murphy, *Congress and the Court*, 154–83; Caro, *Master of the Senate*, 831–41; Rowland Evans and Robert Novak, *Lyndon B. Johnson: The Exercise of Power* (New York: New American Library, 1966), 164–65 ("By 1958, a substantial majority in both the House and Senate favored anti-Court legislation that would have basically altered the federal system").

67. Murphy, *Congress and the Court*, 156 (quote), 157–63, 164 (ABA resolution); Hearings on S 2646 Before the Subcommittee to Investigate the Administration of the Internal Security Act and Other Internal Security Laws, Pt. 2, 85th Cong., 2d Sess. (February-March 1958); *NY Times*, March 10, 1958, "High Court Curb Gets Test Today" ("The first serious effort in a generation to cut down the power of the Supreme Court . . ."). See Powe, *Warren Court,* 131 (ABA resolution "a rather mealymouthed show of support"). In a letter, eighty-six-year-old Learned Hand, "perhaps the most revered of living American judges," voiced opposition to the bill; but Hand's criticism of the Court in lectures given in February—he called it at times "a third legislative chamber"—had been eagerly utilized by the bill's supporters. *NY Times*, May 8, 1958, "Judge Hand Hits Court Curb Bill," February 6, 1958, "Top Court Chided By Learned Hand," and February 5, 1958, "Judge Hand Backs Review by Courts."

68. S. Rept. No. 1586, 85th Cong., 2d Sess. (May 15, 1958); Murphy, *Congress and the Court*, 163–70; Harry McPherson, *A Political Education* (Boston: Little, Brown, 1972), 132 ("a hodgepodge of proposals by Jenner and Butler that struck at the Court from all directions").

69. Hearings on HR 3 Before the House Committee on the Judiciary, 85th Cong., 2d Sess. (May 1958); H. Rept. No. 1878, 85th Cong., 2d Sess. (June 13, 1958); 104 Cong. Rec. 14138–62 (July 17, 1958); Murphy, *Congress and the Court*, 172–74, 182, 194. A Senate counterpart to HR 3, S 337, was approved by Eastland's Judiciary Committee, but Committee liberals succeeded in limiting the bill to subsequently-enacted statutes. S. Rept. No. 2230, 85th Cong., 2d Sess. (July 31, 1958). *Nelson*-only bills: H. Rept. No. 1822, 85th Cong, 2d Sess (May 28, 1958) (H.R. 977); S. Rept. No. 2250, 85th Cong., 2d Sess. (August 8, 1958)) (S. 654).

70. *Cole*: 104 Cong. Rec. 13401–17 (July 10, 1958); H. Rept. No. 2687, 85th Cong., 2d Sess. (August 21, 1958). *Yates*: H. Rept. No. 2495, 85th Cong., 2d Sess. (August 6, 1958); 104 Cong. Rec. 17168–71 (August 12, 1958). *Mallory*: 104 Cong. Rec. 12940–41 (July 2, 1958); Sen. Rept. No. 2252, 85th Cong., 2d Sess. (August 8, 1958). See Murphy, *Congress and the Court*, 174–75, 181–82, 194–96.

71. H. Rept. No. 2684, 85th Cong., 2d Sess. (August 21, 1958); 104 Cong. Rec. 19653–59 (August 23, 1958); *NY Times*, July 17, 1958, "Murphy Pleads for Travel Curb," and July 29, 1958, "City Bar Cautions on Passport Bans." Wayne Morse, a liberal Oregon Democrat, delayed Senate consideration by objecting to hearings being held while the Senate was in session. *NY Times*, July 18, 1958, "Passport Bill Snagged."

72. *NY Times*, August 6, 1958, "Court Curb Bills Gaining in Senate" ("The feeling is that almost anything will pass if it is allowed to reach the floor"), and August 20, 1958, "High Court Curb Voted in Senate" (quote); Robert Mann, *The Walls of Jericho: Lyndon Johnson, Hubert Humphrey, Richard Russell, and the Struggle for Civil Rights* (New York: Harcourt Brace, 1996), 231–32; McPherson, *Political Education*, 132.

73. 104 Cong. Rec. 18432–521 (August 19, 1958) (41–39 vote, 18511; 65–12 vote, 18520); *NY Times*, August 20, 1958, "High Court Curb Voted in Senate."

74. 104 Cong. Rec. 18635–87 (August 20, 1958) (quotes, 18636, 18686) (vote, 18687); *NY*, August 21, 1958, "Critics of Supreme Court Score a Victory in Senate."

75. 104 Cong. Rec. 18691–749 (August 20, 1958); McPherson, *Political Education*, 132–33; Murphy, *Congress and the Court*, 202–4, 210–11. The support for HR 3 may also have reflected an ill-advised attempt by Paul H. Douglas, an Illinois liberal, following the Jenner-Butler vote, to offer a provision praising the *Brown* decision—"a legislative finger in the conservatives' eye." Mann, *Walls of Jericho*, 232.

76. 104 Cong. Rec. 18749–50 (August 20, 1958) (quote); Caro, *Master of the Senate*, 1031; McPherson, *Political Education*, 133; Murphy, *Congress and the Court*, 211–12.

77. Caro, *Master of the Senate*, 1031–32 (quotes); McPherson, *Political Education*, 134 (quote). See Mann, *Walls of Jericho*, 233–34; Evans and Novak, *Lyndon B. Johnson*, 166.

78. 104 Cong. Rec. 18880, 18911–28 (August 21, 1958) (vote, 18928); Caro, *Master of the Senate*, 1032–33 (quote); Murphy, *Congress and the Court*, 212–17 (first quote, 212); Mann, *Walls of Jericho*, 234–35; *NY Times*, August 22, 1958, "41–40 Senate Vote Kills Bills Aimed at Supreme Court" (Lewis quote). In addition to Dirksen, the conservatives

who switched were George ("Molly") Malone (R-Nev.), and Frank Lausche (D-Ohio). The moderates who defected were Albert Gore (D-Tenn.) and Thomas H. Kuchel (R-Calif.).

79. H. Rept. No. 2687, 85th Cong., 2d Sess. (August 21, 1958); 104 Cong. Rec. 19176–78 (August 22, 1968); Murphy, *Congress and the Court*, 218–19.

80. H. Rept. No. 2702, 85th Cong., 2d Sess. (August 23, 1958); 104 Cong. Rec. 19555–57, 19565, 19568–70, 19574–76 (Senate), 19663–64 (House) (August 23, 1958); Murphy, *Congress and the Court*, 219–23; *NY Times*, August 24, 1958, "Aid Bill Is Voted As 85th Congress Winds Up Session."

81. Warren, *Memoirs*, 313. In December, when Frankfurter was hospitalized after a mild heart attack, Lyndon Johnson (who earlier had experienced a severe heart attack) sent words of encouragement, adding: "I closed up the last Session by protecting you and your colleagues from a certain amount of wrath aimed at a few of your decisions. I can't help but wonder what devilment you may be cooking up for me now!" Johnson to Frankfurter, December 6, 1958, Box 533, Frankfurter 1958 file, Harlan Papers.

Chapter 9. *Barenblatt, Uphaus,* and the Court in Retreat

1. *Cooper v. Aaron*, 358 U.S. 1 (1958) (quote, 16); *NY Times*, September 13, 1958, "Court Bars Little Rock Delay," and September 30, 1958, "Supreme Court Bars Evasion or Force to Balk Integration"; Belknap, *Supreme Court under Earl Warren*, 46–48.

2. *NY Times*, October 7, 1958, "Burton Quits High Court on Advice of Physicians," "The Quiet Arbiter" (quote); October 8, 1958, "Justice Burton Retires," "Ohioan Is Chosen for Burton's Post on Supreme Court"; October 9, 1958, "Burton Has Ailment"; October 14, 1958, "Burton, Retiring, Praised by Court"; and October 15, 1958, "Stewart Takes High Court Seat"; Berry, *Stability, Security, and Continuity*, 225–28.

3. *NY Times*, November 5, 1958, "National Election Picture: Democratic Tide Is Strong," and November 6, 1958, "G.O.P. Loser Hits Wisconsin Rival" (quote); Rusk, *Statistical History*, 216, 377; Michael J. Dubin, *United States Congressional Elections, 1788 to 1997* (Jefferson, N.C.: McFarland, 1998), 621. Jenner-Butler vote: see chap. 8, herewith.

4. 1958 term: *Flaxer v. United States*, 358 U.S. 147 (1958); *Vitarelli v. Seaton*, 359 U.S. 535 (1959); *Uphaus v. Wyman*, 360 U.S. 72 (1959); *Barenblatt v. United States*, 360 U.S. 109 (1959); *Raley v. State of Ohio*, 360 U.S. 423 (1959); *Greene v. McElroy*, 360 U.S. 474 (1959); *In re Sawyer*, 360 U.S. 622 (1959). 1959 term: *Nelson v. County of Los Angeles*, 362 U.S. 1 (1960); *Flemming v. Nestor*, 363 U.S. 603 (1960); *Niukkanen v. McAlexander*, 362 U.S. 390 (1960) (per curiam); *Kimm v. Rosenberg*, 363 U.S. 405 (1960) (per curiam).

5. *Jencks* statute: *Palermo v. United States*, 360 U.S. 343 (1959); *Rosenberg v. United States*, 360 U.S. 367 (1959). The Social Security decision was *Nestor*.

6. *Barenblatt*, 360 U.S. 109; *Uphaus*, 360 U.S. 72. *Sweezy*: see chap. 7, herewith.

7. *U.S. News & World Report*, June 22, 1959, 48, "Is the Supreme Court Changing Its Mind?"

8. *Greene*, 360 U.S. 474; *NY Times*, June 30, 1959, "High Court Voids Checks on 'Risks' in Arms Industry."

9. *Scales v. United States*, 360 U.S. 924 (1959), 361 U.S. 952 (1960). Clark each time voiced vigorous objection. 360 U.S. at 925; 361 U.S. at 953. The 1959 term was marked by a rare decision in a case involving a professional Soviet spy, Rudolf Ivanovich Abel, found living in New York City under an assumed identity—a case that presented difficult Fourth Amendment issues. The Court affirmed Abel's conviction, by 5–4 vote, with Warren, Black, Douglas, and Brennan dissenting. Less than two years later, Abel was exchanged for Francis Gary Powers, the pilot of an American U-2 reconnaissance plane shot down over the Soviet Union. *Abel v. United States*, 362 U.S. 217 (1960); *NY Times*, March 29, 1960, "High Court Backs Abel Conviction"; February 10, 1962, "Powers Is Freed by Soviet in An Exchange for Abel"; and February 11, 1962, "Abel Was Agent in Classic Mode."

10. Belknap, *Supreme Court under Earl Warren*, 45 (first quotes); Berry, *Stability, Security, and Continuity*, 225; Schwartz, *Super Chief*. 319–20; *NY Times*, October 8, 1958, "Ohioan Is Chosen for Burton's Post on Supreme Court" (final quotes).

11. Jerold H. Israel, "Potter Stewart" in Friedman and Israel, eds., *Justices*, 2921–23; *NY Times*, October 8, 1958, "Lawyer by Heritage" (quote).

12. Douglas, *The Court Years*, 250 (quote); *Jacobellis v. Ohio*, 378 U.S. 184, 197 (1964) (Stewart, J., concurring) (quote); Israel, "Potter Stewart," in Friedman and Israel, eds., *Justices*, 2925–26; Gayle Binion, "Potter Stewart," in Urofsky, ed., *Supreme Court Justices*, 423 (observer quote). By Israel's count, in forty-two 5–4 decisions "involving issues of individual liberty," Stewart joined the Black-Douglas-Warren-Brennan group only nine times.

13. *Flaxer v. United States*, 358 U.S. 147–50 (quotes). Flaxer's union, which organized public employees, was expelled from the CIO in 1950 as Communist-dominated. Rosswurm, *CIO's Left-Led Unions*, 2–4. Once boasting sixty-one thousand members, its membership had declined to fourteen thousand by the time of its expulsion; 35 to 40 percent were African-Americans.

14. 358 U.S. at 151–52.

15. *Raley*, 360 U.S. 423–34 (quote, 425), *rev'g in part State v. Morgan*, 164 Ohio St. 529 (1956); The defendants were sentenced to ten days in jail and a $500 fine. *NY Times*, June 23, 1959, "High Court Voids 3 Red Convictions."

16. *Raley*, 360 U.S. at 437–40 (quote, 438).

17. *Id.*, 440–42 (Brennan opin.) (quote, 441), 442–44 (Clark opin.) (quote, 443–44). The discussion in published opinions of the merits of a case in which the justices were equally divided was a departure from the usual practice.

18. *Barenblatt*, 360 U.S. at 113–16; *id.*, 134 (Black, J., dissenting). Barenblatt received a six-month prison sentence.

19. *Id.*, 116–25 (quotes, 117–18, 125). See Kalven, *A Worthy Tradition*, 498 ("The outcome in *Barenblatt* makes clear that the pertinency requirement is a slender reed indeed"), 499 ("[HUAC's] authorization is to be defined in terms of what it has actually been doing for so many years").

20. *Barenblatt*, 360 U.S. at 125–34 (quotes, 126–29, 132, 134). See Powe, *The Warren Court and American Politics*, 144 ("How [self-preservation] was involved in asking a

former psychology instructor at Vassar about meetings when he was a graduate student at the University of Michigan was never explained").

21. *Barenblatt*, 360 U.S. at 129.

22. *Id.*, 134–66 (Black, J., dissenting) (quotes, 139, 141, 144).

23. *Id.*, 146–53 (quotes, 146, 149–50) (Black, J., dissenting). Interior quotes are from *Schneiderman*, 320 U.S. 136.

24. *Barenblatt*, 360 U.S. at 166 (Brennan, J., dissenting).

25. *Uphaus*, 360 U.S. 72, 74; *id.*, 86 (Brennan, J., dissenting) (quotes); *NY Times*, June 9, 1959, "High Court Backs Rights of Congress and States in Subversion Inquiries" (first quote); December 15, 1959, "Spirited Pacifist," "Pacifist Is Jailed in Contempt Case"; and October 11, 1983, "Dr. Willard Uphaus, Leader of Pacifist Causes in the 50's" (second quote).

26. *Id.*, *NY Times*, October 11, 1983. (final quote); *Uphaus*, 360 U.S. at 74–76 (quote).

27. *Uphaus*, 360 U.S. at 77–81. The Court held, at the outset, that New Hampshire's anti-subversive statute and resolution authorizing Wyman's investigation were not, as in *Nelson*, preempted by federal legislation, explaining at length that *Nelson* had not "stripped the states of the right to protect themselves." *Id.*, 76–77. But see *Wash. Post*, June 16, 1959, editorial, "Exposure as a Weapon" ("No one seriously contends that New Hampshire was menaced by the pacifists"); Kalven, *A Worthy Tradition*, 507 ("If not a formal university enterprise, the World Fellowship summer camp is surely recognizable as a venture in adult education").

28. 360 U.S. at 82–108 (Brennan, J., dissenting) (quotes, 82, 106).

29. Frankfurter to Brennan, January 7, 1959, Box I:19, Folder 3, Brennan Papers.

30. 360 U.S. at 81–82 (quotes); 364 U.S. 802 (1960) (denying bail); *NY Times*, December 15, 1959, "Pacifist Is Jailed in Contempt Case." Frankfurter as circuit justice denied Uphaus's bail motion in July 1960. 81 S. Ct. 22 (1960); *NY Times*, July 8, 1960, "Uphaus Is Denied Bail." Uphaus's appeal was dismissed during the 1960 term. 364 U.S. 388 (1960); see chap. 10, herewith.

31. *Bates*, 361 U.S. 516 (quotes, 523, 527). Black and Douglas concurred in the judgment "and substantially with the opinion . . ." *Id.*, 527.

32. *Niukkanen*, 362 U.S. 390 (final quote, 391); *id.*, 391–94 (Douglas, J., dissenting) (quotes); *NY Times*, April 19, 1969, "High Court Upholds Finn's Deportation." *Rowoldt*: see chap. 8, herewith.

33. *Niukkanen*, 362 U.S. at 391 (quotes). Niukkanen testified both at INS hearings and before the district judge. *Id.*, 394; *Niukkanen*, 148 F. Supp. 106, 107 (D.Ore. 1956). Author: Frankfurter draft per curiam, recirculated April 5, 1960, Box 637, Niukkanen file, Warren Papers.

34. 362 U.S. at 393–95 (Douglas, J., dissenting) (quotes). Interior quotes are from *Rowoldt*, 355 U.S. 120.

35. Frankfurter mem., April 4, 1960, Box 637, Niukkanen file, Warren Papers; 106 Cong. Rec. 10232–37 (May 13, 1960) (Morse remarks) (S. 3543, 86th Cong.); S. 1894, HR 7942, and HR 8513, 94th Cong. (1975).

36. *Kimm*, 363 U.S. 405–6; *id.*, 409 (Douglas, J., dissenting); *id.*, 413 (Brennan, J., dissenting) (quote); Clark draft per curiam, recirculated June 8, 1960, Box 637, Kimm

file, Warren Papers; *Kimm*, 263 F.2d 773 (9th Cir. 1959); excerpts from Kimm master's thesis, 1933, USC Dept. of Geology, reprinted at http://digitallibrary.usc.edu.

37. *Kimm*, 363 U.S. at 406–8 (quotes, 408). The statutory language was silent on the issue, and the Court relied on an administrative regulation that placed the burden of proof on the applicant. *Id.*, 407.

38. *Id.*, 408–11 (Douglas, J., dissenting) (quote, 410); *id.*, 411–16 (Brennan, J., dissenting) (quote, 414).

39. K. Klein, Korean Heritage Lib., to CIA Info. and Privacy Coordinator, March 21, 1988, reprinted at http://digitallibrary.usc.edu.

40. Pub. L. 761, 68 Stat. 1052, 1083 (September 1, 1954) (quote); *Nestor*, 363 U.S. 603, 604–5, 618 and n10. The provision was included in omnibus legislation titled "Social Security Amendments of 1954."

41. 363 U.S. at 605; *id.*, 621–22 (Black, J., dissenting), 628–29 (Douglas, J., dissenting); *Nestor*, 169 F. Supp. 922, 934 (D.D.C. 1959) (quote); *NY Times*, June 21, 1960. "High Court Rejects Pension Plea."

42. *Nestor*, 363 U.S. at 604–21 (quotes, 610–13).

43. *Id.*, 621–28 (Black, J., dissenting); *id.*, 628–34 (Douglas, J., dissenting) (quotes, 629, 630); *id.*, 634–40 (Brennan, J., dissenting, joined by Warren and Douglas) (quote, 635);

44. *Greene*, 360 U.S. 474, 475–91; *NY Times*, June 30, 1959, "High Court Voids Checks on 'Risks' in Arms Industry."

45. *Greene*, 360 U.S. at 475–90 (quotes, 478 n. 5, 479, 484 n. 14).

46. *Id.*, 492–508 (quotes, 495, 496, 499–500, 508). Warren's opinion was joined by Black, Douglas, Brennan, and Stewart.

47. *Id.*, 508 (three-justice concurring statement) (quote); *id.*, 509–10 (Harlan, J., concurring specially).

48. *Id.*, 510–24 (Clark, J., dissenting) (quotes, 524).

49. *Taylor v. McElroy*, 360 U.S. 709 (1959) (quotes); *NY Times*, June 30, 1959, "High Court Voids Checks on 'Risks' in Arms Industry." In Greene's case, however, the government resisted his claim for income lost due to revocation of his clearance; in 1964 the Court, by 7–2 vote, ruled in his favor. *Greene v. United States*, 376 U.S. 149.

50. H. Rept. No. 1122, Sept 2, 1959, 86th Cong., 1st Sess., 1 (quote); *NY Times*, February 21, 1960, "Security Procedures Reflect Calmer Era" (quote), and January 17, 1960, "Defense Workers to Get New Right in Security Cases"; Exec. Order 10865, 25 Fed. Reg. 1583 (1960). Exceptions to the rule affording the employee "an opportunity to cross-examine persons who have made oral or written statements adverse to" him required specific approval by the department head. *Id.*, §4. The administration, however, did not adopt similar confrontation rules for federal-employee loyalty-security cases. Walter's bill was HR 8121, 86th Cong., 1st Sess.; three Senate bills, S 776 (Butler), S 2392 (Johnston, Eastland), and S 2416 (Keating), were introduced.

51. *Vitarelli*, 359 U.S. 535, 536–37 (quote); *NY Times*, June 2, 1959, "High Court Voids Ouster of 'Risk'"; *Honolulu Star-Bulletin*, January 26, 2010, "Official built schools, businesses on Palau." Vitarelli was also charged with having registered as a supporter of the American Labor Party (a left-labor political party in New York) and purchased copies of the *Daily Worker* and *New Masses*.

52. *Vitarelli*, 359 U.S. 535, 539–45 (quotes). The Court cited *Service v. Dulles* (see chap. 7, herewith). The regulations required, for example, that hearings be limited by relevance; but Vitarelli's hearing "developed into a wide-ranging inquisition into this man's educational, social, and political beliefs, encompassing even a question as to whether he was 'a religious man.'" 359 U.S. at 543.

53. *Id.*, 545–46 (quotes).

54. *Id.*, 546–49 (Frankfurter, J., dissenting).

55. *Honolulu Star-Bulletin*, January 26, 2010, "Official built schools, businesses on Palau"; *The Maui News*, January 23, 2010, "William Vitarelli, 'King of Maui,' Dies at 99."

56. *Nelson*, 362 U.S. 1.

57. *Id.*, 2–5 (second quote, 3); *Globe*, 163 Cal.App.2d 595 (1958) (596, first and final quotes, 597, quoting Calif. statute); *Nelson*, 163 Cal.App.2d 607 (1958). The employees also invoked their First Amendment rights, a position foreclosed by *Barenblatt* and *Uphaus*.

58. *Nelson*, 362 U.S. at 2–9 (quotes, 7).

59. *Id.*, 9–10 (Black, J., dissenting) (quote); *id.*, 10–16 (Brennan, J., dissenting) (quotes, 12–13). In Nelson's case, Whittaker was likely the fourth justice who joined Black, Douglas, and Brennan in opposing affirmance. At conference, he said "he would let [Nelson] have a new hearing." Harlan also said he would "remand for hearing," but he expressly changed his vote. Conf. notes, January 15, 1960, and Harlan to Black, January 18, 1960, Box 1215, Argued Cases 150–199 file, Douglas Papers.

60. *NY Times*, March 2, 1960, editorial, "A Regrettable Decision."

61. *Nostrand v. Little*, 362 U.S. 474 (1960) (quotes) *vacating Nostrand v. Balmer*, 53 Wn.2d 460 (1959). The per curiam was written by Clark. Clark draft, recirculated April 15, 1960, Box 637, Nostrand file, Warren Papers. The case returned in the 1961 term (see chap. 11, herewith).

62. *Sawyer*, 360 U.S. 622. The meeting was sponsored by the ILWU (Harry Bridges' union), some of whose officers or members were defendants in the Smith Act case, and was attended "in large part" by union members. *Id.*, 627. The trial ended in the conviction of all seven defendants. *NY Times*, June 20, 1953, "7 in Hawaii Guilty of Red Conspiracy," and July 5, 1953, "6 Hawaii Reds in Jail." The convictions were reversed after *Yates*. *Fujimoto v. United States*, 251 F.2d 342 (9th Cir. 1958).

63. *Sawyer*, 360 U.S. at 636, 640–46 (quotes). A second charge, relating to Sawyer's posttrial interview of a juror, was not, in the Court's view, punished by the Hawaii court. *Id.*, 636–38.

64. *Id.*, 623–46 (quotes, 628, 631, 632). On June 24, 1959, five days before the decision was issued, Brennan circulated a draft "opinion of the Court"; the next day, Stewart circulated his draft concurrence, evidently for the first time. Brennan draft opinion, June 24, 1959, and Stewart draft concurrence, June 25, 1959, Box I:25, Folder 4, Brennan Papers.

65. 360 U.S. at 647–69 (Frankfurter, J., dissenting) (quotes, 653, 663, 664). Clark, while joining Frankfurter, also filed a dissent. *Id.*, 669–71.

66. *Id.*, 646–47 (Stewart, J., concurring in the result) (quotes).

67. *Palermo*, 360 U.S. 343; *Rosenberg*, 360 U.S. 367; 18 U.S.C. § 3500.

68. *Palermo*, 360 U.S. 343–59 (quotes, 345, 351, 352, 356). See Murphy, *Congress and the Court*, 246 ("Frankfurter's majority opinion in *Palermo* . . . almost totally relinquished to congressional discretion questions as to when and under what circumstances FBI files could be made available to criminal defendants").

69. *Rosenberg*, 360 U.S. 367, 368–73 (quote, 370).

70. *Palermo*, 360 U.S. at 360–66 (Brennan, J., concurring in the result) (quotes, 361, 362–63); *Rosenberg*, 360 U.S. at 373–77 (Brennan, J., dissenting) (quote, 375).

71. *NY Times*, February 26, 1959, "Early House Vote on Court Sought."

72. *U.S. News & World* Report, October 3, 1958, 92–102, "What 36 State Chief Justices Said About the Supreme Court," reprinting text of resolution and accompanying committee report (quote, 92); 106 Cong. Rec. 3998–4002 (March 1, 1960) (Byrd remarks); *NY Times*, August 24, 1958, "Jurists Endorse Court Criticism." See Friedman, *Will of the People*, 256 ("The report was anything but respectful").

73. 105 Cong. Rec. 3361–80 (March 5, 1959) (Eastland; reprinting ABA recommendations and committee report) (quotes, 3363, 3364, 3365); *NY Times*, February 22, 1959, "Bar Heads Favor Reversing Court on Red Decisions"; February 25, 1959, "Bar Bids Congress Tighten Red Laws," "Text of Bar Association's Stand on Communism"; and March 1, 1959, "High Court Debate Is Given New Impetus" (Lewis quote). When HUAC issued a report on "Communist Legal Subversion," including "Case histories" of dozens of "identified Communist lawyers," the ABA's president, Ross L. Malone of New Mexico, announced that "disbarment proceedings against lawyers who had been proven to be Communist party members would take place immediately." H. Rept. No. 41, 86th Cong., 1st Sess. (February 16, 1959); *NY Times*, February 17, 1959, "Bar Head Predicts Fast Action on Reds."

74. "Organize" (HR 2369): H. Rept. No. 39, 86th Cong., 1st Sess. (February 18, 1959); 105 Cong. Rec. 3157 (March 2, 1959). HR 3: H. Rept. No. 422, 86th Cong., 1st Sess. (June 2, 1959); 105 Cong. Rec. 11789–808 (June 24, 1959). *Mallory* (HR 4957): H. Rept. No. 352, 85th Cong., 1st Sess. (May 11, 1959); 105 Cong. Rec. 12861–89 (July 7, 1959). A *Nelson*-only bill, which was separately approved by the Judiciary Committee in June (H. Rept. No. 432, 86th Cong., 1st Sess. [June 3, 1959]), was passed by the House as a section of HR 3. A *Yates*-"organize" bill was part of an omnibus bill (S 2652) reported favorably by the Senate Judiciary Committee in June 1960. S. Rept. No. 1811, 86th Cong., 2d Sess. (June 30, 1960); *NY Times*, July 1, 1960, "Senators Favor Passport Curbs."

75. H. Rept. No. 1151, 86th Cong., 1st Sess. (September 4, 1959) (HR 9069); 105 Cong. Rec. 18443–53, 18611–25 (September 7–8, 1959); S. Rept. No. 1811, 86th Cong., 2d Sess. (June 30, 1960); *NY Times*, September 8, 1959, "Congress Weighs Passport Bills," September 9, 1959, "House Approves a Passport Bill," and July 1, 1960, "Senators Favor Passport Curbs." The Dodd-Keating bill (S 2652) provided that the secretary's decision "shall be final"; it made the department's files "part of the evidence" but provided that "[s]uch files may not be examined by the applicant."

76. 106 Cong. Rec. 1783 (February 2, 1960); *NY Times*, February 3, 1960, "Opponents 'Goof,' Risk Bill Slips By." Walter's bill, HR 8121, was reported by HUAC. H. Rept. No. 1122, 86th Cong., 1st Sess. (September 2, 1959). Senator Keating continued to press for passage of a *Greene* bill even after the President's executive order, contending that the

order "does not obviate the necessity for legislation." 106 Cong. Rec. 3172 (February 23, 1960); *NY Times*, February 24, 1960, "Congress Prodded on Security."

77. *NY Times*, September 2, 1960, "Congress Closes."

Chapter 10. *Scales* and *CPUSA*, *Wilkinson* and *Braden*, and *Konigsberg II* and *Anastaplo*—a Full-Scale Retreat

1. *Scales v. United States*, 367 U.S. 203 (1961) (Smith Act); *Noto v. United States*, 367 U.S. 291 (1961) (same); *Communist Party v. SACB*, 367 U.S. 1 (1961) (Internal Security Act); *Wilkinson v. United States*, 365 U.S. 399 (1961) (contempt); *Braden v. United States*, 365 U.S. 431 (1961) (same); *McPhaul v. United States*, 364 U.S. 372 (1960) (same); *Deutch v. United States*, 367 U.S. 456 (1961) (same); *Slagle v. Ohio*, 366 U.S. 259 (1961) (same); *Konigsberg v. State Bar of California*, 366 U.S. 36 (1961) (bar admission); *In re Anastaplo*, 366 U.S. 82 (1961) (same); *Chaunt v. United States*, 364 U.S. 250 (1960) (denaturalization); *Polites v. United States*, 364 U.S. 426 (1960) (same); *Travis v. United States*, 364 U.S. 631 (1961) (Taft-Hartley affidavit); *Cafeteria and Restaurant Workers Union v. McElroy*, 367 U.S. 886 (1961) (loyalty discharge); *Communist Party, U.S.A. v. Catherwood*, 367 U.S. 389 (1961) (Communist Control Act). The Court dismissed on procedural grounds the appeal of Robert G. Thompson, a *Dennis* defendant, challenging the VA's termination of his disability benefits. *Thompson v. Whittier*, 365 U.S. 465 (1961).

2. Election: Rusk, *Statistical History*, 216, 377. Kennedys and McCarthy: Cook, *Nightmare Decade*, 283–88; Reeves, *Life and Times of Joe McCarthy*, 442–44; Arthur M. Schlesinger Jr., *Robert Kennedy and His Times* (Boston: Houghton Mifflin, 1978), 99–115; Richard J. Whalen, *The Founding Father: The Story of Joseph P. Kennedy* (New York: New American Library, 1964), 426–29, 436–38; Arthur M. Schlesinger Jr., *A Thousand Days: John F. Kennedy in the White House* (Boston: Houghton Mifflin, 1965), 12 (quote). Hoover: *NY Times*, January 17, 1960, "F.B.I. Chief Warns of Red Resurgence"; April 19, 1960, "J. E. Hoover Warns of Threat By Reds"; July 18, 1960, "F.B.I. Chief Says Reds Incite Youth"; November 11, 1960, "6 Aides Appointed"; and December 23, 1960, "J. Edgar Hoover Asserts Reds Are Planning New Youth Group."

3. *Uphaus v. Wyman*, 364 U.S. 388 (1960) (dismissal of appeal), 364 U.S. 802 (1960) (denying bail), 81 S. Ct. 22 (1960) (Frankfurter as circuit justice denying bail); Leo Mayer to Frankfurter, November 16, 1960, and Frankfurter to Mayer, November 22 and December 20, 1960, Pt. 2, microfilm reel 73, Frankfurter Papers (quote); Douglas mem., November 21, 1960, Box 1234, Douglas memoranda file, Douglas Papers (quote); *NY Times*, November 15, 1960, "Contempt Cases Stir High Court," and April 25, 1961, "Warren Says Frankfurter Degrades Court in Dissent" (quote).

4. *Uphaus*, 364 U.S. 388–89 (opinion of Brennan, J.) (quote); *id.*, 389–401 (Black, J., dissenting) (quote, 395); *id.*, 401–08 (Douglas, J., dissenting) (quotes, 406, 408); Frankfurter to Clark, Harlan, Whittaker, and Stewart, November 7, 1960, and Frankfurter handwritten Per Curiam on Brennan draft opinion, October 1960, Pt. 2, microfilm reel 73, Frankfurter Papers.

5. *Shelton v. Tucker*, 364 U.S. 479 (1960) (quote, 490); *id.*, 490–96 (Frankfurter, J., dissenting) (quote, 496). In a second decision, the Court (without dissent but with only

five justices joining its opinion) struck down a Louisiana statute aimed at the NAACP, which required "non-trading" associations with an out-of-state affiliate to file annually an affidavit stating that no officer or director of the affiliate was a member of a "Communist, Communist-front or subversive organization[]." *Louisiana ex rel. Gremillion v. NAACP*, 366 U.S. 293, 294–95 (1961).

6. Atlanta hearing cases: *Wilkinson*, 365 U.S. 399; *Braden*, 365 U.S. 431.

7. *Wilkinson*, 365 U.S. at 402–7, (quote, 404); *id.*, 415–16 and n2 (Black, J., dissenting); Robert Sherill, *First Amendment Felon: The Story of Frank Wilkinson, His 132,000-Page FBI File, and His Epic Fight for Civil Rights and Liberties* (New York: Nation, 2005), 24, 178–90. The organization Wilkinson represented was the Emergency Civil Liberties Committee, founded in 1951 by a group that included former ACLU board members unhappy with the ACLU's performance during the McCarthy era. *Id.*, 143; Klingaman, *Encyclopedia of the McCarthy Era*, 136. According to his biographer, Wilkinson joined the CPUSA in 1942 and remained a dissident member. Sherill, *First Amendment Felon*, 77–84.

8. *Wilkinson*, 365 U.S. at 407–15 (quotes, 409–10, 412, 413–14). The Court also rejected Wilkinson's challenge to HUAC's authorizing resolution and his pertinency claim.

9. *Id.*, 415–23 (Black, J., dissenting) (quotes, 417, 423); *id.*, 423–29 (Douglas, J., dissenting); *id.*, 429–30 (Brennan, J., dissenting) (quotes).

10. *Braden*, 365 U.S. at 438–39 and n1 (Black, J., dissenting); Catherine Fosl, *Subversive Southerner: Anne Braden and the Struggle for Racial Justice in the Cold War South* (New York: Palgrave Macmillan, 2002), 135–73, 177, 185–88; Sherill, *First Amendment Felon*, 169–74; *NY Times*, October 2, 1954, "Six Are Indicted on Sedition Count"; October 10, 1954, "Bomb Shattered Racial Harmony"; and December 14, 1954, "Newsman Guilty in Sedition Case." Anne Braden had not yet been tried when *Nelson* was decided.

11. *Braden*, 365 U.S. at 432–34; *id*,. 438–40 (Black, J., dissenting); H. Rept. No. 2684, 85th Cong., 2d. Sess. (August 13, 1958), 2, 18; Fosl, *Subversive Southerner*, 230–37; Sherill, *First Amendment Felon*, 180–81. He received a one-year prison sentence. In the sedition case the Bradens received financial and other support from the Emergency Civil Liberties Committee. Fosl, 185–87.

12. *Braden*, 365 U.S. at 432–38 (quotes, 437–38). The Court found, as in *Wilkinson*, that HUAC "had reason to believe" Braden was a CPUSA member—an informant named him (*id.*, 439n2).

13. *Id.* 438–46 (quote, 444) (Black, J., dissenting); *id.* 446–57 (quote, 449) (Douglas, J., dissenting).

14. *NY*, February 28, 1961 "High Court Backs House Committee in Contempt Issue" (quotes).

15. *McPhaul*, 364 U.S. 372, 373–78 (quote, 373); Gerald Horne, *Communist Front? The Civil Rights Congress, 1946–1956* (Rutherford, N.J.: Fairleigh Dickinson University Press, 1988), 39, 291, 354–58; *NY Times*, November 15, 1960, "Contempt Cases Stir High Court."

16. *McPhaul*, 364 U.S. at 373, 378–80 (quote, 379).

17. *Id.*, 383–87 (Douglas, J., dissenting) (quotes, 384). Black, Warren, and Brennan joined Douglas's dissent.

18. *Deutch*, 367 U.S. 456. See *NY Times*, June 13, 1961, "High Court Voids Contempt Finding" ("Some observers thought a significant factor in the decision was Mr. Deutch's refusal to tell on others").

19. *Deutch*, 367 U.S. at 457–62 (quotes).

20. *Id.*, 463–72 (quotes, 467, 470). The Court distinguished between two types of pertinency issues: the first whether the pertinency of the questions has been "brought home to the witness" and the second (with which *Deutch* was concerned) whether the prosecution proved that the questions were "in fact" pertinent to the subject under inquiry. *Id.*, 467–69.

21. *Id.*, 472–75 (Harlan, J., dissenting) (quote, 473); *id.*, 475–85 (Whittaker, J., dissenting) (quote, 475).

22. *Slagle*, 366 U.S. 259 (quote, 265).

23. *Id.*, 264–68 (quote, 266); *NY Times*, May 16, 1961, "Contempt Ruling For 2 Is Reversed." The convictions of Laverne Slagle and Paul Bohus were reversed entirely, and those of Olga Perry, Eula Ann Cooper, and Rose Mladajan were affirmed in part.

24. *Polites*, 364 U.S. 426 (quote, 434); 127 F. Supp. 768 (E.D.Mich. 1953); Nationality Act of 1940, § 305, 54 Stat. 1137, 1141 (October 14, 1940). *Nowak* and *Maisenberg*: see chap. 8, herewith.

25. *Polites*, 364 U.S. 426–37 (quotes, 434 and n10, 435, 436).

26. *Id.*, 437–40 (Brennan, J., dissenting). Brennan argued that a federal procedural rule afforded discretion to the trial judge, not exercised by him, in cases where it was "no longer equitable" that a "judgment should have prospective application" (Rule 60(b)(5), F.R.Civ.P., 28 U.S.C.A.).

27. *Chaunt*, 364 U.S. 350, *rev'g* 270 F.2d 179 (9th Cir. 1959).

28. 364 U.S. 350–56 (quotes, 353, 354); Act of June 29, 1906, § 4, 34 Stat. 598, as amended, 45 Stat. 1513–14 (March 2, 1929). The government contended that if the arrests had been disclosed it "might well have discovered that [Chaunt] in 1929 was 'a district organizer' of the Communist Party." 364 U.S. at 354–55. It also charged Chaunt with failing to disclose CPUSA membership, but the Court did not reach the issue.

29. *Id.*, 356–60 (Clark, J., dissenting) (quote, 357).

30. Smith Act, 54 Stat. 670, 671; Internal Security Act, § 4(f), 64 Stat. 987, 992; Belknap, *Cold War Political Justice*, 261–72.

31. *Scales*, 350 U.S. 992 (1956), 353 U.S. 979 (1957), 355 U.S. 1 (1957), 358 U.S. 917 (1958), 360 U.S. 924 (1959), 361 U.S. 952 (1960); Telford Taylor, Foreword (original edition), in Junius Scales and Richard Nickson, *Cause at Heart: A Former Communist Remembers* (Athens: University of Georgia Press, 1987, paperbound, 2005), xxxiii; Belknap, *Cold War Political Justice*, 266 (quote). *Lightfoot v. United States* was initially a companion case to *Scales*, 350 U.S. 992 (1956), and was remanded on *Jencks* grounds at the same time, 355 U.S. 2 (1957); but Claude Lightfoot, an Illinois CPUSA official, was not retried. Belknap, 265.

32. Scales and Nickson, *Cause at Heart*; Mickey Friedman, *A Red Family: Junius, Gladys, and Barbara Scales* (Urbana: University of Illinois Press, 2009). Quit the party: Scales and Nickson, *Cause at Heart*, 307–21; Belknap, *Cold War Political Justice*, 265–66.

33. *Scales*, 367 U.S. 203, 206–19 (quotes, 209) ; ISA §4(f) (quote; emphasis added).

At the justices' first conference (there were six) in October 1956, as many as six of the nine justices present, including Burton, seemed to favor reversal on the § 4(f) ground. Harlan was uncertain ("I am inclined to think it [§ 4(f)] is a repealer. I very tentatively vote to reverse"); Frankfurter was "not yet prepared to vote definitively." Dickson, ed., *Supreme Court in Conference*, 301.

34. 367 U.S. at 219-30 (quotes, 220). The parties' respective positions on the constitutional issue created an anomalous situation in which the prosecution argued that a criminal statute required *additional* elements of proof (and thus satisfied constitutional requirements) and the defense the converse.

35. *Id.*, 230-55 (quotes, 231, 232, 237, 250, 251).

36. *Id.*, 259-62 (Black, J., dissenting); *id.*, 262-78 (Douglas, J., dissenting) (quotes, 265, 268); *id.*, 278-89 (Brennan, J., dissenting) (quotes, 280).

37. Dickson, ed., *The Supreme Court in Conference*, 304-07 (first quote, 307); Stewart to Harlan, February 2, 1961, and Mem. of Mr. Justice Stewart (quote, 1), Harlan to Stewart, February 13, 1961 (quote), Stewart to Harlan, April 13, 1961, Box 105, Scales Memoranda etc. file, Harlan Papers; Stewart to Harlan, April 26, 1961, Box 181, Folder 1696, Stewart Papers (quote); Yarbrough, *John Marshall Harlan*, 193-94; see Box 180, Folder 1694, Stewart Papers.

38. *Noto*, 367 U.S. 290.

39. *Id.*, 291-300 (quotes, 297-98, 299). Clark joined Harlan's opinion, explaining he was "a captive of *Yates*—which I continue to believe wrong." Clark to Harlan, February 21, 1961, Box 1235, Argued Cases Nos. 400-869 file, Douglas Papers. See Kalven, *A Worthy Tradition*, 225 ("the differences between the evidence that failed in *Noto* and the evidence that persuaded in *Scales* are pretty subtle").

40. 367 U.S. at 300-302.

41. *NY Times*, June 6, 1961, "High Court Puts Curb on U.S. Reds in 2 Major Cases" (quote); Belknap, *Cold War Political Justice*, 269-70, 271-72. In 1962 a court of appeals reversed the membership-clause conviction of John Cyril Hellman, a party official in Montana and Idaho, finding the evidence insufficient to show he had a specific intent to achieve violent overthrow. *Hellman v. United States*, 298 F.2d 810 (9th Cir.).

42. Belknap, *Cold War Political Justice*, 269-70, 272 (quotes); Scales and Nickson, *Cause at Heart*, 412-15; *NY Times*, February 7, 1962, "The Scales Case," and December 28, 1962, "Clemency for Scales."

43. *CPUSA*, 367 U.S. 1, 19-22. Remands: 351 U.S. 115 (see chap. 6, herewith); 254 F.2d 314 (D.C.Cir. 1958).

44. *CPUSA*, 367 U.S. at 5-8; ISA, §§ 2 (quote), 2(15) (quote), 3(3) (quote). The registration provisions were contained in Title I of the act, titled and often referred to as the "Subversive Activities Control Act." 64 Stat. 987.

45. *CPUSA*, 367 U.S. at 8-14; ISA, §§ 7(a), 7(d), 7(e), 7(h), 8; 28 CFR § 11.200; see Dept. of Justice, Form ISA-1. The form also called for an accounting of "all moneys received and expended" and "a listing of all printing presses and machines." Once registered the organization was required annually to submit updated information. An officer's failure to register the organization was a crime.

46. *CPUSA*, 367 U.S. at 15-18; ISA, §§ 5(a), 6, 11; Immigration & Nationality Act, §§

313(a), 340(c), 66 Stat. 240, 261 (June 27, 1952). Employees of the organization were excluded from the social security system.

47. *CPUSA,* 367 U.S. at 4–115 (quote, 71). The registration provision was ISA, § 7. See discussion in Kalven, *A Worthy Tradition,* 264–87. The Party's most serious claim of procedural error was the board's refusal to require production of memoranda supplied to the FBI by a key government witness, Benjamin Gitlow, a former top party official. The Court, however, declined to consider the claim because the Party had not asserted it in the 1956 appeal. 367 U.S. at 29–32. A second claim involved belatedly produced statements to the FBI of Louis Budenz, also an important witness, who had already completed his testimony and was unable for health reasons to be recalled. The Court upheld the board's refusal to strike Budenz's testimony. *Id.,* 22–29.

48. *CPUSA,* 367 U.S. at 81–105 (quotes, 86, 89, 90, 91, 94).

49. *Id.,* 105–10 (quotes, 106, 107). The Court found "[m]anifestly" premature the claim that the provision of the Act (§ 7(h)) obligating officers to register the Party should it fail to register compelled self-incrimination. *Id.,* 106.

50. *Id.,* 71–81 (quotes, 78–79). The Court relied on a 1938 decision involving registration of holding companies under the Public Utility Holding Company Act of 1935, *Electric Bond & Share Co. v. SEC,* 303 U.S. 419 (1938), where it declined to decide constitutional issues—a precedent, it said, "that controls the present case." 367 U.S. at 77.

51. *Id.,* 115–37 (Warren, C.J., dissenting), 169–90 (Douglas, J., dissenting) (quotes, 174, 175), 191–202 (Brennan, J., joined by Warren, dissenting in part).

52. *Id.,* 137–69 (Black, J., dissenting) (quotes, 146, 147, 160). Black, like the other dissenters, found the Act in "direct conflict with the self-incrimination provisions of the Fifth Amendment." *Id.,* 146. The act was also a bill of attainder, he said, because "[t]he legislative fact-findings . . . supply practically all the proof needed." *Id.* See Powe, *Warren Court,* 151 ("Douglas and Black voted differently on the First Amendment for the first time since 1947").

53. *Communist Party v. United States,* 331 F.2d 807 (D.C.Cir. 1963), 384 F.2d 957 (D.C.Cir. 1967); *Albertson v. SACB,* 382 U.S. 70 (1965) (quote, 77); *NY Times,* December 2, 1961, "Communist Party Indicted after Failing to Register"; December 18, 1962, "Communist Party Convicted By U.S"; December 18, 1963, "Communist Party in U.S. Wins Plea on Registration"; November 20, 1965, "Red Party Guilty on Registration"; and March 4, 1967, "Communists Win Second Reversal on M'Carran Act." The party was sentenced to pay a fine of $120,000 at the first trial and $230,000 at the second. Henry O. Marriott and Lula Mae Thompson, produced as witnesses at the party's second trial, were former party members "who had served as paid informers of the [FBI] throughout their entire periods of membership." 384 F.2d at 967 (quote)

54. *NY Times,* April 4, 1967, "U.S. Drops Fight to Register Reds."

55. *NY Times,* June 6, 1961, "High Court Puts Curb on U.S. Reds in 2 Major Cases" (Lewis quote), and A. Krock, "Supreme Court Strengthens the National Defenses"; June 11, 1961, "U.S. Set to Press Red Registration" (Kennedy quote). Lewis's report cited the pendency of "a large number" of cases to compel registration by alleged "Communist front" organizations; but when the first cases reached the Court in the 1964 term, it vacated the SACB's orders because the hearing records had become "stale." *American*

Committee for Protection of Foreign Born v. SACB, 380 U.S. 503 (1965); *Veterans of Abraham Lincoln Brigade v. SACB*, 380 U.S. 513 (1965).

56. Communist Control Act of 1954, §§ 2, 3 (quotes), 68 Stat. 775, 776 (August 24, 1954).

57. *Communist Party*, 367 U.S. 389 (quotes, 390, 393); chap. 5, herewith; A. Lewis, *NY Times*, June 11, 1961, "Law Tightens on U.S. Communists" (quote).

58. 367 U.S. at 393–95 (quotes); *NY Times*, June 13, 1961, "State Overruled on Taxing Reds." The Court cited as "good indications" the IRS's continued collection of taxes from the Party under the federal unemployment act, along with subsequent actions by the Congress. Black concurred only in the result.

59. *Travis*, 364 U.S. 631, 632–34.

60. *Id.*, 632–35; 18 U.S.C. §§ 1001 (quote), 3237(a) (quote); Taft-Hartley provision, 61 Stat. 136, 146 (June 23, 1947) (quote). The affidavit requirement was repealed in an omnibus labor statute enacted in 1959, replaced by a criminal provision barring present and former (in the preceding five years) Communists from holding union office. Labor-Management Reporting and Disclosure Act of 1959, §§ 201(d), 504(a), 73 Stat. 519, 525, 536–37 (September 14, 1959); *NY Times*, September 15, 1959, "Main Provisions in Labor Reform."

61. *Travis*, 364 U.S. at 635–37 (quotes, 635, 636); *id.*, 637–41 (Harlan, J., dissenting).

62. 1956-term decisions: see chap. 7, herewith.

63. *Konigsberg*, 366 U.S. 36, 37–39 (final quote). First time: 353 U.S. 252 (1957); *id.*, 282 (Harlan quote).

64. *Konigsberg*, 366 U.S. at 40–56 (quotes, 44, 49, 51, 52).

65. *Id.*, 56–80 (Black, J., dissenting) (quotes, 61, 74). Both Black and Brennan, in a separate dissent (*id.*, 80–81), contended that reversal was also required by *Speiser* (which held unlawful the state's imposition of the burden of proof upon the individual). *Speiser*: see chap. 8, herewith.

66. Edward Mosk, "Raphael Konigsberg," 52 *S. Cal. L. Rev.* 665, 666–67 (1979).

67. *Anastaplo*, 366 U.S. 82, 83–84; *id.*, 98–107 (Black, J., dissenting) (quotes, 99, 103); Andrew Patner, "The Quest of George Anastaplo," *Chicago*, December 1982, 185; Abner Mikva, "George Anastaplo," http:www.hydeparkhistory.org/herald/GeorgeAnastaplo.pdf (undated); William J. Martin, "The Anastaplo Case: A Review," *Loyola Law Times*, vol. 2, no. 1 (winter 1962), 9–14, in Box 117, Memoranda file, Harlan Papers; Fred J. Cook, "How They Shortchanged an American," *Saga*, March 1962, 18.

68. 348 U.S. 946 (1955) (denying review), Black and Douglas dissenting; 366 U.S. at 84n2 (quote). The state supreme court's first ruling against Anastaplo was unanimous, 3 Ill.2d 471 (1954); its second was by 4–3 vote, 18 Ill.2d 182 (1959).

69. 366 U.S. at 88–97 (quotes, 89–90, 96–97). The Court decided other issues—whether Anastaplo received "adequate warning" and whether his rejection was "arbitrary or discriminatory"—adversely to him.

70. *Id.*, 97–116 (Black, J., dissenting) (quotes, 98, 107, 112, 114). Brennan, in a one-sentence dissent in which Warren joined, added that he would also reverse on *Speiser* grounds. *Id.*, 116.

71. Patner, "The Quest of George Anastaplo," *Chicago*, 188 (quote). Shortly after the

Court's decision, Anastaplo wrote to the Illinois Supreme Court, "I do not anticipate any further attempt, on my own initiative, to secure admission to the bar of any state." Anastaplo to Chief Justice, October 13, 1961, Box I:53, Folder 5, Brennan Papers.

72. *Cafeteria and Restaurant Workers,* 367 U.S. 886, 887–89 (quotes, 888); 284 F.2d 173, 175 (D.C.Cir. 1960) (en banc) (first quote).

73. 367 U.S. at 889–94 (quote, 892).

74. *Id.*, 894–99 (quotes, 895–96, 898, 899).

75. *Id.*, 899–902 (Brennan, J., dissenting) (quotes, 900–901).

76. H.R. 3: H. Rept. No. 1820, June 13, 1962, 87th Cong., 2d Sess. *Yates* "organize" (HR 3247): 107 Cong. Rec. 7966–67 (May 15, 1961); H. Rept. No. 248, April 18, 1961, 87th Cong., 1st Sess. *Mallory* (HR 7053): 107 Cong. Rec. 10068–81 (June 12, 1961); H. Rept. No. 460, June 7, 1961, 87th Cong., 1st Sess.

77. Powe, *Warren Court,* 154.

Chapter 11. Frankfurter's Departure, a Near-Decision in *Gibson*, and the Era's End

1. Warren mem. to Justices, April 25, 1962, Box 354, Frankfurter 1962 to 1974 file, Warren Papers (quotes). Whittaker: *NY Times,* March 29, 1962, "Whittaker Must Rest," and March 30, 1962, "Ailing Justice Whittaker Leaving Supreme Court"; Garrow, "Mental Decrepitude," 1045–50. Frankfurter: *NY Times,* April 6, 1962, Justice Frankfurter Taken to Hospital," and August 30, 1962, "Justice Frankfurter Retires."

2. *Killian v. United States,* 368 U.S. 231 (1961) (false Taft-Hartley affidavit); *Cramp v. Board of Public Instruction,* 368 U.S. 278 (1961) (loyalty oath); *Russell v. United States,* 369 U.S. 749 (1962) (contempt of Congress). Per curiam: *DeGregory v. Attorney General of New Hampshire,* 368 U.S. 19 (1961); *Nostrand v. Little,* 368 U.S. 436 (1962); *Silber v. United States,* 370 U.S. 717 (1962). The Court refused to review the denial of a preliminary injunction in a lawsuit by blacklisted Hollywood talent against major Hollywood studios challenging the blacklist as a violation of federal antitrust law. *Young v. Motion Picture Association of America,* 370 U.S. 922 (1962).

3. Conf. notes, December 8, 1961, and Harlan draft opinion, circulated March 13, 1962 ("Harlan draft *Gibson* opin."), Box 1288, Gibson memos file, Douglas Papers. The case was one of twelve ordered to be reargued four days after Whittaker's retirement. *Gibson,* 369 U.S. 834 (1962); *NY Times,* April 3, 1962, "Supreme Court Defers 12 Cases."

4. 108 Cong. Rec. 7600–7604 (May 2, 1962) (first quotes); *NY Times,* May 3, 1962, "Eastland Calls Warren Pro-Red" (quoting attack on Warren), and May 4, 1962, "Eastland Charge on Court Scored" (AP dispatch) (quote). Eastland's attack on Warren, quoted verbatim in the *Times,* does not appear in the bound Congressional Record.

5. *Killian,* 368 U.S. 231.

6. *Killian,* 368 U.S. at 244–58 (quotes, 246n5, 247); *id.,* 261–62 (Douglas, J., dissenting) (quote, 261). The same jury-instruction issue had been raised in *Jencks,* also a false Taft-Hartley affidavit prosecution, but was addressed only in Burton's concurring opinion (see chap. 7, herewith). The words of the Taft-Hartley oath created an "affiliation" issue, parallel to the "membership" issue. 368 U.S. at 254–58. The case also presented

Jencks issues, requiring a factual determination concerning FBI agents' destruction of their notes. *Id.*, 236–44.

7. *Id.*, 244–54 (quote, 249). The Court also sustained the trial judge's separate instruction on affiliation with the Party. *Id.*, 254–58. On the *Jencks* issues, it adopted the solicitor general's proposal that the Court vacate Killian's conviction and remand the case to the trial judge for a hearing, after which the judge would either reinstate the conviction or order a new trial. *Id.*, 241, 244.

8. *Id.*, 258–60 (Black, J., dissenting) (quote, 259); *id.*, 261–67 (Douglas, J., dissenting) (quote, 264); *id.*, 267–77 (Brennan, J., dissenting) (quote, 270). *Douds*: see chap. 2, herewith.

9. *Cramp*, 368 U.S. 278 (quotes, 279, 279n1).

10. *Id.*, 279–88 (quotes, 286).

11. *Nostrand*, 368 U.S. 436; *id.*, 436–38 (Douglas, J., dissenting). 1960 ruling: see chap. 9 herewith.

12. Garrow, "Mental Decrepitude," 1045–47; Craig Alan Smith, *Charles Evans Whittaker, Associate Justice of the Supreme Court* (unpublished master's thesis, University of Missouri-Kansas City, 1997), 30, quoted in Garrow, "Mental Decrepitude," 1046 (first quote).

13. Warren mem. to Justices, April 25, 1962, Box 354, Frankfurter 1962 to 1974 file, Warren Papers ("We did not have the services of Charley since about February 1st"); Dennis J. Hutchinson, *The Man Who Once Was Whizzer White: A Portrait of Justice Byron R. White* (New York: Free Press, 1998), 311–12 (first quote); Garrow, "Mental Decrepitude," 1046–49; Medical Bd. certif. (quote), Whittaker to Kennedy (quote), Warren certif., and Warren to Kennedy, all March 16, 1962, Box 358, Whittaker file, Warren Papers; *NY Times*, March 29, 1962, "Whittaker Must Rest" (final quotes) and March 30, 1962, "Ailing Justice Whittaker Leaving Supreme Court." As early as June 1957, shortly after Whittaker joined the Court, Burton noted that he "has been on the verge of a nervous breakdown." Garrow, 1045. Afterward, in 1963, after another Walter Reed board found Whittaker "medically qualified" to serve on courts "other than the Supreme Court," Warren agreed to assign him to serve on lower federal courts. Medical Bd. certif., March 13, 1963, and Warren to Hunter, March 18, 1963, Box 358.

14. *NY Times*, March 30, 1962, "Ailing Justice Whittaker Leaving Supreme Court" (Whittaker quotes), "Transcript of the President's News Conference" (JFK quote).

15. Hutchinson, *Man Who Once Was Whizzer White*; Fred L. Israel, "Byron R. White," in Friedman and Israel, eds., *Justices*, 2951–61; *NY Times*, March 31, 1962, "Byron White Gets Whittaker's Seat," ("All-Round Nominee").

16. Hutchinson, *The Man Who Once Was Whizzer White*, 326; Friedman and Israel, eds., *Justices*, 2957 (observer quote). Votes for the government: *Gibson*, 372 U.S. 539 (1963); *Yellin*, 374 U.S. 109 (1963); *Gastelum-Quinones*, 374 U.S. 469 (1963); *Greene*, 376 U.S. 149 (1964); *Aptheker*, 378 U.S. 500 (1964); *Brown*, 381 U.S. 437 (1965); *DeGregory*, 383 U.S. 825 (1966); *Elfbrandt*, 384 U.S. 11 (1966); *Keyishian*, 385 U.S. 589 (1967); *Whitehill*, 389 U.S. 54 (1967); *Robel*, 389 U.S. 258 (1967).

17. *NY Times*, April 12, 1962, "Senate Approves White for Bench"; April 17, 1962,

"White Takes Supreme Court Seat"; May 1, 1962, "Longer Rest Set for Frankfurter"; and July 2, 1962, A. Lewis, "Supreme Court's Term Viewed as One of Most Significant."

18. *NY Times*, April 6, 1962, "Justice Frankfurter Taken to Hospital"; April 7, 1962, "Rest Prescribed for Frankfurter" (quote); April 24, 1962, "Frankfurter Gaining" (quotes); May 1, 1962, "Longer Rest Set for Frankfurter"; and August 30, 1962, "Justice Frankfurter Retires" (second-stroke quote).

19. McHugh to Warren, August 16, 1962, Box 354, Frankfurter 1962 to 1974 file, Warren Papers; *NY Times*, July 27, 1962, "Kennedy Pays Courtesy Call on Frankfurter at Home"; August 30, 1962, "Justice Frankfurter Retires," and "Text of Frankfurter-Kennedy Letters" (quote).

20. *Baker v. Carr*, 369 U.S. 186 (1962); *id.*, 266 (Frankfurter, J., dissenting) (quote, 267); *NY Times*, August 30, 1962, "Justice Frankfurter Retires" (Lewis quote). Schwartz speculated that there may have been "a cause and effect relationship between his defeat in [*Baker v. Carr*] and the Justice's physical collapse." (*Super Chief*, 427). Frankfurter himself reportedly believed the decision was "responsible for his stroke." Stern and Wermiel, *Justice Brennan*, 191.

21. David L. Stebenne, *Arthur J. Goldberg, New Deal Liberal* (New York: Oxford University Press, 1996), 4–19, 25–44, 65–66, 110–25, 215–35, 309–10, (quote, 217); Stephen J. Friedman, "Arthur J. Goldberg," in Friedman and Israel, eds., *Justices*, 2977–79. As the CIO's general counsel, Goldberg played a major role in its expulsion of eleven unions as Communist-dominated. Stebenne, *Arthur J. Goldberg*, 73–74, 79–80. See Robert M. Lichtman, "Goldberg and Hoover: How Two Disparate Washington Insiders Resolved a McCarthy-Era Problem to Mutual (and the Nation's) Advantage," 10 *Amer. Comm. Hist.* 205, 212–13 (2011).

22. Friedman, "Arthur J. Goldberg," in Friedman and Israel, eds., *Justices*, 2979–83; Belknap, *Supreme Court under Earl Warren*, 75 (quote); Schwartz, *Super Chief*, 445–57 (final quote, 448). Frankfurter, in a 1963 letter to Alexander Bickel, his former law clerk, for example, criticized "such wholly inexperienced men as Goldberg . . . without familiarity with the jurisdiction or the jurisprudence of the Court either as practitioners or scholars or judges." Schwartz, *Super Chief*, 448, 815n8.

23. *NY Times*, April 3, 1962, "Supreme Court Defers 12 Cases," and June 26, 1962, "Supreme Court Will Rehear Contempt of Congress Case"; *Russell*, 369 U.S. 749. At the start of the term, the Court by per curiam order affirmed, by its usual 5–4 split, a judgment in a state contempt case holding Hugo DeGregory, a bookkeeper from Hudson, New Hampshire, in civil contempt for refusing to answer the question "Are you presently a member of the Communist Party?" *DeGregory*, 368 U.S. 19, *aff'g Wyman v. DeGregory*, 103 N.H. 214 (1961); see *NY Times*, April 5, 1966, "High Court Voids Contempt Finding"); *DeGregory v. New Hampshire Atty. Gen.*, 383 U.S. 825, 826n1 (1966). In 1966, the Court reversed another judgment of contempt against DeGregory, citing the "guarantee of the First Amendment that a person can speak or not, as he chooses, free of all governmental compulsion." *Id.*,830.

24. *NY Times*, July 8, 1955, "5 Newsmen Called by Senate Inquiry"; July 16, 1955, "Red 'Leads' Goal of Press Inquiry"; November 19, 1955, "New Inquiry Set on Reds in Press"; December 7, 1955, "Press Inquiry Hears 12"; December 8, 1955, "14 More Tes-

tify in Press Inquiry"; January 5, 1956, "The Voice of a Free Press" (editorial) (quote); "Eastland Again Denies the Times Is His Target"); January 6, 1956, "4 Witnesses Balk at Press Hearing"; January 7, 1956, "2 Senators Say Red Tried to Penetrate Newspapers"; January 8, 1956, "Eastland Committee Plans a New Inquiry"; November 27, 1956, "6 Indicted in Senate Inquiry"; and May 22, 1962, "Contempt Convictions of 6 Voided by Supreme Court"; Caute, *Great Fear*, 451–53. The *Times* reportedly told its subpoenaed employees they would be fired if they invoked the Fifth Amendment; employees who admitted past CPUSA membership but refused to name others or who invoked the First Amendment usually retained their jobs but had to face contempt prosecutions. *Id.*, 453.

25. *Russell*, 369 U.S. at 751–54 (quotes). At the justices' conferences on December 8 and 15, Frankfurter and Whittaker voted to affirm some or all of the convictions. Conf. notes, Box 1260, Argued Cases Nos. 1–25 file and Box 1268, Russell memos file, Douglas Papers.

26. 369 U.S. at 754–72 (quotes, 766, 768, 770). Douglas, in a concurring opinion, argued that no indictment could "be sustained under the requirements of the First Amendment" in the four SISS cases because the hearing "was concededly an investigation of the press." *Id.*, 773.

27. *Id.*, 779–81 (Clark, J., dissenting) (quote); *id.*, 781–94 (Harlan, J., dissenting).

28. *Grumman v. United States*, 370 U.S. 288 (1962); *Silber*, 370 U.S. 717 (quote); *Hartman v. United States*, 370 U.S. 724 (1962); *NY Times*, June 20, 1962, "Conviction Voided in Contempt Case," and June 26, 1962, "2 Contempt-of-Congress Cases Voided Over Faulty Indictments." Author: see draft circulated June 4, 1962, Box 20, Folder 184, Stewart Papers.

29. *NY Times*, June 2, 1962, "6 in Contempt Case Face New Charges"; September 25, 1962, "U.S. Seeks Retrial of 8 for Contempt" (quote); and October 1, 1962, "8 Are Re-Indicted in Contempt Cases."

30. *Shelton v. United States*, 327 F.2d 601 (D.C. Cir. 1963) (quote, 606); *Gojack v. United States*, 394 U.S. 702 (1966); *NY Times*, March 22, 1964, "Courts Settling 8 Contempt Cases," and November 30, 1965, "U.S. Drops Contempt Case against Times Newsman." The Court in *Gojack* held that HUAC failed to comply with its rules requiring that the subject of inquiry be authorized by the committee and that subcommittee hearings be authorized by the full committee. After *Russell* and its progeny were decided, the only contempt-of-Congress case that had been argued but not decided in the 1961 term, *Yellin v. United States*, was ordered to be reargued; in 1963, the Court reversed Yellin's conviction, by 5–4 vote, on the ground that HUAC violated its own rule concerning non-public hearings. *Yellin v. United States*, 370 U.S. 931 (1962), 374 U.S. 109 (1963).

31. Belknap, *Supreme Court Under Earl Warren*, 150 (quote); *Uphaus*, 364 U.S. 408 (Douglas, J., dissenting) (quote). String of cases: see chaps. 8, 9, and 10 herewith.

32. Harlan draft *Gibson* opinion, 1–6 (quotes); *Gibson*, 372 U.S. 539, 540–43 (1963).

33. Harlan draft *Gibson* opinion, 1, 3–6 (quotes); *Gibson*, 372 U.S. at 542–43. Gibson was shown photographs of the fourteen individuals the investigator named as having been both CPUSA and NAACP members. According to Harlan's draft opinion (at 5), he said he recognized "only one as having been at any time a member of the N.A.A.C.P."; but according to the Court's 1963 decision, he "said that he could associate none of them with the N.A.A.C.P." (372 U.S. at 543). The committee initially sought unconditional

production of the Miami branch's membership list; but the Florida Supreme Court, citing pertinency "limitations," outlined the more nuanced approach ultimately employed. *Id.*, 540–41; *Gibson*, 108 So.2d 729, 744 (Fla. 1958); see Mark V. Tushnet, *Making Civil Rights Law: Thurgood Marshall and the Supreme Court, 1936-1961* (New York: Oxford University Press, 1994), 296–98.

34. Conf. notes, December 8, 1961, Box 1288, Gibson memos file, Douglas Papers (quotes); Schwartz, *Super Chief*, 452–53.

35. Harlan draft *Gibson* opinion, 6–11 (quotes, 8); see Frankfurter to Warren, undated note, Box 354, Frankfurter 1958 thru 1961 file, Warren Papers (Frankfurter initially assigned *Gibson* opinion to himself).

36. *Gibson*, 369 U.S. 834 (reargument), 372 U.S. 539 (quotes, 549, 554–55); *id.*, 558–59 (Black, J., concurring) (quotes); *id.*, 559–76 (Douglas, J., concurring); Harlan mem., October 4, 1962 (quote), and draft opinion, Box I:80, Folder 2, Brennan Papers.

37. *NY Times*, June 26, 1962, "Black Is Honored By Supreme Court" (quotes), "A Liberal From Dixie."

38. 1963 term: *Apteker v. Secretary of State*, 378 U.S. 500 (1964); *NY Times*, June 23, 1964 "Ruling Ends Passport Ban Restricting Travel by Reds." Travel abroad was held to be a protected "liberty" interest. 1964 term: *United States v. Brown*, 381 U.S. 437 (1965); *NY Times*, June 8, 1965, "Court Upsets Ban on Reds as Officials of Unions." The provision was added when the Taft-Hartley affidavit requirement was repealed (see chap. 10 herewith). 1965 term: *Albertson v. Subversive Activities Control Board*, 382 U.S. 70 (1965) (see chap. 10 herewith); *NY Times*, November 16, 1965, "High Court Limits Law to Register Individual Reds"; 1967 term: *United States v. Robel*, 389 U.S. 258 (1967) (quotes, 266); *NY Times*, December 12, 1967 "High Court Voids Job Ban on Reds in Defense Units." The defendant, Frank Robel, was a machinist at the Seattle shipyard of Todd Shipyards Corporation and a CPUSA member.

39. Frankfurter: *NY Times*, Feburary 23, 1965, "Felix Frankfurter Is Dead." Fortas: *NY Times*, July 28, 1965, "Fortas Taking Goldberg Seat on High Court," and "The New Justice"; see Laura Kalman, *Abe Fortas: A Biography* (New Haven, Conn.: Yale University Press, 1990). Vietnam War decision: *Bond v. Floyd*, 385 U.S. 116 (1966).

Epilogue

1. Mocking symbols: *Schacht v. United States*, 398 U.S. 58 (1970); *Smith v. Goguen*, 415 U.S. 566 (1974); *Spence v. Washington*, 418 U.S. 405 (1974); *NY Times*, May 26, 1970, "Court Upsets Ban on Uniforms Worn by Actors Mocking Army." Disorderly conduct: *Cohen v. California*, 403 U.S. 15 (1971); *Hess v. Indiana*, 414 U.S. 105 (1973). In an earlier decision, however, the Court upheld the conviction of a defendant who burned his draft card before a crowd on the steps of the South Boston Courthouse. *United States v. O'Brien*, 391 U.S. 367 (1968).

2. *New York Times Co. v. United States*, 403 U.S. 713 (1971); *id.*, 717 (Black, J., concurring) (first quote); Peter Irons and Stephanie Guitton, eds., *May It Please the Court: The Most Significant Oral Arguments before the Supreme Court Since 1955* (New York: New Press, 1993), 170 (quotes); Stone, *Perilous Times*, 500–16. The *Post* began to publish the study after the government obtained a temporary restraining order against the *Times*.

3. 403 U.S. at 714–48. Prior restraints: *Near v. Minnesota*, 283 U.S. 697 (1931); *Bantam Books, Inc. v. Sullivan*, 372 U.S. 58 (1963) (quote, 70); *Organization for a Better Austin v. Keefe*, 402 U.S. 415 (1971).

4. *Brandenburg v. Ohio*, 395 U.S. 444 (1969) (quotes, 446, 447); *Whitney v. California*, 274 U.S. 357 (1927).

5. 395 U.S. 444–49 (quote, 447); The per curiam was written by Brennan. Draft opinion, by Brennan, circulated May 20, 1969, Box 404, Brandenburg file, Black Papers. It began as a signed opinion by Fortas, who left the Court (on May 15th) before it could be issued. *Id.*, Fortas draft opinion, recirculated April 18, 1969; see *NY Times*, May 16, 1969, "Fortas Quits the Supreme Court."

6. Stone, *Perilous Times*, 418–19 (quote); Gunther, "Reflections on *Robel*," 1149 (quote). There was substantial identity among the justices during the two periods: Douglas, Brennan, and Stewart continued on the Court for the entire Vietnam War period, Black and Harlan for most of it, and Warren for part of it. *NY Times*, June 23, 1969, "Warren Era Ending Today after 16 Years of Reform"; September 18, 1971, "Justice Black, 85, Quits High Court"; and September 24, 1971, "Harlan Retires."

7. Brennan, "Quest to Develop," 8.

8. Schwartz, *Super Chief*, 448 (Goldberg quote); Fred Rodell, *NY Times Magazine*, May 28, 1960, "Crux of the Court Hullabaloo" (quote).

9. In *Sweezy*, where there was no opinion of the Court, Frankfurter's concurring opinion was if anything more far reaching than Warren's plurality opinion.

10. Friedman, *Will of the People*, 253 (quote).

11. Black to Rodell, September 7, 1962, Box 47, Rodell 1956–63 file, Black Papers (quote). The internal quotations and ellipsis in Black's letter are taken from Rodell's law review article on judicial deference, the subject of the letter. Rodell, "For Every Justice, Judicial Deference Is a Sometime Thing," 50 *Georgetown L. J.* 700, 701 (1962) ("[T]he *Georgetown Law Journal* asked me to write 'an article examining the extent to which the judiciary should defer to legislative judgment without abdicating its own responsibilities'").

12. David H. Souter, Commencement Address, Harvard University, May 27, 2010 (quotes).

Selected Bibliography

Justices' Papers

Hugo L. Black Papers, Manuscript Division, Library of Congress, Washington, D.C.
William J. Brennan Jr. Collection, Manuscript Division, Library of Congress, Washington, D.C.
Harold H. Burton Collection, Manuscript Division, Library of Congress, Washington, D.C.
Tom C. Clark Papers, Rare Books and Special Collections, Tarlton Law Library, University of Texas at Austin.
William O. Douglas Collection, Manuscript Division, Library of Congress, Washington, D.C.
Felix Frankfurter Papers, Harvard Law School Library, Parts 1 and 2, microfilm.
John M. Harlan Papers, Seeley G. Mudd Manuscript Library, Princeton University, Princeton, N.J.
Robert H. Jackson Papers, Manuscript Division, Library of Congress, Washington, D.C.
Stanley Forman Reed Collection, University of Kentucky, Special Collections Library, Lexington.
Potter Stewart Papers, Sterling Memorial Library, Yale University, New Haven.
Frederick Moore Vinson Collection, University of Kentucky, Special Collections Library, Lexington.
Earl Warren Papers, Manuscript Division, Library of Congress, Washington, D.C.

Books

Alsop, Joseph, and Turner Catledge. *The 168 Days* (Garden City, N.Y.: Doubleday/Doran, 1938)
American Bar Association. *An Independent Judiciary,* Report of the Commission on Separation of Powers and Judicial Independence (1997).

Bartley, Numan V. *The Rise of Massive Resistance: Race and Politics in the South During the 1950s* (Baton Rouge: Louisiana State University Press, 1969).
Belknap, Michal. *Cold War Political Justice: The Smith Act, the Communist Party, and American Civil Liberties* (Westport, Conn.: Greenwood, 1977).
Belknap, Michal. *The Supreme Court under Earl Warren, 1953–1969* (Columbia: University of South Carolina Press, 2005).
Belknap, Michal. *The Vinson Court: Justices, Rulings, and Legacy* (Santa Barbara, Calif.: ABC-CLIO, 2004).
Belknap, Michal, ed., *American Political Trials* (Westport, Conn.: Greenwood, 1981).
Berger, Raoul. *Congress v. The Supreme Court* (Cambridge: Harvard University Press, 1969).
Berry, Mary Frances. *Stability, Security and Continuity: Mr. Justice Burton and Decision-Making in the Supreme Court 1945–1958* (Westport, Conn.: Greenwood, 1978).
Blasi, Vincent, ed. *The Burger Court: The Counter-Revolution That Wasn't* (New Haven: Yale University Press, 1983).
Bontecou, Eleanor. *The Federal Loyalty-Security Program* (Ithaca, N.Y.: Cornell University Press, 1953).
Broadwater, Jeff. *Adlai Stevenson and American Politics: The Odyssey of a Cold War Liberal* (New York: Twayne, 1994).
Broadwater, Jeff. *Eisenhower and the Anti-Communist Crusade* (Chapel Hill: University of North Carolina Press, 1992).
Brown, Ralph S. Jr. *Loyalty and Security: Employment Tests in the United States* (New Haven: Yale University Press, 1958).
Brownell, Herbert, with John P. Burke. *Advising Ike: The Memoirs of Attorney General Herbert Brownell* (Lawrence: University Press of Kansas, 1993).
Caro, Robert A. *The Years of Lyndon Johnson: Master of the Senate* (New York: Knopf, 2002).
Carpenter, William S. *Judicial Tenure in the United States* (New Haven: Yale University Press, 1918).
Caute, David. *The Great Fear: The Anti-Communist Purge Under Truman and Eisenhower* (New York: Simon & Schuster, 1978).
Chernow, Ron. *Alexander Hamilton.* (New York: Penguin, 2004).
Clark, Hunter R. *Justice Brennan: The Great Conciliator* (New York: Birch Lane, 1995).
Cook, Fred J. *The Nightmare Decade: The Life and Times of Senator Joe McCarthy* (New York: Random House, 1971).
Cray, Ed. *Chief Justice: A Biography of Earl Warren (New York: Simon & Schuster, 1997).*
Dickson, Del, ed. *The Supreme Court in Conference (1940–1985): The Private Discussions Behind Nearly 300 Supreme Court Decisions* (New York: Oxford University Press, 2001).
Donovan, Robert J. *My First Fifty Years in Politics* (New York: McGraw Hill, 1960).
Douglas, William O. *The Court Years, 1939–1975: The Autobiography of William O. Douglas* (New York: Random House, 1980).
Douglas, William O. *Go East, Young Man: The Early Years; The Autobiography of William O. Douglas* (New York: Random House, 1974).

Duberman, Martin Bauml. *Paul Robeson* (New York: Knopf, 1988).
Dubin, Michael J. United States Congressional Elections, 1788–1977 (Jefferson, N.C.: McFarland, 1998).
Eisenhower, Dwight D. *The White House Years: Mandate for Change 1953–1956* (New York: Doubleday, 1963).
Eisler, Kim Isaac. *A Justice for All: William J. Brennan, Jr., and the Decisions That Transformed America* (New York: Simon & Schuster, 1993).
Ellis, Joseph J. *American Sphinx: The Character of Thomas Jefferson* (New York: Vintage Books, 1996).
Ellis, Richard E. *The Jeffersonian Crisis: Courts and Politics in the Young Republic* (New York: Oxford University Press, 1971).
Ernst, Morris L., and David Loth. *Report on the American Communist* (New York: Holt, 1952).
Evans, Rowland, and Robert Novak. *Lyndon Johnson: The Exercise of Power* (New York: New American Library, 1966).
Fairman, Charles. *History of the Supreme Court of the United States*, vol. VI: *Reconstruction and Reunion, 1864–88, Part One* (New York: Macmillan, 1971).
Fassett, John D. *New Deal Justice: The Life of Stanley Reed of Kentucky* (New York: Vantage, 1994).
Feldman, Noah. *Scorpions: The Battles and Triumphs of FDR's Great Supreme Court Justices* (New York: Twelve, 2010).
Fosl, Catherine. *Subversive Southerner: Anne Braden and the Struggle for Racial Justice in the Cold War South* (New York: Palgrave Macmillan, 2002).
Frank, John P. *Mr. Justice Black: The Man and His Opinions* (New York: Knopf, 1949).
Frank, John P. *The Warren Court* (New York: Macmillan, 1964).
Frankfurter, Felix. *The Case of Sacco and Vanzetti* (New York: Universal Library, 1962).
Freyer, Tony, ed. *Justice Hugo Black and Modern America* (Tuscaloosa: University of Alabama Press, 1990).
Fried, Richard M. *Nightmare in Red: The McCarthy Era in Perspective* (New York: Oxford University Press, 1990).
Friedman, Barry. *The Will of the People: How Public Opinion Has Influenced the Supreme Court and Shaped the Meaning of the Constitution* (New York: Farrar, Straus and Giroux, 2009).
Friedman, Leon, and Fred L. Israel, eds. *The Justices of the United States Supreme Court: Their Lives and Major Opinions*, vol. IV (New York: Bowker and Chelsea House, 1969).
Friedman, Mickey. *A Red Family: Junius, Gladys & Barbara Scales* (Urbana: University of Illinois Press, 2009).
Gentry, Curt. *J. Edgar Hoover: The Man and the Secrets* (New York: Norton, 1991).
Gerhart, Eugene. *America's Advocate: Robert H. Jackson* (Indianapolis: Bobbs-Merrill, 1958).
Geyh, Charles Gardner. *When Congress and the Courts Collide: The Struggle for Control of America's Judicial System* (Ann Arbor: University of Michigan Press, 2006)
Ginger, Ann Fagan, and Eugene M. Tobin, eds. *The National Lawyers Guild: From Roosevelt through Reagan* (Philadelphia: Temple University Press, 1988).

Goldberg, Arthur J. *AFL-CIO: Labor United* (New York: McGraw Hill, 1956).
Goldstein, Robert Justin. *American Blacklist: The Attorney General's List of Subversive Organizations* (Lawrence: University Press of Kansas, 2008).
Goldstein, Robert Justin. *Political Repression in Modern America: From 1870 to 1976* (Urbana: University of Illinois Press, 2001).
Goodman, Walter. *The Committee: The Extraordinary Career of the House Committee on Un-American Activities* (New York: Farrar, Straus, 1968).
Griffith, Robert. *The Politics of Fear: Joseph R. McCarthy and the Senate*, 2nd ed. (Amherst: University of Massachusetts Press, 1987).
Griffith, Robert, and Athan Theoharis, eds., *The Specter: Original Essays on the Cold War and the Origins of McCarthyism* (New York: New Viewpoints, 1974).
Gugin, Linda C., and James E. St. Clair. *Sherman Minton: New Deal Senator, Cold War Justice* (Indianapolis: Indiana Historical Society, 1997).
Haynes, John Earl, and Harvey Klehr. *Venona: Decoding Soviet Espionage in America* (New Haven: Yale University Press, 1999).
Haynes, John Earl, Harvey Klehr, and Alexander Vassiliev. *Spies: The Rise and Fall of the KGB in America* (New Haven: Yale University Press, 2009).
Horne, Gerald. *Communist Front? The Civil Rights Congress, 1946–1956* (Rutherford, N.J.: Fairleigh Dickinson University Press, 1988).
Hutchinson, Dennis J. *The Man Who Once Was Whizzer White: A Portrait of Justice Byron R. White* (New York: Free Press, 1998).
Irons, Peter. *Justice at War: The Story of the Japanese American Internment Cases* (Berkeley: University of California Press, 1983).
Irons, Peter, and Stephanie Guitton, eds. *May It Please the Court: The Most Significant Oral Arguments before the Supreme Court Since 1955* (New York: New Press, 1993).
Isserman, Maurice. *Which Side Were You On? The American Communist Party during the Second World War* (Urbana: University of Illinois Press, 1993).
Jackson, Robert H. *The Struggle for Judicial Supremacy: A Study of a Crisis in American Power Politics* (New York: Vintage [paperbound], 1941).
Jackson, Robert H. *The Supreme Court in the American System of Government* (New York: Harper & Row, 1955).
Kalman, Laura. *Abe Fortas: A Biography* (New Haven: Yale University Press, 1990).
Kalven, Harry Jr. *The Negro and the First Amendment* (Chicago: University of Chicago Press, 1965).
Kalven, Harry Jr. *A Worthy Tradition: Freedom of Speech in America* (New York: Harper & Row, 1988).
Karabell, Zachary. *The Last Campaign: How Harry Truman Won the 1948 Election* (New York: Vintage, 2000).
Keck, Thomas M. *The Most Activist Supreme Court in History: The Road to Modern Judicial Conservatism* (Chicago: University of Chicago Press, 2004)
Klarman, Michael. *From Jim Crow to Civil Rights: The Supreme Court and the Struggle for Racial Equality* (New York: Oxford University Press, 2004).
Klehr, Harvey. *The Heyday of American Communism: The Depression Decade* (New York: Basic Books, 1984).

Klehr, Harvey, and John Earl Haynes. *The American Communist Movement: Storming Heaven Itself* (New York: Twayne, 1992).

Klehr, Harvey, John Earl Haynes, and Kyrill M. Anderson. *The Soviet World of American Communism* (New Haven: Yale University Press, 1998).

Klehr, Harvey, and Ronald Radosh. *The Amerasia Spy Case: Prelude to McCarthyism* (Chapel Hill: University of North Carolina Press, 1996).

Klingaman, William K. *Encyclopedia of the McCarthy Era* (New York: Facts on File, 1996).

Kluger, Richard. *Simple Justice: The History of* Brown v. Board of Education *and Black America's Struggle for Equality* (New York: Vintage Books, 2004).

Knauff, Ellen Raphael. *The Ellen Knauff Story* (New York: Norton, 1952).

Kutler, Stanley I. *The American Inquisition: Justice and Injustice in the Cold War* (New York: Hill and Wang, 1982).

Kutler, Stanley I. *Judicial Power and Reconstruction Politics* (University of Chicago Press, 1968).

Larrowe, Charles P. *Harry Bridges: The Rise and Fall of Radical Labor in the United States* (New York: Lawrence Hill, 1972).

Lash, Joseph P. *Diaries of Felix Frankfurter* (New York: Norton, 1975).

Latham, Earl. *The Communist Controversy in Washington: From the New Deal to McCarthy* (Cambridge: Harvard University Press, 1966).

Leab, Daniel J. *I Was a Communist for the FBI: The Unhappy Life and Times of Matt Cvetic* (University Park: Pennsylvania State University Press, 2000).

Leuchtenburg, William E. *The Supreme Court Reborn: The Constitutional Revolution in the Age of Roosevelt* (New York: Oxford University Press, 1995).

Lewis, Anthony. *Freedom for the Thought That We Hate: A Biography of the First Amendment* (New York: Basic, 2007)

Lewis, George. *The White South and the Red Menace: Segregationists, Anticommunism, and Massive Resistance, 1945–1965* (Gainesville: University Press of Florida, 2004).

Lichtman, Robert M., and Ronald D. Cohen. *Deadly Farce: Harvey Matusow and the Informer System in the McCarthy Era* (Urbana: University of Illinois Press, 2004).

Linfield, Michael. *Freedom Under Fire: U.S. Civil Liberties in Times of War* (Boston: South End, 1990).

Lorence, James J. *The Suppression of* Salt of the Earth: *How Hollywood, Big Labor, and Politicians Blacklisted a Movie in Cold War America* (Albuquerque: University of New Mexico Press, 1999).

Madison, James, Alexander Hamilton, and John Jay. *The Federalist Papers,* Isaac Kramnick ed. (London: Penguin, 1987).

Mann, Robert. *The Walls of Jericho: Lyndon Johnson, Hubert Humphrey, Richard Russell, and the Struggle for Civil Rights* (New York: Harcourt, Brace. 1996).

Martin, Joe (as told to Robert J. Donovan). *My First Fifty Years in Politics* (New York: McGraw Hill, 1960).

May, Gary. *Un-American Activities: The Trials of William Remington* (New York: Oxford University Press, 1994).

McCloskey, Robert G. *The American Supreme Court,* 4th ed. (Chicago: University of Chicago Press, 2005).

McCullough, David. *Truman* (New York: Simon & Schuster, 1992).
McPherson, Harry. *A Political Education* (Boston: Little, Brown, 1972).
Mendelson, Wallace. *Justices Black and Frankfurter: Conflict in the Court* (Chicago: University of Chicago Press, 1961).
Miller, Arthur. *Timebends: A Life* (New York: Grove, 1987).
Miller, Merle. *Plain Speaking: An Oral History of Harry S. Truman* (New York: Berkley, 1974).
Mitchell, Greg. *Tricky Dick and the Pink Lady: Richard Nixon vs. Helen Gahagan Douglas-Sexual Politics and the Red Scare, 1950* (New York: Random House, 1998).
Morgan, Ted. *Reds: McCarthyism in Twentieth-Century America* (New York: Random House, 2003).
Morris, Roger. *Richard Milhous Nixon: The Rise of an American Politician* (New York: Holt, 1990).
Murphy, Bruce Allen. *The Brandeis/Frankfurter Connection: The Secret Political Activities of Two Supreme Court Justices* (New York: Oxford University Press, 1982).
Murphy, Bruce Allen. *Wild Bill: The Legend and Life of William O. Douglas* (New York: Random House, 2003).
Murphy, Walter F. *Congress and the Court: A Case Study in the American Political Process* (Chicago: University of Chicago Press, 1962).
Musmanno, Michael A. *Across the Street from the Courthouse* (Philadelphia: Dorrence, 1954).
Myrdal, Gunnar. *An American Dilemma: The Negro Problem and American Democracy* (New York: Harper, 1944).
Nelson, Steve. *The 13th Juror: The Inside Story of My Trial* (New York: Masses and Mainstream, 1955).
Nelson, Steve, James R. Barrett, and Rob Ruck. *Steve Nelson, American Radical* (Pittsburgh: University of Pittsburgh Press 1981).
Newman, Roger K. *Hugo Black: A Biography* (New York: Fordham University Press, 2d ed., 1997).
Newton, Jim. *Justice for All: Earl Warren and the Nation He Made* (New York: Riverhead, 2006).
Olmsted, Kathryn S. *Red Spy Queen: A Biography of Elizabeth Bentley* (Chapel Hill: University of North Carolina Press, 2002).
Oshinsky, David M. *A Conspiracy So Immense: The World of Joe McCarthy* (New York: Free Press, 1983).
Palmer, Jan. *The Vinson Court Era: The Supreme Court's Conference Votes: Data and Analysis* (New York: AMS, 1990).
Parrish, Michael E. *Felix Frankfurter and His Times: The Reform Years* (New York: Free Press, 1982).
Powe, Lucas A. *The Warren Court and American Politics* (Cambridge: Harvard University Press, 2000).
Powers, Richard Gid. *Not Without Honor: The History of American Anticommunism* (New York: The Free Press, 1995).
Powers, Richard Gid. *Secrecy and Power: The Life of J. Edgar Hoover* (New York: Free Press, 1987).

Pritchett, C. Herman. *Civil Liberties and the Vinson Court* (Chicago: University of Chicago Press, 1966).
Radosh, Ronald, and Joyce Milton. *The Rosenberg File: Second Edition* (New Haven: Yale University Press, 1997).
Reeves, Thomas C. *The Life and Times of Joe McCarthy: A Biography* (New York: Stein & Day, 1982).
Rehnquist, William H. *All the Laws but One: Civil Liberties in Wartime* (New York: Vantage, 1998).
Rehnquist, William H. *Grand Inquests: The Historic Impeachments of Justice Samuel Chase and President Andrew Johnson* (New York: Morrow, 1992).
Robertson, David. *Sly and Able: A Political Biography of James F. Byrnes* (New York: Norton, 1994).
Rodell, Fred. *Nine Men: A Political History of the Supreme Court from 1790 to 1955* (New York: Random House, 1955).
Rosswurm, Steve, ed. *The CIO's Left-Led Unions* (New Brunswick, N.J.: Rutgers University Press, 1992).
Rovere, Richard H. *The American Establishment and Other Reports, Opinions, and Speculations* (New York: Harcourt, Brace & World, 1962).
Rovere, Richard H. *Senator Joe McCarthy* (New York: Harcourt, Brace, 1959)
Rusk, Jerrold G., *A Statistical History of the American Electorate* (Washington: CQ, 2001).
Sabin, Arthur J. *In Calmer Times: The Supreme Court and Red Monday* (Philadelphia: University of Pennsylvania Press, 1999).
Sabin, Arthur J. *Red Scare in Court: New York versus the International Workers Order* (Philadelphia: University of Pennsylvania Press, 1993).
Scales, Junius, and Richard Nickson. *Cause at Heart: A Former Communist Remembers* (Athens, Ga.: University of Georgia Press, 1987/2005).
Schlesinger, Arthur M. Jr. *Robert Kennedy and His Times* (Boston: Houghton Mifflin, 1978).
Schlesinger, Arthur M. Jr. *A Thousand Days: John F. Kennedy in the White House* (Boston: Houghton Mifflin, 1965).
Schrecker, Ellen. *Many Are the Crimes: McCarthyism in America* (Boston: Little, Brown, 1998).
Schwartz, Bernard. *A History of the Supreme Court* (New York: Oxford University Press, 1993).
Schwartz, Bernard. *Super Chief: Earl Warren and His Supreme Court—A Judicial Biography* (New York: New York University Press, 1983).
Schwartz, Bernard. *The Unpublished Opinions of the Warren Court* (New York: Oxford University Press, 1985).
Sherill, Robert. *First Amendment Felon: The Story of Frank Wilkinson, His 132,000-Page FBI File, and His Epic Fight for Civil Rights and Liberties* (New York: Nation, 2005).
Silber, Norman I. *With All Deliberate Speed: The Life of Philip Elman*, (Ann Arbor: University of Michigan Press, 2004).
Simon, James F. *The Antagonists: Hugo Black, Felix Frankfurter and Civil Liberties in Modern America* (New York: Simon & Schuster, 1989).

Simon, James F. *Independent Journey: The Life of William O. Douglas* (New York: Harper & Row, 1980).

Smith, Richard Norton. *Thomas E. Dewey and His Times* (New York: Simon & Schuster, 1982).

St. Clair, James E., and Linda C. Gugin. *Chief Justice Fred M. Vinson of Kentucky: A Political Biography* (Lexington: University Press of Kentucky, 2002).

Stebenne, David L. *Arthur J. Goldberg, New Deal Liberal* (New York: Oxford University Press, 1996).

Stern, Seth, and Stephen Wermiel. *Justice Brennan: Liberal Champion* (Boston: Houghton Mifflin Harcourt, 2010).

Stone, Geoffrey R. *Perilous Times: Free Speech in Wartime from the Sedition Act of 1798 to the War on Terrorism.* (New York: Norton, 2004).

Stone, I. F. *The Haunted Fifties, 1953–1963* (Boston: Little Brown, 1963).

Stouffer, Samuel A. *Communism, Conformity, and Civil Liberties* (New York: Doubleday, 1955).

Tanenhaus, Sam. *Whittaker Chambers: A Biography* (New York: Random House, 1997).

Theoharis, Athan G., and John Stuart Cox. *The Boss: J. Edgar Hoover and the Great American Inquisition* (Philadelphia: Temple University Press, 1988).

Tushnet, Mark V. *Making Civil Rights Law: Thurgood Marshall and the Supreme Court, 1936–1961* (New York: Oxford University Press, 1994).

Urofsky, Melvin I. *Division and Discord The Supreme Court under Stone and Vinson, 1941–1953* (Columbia: University of South Carolina Press, 1997).

Urofsky, Melvin I. *Felix Frankfurter: Judicial Restraint and Civil Liberties (Boston: Twayne, 1991).*

Urofsky, Melvin I. *Louis D. Brandeis: A Life* (New York: Pantheon, 2009)

Urofsky, Melvin I. ed. *The Douglas Letters: Selections from the Private Papers of Justice William O. Douglas*, (Bethesda, Md.: Adler & Adler, 1987).

Urofsky, Melvin I. ed. *The Supreme Court Justices: A Biographical Dictionary* (New York: Garland, 1994).

Warren, Earl. *The Memoirs of Chief Justice Earl Warren.* (Garden City, N.Y.: Doubleday, 1977).

Weinstein, Allen, *Perjury: The Hiss-Chambers Case* (New York: Knopf, 1978).

Weaver, John D. *Warren: The Man, The Court, The Era* (Boston: Little, Brown, 1967).

Whalen, Richard J. *The Founding Father: The Story of Joseph P. Kennedy* (New York: New American Library, 1964).

White, G. Edward. *Earl Warren: A Public Life* (New York: Oxford University Press, 1982).

White, John Kenneth. *Still Seeing Red: How the Cold War Shapes the New American Politics* (Boulder, Colo.: Westview, 1997).

Wicker, Tom. *One of Us: Richard Nixon and the American Dream* (New York: Random House, 1991).

Wicker, Tom. *Shooting Star: The Brief Arc of Joe McCarthy* (Orlando: Harcourt, 2006).

Wiecek, William M. *The Birth of the Modern Constitution: The United States Supreme Court, 1941–1953,* vol. XII, History of the Supreme Court (Cambridge: Cambridge University Press, 2006).

Wills, Garry. *Inventing America: Jefferson's Declaration of Independence*. (New York: Vintage, 1978).
Woods, Jeff. *Black Struggle, Red Scare: Segregation and Anti-Communism in the South, 1948–1968* (Baton Rouge: Louisiana State University Press, 2004).
Yarbrough, Tinsley E. *John Marshall Harlan: Great Dissenter of the Warren Court* (New York: Oxford University Press, 1992).
Ybarra, Michael J. *Washington Gone Crazy: Senator Pat McCarran and the Great American Communist Hunt* (Hanover, N.H.: Steerforth, 2004).
Young, Evan A. *Lone Star Justice: A Biography of Justice Tom C. Clark* (Dallas: Hendrick-Long, 1998).

Journal Articles

Alsop, Joseph. "The Strange Case of Louis Budenz," *Atlantic Monthly*, April 1952.
Atkinson, David N. "Justice Sherman Minton and Behavior Patterns Inside the Supreme Court," 69 *Nw. U. L. Rev.* 716 (1974).
Balkin, Jack M. "*Bush v. Gore* and the Boundary Between Law and Politics," 110 *Yale L. J.* 1407 (2001).
Black, Hugo L. "The Bill of Rights," 35 *N.Y.U. L. Rev.* 865 (1960).
Boudin, Leonard B. "The Constitutional Right to Travel," 56 *Colum. L. Rev.* 47 (1956).
Brown, Ralph S. Jr., and Fassett, John D. "Loyalty Tests for Admission to the Bar," 20 *U. Chi. L. Rev.* 480 (1953).
Byrnes, James F. "'The Supreme Court Must Be Curbed,'" *U.S. News & World Report*, May 18, 1956, 50–58.
Cohen, William. "Douglas and the *Rosenberg* Case: Setting the Record Straight," 70 *Cornell L. Rev.* 211 (1985).
Culp, Maurice S. "A Survey of the Proposals to Limit or Deny the Power of Judicial Review by the Supreme Court of the United States," 4 *Indiana L. J.* 386 (1929).
Culp, Maurice S. "A Survey of the Proposals to Limit or Deny the Power of Judicial Review by the Supreme Court of the United States—II," 4 *Indiana L. J.* 474 (1929).
Deery, Phillip. "'A Blot upon Liberty': McCarthyism, Dr. Barsky, and the Joint Anti-Fascist Refugee Committee," 8 *Amer. Comm. Hist.* 167 (2009).
Elliott, Shelden D. "Court-Curbing Proposals in Congress," 33 *Notre Dame Lawyer* 597 (1958).
Frank, John P., "Fred Vinson and the Chief Justiceship," 21 *U. Chi. L. Rev.* 212 (1954).
Frank, John P. "The United States Supreme Court: 1949–50," 18 *U. Chi. L. Rev.* 1 (1950).
Frank, John P. "The United States Supreme Court: 1950–51," 19 *U. Chi. L. Rev.* 165 (1952).
Frankfurter, Felix. "Mr. Justice Jackson," 68 *Harv. L. Rev.* 937 (1955).
Friedman, Barry. "The History of the Countermajoritarian Difficulty. Part One: The Road to Judicial Supremacy," 73 *N.Y.U. L. Rev.* 333 (1998).
Friedman, Barry. "The History of the Countermajoritarian Difficulty, Part II: Reconstruction's Political Court," 91 *Georgetown L. J.* 1 (2002).
Friedman, Barry. "The History of the Countermajoritarian Difficulty, Part Four: Law's Politics," 148 *U. Pa. L. Rev.* 971 (2000).

Friedman, Barry. "The Birth of An Academic Obsession: The History of the Counter-majoritarian Difficulty, Part Five," 112 *Yale L. J.* 153 (2002).
Garrow, David J. "Mental Decrepitude on the U.S. Supreme Court: The Historical Case for a 28th Amendment," 67 *U. Chi. L. Rev.* 995 (2000).
Gunther, Gerald. "Reflections on *Robel*: 'It's Not What the Court Did but the Way It Did It,'" 20 *Stanford L. Rev.* 1140 (1968).
Harper, Fowler V., and Alan S.Rosenthal. "What the Supreme Court Did Not Do in the 1949 Term: An Appraisal of Certiorari," 99 *U. Pa. L. Rev.* 293 (1950).
Hart, Henry M. Jr. "The Power of Congress to Limit the Jurisdiction of the Federal Courts: An Exercise in Dialectic," 66 *Harv. L. Rev.* 1362 (1953).
Hennings, Thomas C. Jr. "'Equal Justice Under Law,'" 47 *Georgetown L. J.* 1 (1957).
Hutchinson, Dennis J. "The Black-Jackson Feud," 1988 *Sup. Ct. Rev.* 203.
Kalven, Harry. "Professor Ernst Freund *and Debs v. United States*," 40 *U. Chi. L. Rev.* 235 (1973).
Kutler, Stanley I. "*Ex parte McCardle*: Judicial Impotency? The Supreme Court and Reconstruction Reconsidered," 72 *American Hist. Rev.* 835 (1967).
Lewis, Anthony. "Justice Black and First Amendment 'Absolutes': A Public Interview," 37 *N.Y.U. L. Rev.* 549 (1962).
Lichtman, Robert M. "Goldberg and Hoover: How Two Disparate Washington Insiders Resolved a McCarthy-Era Problem to Mutual (and the Nation's) Advantage," 10 *Amer. Comm. Hist.* 205 (2011).
Lichtman, Robert M. "J. B. Matthews and the 'Counter-subversives': Names as a Political and Financial Resource in the McCarthy Era," 5 *Amer. Comm. Hist.* 1 (2006).
Lichtman, Robert M. "Louis Budenz, the FBI, and the 'List of 400 Concealed Communists': An Extended Tale of McCarthy-Era Informing," 3 *Amer. Comm. Hist.* 25 (2004).
Long, Edward R. "Earl Warren and the Politics of Anti-Communism," 51 *Pacific Hist. Rev.* 51 (1982).
McCloskey, Robert G. "The Supreme Court Finds a Role," 42 *Va. L. Rev.* 735 (1956).
McCloskey, Robert G. "Useful Toil or Paths of Glory? Civil Liberties in the 1956 Term of the Supreme Court," 43 *Va. L. Rev.* 803 (1957).
Mollan, Robert. "Smith Act Prosecutions: The Effect of the *Dennis* and *Yates* Decisions," 26 *University Pittsburgh L. Rev.* 705 (1965).
Murphy, Walter F. "The South Counterattacks: The Anti-NAACP Laws," 12 *Western Pol. Quar.* 371 (1959).
Parrish, Michael E. "Cold War Justice: The Supreme Court and the Rosenbergs," 82 *Amer. Hist. Rev.* 805, (1977).
Powe, L. A. Jr. "Justice Douglas After Fifty Years: The First Amendment, McCarthyism and Rights," 6 *Const. Comm.* 267, 269–71 (1989).
Redish, Martin E. "Congressional Power to Regulate Supreme Court Appellate Jurisdiction Under the Exceptions Clause: An Internal and External Examination," 27 *Villanova L. Rev.* 900 (1982).
Rodell, Fred. "For Every Justice, Judicial Deference Is a Sometime Thing," 50 *Georgetown L. J.* 700 (1962).

Schrecker, Ellen. "Immigration and Internal Security: Political Deportations During the McCarthy Era," 60 *Sci. & Soc.* 393 (1997).

Schwartz, Bernard. "Felix Frankfurter and Earl Warren: A Study of a Deteriorating Relationship," 2000 *Sup. Ct. Rev.* 115.

Steamer, Robert J. "Statesmanship or Craftsmanship: Current Conflict Over the Supreme Court," 11 *Western Pol. Quar.* 265 (1958).

Stone, Geoffrey R. "Free Speech in the Age of McCarthy: A Cautionary Tale," 93 *Calif. L. Rev.* 1387 (2005).

Urofsky, Melvin I. "Conflict Among the Brethren: Felix Frankfurter, William O. Douglas and the Clash of Personalities and Philosophies on the United States Supreme Court," 1988 *Duke L. J.* 71.

Wermiel, Stephen J. "The Nomination of Justice Brennan: Eisenhower's Mistake? A Look at the Historical Record," 11 *Const. Comm.* 515 (1994).

Wiecek, William M. "The Legal Foundations of Domestic Anticommunism: The Background of *Dennis v. United States*," 2001 *Sup. Ct. Rev.* 375.

Addresses and Speeches

William J. Brennan Jr. "The Quest to Develop a Jurisprudence of Civil Liberties in Times of Security Crises," Address, Law School of Hebrew University, Jerusalem, Israel, Dec. 22, 1987; available at (at http://www.hofstra.edu/PDF/law_civil_hafetz_article1.pdf), accessed November 27, 2011.

David H. Souter, Commencement Address, Harvard University, May 27, 2010, reprinted at http://news.harvard.edu/gazette, accessed November 27, 2011.

Index of Supreme Court Decisions

Abbott Laboratories v. Gardner, 387 U.S. 136 (1967), 206n30
Abel v. United States, 362 U.S. 217 (1960), 237n9
Abrams v. United States, 250 U.S. 616 (1919), 9, 181n28, 181nn30–31
Adamson v. California, 332 U.S. 46 (1947), 191n9
Adler v. Board of Education, 342 U.S. 485 (1952), 48, 53–54, 203n1, 206nn28–31
Albertson v. Millard, 345 U.S. 242 (1953), 206n30
Albertson v. SACB, 382 U.S. 70 (1965), 155, 169–70, 246n53, 252n38
Amalgamated Meat Cutters v. NLRB, 352 U.S. 153 (1956), 103, 222n2, 226n58
American Committee for the Protection of Foreign Born v. SACB, 380 U.S. 503 (1965), 246–47n55
American Communications Ass'n v. Douds, 339 U.S. 382 (1950), 24, 35–36, 163, 190n2, 193n17, 197nn47–53, 249n8
Anastaplo, In re, 366 U.S. 82 (1961), 157–59, 189n48, 242n1, 247nn67–70
Aptheker v. Secretary of State, 378 U.S. 500 (1964), 169, 249n16, 252n38
Arndstein v. McCarthy, 254 U.S. 71 (1920), 199n16
Ashton v. Cameron County Water Improvement Dist., 298 U.S. 513 (1936), 182n37
Automobile Workers v. Russell, 356 U.S. 634 (1958), 229n6

Bailey v. Richardson, 341 U.S. 918 (1951), 37, 38–39, 71, 73, 188n40, 198n1, 198n4, 198n9
Baker v. Carr, 369 U.S. 186 (1962), 165, 250n20
Bantam Books, Inc. v. Sullivan, 372 U.S. 58 (1963), 252n3
Barenblatt v. United States, 360 U.S. 109 (1959), 128, 129, 130–32, 144, 147, 169, 174, 189n49, 196n38, 236n4, 23n6, 237–38nn18–24, 242n1
Barsky v. Board of Regents, 347 U.S. 442 (1954), 66, 212nn8–10
Bart v. United States, 349 U.S. 219 (1955), 70, 71, 214n27
Barton v. Sentner, 353 U.S. 963 (1957), 102–3, 226n54
Bates v. Little Rock, 361 U.S. 516 (1960), 133, 168, 169, 238n31
Baumgartner v. United States, 322 U.S. 665 (1944), 181–82n33
Beilan v. Board of Public Education, 357 U.S. 399 (1958), 113–14, 139, 145, 174, 189n47, 222n2, 231nn22–24, 231n28
Berger v. United States, 255 U.S. 22 (1921), 181n29
Black v. Cutter Laboratories, 351 U.S. 292 (1956), 83, 217n1, 219nn22–24
Blau (Irving) v. United States, 340 U.S. 332 (1951), 37, 40–41, 198n1, 199n17
Blau (Patricia) v. United States, 340 U.S. 159 (1950), 37, 40, 47, 198n1, 199nn13–15

Bolling v. Sharpe, 347 U.S. 497 (1954), 215n43

Bond v. Floyd, 385 U.S. 116 (1966), 170, 252n39

Bonetti v. Rogers, 356 U.S. 691 (1958), 115–16, 222n2, 232nn33–36

Boumediene v. Bush, 553 U.S. 723 (2008), 7, 180n20

Braden v. United States, 365 U.S. 431 (1961), 146–47, 174, 242n1, 243nn10–13

Brandenburg v. Ohio, 395 U.S. 444 (1969), 172, 253nn4–5

Bridges v. California, 314 U.S. 252 (1941), 202n37

Bridges v. United States, 346 U.S. 209 (1953), 53, 117, 203n1, 205–6nn25–26

Bridges v. Wixon, 326 U.S. 135 (1945), 205n25

Brown v. Board of Education, 347 U.S. 483 (1954), 10, 65, 74–75, 76, 175, 182n37, 212n7, 215nn43–44, 222n2

Brown v. Board of Education, 349 U.S. 294 (1955), 65, 74, 75, 76, 212n7, 215n45

Brown v. United States, 356 U.S. 148 (1958), 109, 111–12, 229n2, 230nn13–15

Brown v. Walker, 161 U.S. 591 (1896), 79, 217n3

Bryant v. Zimmerman, 278 U.S. 63 (1928), 218n16

Buckley v. Valeo, 424 U.S. 1 (1976), 10–11, 182n38

Bush v. Gore, 531 U.S. 98 (2000), 11, 182n39

Cafeteria and Restaurant Workers Union v. McElroy, 367 U.S. 886 (1961), 159–60, 242n1, 248nn72–75

Cammer v. United States, 350 U.S. 399 (1956), 79–80, 217n1, 217nn6–7

Carlson v. Landon, 342 U.S. 524 (1952), 49–50, 203n1, 204nn8–10

Carter v. Carter Coal Co. 298 U.S. 238 (1936), 182n37

Chaunt v. United States, 364 U.S. 350 (1960), 149–50, 242n1, 244nn27–29

Cherokee Nation v. Georgia, 30 U.S. (5 Pet.) 1 (1831), 7–8, 180n25

Christoffel v. United States, 338 U.S. 84 (1949), 189n50

Citizens United v. Federal Election Commission, 558 U.S. 50 (2010), 182–83n40

Cohen v. California, 403 U.S. 15 (1971), 171, 252n1

Cole v. Young, 351 U.S. 536 (1956), 69, 84–85, 90, 105–6, 107, 110, 123, 125, 142, 173, 174, 188n41, 213n22, 217n1, 219nn29–32

Collins v. Hardyman, 341 U.S. 651 (1951), 37, 41–42, 198n1, 200n21, 200n23

Communist Party v. SACB, 351 U.S. 115 (1956), 81–83, 206n27, 217n1, 218n15, 218nn19–20

Communist Party v. SACB, 367 U.S. 1 (1961), 129, 144, 153–55, 173, 188n39, 242n1, 244–45nn43–52

Communist Party, U.S.A. v. Catherwood, 367 U.S. 389 (1961), 155–56, 242n1, 247nn57–58

Cooper v. Aaron, 358 U.S. 1 (1958), 127, 229n5, 236n1

Counselman v. Hitchcock, 142 U.S. 547 (1892), 199n16

Cramp v. Board of Public Instruction, 368 U.S. 278 (1961), 161, 163, 189n47, 248n2, 249nn9–10

Cummings v. Missouri, 71 U.S. (4 Wall.) 277 (1866), 201n32

Dayton v. Dulles, 357 U.S. 144 (1958), 119–20, 174, 189n45, 222n2, 232nn49–50

Debs v. United States, 249 U.S. 211 (1919), 8–9, 181nn28–29

DeGregory v. Attorney General of New Hampshire, 368 U.S. 19 (1961), 248n2, 250n23

DeGregory v. Attorney General of New Hampshire, 383 U.S. 825 (1966), 249n16, 250n23

Dennis v. United States, 339 U.S. 162 (1950), 25, 31–32, 190n3, 195nn30–34

Dennis v. United States, 341 U.S. 494 (1951), 37, 44–47, 48, 95, 160, 172, 173, 188n38, 193n17, 198n2, 201nn37–41

Deutch v. United States, 367 U.S. 456 (1961), 148, 242n1, 244nn18–21

Electric Bond & Share Co. v. SEC, 303 U.S. 419 (1938), 246n50

Elfbrandt v. Russell, 384 U.S. 11 (1966), 249n16

Emspak v. United States, 349 U.S. 190 (1955), 68, 69–71, 189n49, 214n26, 214n28

Endo, Ex parte, 323 U.S. 283 (1944), 9, 182n34

Feiner v. New York, 340 U.S. 315 (1951), 37, 42, 198n1, 200nn24–25

First Unitarian Church v. County of Los An-

geles, 357 U.S. 545 (1958), 121, 222n2, 232nn58–59

Flaxer v. United States, 358 U.S. 147 (1958), 129–30, 236n4, 237nn13–14

Flemming v. Nestor, 363 U.S. 603 (1960), 128, 135–36, 236nn4–5, 239nn41–43

Frazier v. United States, 335 U.S. 497 (1949), 32, 195n32

Frohwerk v. United States, 249 U.S. 204 (1919), 181n28

Galvan v. Press, 347 U.S. 522 (1954), 66–67, 110, 115, 189n44, 212nn11–12, 231n30

Garland, Ex parte, 71 (4 Wall.) 333 (1866), 201n32

Garner v. Board of Public Works, 341 U.S. 716 (1951), 37, 42–44, 47, 189n47, 198n1, 200nn27–32

Gastelum-Quinones v. Kennedy, 374 U.S. 469 (1963), 249n16

Gerende v. Board of Supervisors of Elections, 341 U.S. 56 (1951), 201n33

Gibson v. Florida Legislative Committee, 372 U.S. 539 (1963), 161–62, 168–69, 249n16, 251–52nn32–33, 251n36

Gilbert v. Minnesota, 254 U.S. 325 (1920), 181n28

Gitlow v. New York, 268 U.S. 652 (1925), 224n20

Gojack v. United States, 394 U.S. 702 (1966), 168, 251n30

Gold v. United States, 352 U.S. 985 (1957), 103, 222n2, 226n56

Gordon v. United States, 344 U.S. 414 (1953), 104, 227n61

Green v. United States, 356 U.S. 165 (1958), 47, 112, 203n45, 222n2, 230nn16–18

Greene v. McElroy, 360 U.S. 474 (1959), 128, 136–37, 143, 159, 173, 188n42, 194n27, 236n4, 236n8, 239nn44–48

Greene v. United States, 376 U.S. 149 (1964), 239n49, 249n16

Grumman v. United States, 370 U.S. 288 (1962), 167, 251n28

Hamdan v. Rumsfeld, 548 U.S. 557 (2006), 6–7, 180n20

Harisiades v. Shaughnessy, 342 U.S. 580 (1952), 49, 66, 189n44, 203n1, 203–4nn4–7, 212n12

Harmon v. Brucker, 355 U.S. 579 (1958), 109, 121–22, 189n43, 234n61, 234nn63–65

Hartman v. United States, 370 U.S. 724 (1962), 167, 251n28

Hartzell v. United States, 322 U.S. 680 (1944), 181n33

Heikkila v. Barber, 345 U.S. 229 (1953), 52–53, 203n1, 205nn21–23

Heikkinen v. United States, 355 U.S. 273 (1958), 116, 222n2, 232nn37–38

Hess v. Indiana, 414 U.S. 105 (1973), 252n1

Hirabayashi v. United States, 320 U.S. 81 (1943), 9, 181n33

Hoffman v. United States, 341 U.S. 479 (1951), 199n16

Hudgings, Ex parte, 249 U.S. 378 (1919), 230n14

Hyun v. Landon, 350 U.S. 990 (1956), 81, 218n14

Isserman, In re, 345 U.S. 286 (1953), 55–56, 193n17, 203n1, 207nn40–42

Isserman, In re Disbarment of, 348 U.S. 1 (1954), 73, 215n39

Jacobellis v. Ohio, 378 U.S. 184 (1964), 237n12

Jay v. Boyd, 351 U.S. 345 (1956), 80–81, 217n54, 217n1, 218nn8–10

Jencks v. United States, 353 U.S. 657 (1957), 91–92, 104–5, 106, 107, 108, 173, 174, 194n27, 222n2, 222n4, 227nn60–64

Jewell Ridge Coal Corp. v. Local No. 6167, UMW, 325 U.S. 161 (1945), 28, 192–93n16

Joint Anti-Fascist Refugee Committee v. McGrath, 341 U.S. 123 (1951), 37, 38–39, 47, 194n25, 198n1, 198nn4–10

Kent v. Dulles, 357 U.S. 116 (1958), 118–20, 174, 189n45, 222n2, 232–33nn45–48

Kessler v. Strecker, 307 U.S. 22 (1939), 204n5

Keyishian v. Board of Regents, 385 U.S. 589 (1967), 206n29, 249n16

Killian v. United States, 368 U.S. 231 (1961), 161, 162–63, 248n2, 248–49nn5–8

Kimm v. Rosenberg, 363 U.S. 405 (1960), 135, 236n4, 238–39nn36–38

Knauer v. United States, 328 U.S. 654 (1946), 181–82n33

Konigsberg v. State Bar of California, 353 U.S. 252 (1957), 91, 100–101, 158, 160, 189n48, 194n25, 222n2, 225nn41–43

Konigsberg v. State Bar of California, 366 U.S.

36 (1961), 156–57, 158, 189n48, 191n9, 242n1, 247nn64–65
Korematsu v. United States, 323 U.S. 214 (1944), 9, 182n34
Kremen v. United States, 353 U.S. 346 (1957), 47, 96–97, 203n45, 222n2, 224nn22–23, 224nn26–27
Kwang Hai Chew v. Colding, 344 U.S. 590 (1953), 51, 203n1, 205n20

Lawson and Trumbo, 339 U.S. 934 (1950), 33, 196n38
Leedom v. International Union of Mine, Mill and Smelter Workers, 352 U.S. 145 (1956), 103, 222n2, 226n57
Lerner v. Casey, 357 U.S. 468 (1958), 113–14, 139, 145, 174, 189n47, 222n2, 231n22, 231nn25–27
Levy, In the Matter of Application of Ben G., 348 U.S. 978 (1955), 73, 215n40
Lightfoot v. United States, 355 U.S. 2 (1957), 110, 229n4
Linehan v. Waterfront Commission, 347 U.S. 439 (1954), 212–13n14
Louisiana ex rel. Gremillion v. NAACP, 366 U.S. 293 (1961), 243n5
Louisville Bank v. Radford, 295 U.S. 555 (1935), 182n37

Machinists v. Gonzales, 356 U.S. 617 (1958), 229n6
Maisenberg v. United States, 356 U.S. 668 (1958), 117, 149, 222n2, 232nn39–41, 244n24
Mallory v. United States, 354 U.S. 449 (1957), 106, 110, 123, 124, 125, 142–43, 228n72
Mapp v. Ohio, 367 U.S. 643 (1961), 194n27
Marbury v. Madison, 5 U.S. (1 Cranch.) 137 (1803), 4, 178n12
Marshall v. Brucker, 356 U.S. 34 (1958), 234n65
McCardle, Ex parte, 74 U.S. (7 Wall) 506 (1868), 6, 10, 11, 179n18
McPhaul v. United States, 364 U.S. 372 (1960), 147–48, 242n1, 243nn15–17
Mesarosh v. United States, 352 U.S. 1 (1956), 94, 222n2, 223nn12–14
Milligan, Ex parte, 71 U.S. (7 Wall.) 2 (1866), 6, 179n18
Miranda v. Arizona, 384 U.S. 436 (1966), 10, 182n37
Mooney v. Holohan, 294 U.S. 103 (1935), 209n58

Morehead v. New York ex rel. Tipaldo, 298 U.S. 587 (1936), 182n37
Morford v. United States, 339 U.S. 258 (1950), 195n32

NAACP v. Alabama, 357 U.S. 449 (1958), 110, 114, 133, 145, 168, 169, 229n5, 231n28
Near v. Minnesota, 283 U.S. 697 (1931), 252n3
Nelson v. County of Los Angeles, 362 U.S. 1 (1960), 139, 174, 236n4, 240nn56–59
New York Times Co. v. United States, 403 U.S. 713 (1971), 171–72, 252nn2–3
Niukkanen v. McAlexander, 362 U.S. 390 (1960), 134–35, 174, 236n4, 238nn32–34
Nostrand v. Little, 362 U.S. 474 (1960), 139–40, 240n61
Nostrand v. Little, 368 U.S. 436 (1962), 163–64, 248n2, 249n11
Noto v. United States, 367 U.S. 291 (1961), 152, 160, 173, 188n38, 242n1, 245nn38–40
Nowak v. United States, 356 U.S. 650 (1958), 117, 149, 222n2, 232nn39–41, 244n24
Nukk v. Shaughnessy, 350 U.S. 869 (1955), 218n14

Organization for a Better Austin v. Keefe, 402 U.S. 415 (1971), 252n3
Orloff v. Willoughby, 345 U.S. 83 (1952), 48, 56–57, 203n1, 207nn46–48
Osman v. Douds, 339 U.S. 846 (1950), 197n52

Palermo v. United States, 360 U.S. 343 (1959), 141–42, 236n5, 240–41nn67–68, 241n70
Pennsylvania v. Nelson, 350 U.S. 497 (1956), 67, 86–87, 123, 124, 125, 142, 147, 173, 174, 189n46, 217n1, 219–20nn35–38, 243n10
Peters v. Hobby, 349 U.S. 331 (1955), 71–73, 188n40, 214–15nn30–31, 35–37
Pierce v. United States, 252 U.S. 239 (1920), 181n28
Plessy v. Ferguson, 163 U.S. 537 (1896), 69, 213n20
Polites v. United States, 364 U.S. 426 (1960), 149, 242n1, 244nn24–25

Quinn v. United States, 349 U.S. 155 (1955), 70–71, 189n49, 214n25, 214n28
Quirin, Ex parte, 317 U.S. 1 (1942), 9, 181n33

Railway Employes' Department v. Hanson, 351 U.S. 225 (1956), 220–21n42

Raley v. State of Ohio, 360 U.S. 423 (1959), 130, 236n4, 237nn15–17

Rasul v. Bush, 542 U.S. 466 (2004), 6, 180n20

Remmer v. United States, 350 U.S. 377 (1956), 226n56

Retirement Board v. Alton R. Co., 295 U.S. 330 (1935), 182n37

Reynolds v. Sims, 377 U.S. 533 (1964), 10, 182n37

Roe v. Wade, 410 U.S. 113 (1973), 11, 182n38

Rogers v. United States, 340 U.S. 367 (1951), 37, 41, 198n1, 199–200nn19–20

Rosenberg v. United States, 346 U.S. 273 (1953), 48, 57–63, 175, 203n2, 210nn66–67, 210n69

Rosenberg v. United States, 360 U.S. 367 (1959), 141–42, 236n5, 241nn69–70

Rowoldt v. Perfetto, 355 U.S. 115 (1957), 109–10, 115, 134, 174, 222n2, 231–32nn29–32, 238n34

Russell v. United States, 369 U.S. 749 (1962), 161, 166–67, 248n2, 250n23, 251nn25–27

Sacher v. Association of the Bar of City of N.Y., 347 U.S. 388 (1954), 67, 212–13n14

Sacher v. United States, 343 U.S. 1 (1952), 47, 54–55, 203n1, 207nn37–39

Sacher v. United States, 356 U.S. 576 (1958), 109, 112–13, 229n2, 230–31nn19–20

Sawyer, In re, 360 U.S. 622 (1959), 140–41, 236n4, 240nn63–66

Scales v. United States, 355 U.S. 1 (1957), 110, 150, 229n4, 244n31

Scales v. United States, 367 U.S. 203 (1961), 129, 144, 150–52, 153, 155, 160, 173, 188n38, 242n1, 244–45nn33–36

Schacht v. United States, 398 U.S. 58 (1970), 171, 252n1

Schaefer v. United States, 251 U.S. 466 (1920), 181n28

Schechter Corp. v. United States, 295 U.S. 495 (1935), 182n37

Schenck v. United States, 249 U.S. 47 (1919), 181n28, 181n31

Schneiderman v. United States, 320 U.S. 118 (1943), 116, 232n39, 238n23

Schware v. Board of Bar Examiners, 353 U.S. 232 (1957), 91, 100, 158, 189n48, 194n25, 222n2, 225nn39–40

Service v. Dulles, 354 U.S. 363 (1957), 101, 222n2, 223n11, 225–26nn45–49

Shaughnessy v. United States ex rel. Mezei, 345 U.S. 206 (1953), 51–52, 193n17, 197n46, 203n1, 205nn17–19

Shelton v. Tucker, 364 U.S. 479 (1960), 145–46, 168, 242–43n5

Silber v. United States, 370 U.S. 717 (1962), 167, 248n2, 251n28

Slagle v. Ohio, 366 U.S. 259 (1961), 148–49, 242n1, 244nn22–23

Slochower v. Board of Higher Education, 350 U.S. 551 (1956), 84, 106, 109, 113–14, 139, 160, 174, 189n47, 194n27, 217n1, 219nn25–27

Smith v. Goguen, 415 U.S. 566 (1974), 252n1

Speiser v. Randall, 357 U.S. 513 (1958), 120–21, 222n2, 232nn55–57

Spence v. Washington, 418 U.S. 405 (1974), 252n1

Stack v. Boyle, 342 U.S. 1 (1951), 56, 203n1, 207nn44–45

Sweezy v. New Hampshire, 354 U.S. 234 (1957), 91, 98–99, 107, 128, 133, 147, 174, 189n49, 222n2, 225nn33–37, 236n6, 253n9

Taylor v. McElroy, 360 U.S. 709 (1959), 137, 188n42, 239n49

Taylor v. State of Mississippi, 319 U.S. 584 (1943), 181n33

Tenney v. Brandhove, 341 U.S. 367 (1951), 37, 41, 198n1, 200nn21–22

Thompson v. Whittier, 365 U.S. 465 (1961), 242n1

Travis v. United States, 364 U.S. 631 (1961), 156, 242n1, 247nn59–61

Trop v. Dulles, 356 U.S. 86 (1958), 11, 183n41

Ullmann v. United States, 350 U.S. 422 (1956), 79, 217n1, 217nn3–5

United Mine Workers v. Arkansas Oak Flooring Co., 351 U.S. 62 (1956), 221n42

United States ex rel. Knauff v. Shaughnessy, 338 U.S. 537 (1950), 33–35, 190n4, 193n17, 196nn39–45

United States ex rel. Milwaukee Social Democratic Pub. Co. v. Burleson, 255 U.S. 407 (1921), 8, 181n28

United States ex rel. Toth v. Quarles, 350 U.S. 11 (1955), 178n7

United States v. Brown, 381 U.S. 437 (1965), 169, 249n16, 252n38

United States v. Bryan, 339 U.S. 323 (1950), 32–33, 190n4, 195nn35–36

United States v. Butler, 297 U.S. 1 (1936), 182n37
United States v. Fleischman, 339 U.S. 349 (1950), 32–33, 190n4, 195n35, 195n37
United States v. Gaudin, 515 U.S. 506 (1995), 204n14
United States v. Harriss, 347 U.S. 612 (1954), 218n16
United States v. Lovett, 328 U.S. 303 (1946), 198n7
United States v. O'Brien, 391 U.S. 367 (1968), 252n1
United States v. Robel, 389 U.S. 258 (1967), 170, 249n16, 252n38
United States v. Spector, 343 U.S. 169 (1952), 50–51, 116, 203n1, 204nn13–14
United States v. Will, 449 U.S. 200 (1980), 178n6
United States v. Witkovich, 353 U.S. 194 (1957), 102, 106, 142, 174, 222n2, 226nn50–53
United States v. Zucca, 351 U.S. 91 (1956), 81, 117, 217n1, 218nn11–13
Uphaus v. Wyman, 360 U.S. 72 (1959), 128, 129, 130, 132–33, 145, 168, 169, 174, 189n49, 236n4, 236n6, 238nn25–30, 251n31
Uphaus v. Wyman, 364 U.S. 388 (1960), 145, 242nn3–4

Veterans of Abraham Lincoln Brigade v. SACB, 380 U.S. 513 (1965), 247n55
Vitarelli v. Seaton, 359 U.S. 535 (1959), 138, 236n4, 239–40nn51–54

Watkins v. United States, 354 U.S. 178 (1957), 91, 97–98, 106, 107, 108, 113, 123, 131, 147, 160, 174, 189n49, 222n2, 224–25nn28–32

Wellman v. United States, 354 U.S. 931 (1957), 224n21
Wesberry v. Sanders, 376 U.S. 1 (1964), 10, 182n37
West Virginia Board of Education v. Barnette, 319 U.S. 624 (1943), 202n38
Whitehill v. Elkins, 389 U.S. 54 (1967), 249n16
Whitney v. California, 274 U.S. 357 (1927), 45, 172, 202n37, 253n4
Wieman v. Updegraff, 344 U.S. 183 (1952), 48, 54, 189n47, 194n27, 203n1, 206–7nn33–35
Wilkinson v. United States, 365 U.S. 399 (1961), 146, 147, 174, 242n1, 243nn7–8
Wilson v. Loew's Incorporated, 355 U.S. 597 (1958), 222n2
Worcester v. Georgia, 31 U.S. (6 Pet.) 515 (1832), 7–8, 180n25

Yasui v. United States, 320 U.S. 115 (1943), 9, 181n33
Yates v. United States, 354 U.S. 298 (1957), 69, 91, 94–96, 106, 108, 110, 123, 150, 160, 173, 174, 175, 188n33, 213n22, 222n2, 223–24nn15–19, 224n21
Yates v. United States, 355 U.S. 66 (1957), 110–11, 222n2, 230nn8–9
Yates v. United States, 356 U.S. 363 (1958), 111, 230n10
Yellin v. United States, 374 U.S. 109 (1963), 249n16, 251n30
Yerger, Ex parte, 75 U.S. (8 Wall.) 85 (1869), 11, 183n42
Young v. Motion Picture Association of America, 370 U.S. 922 (1962), 248n2

Index

1946 elections, 16
1948 elections, 19
1950 elections, 19, 47
1952 elections, 187–88n34
1954 elections, 70, 77
1956 elections, 92
1958 elections, 127, 142, 174
1960 elections, 144

ABA (American Bar Association), 105–6, 142
Abel, Rudolf Ivanovich, 237n9
Abramowitz, Howard D., 121–22, 234n61
Abrams v. United States, 9
Acheson, Dean, 101, 225n47
Adler, Irving, 54, 173, 206n32
Administrative Procedure Act (APA), 52
advocacy of action, 44, 95–96, 150–52
affidavits, non-Communist. *See* Taft-Hartley Act non-Communist-affidavits
Alien and Sedition Acts (1789), 2
Alsop, Joseph, 19
Amerasia (magazine), 101, 183–84n3
American Bar Association (ABA), 105–6, 142
American Dilemma, An (Myrdal), 75
American Nazis, 181–82n33
anarchists, 9
Anastaplo, George, 157–59, 247nn68–71
Andrews, George W., 83
anti-war speech or publication cases, 2, 8–9, 171–72, 181n29

Army, Department of the, 20, 22, 56–57, 121–22, 234n61
atomic bomb, 14, 57, 184n5
Atomic Energy Act (1946), 60–61, 209–10n62, 210n64
attorney general's list of "subversive" organizations, 39, 199n12; accuracy of, 184n9; Civil Rights Congress, 147; Independent Socialist League, 199n12; JAFRC, 32–38, 47, 66, 195n35; *Joint Anti-Fascist*, 38–39, 66; and loyalty program, 38, 198n4; National Lawyers Guild, 199n12; Nature Friends of America, 85; origins of, 16, 30; and public housing, 217n1

bail, 49–50, 56
Bailey, Dorothy, 38–39
balancing tests: *Anastaplo*, 158; *Barenblatt*, 131–32; *CPUSA v. SACB*, 153–54; *Douds*, 35; *Konigsberg II*, 157; *Uphaus*, 133; *Wilkinson*, 146–47
bar admissions and disbarment, 55–56, 100–101, 140–41, 144, 156–57, 207n43, 241n73
Barenblatt, Lloyd, 130–32
Barenblatt contempt-of-Congress case, 128, 130–32, 225n32, 237n19
Barsky, Edward K., 65, 212n8
Beilan, Herman, 113, 173, 231n23
Belknap, Michal: on Goldberg, 166; on NAACP litigation, 168; on Smith Act and Smith Act cases, 46, 95, 152; on Supreme Court Justices, 25–30, 65, 190n1

Bennett, Wallace, 125
Bentley, Elizabeth, 13, 16, 79, 203n1
Berger, Victor L., 181n29
bills of attainder, 43, 136, 154, 169, 198n7
Black, Hugo L.: background information, 25–26, 190–91n7; on Communist Party, 132; feud with Jackson, 28, 192–93nn16–17; First Amendment views, 26, 131–32, 175, 191n9; and Frankfurter, 27; and Japanese Internment, 191n8; Ku Klux Klan membership, 26; liberal alliances, 25, 47, 65, 67–68, 93, 144; and the Rosenberg case, 61–62
Black, Hugo L., published opinions: *Adler* dissent, 54; *Anastaplo* dissent, 158; *Barenblatt* dissent, 131–32; *Barsky* dissent, 66; *Blau* (Patricia and Irving) opinions; 40; *Braden* dissent, 146–47; *Brown* dissent, 112; *Bryan* dissent, 33; *Cammer* opinion, 80; *CPUSA v. SACB* dissent, 154; *Dennis* contempt-of-Congress dissent, 32; *Douds* dissent, 197n49; *First Unitarian Church* concurrence, 121; *Fleischman* dissent, 33; *Galvan* dissent, 67; *Gibson* concurrence, 169; *Isserman* dissent, 56; *Jay* dissent, 80; *Joint Anti-Fascist* opinion, 38–39; *Killian* dissent, 162; *Knauff* dissent, 34; *Konigsberg I* opinion, 100; *Konigsberg II* dissent, 157, 247n65; *Mezei* dissent, 52; *Nelson/Globe* dissent, 139; *Noto* concurrence, 152; *Orloff* dissent, 57; *Rogers* dissent, 41; *Rosenberg* dissent, 61; *Sacher* dissent, 55; *Scales* dissent, 151; *Schware* opinion, 100; *Spector* dissent, 51; *Speiser* concurrence, 121; *Wieman* concurrence, 54; *Wilkinson* dissent, 146–47
Black Monday, 222n2
Blackmun, Harry, 182n38
Blasi, Vincent, 10, 27
Blau, Irving, 40–41
Blau, Patricia, 40, 47
Bloch, Emanuel, 61
Bohus, Paul, 244n23
Bond, Julian, 170
Bonetti, Frank, 115–16
Braden, Carl, 146–47, 173, 243n11
Brandeis, Louis D., 9, 26, 28, 45, 172
Brandenburg, Clarence, 172
Brawner, Rachel, 159, 173
Brennan, William J.: appointment of, 222–23n8; background information, 92–93; and Frankfurter, 93, 107; liberal alliances, 93, 144; on McCarthy-era fears, 173; on repression in America, 1

Brennan, William J., published opinions: *Anastaplo* dissent, 247n70; *Barenblatt* dissent, 132–33; *Brandenburg per curiam*, 253n5; *Brawner* dissent, 160; *CPUSA v. SACB* dissent, 154; *First Unitarian Church* opinion, 121; *Jencks* opinion, 92, 104; *Killian* dissent, 162; *Konigsberg II dissent*, 247n65; *Lerner* dissent, 114; *Noto* dissent, 152; *Palermo* concurrence, 141; *Polites* dissent, 149, 244n26; *Raley* opinion, 130; *Rosenberg* dissent, 141; *Sawyer* opinion, 140; *Spieser* opinion, 120; *Uphaus* dissent, 133
Bridges, Harry, 53, 240n62
Bridges, Styles, 87, 205–6n25, 206n27
Briehl, Walter, 232n45
Broadwater, Jeff, 15
Browder, Earl, 19
Brown, Paul, 88
Brown, Stefena, 111–12, 230n13
Brownell, Herbert, 39, 52, 60–61, 85, 92
Brown v. Board of Education I and *II*, 65, 74–76
Bryan, Helen R., 32–33
Bryson, Hugh, 103, 226n55
Budenz, Louis F., 19, 246n47
Burger, Warren E., 10–11, 72
Burton, Harold H.: background information, 25, 30; and conservative bloc, 30; retirement of, 127; and *Rosenberg*, 208n51
Burton, Harold H., published opinions: *Barsky* opinion, 66; *Beilan* opinion, 113; *Bridges* opinion, 53; *Carlson* dissent, 50; *Collins* dissent, 200n23; *Garner* concurrence, 43; *Isserman* dissent, 73; *Jencks* concurrence, 104, 227n63, 246n6; *Joint Anti-Fascist* opinion, 38–39; *Kwong Hai Chew* opinion, 51; *Nowak* dissent, 117; *Yates* contempt-of-court dissent, 111
Butler, John Marshall, 123, 216–17n52
Byrd, Harry F., 88, 142

Cain, Harry P., 77, 184n9
Cammer, Harold I., 79–80
Caro, Robert, 125
Carroll, John, 125
Celler, Emanuel, 89, 107
Chambers, Whittaker, 16
Chaunt, Peter, 149, 244n28
Chelf, Frank L., 62
Chew, Kwong Hai, 51, 204n16
China, 13–14, 17, 101
CIO expulsion of Communist-dominated

unions, 103, 214n24, 224–25n29, 237n13, 250n21
Civil Rights Congress, 147
Civil Service Commission, 85, 188–89nn41–42
Civil War era, 2, 7, 9–10
Clark, Tom C.: appointment of, 24; as Attorney General, 16; background information, 30, 194n27; and Knauff case, 34; support for government agenda, 108
Clark, Tom C., published opinions: *Black* opinion, 83; *Bonetti* dissent, 116; *Chaunt* dissent, 150; *Cole* dissent, 85; *CPUSA v. SACB* dissent, 83; *Dayton* dissent, 119; *Garner* opinion, 43, 200n27; *Greene* dissent, 137; *Harmon* dissent, 122, 234n65; *Heikkila* opinion, 52; *Jencks* dissent, 92, 105, 198; *Kent* dissent, 119; *Kimm* per curiam, 135; *Mezei* opinion, 51, 205n18; *Nelson/Globe* opinion, 139; *Nowak* dissent, 117; *Rosenberg* concurrence, 61; *Russell* dissent, 166–67; *Sacher* dissent, 113; *Slochower* opinion, 84; *Spieser* dissent, 121; *Sweezy* dissent, 99, 225n37; *Uphaus* opinion, 132–33; *Watkins* dissent, 98, 108; *Wieman* opinion, 54; *Witkovich* dissent, 103; *Yates* contempt-of-court dissent, 111; *Yates* Smith Act dissent, 97; *Zucca* dissent, 81
clear-and-present danger test: *Abrams*, 9; *Brandenburg*, 172; *Dennis* Smith Act case, 37, 172, 202n39; *Douds*, 35, 37, 197n50; Holmes-Brandeis test, 9, 45, 172; *Schenck*, 181n31; *Whitney*, 202n37
Cole, Kendrick, 84–85
Coleman, Dora, 49
Coleman, Samuel I., 96
Cole v. Young bills, 85–86, 90, 105–6, 123–25, 142
Cole v. Young federal-employee loyalty case, 84–86
Colmer, William M., 88
"communist-action" organizations, 21, 81–83, 144, 153–55, 241n45
"Communist" cases, defined, 183n45
Communist Control Act (1954), 77, 87, 155–56, 216–17n52, 216n50
"communist front" organizations, 14–15, 21, 38–39, 132–33. *See also* attorney general's list of "subversive" organizations
"Communist-infiltrated" organizations, 216–17n52
Communist Party, U. S. *See* CPUSA

compelled disclosure: of Communist affiliations, 33, 68, 91, 98, 128, 144, 154, 160, 246n49; of NAACP members, 114, 133
Conference of Chief Justices, 106, 142
Conference of State Governors, 89
Congress, 35, 78–90, 98, 105–8. *See also* House of Representatives; Senate
conservatives, defined, 182n37
contempt-of-Congress cases: *Barenblatt*, 128, 130–32, 225n32, 237n19; *Bart*, 70–71; *Braden*, 146–47, 243nn11–12; *Bryan* and *Fleischman*, 32–33; *Dennis*, 25, 31–32, 195nn30–33; *Deutch*, 148; *Emspak*, 68, 70; Fifth Amendment privilege, 23; *Gojack*, 251n30; *Grumman*, 167; *Hartman*, 167; *McPhaul*, 147–48; overview of, 189n49; *Quinn*, 70; *Russell*, 166–68, 251n30; *Sacher*, 112–13; *Silber*, 167; *Trumbo* and *Lawson*, 33; *Watkins*, 91, 97–98, 106, 113, 147, 160; *Wilkinson*, 146; *Yellin*, 251n30
contempt-of-court cases: *Blau* and *Rogers*, 41–42; *Brown v. United States*, 111–12; *Cammer*, 79–80; *Green*, 112; *Ullmann*, 79; *Yates* contempt case, 110–11
Cooper, Eula Ann, 244n23
Coplon, Judith, 17
court-curbing legislation: *Cole v. Young* bills, 85–86, 90, 105–6, 123–25, 142; *Greene* bills, 137; HR 3 anti-preemption bill, 78, 86–89, 107, 110, 123–24, 142–43, 160; Jencks Act, 92, 105–8, 128, 141–42, 173, 228n75; Jenner bill, 107–8, 110, 123, 139; Jenner-Butler bill, 123–24, 127; and judicial independence, 109; *Mallory* bills, 110, 123–26, 142–43, 160; *Nelson* bills, 87–88, 123–25, 142, 147; overview of, 87–90, 220–21n42; passport bills, 123, 125, 142–43; *Yates* bills, 105–6, 110, 123–25, 142, 160. *See also* jurisdiction-stripping legislation
court-packing, 7, 190n5
Cox, Archibald, 169
CPUSA: character of, 13–14, 95; *CPUSA v. Catherwood*, 155–56; *CPUSA v. SACB*, 81–83, 153–55, 160, 173, 246n47, 246n49; denaturalization of members, 22, 117, 149, 135–36; deportation of members, 22, 67, 102, 115–16, 203–4n5; indictment of officials under Smith Act, 16, 24–25, 201nn34–35; and labor unions, 35–36, 103, 169; meaningful association with, 115, 134; membership numbers, 184n8; and the NAACP, 162, 168–69, 251n33;

outlawing of, 77, 216–17n52; refusal to obey registration order, 154–55; registration requirement, 16, 115, 206n30
Cramp, David Walton, 163
Crouch, Paul, 82–83, 206n27
Cvetic, Matt, 86, 219–20n25

Daily, Joseph E., 159
Dayton, Weldon Bruce, 119
Debs, Eugene V., 8–9, 181n29
Debs v. United States, 8–9
defense industry employees and loyalty screenings, 21–22, 136–38
DeGregory, Hugo, 250n23
Democratic Party: 1946 elections, 16; 1948 elections, 19; 1952 elections, 19–20, 48; 1954 elections, 70, 77; 1958 elections, 127, 175; 1960 elections, 144; "soft on communism" charges, 15–17, 48, 77, 155; southern Democrats alliance with Republicans, 78, 87–88, 110
denaturalization: *Bridges*, 116; *Brown v. United States*, 111–12; *Chaunt*, 244n28; and CPUSA membership, 22, 117, 149; *Maisenberg*, 117, 149; of members of "communist-action" organizations, 153–54; *Nowak*, 117, 149; *Polites*, 149, 244n26; of pro-Nazi German-Americans, 181–82n33; *Schneiderman*, 116; *Zucca*, 81, 116
Dennis, Eugene, 25, 31–32, 195n30
Dennis contempt-of-Congress case, 25, 31–32, 195nn30–33
Dennis Smith Act case: about, 24–25, 37, 44–47, 201–2nn37–38; bail for defendants, 56, 203n45; clear-and-present danger test, 37, 45–46, 172; compared to *Yates* Smith Act case, 95; contempt charges for defense lawyers, 54–55, 67, 73; Department of Defense, 22–23, 137; flight of four defendants, 47, 96–97, 112
Department of the Army, 20, 22, 56–57, 121–22, 234n61
deportation cases: and Administrative Procedure Act (APA), 52; of alien members, 22, 67, 102, 115–16, 189n44, 203–4n5; *Bonetti*, 115–16; *Bridges*, 53; *Galvan*, 66–67, 110, 115; *Harisiades*, 49, 212n12; *Heikkila*, 52; *Heikkinen*, 116; *Hyun*, 218n14; and the Internal Security Act, 212n11; *Jay*, 80; *Kimm*, 135; *Knauff*, 33–35, 196n40, 196n44; *Kwong Hai Chew*, 51, 204n16; *Mezei*, 51–52, 173, 205n18; *Nestor*, 135–36; *Niukkanen*, 134; *Rowoldt*, 115, 231–32n32; *Spector*, 50–51, 116, 204n12; and supervision of deportees, 102, 218n14
desegregation cases. *See* school-desegregation
Dethmers, John R., 106
Deutch, Bernhard, 148
Dewey, Thomas E., 16–17, 186nn19–20
Dirksen, Everett J., 19, 125
disbarment and bar admissions, 55–56, 100–101, 140–41, 144, 156–59, 207n43, 241n73
disorderly-conduct cases, 163, 171
doctors, 56–57
Dodd, Thomas J., 143
Douds Taft-Hartley case, 35–37, 197nn49–52
Douglas, Paul H., 77, 235n75
Douglas, William O.: accident, 24, 190n1; antagonistic relationship with Frankfurter and Jackson, 27, 145, 191–92n12, 208n55; background information, 27, 192nn13–14; and *Dennis* record, 44, 201n35; on influence of public opinion, 2; and *Kremen*, 97; liberal alliances, 47, 65, 67–68, 93, 144; and *Rosenberg*, 58–64, 175, 210n65, 210n69.
Douglas, William O., published opinions: *Adler* dissent, 54; *Beilan* dissent, 114; *Black* dissent, 83; *Chaunt* opinion, 150; *CPUSA v. SACB* dissent, 154; *Dennis* dissent, 44–46; *Flaxer* opinion, 130; *Garner* opinion, 43; *Gibson* concurrence, 169; *Harisiades* dissent, 49; *Isserman* dissent, 56; *Jay* dissent, 80; *Joint Anti-Fascist* opinion, 38; *Kent* and *Dayton* opinions, 118–20; *Killian* dissent, 162; *Kimm* dissent, 135; *Lerner* dissent, 114; *McPhaul* dissent, 148; *Mine*-Mill and *Meat Cutters* opinions, 103; *Nestor* dissent, 136; *Niukkanen* dissent, 134; *Nostrand* dissent, 140, 163; *Noto* concurrence, 152; *Peters* concurrrence, 215n35; *Rosenbergs's* stay opinion and dissent, 48, 60–61; *Russell* concurrence, 251n26; *Sacher* dissent, 55; *Scales* dissent, 151–52; *Spector* opinion, 50–51; *Tenney* dissent, 200n22; *Travis* opinion, 103, 156; *Ullmann* dissent, 79; *Uphaus* dissent, 145, 168; *Yates* contempt case dissent, 111, 230n9
draft, the, 56–57, 121–22

Eastland, James O.: and *Cole v. Young* bill, 86; and court-curbing legislation, 69–70, 108, 120, 123; criticism of the Supreme Court,

88, 142, 162; and school-desegregation cases, 75–76; and SISS, 216n48
Edelman, Irwin, 60–61
Eighth Amendment, 49–50
Eisenhower, Dwight D.: and Communist Control Act, 155, 216–17n52; court-curbing legislation, 106–7, 120, 123; on Court's 1956-term decisions, 105; election of, 20; federal troops to Little Rock, 110; issuance of industrial security procedures, 21–22, 137–38, 173; loyalty-security regulation, 21, 73, 215n37; and the Rosenbergs, 62; Supreme Court appointees, 64, 68, 92, 127, 129, 211n2, 222–23n8
Emergency Civil Liberties Committee, 243n7, 243n11
Emspak, Julius, 68, 70, 214n24, 214n26
Endo, Mitsuye, 9
Equal Protection Clause, 74–75, 215n43
ERCO, 136–37
Ernst, Morris, 14
espionage, 13–14, 17, 19, 101, 183–84n3, 208n50, 237n9. *See also* Rosenberg, Ethel and Julius
Espionage Act (1917), 60–61
exclusion cases: *Knauff,* 33–35, 196n40, 196n44; *Kwong Hai Chew,* 51, 204n16; *Mezei,* 51–52, 173, 205n18
exposure of Communist affiliations, 79, 98, 131–33, 160

Farmer, Fyke, 60, 209n59
FBI, 96–97, 103, 226n56
FBI informants: Bentley, 13, 16, 79, 203n1; Budenz, 19, 246n47; Chambers, 16; Crouch, 82–83, 206n27; Cvetic, 86, 219–20n25; Ford, 104; Gitlow, 246n47; Johnson, 82–83, 206n27; Marriott, 246n53; Matusow, 82–83, 104–5, 112–13, 227n60, 227n65, 230–31n19; Mazzei, 94, 223n12; and Sixth Amendment rights, 137–38; Thompson, 246n53. *See also* witnesses
federal campaign reform statute, 182–83n40
federal-employee loyalty screenings: *Cole,* 84–85, 173; *Bailey* and *Joint Anti-Fascist,* 38–39; non-sensitive government employees, 85; *Peters,* 71; *Service,* 101; standard of proof, 198–99n10; subversive organization membership, 16, 21, 188–89nn41–42, 198n4; summary dismissal, 21, 85; *Vitarelli,* 138. *See also* Loyalty Review Board; public-employee loyalty screenings

Federalist Papers, The (Hamilton), 4, 32, 178n8
federal-preemption cases. *See* HR 3 anti-preemption bill; *Nelson* preemption case; preemption of state laws
Feinberg, Benjamin, 206n28
Feinberg Law, 53–54, 206n28
Fifth Amendment. *See* self-incrimination
"Fifth Amendment Communists," 23, 189n49. *See also* self-incrimination (Fifth Amendment privilege)
Finerty, John F., 59, 61, 209n58
First Amendment cases: *Barenblatt,* 128, 130–32, 225n32, 237n19; *Bates,* 133; *Dennis,* 44–46; *Douds,* 35–37, 197n52, 197nn49–50; *Feiner,* 42; freedom of association, 168; *Gibson,* 161–62, 168–69; and Internal Security Act's registration requirement, 150–54, 160, 241n45; and loyalty screenings, 38–39; after McCarthy era, 170; *NAACP v. Alabama,* 110, 114, 133, 145, 168; and Smith Act, 44–47, 150–52; *Speiser,* 121; *Sweezy,* 98–99, 128, 131; and Taft-Hartley Act, 35; *Uphaus,* 128, 132–33; during Vietnam War, 171–72. *See also* balancing tests; *Dennis* Smith Act case
Fitzpatrick, Thomas J., 70
Flanders, Ralph, 76
Flaxer, Abram, 129–30, 225n32
Fleischman, Ernestina, 32–33
footnote 11. *See Brown v. Board of Education I*
Ford, Gerald, 10, 182n38
Ford, J. W., 104
Fortas, Abe, 170
Foster, William Z., 201n34
Fourth Amendment cases, 96–97, 237n9
Frank, Jerome, 209–10n62
Frankfurter, Felix: antagonism towards Black and Douglas, 27, 145, 191–92n12, 208n55; background information, 26–27, 191n10; and Burton, 191–92n12; at center of Court, 79, 109–10, 174; and *Dayton,* 119–20; and Goldberg, 166, 250n22; and Harlan, 69, 191–92n12; and *Harmon,* 122; health issues and retirement of, 161, 165, 250n20; and Hiss, 193n20; on influence of public opinion, 2–3; and Jackson, 28, 191–92n12; and *Jencks,* 107; judicial philosophy, 26–27, 174, 191n11, 231n29; and *Kremen,* 97; as leader of the Court's retreat, 23, 109, 128–34; and "meaningful association," 115, 134; and *Rosenberg,* 58–64; and *Sweezy,* 99; and *Uphaus* imprison-

ment, 145; and Vinson, 27, 191–92n12; and Warren, 27, 67, 145, 213n16
Frankfurter, Felix, published opinions: *Adler* dissent, 54; *Baker v. Carr* dissent, 165; *Barsky* dissent, 66; *Beilan* concurrence, 231n26; *Brown* contempt-of-court opinion, 111–12; *Carlson* dissent, 50; *CPUSA v. SACB* opinions, 82–83, 153–54; *Dennis* contempt-of-Congress dissent, 32; *Dennis* Smith Act concurrence, 45–46, 202n39; *Douds* concurrence, 36; *Feiner* concurrence, 200n25; *Galvan* opinion, 67; *Garner* concurrence, 43, 200n27, 200n30; *Gerende per curiam*, 201n33; *Greene* concurrence, 137, 230n17; *Harisiades* concurrence, 204n6; *Heikkila* dissent, 52; *Jay* dissent, 80; *Joint Anti-Fascist* opinion, 38; *Knauff* dissent, 34; *Konigsberg I* dissent, 101, 225n43; *Lerner* concurrence, 231n26; *Niukkanen per curiam*, 134; *Orloff* dissent, 57; *Palermo/Rosenberg* opinions, 141; *Rosenberg* dissent, 48, 61, 62; *Rowoldt* opinion, 115; *Sacher* dissent, 55, 207n39; *Sacher per curiam*, 113; *Shelton* (NAACP) dissent, 145; *Sweezy* concurrence, 99; *Tenney* opinion, 41; *Ullmann* opinion, 79; *Wieman* concurrence, 54; *Witkovich* opinion, 102; *Yates* contempt *per curiam*, 111
freedom of association cases. *See* First Amendment cases
freedom of speech cases. *See* First Amendment cases
freedom of the press, 171–72
Fried, Richard, 12
Friedman, Barry, 174
Friedman, Leon, 93
Fur and Leather Workers Union, 103, 226n58

Galvan v. Press, 66–67
Gambrell, E. Smythe, 89
Gerende, Thelma, 201n33
Gibson, Theodore R., 161–62, 168–69
Gideonse, Harry D., 84
Gitlow, Benjamin, 246n47
Globe, Arthur, 139, 173
Gojack, John T., 166–68
Gold, Ben, 79–80, 103, 226n56
Goldberg, Arthur J.: appointment of, 23; background information, 165–66; and CIO, 250n21; on Frankfurter, 174; *Gibson* opinion, 169; liberal alliances, 166

Gore, Albert, 235–36n78
Green, Gilbert, 112
Greene, Graham, 204n6
Greene, William L., 136–37, 239n49
Greenglass, David and Ruth, 57, 208n50
Greenhouse, Linda, 93
Griffith, Robert, 18–19, 76
Gruening, Ernest, 127
Grumman, Frank, 166–67
Gunther, Gerald, 172
Gwinn Amendment, 217n1

habeas corpus, writ of, 2, 6–7, 9, 34–35
Hallinan, Vincent, 205–6n25
Hamilton, Alexander, 4, 32, 175, 178n8
Hammett, Dashiell, 203n45
Hand, Learned, 45, 201–2n37, 227n62, 234n67
Harding, Warren G., 181n29
Harisiades, Peter, 49
Harlan, John Marshall: alliance with Frankfurter, 69, 73; background information, 69–70; and *Dayton*, 119–20; and *Gibson*, 168–69, 251n33; and *Kremen*, 97
Harlan, John Marshall, published opinions: *Anastaplo* opinion, 158; *Barenblatt* opinion, 131; *Bart* dissent, 71; *Cole* opinion, 85; *CPUSA v. Catherwood* opinion, 155–56; *Deutch* dissent, 148; *Greene* concurrence, 239n47; *Green* opinion, 112; *Konigsberg I* dissent, 100, 157; *Konigsberg II* opinion, 157; *Kremen per curiam*, 97; *Lerner* opinion, 114; *Mesarosh* dissent, 94; *Nestor* opinion, 135–36; *Noto* opinion, 152; *Nowak* and *Maisenberg* opinions, 117; *Quinn* dissent, 214n28; *Rowoldt* dissent, 115, 231–32n32; *Scales* opinion, 151–52; *Service* opinion, 101; *Slochower* dissent, 84; *Sweezy* concurrence, 97; *Travis* dissent, 156; *Vitarelli* opinion, 138; *Yates* Smith Act opinion, 95–96, 175
harmless-error doctrine, 141–42
Harmon, John Henry, III, 121–22, 234n61
Hart, Philip, 127
Hartman, Louis, 166–67
Haynes, John Earl, 14
Heckler's veto, 42, 200n26
Heikkila, William, 52–53
Heikkinen, Knut Einar, 116
Hellman, John Cyril, 245n41
Hemingway, Ernest, 212n8
Hennings, Thomas C., Jr., 108, 124

Hiss, Alger, 13, 15–17, 19–20, 193n120
Hollywood, 16, 204n6, 229n2, 248b2
Hollywood Ten, 33
Holmes, Oliver Wendell, 9, 26, 172, 181n31
Holmes-Brandeis clear-and-present-danger test, 9, 45, 172. *See also* clear-and-present danger test
Hoover, J. Edgar, 16–17, 77, 106, 145, 208n50. *See also* FBI; House Committee on Un-American Activities
House Committee on Un-American Activities (HUAC), 15, 98, 131–32, 146–47, 237n19. *See also* contempt-of-Congress cases
House of Representatives, 5, 87–88, 91, 107, 122–23, 142–43. *See also* court-curbing legislation; HR 3 anti-preemption bill
HR 3 anti-preemption bill, 78, 86–89, 107, 110, 123–24, 142–43, 160
Hughes, Charles Evans, 28, 180n22
Humphrey, Hubert H., 77, 124–25, 155, 216–17n52
Humphreys, West H., 179n15
Hyun, David, 81, 218n14

Immigration Act (1917), 205n22
Immigration & Nationality Act (1952), 135–36
Immigration & Naturalization Service, 34–35, 52
imminence in clear-and-present-danger test, 45, 172
Immunity Act (1954), 79, 216n50
impeachment of judges, 4–5, 62, 178n11, 179n15
in camera inspections of witness testimony, 104–7
Independent Socialist League, 39, 199n12
Institute of Pacific Relations, 216n48
Internal Security Act (1950): about, 21, 153, 188n39; "communist-action" organizations, 81–83, 144, 153; "communist front" organizations, 14–15, 21, 38–39, 132–33; "Communist-infiltrated" organizations, 216–17n52; *CPUSA v. SACB*, 81–83, 153–55, 160, 173, 246n47, 246n49; deportation provisions, 49–50, 102, 189n44, 231–32n32; enforcement of, 37–38; government's inability to compel registration, 154–55, 160, 169–70, 173; registration requirement, 21, 153, 245nn44–45; Truman veto, 36. *See also* Smith Act (1940)

International Workers Order, 38, 52
Isserman, Abraham, 55–56, 73, 207n43
I Was a Communist for the FBI (motion picture), 86

Jackson, Robert H.: advocacy of different constitutional rules for Communists, 28, 35–36, 45, 202n38; alliance with Frankfurter, 28, 191–92n12; background information, 27–28; and *Brown I*, 74; death of, 68; and hostility toward Douglas, 27, 59, 208n55; feud with Black, 28, 192–93nn16–17; and *Rosenberg*, 59–61
Jackson, Robert H., published opinions: *Bryan* concurrence, 195n35; *Collins* opinion, 42; *Dennis* contempt-of-Congress concurrence, 32, 195n33; *Dennis* Smith Act concurrence, 45, 201–2nn37–38; *Douds* concurrence, 35–36, 38; *Harisiades* opinion, 49, 204n6; *Isserman* opinion, 56; *Joint Anti-Fascist* opinion, 38; *Knauff* dissent and orders, 33–34; *Mezei* dissent, 51–52; *Orloff* opinion, 57; *Rosenberg* concurrence, 61; *Sacher* opinion, 55; *Spector* dissent, 50, 204n14
Japanese internment, 1–2, 9, 29, 65, 177n1
Jay, Cecil Reginald, 80
Jay, John, 178n8
Jefferson, Thomas, 3, 177n1
Jehovah's Witnesses, 181–82n33
Jencks, Clinton, 104–5
Jencks Act (1957), 92, 105–8, 128, 141–42, 173, 228n75
Jencks non-Communist-affidavit case, 91–92, 104–7, 110, 173, 227n63, 227n65, 248–49nn6–7
Jenner, William E., 107–8
Jenner bill, 107–8, 110, 123, 139
Jenner-Butler bill, 123–24, 127
Johnson, Andrew, 10
Johnson, Lyndon, 110, 123, 124–26, 236n82
Johnson, Manning, 82–83, 206n27
Johnston, Olin D., 125
Joint Anti-Fascist Refugee Committee (JAFRC), 32, 38, 47, 66, 195n35
judicial activism, 10–11, 75, 105–8, 182–83n40, 182n37
judicial independence, 3–4, 11–12, 109, 178n7
judicial restraint, philosophy of, 10–11, 142, 191n11, 231n29
judicial review, principle of, 4

280 · INDEX

juries, 80, 103, 226n56
jurisdiction-stripping legislation, 5–7, 107–8, 110, 123–24, 127, 139, 179n17. *See also* court-curbing legislation

Kalven, Harry, 9, 95
Kaufman, Irving R., 58–60, 62–63, 209n61
Keating, Kenneth, 120, 143, 241–42n76
Kelser, Gregory A., 165
Kennedy, John F., 144, 152, 164–66
Kennedy, Joseph P., 144
Kennedy, Robert F., 144, 155
Kent, Rockwell, 118
Kent and *Dayton* passport cases, 118–20
Kerr, Robert, 125
Killian, John J., 162–63
Kimm, Diamond, 135
Kirkendall, Richard, 30
Klehr, Harvey, 14
Knauff, Ellen Raphael, 33–35, 196n40, 196n44
Knight, Frances G., 118
Konigsberg, Raphael, 100–101, 156–59
Korean War, 14, 17
Korematsu, Fred, 9
Krock, Arthur, 20, 39, 62, 73, 87, 120, 155
Kuchel, Thomas H., 235–36n78
Ku Klux Klan, 26, 41, 172
Kutler, Stanley I., 11, 119

labor unions: anti-union sentiment, 16; *Cafeteria Workers*, 159–60; and CPUSA members, 103, 169, 205–6n25, 206n27; Fur and Leather Workers Union, 103, 226n58; longshoremen's, 53; membership lists, 129–30; Mine-Mill union, 103–4; political strikes, 35, 197n48; and Taft-Hartley non-Communist-affidavits, 35–36, 91, 247n60; United Public Workers union, 129–30, 237n13. *See also* CIO expulsion of Communist-dominated unions
Latham, Earl, 17
Lattimore, Owen, 19
Lausche, Frank, 235–36n78
Lawrence, David, 120
Lawson, John Howard, 33
lawyers: bar admissions and disbarments, 55–56, 67, 73, 100–101, 140–41, 144, 156–59, 207n43, 241n73; and contempt charges against *Dennis* lawyers, 54–55, 112–13; Vincent Hallinan, 205n25
Lehman, Herbert, 76
Lerner, Max, 113–14, 173

less-than-honorable discharges, 121–22, 234n61
Levy, Ben G., 73, 215n40
Lewin, Nathan, 69
Lewis, Anthony: on ABA's critique of the Supreme Court, 142; on Black, 26, 67–68; on Communist Control Act, 155; on contempt-of-Congress cases, 147; on court-curbing legislation, 124; on *CPUSA v. SACB* and *Scales*, 155, 246–47n55; on Douglas, 27; on Frankfurter, 165; on industrial security regulations, 138; on judicial activism, 11; and Lyndon Johnson, 125; on Warren, 65, 67–68
Lewis, George, 76
liberals, defined, 182n37
lifetime tenure, 4
Lightfoot, Claude, 244n31
Liveright, Herman, 166
longshoremen, 53
Loth, David, 14
loyalty and non-Communist oaths, 42–44, 54, 120–21, 163, 189n47. *See also* federal-employee loyalty screenings; private-employee loyalty screenings; public-employee loyalty screenings; Taft-Hartley Act non-Communist-affidavits
Loyalty Review Board, 72–73, 101, 198n4, 215n37, 225n47
Lucas, Scott, 19

Madison, James, 178n8
Maisenberg, Rebecca, 117, 232n40
Mallory, Andrew, 106
Mallory bills, 110, 123–26, 142–43, 160
Malone, George "Molly," 235–36n78
Malone, Ross L., 241n73
Mandel, Benjamin, 108
Mariott, Henry O., 246n53
Marshall, John, 4
Marshall, Thurgood, 74
Marshall Plan, 41–42, 200n23
Martin, Joseph W., Jr., 17
Masciti, Luigi, 49
Mason, Noah, 87
Mathes, William C., 110–11, 230n7
Matusow, Harvey, 82–83, 104–5, 112–13, 227n60, 227n65, 230–31n19
Maxwell, David F., 105
Mazzei, Joseph D., 94, 223n12
McCarran, Pat, 21, 115, 196n44, 213–14n23
McCarran Rider, 101, 226n48
McCarthy, Eugene, 127

McCarthy, Joseph: Army-hearings, 20, 188n35; and Brennan, 92, 222-3n8; career and role in American politics, 17-20; censure resolution, 20, 76; court bashing, 87-88, 220n41; and court-curbing bills, 87-88; death of, 92; ties to Kennedys, 144
McCarthy era, 1, 13-20, 169-70, 174-75, 183n45, 189n50
McClellan, John L., 124
McCloskey, Robert G., 91
McCullough, David, 15
McGohey, John F. X., 201n34
McGrath, J. Howard, 35, 37, 46, 204n12
McInerney, James M., 46
McPhaul, Arthur M., 147
McPherson, Harry, 125
Medina, Harold R., 44, 46, 55, 201n34, 202n42, 207n39
"membership" clause of Smith Act, 96, 129, 144, 150-52, 245n41
Merryman, Ex parte, 10
Mezei, Ignatz, 51-52, 173, 205n18
Miller, Arthur, 118
Milton, Joyce, 57
Mine, Mill & Smelter Workers, 103-5
Minton, Sherman: appointment of, 24, 194-95n28; background information, 31, 194-95nn28-29; on Communism, 82; health issues, 222n7; retirement of, 92
Minton, Sherman, published opinions: *Adler* opinion, 53; *Bart* dissent, 71; *Blau (Irving)* dissent, 41, 199n17; *Dennis* contempt-of-Congress opinion, 32; *Knauff* opinion, 34, 196n42; *Kwong Hai Chew* dissent, 204n16
Mladajan, Rose, 244n23
M & M Restaurants, 159
monetary damages actions, 41-42
Mooney, Tom, 209n58
Morse, Wayne, 134
motion picture industry, 16. *See also* Hollywood
Mundt, Karl, 16, 85
Murphy, Frank, 24, 30, 190n1
Murphy, Thomas F., 202n42
Murphy, Walter F., 78, 90, 105, 123
Murray, Tom, 125
Musmanno, Michael, 86, 173
Myrdal, Gunnar, 75

NAACP litigation: *Bates*, 133, 168-69; *Gibson*, 161-62, 168-69; membership lists, 110, 114, 133, 162, 168-69, 231n28;

NAACP v. Alabama, 114, 145, 168-69; non-Communist affidavits, 242-43n15; relationship between NAACP and Communists, 145, 162, 168-69, 251n33; and school-desegregation cases, 74; *Shelton*, 145-46, 168
National Association of Attorneys General, 89, 106
National Council for American-Soviet Friendship, 38
National Labor Relations Board, 35, 103, 156
National Lawyers Guild, 199n121
Nature Friends of America, 85
Nazis, American, 9, 181-82n33
Nelson, Steve, 78, 86-87, 94, 173, 219-20n25
Nelson bills, 87-88, 123-25, 142, 147
Nelson preemption case, 78, 86-89, 94, 147, 173. *See also* preemption of state laws
Nestor, Ephram, 135-36
New Deal, 7, 10, 15, 191n10
newspapers, anti-communist agenda of, 17, 202n42
New York Times journalists contempt-of-Congress cases, 166-67, 250-51n24
"next friend," 60, 209n59
Niukkanen, Willia, 134, 173
Nixon, Richard M., 10, 16, 20, 125, 182n38
non-sensitive government employees, 85, 107
Noto, John Francis, 152
Noto Smith Act case, 152, 245n41
Nowak, Stanislaw, 117
Nugent, Charles A., 57, 207n49

O'Conor, Herbert R., 105
Ohio's "little HUAC" commission, 130, 148-49, 225n37
O'Mahoney, Joseph C., 77
Orloff, Stanley, 56-57

Palermo tax evasion case, 141
partial sanctions, 37
passports: denials, 22, 109-10, 117-20, 143, 153-54, 169, 174, 233n49; legislation, 123, 125, 142-43
patriotic symbols, 171, 253n1
Pauling, Linus, 119
Pennsylvania Sedition Act, 86-87, 220n36
Pentagon Papers, 171-72
Perl, William, 58, 208n51
Perry, Olga, 244n23
pertinency rationale: *Barenblatt*, 131, 237n19; *Bart*, 71; *Deutch*, 148, 244n20;

Sacher contempt-of-Congress, 112–13; *Sweezy*, 99; *Watkins*, 174
Peters, John P., 71–73
Pickering, John, 179n15
Plessy v. Ferguson, 69, 74–75
Polites, Gus, 149
political repression, 1–2, 8–10.
post-audits, by Loyalty Review Board, 72–73, 101
Powe, Lucas A., 27, 91, 109, 160
Powell, Lewis, 182n38
Powers, Francis Gary, 237n9
Powers, Richard Gid, 17
preemption of state laws, 22, 86–90, 220–21n42. *See also* HR 3 anti-preemption bill; *Nelson* bills; *Nelson* preemption case
pretrial bail, 56
Price, William A., 166–67
prior restraint on speech, 171–72
Pritchett, C. Herman, 26
private-employee loyalty screenings, 21–22, 83, 128, 136–37, 159–60
Progressive Party, 14, 205–6n25
Proxmire, William, 127
public-employee loyalty screenings: *Adler*, 53–54; *Beilan*, 113, 139; *Cole*, 84–85; *Cramp*, 163; *Garner*, 42–44; *Lerner*, 113, 139; and longshoremen, 212–13n14; loyalty discharges, 113–14, 138–40; loyalty oaths, 42–44, 201n33; *Nelson/Globe*, 139–40; *Nostrand*, 163; and public school teachers, 53–54, 145–46; *Slochower*, 84, 113, 139, 160; *Vitarelli*, 138
public housing, 217n1
public opinion, influence of, 2–3, 20–21
Public Utility Holding Company Act (1935), 246n50

Quinn, Thomas, 70, 214n24

Radosh, Ronald, 57
Rankin, John E., 100n16
Reagan, Ronald, 177n1
Red Monday, 91, 94, 97–98, 101, 108, 222n2
Reed, Chauncey W., 62
Reed, Stanley F.: background information, 25, 28–29, 193nn19–20; on Japanese internment, 29; retirement of, 92
Reed, Stanley F., published opinions: *Bart* dissent, 71; *Bridges* dissent, 53; *Carlson* opinion, 49–50; *Emspak* draft opinion and dissent, 68, 71; *Gold* dissent, 103; *Jay* opinion, 80; *Joint Anti-Fascist* dissent, 39; *Nelson* dissent, 87; *Peters* dissent, 73; *Slochower* dissent, 84
Rehnquist, William H., 5, 11, 182n38, 233n53
Remington, William, 203n1
repressive eras in U.S. history, 1–3
Republican Party, 16–17, 19–20, 48, 76–78, 87–88, 110
ripeness, 54, 206n30
Robel, Frank, 253n38
Roberts, John G., 182–83n40
Roberts, Owen, 30, 180n22, 190n5
Robeson, Paul, 118, 120
Robinson, Joseph T., 190–91n7
Rodell, Fred, 26, 29, 174
Rogers, Jane, 41
Rogers, William P., 129
Roosevelt, Franklin Delano, 1, 7, 15, 25–29, 190n5
Rosenberg, Ethel and Julius, 17, 48, 57–63, 175, 208nn50–51, 209–10n62, 210n65, 210n69
Rovere, Richard H., 18
Rowoldt, Charles, 115, 231–32n32
Russell, Bertrand, 204n6
Russell, Norton Anthony, 166–68
Rutledge, Wiley B., 24, 190n1

Sacher, Harry, 67, 112–13, 225n32
Salt of the Earth (motion picture), 104
Sawyer, Harriet Bouslog, 140–41
Saypol, Irving, 58–59
Scales, Junius Irving, 150–51
Scales Smith Act case, 144, 150–52, 173, 244–45nn33–34
Scalia, Antonin, 11
Schlesinger, Arthur M., Jr., 144
school-desegregation, 8, 65, 74–76, 89, 110, 215n43
Schrecker, Ellen, 104
Schware, Rudolph, 100
Schwartz, Bernard, 29, 65, 67, 69, 74
Scott, Hugh, 17
security clearances, 128, 136–37
Security Risk Law (New York), 113–14
Sedition Act (1798), 177n1, 207n35
sedition statutes, federal, 1–2, 8–9, 21, 44
sedition statutes, state, 86–90. *See also* preemption of state laws
self-incrimination (Fifth Amendment privilege): *Beilan*, 113, 231n23; *Blau (Irving)*, 40–41; *Blau (Patricia)*, 40, 100n16; *CPUSA v. SACB*, 153–55, 160; *DeGreg-*

ory, 250n23; *Emspak*, 70–71; *Globe*, 139; *Kimm*, 135; *Lerner*, 113–14; *McPhaul*, 147–48; overview of, 189n49; *Quinn*, 70; *Rogers*, 41; *Slochower*, 84, 113, 160; *Ullmann*, 79. *See also* compelled disclosure; contempt-of-Congress cases; CPUSA
Senate, 5, 19, 20, 76–77, 124–26. *See also* court-curbing legislation; SISS (Senate Internal Security Subcommittee)
Sentner, Antonia, 102
Sentner, William, 226n54
Service, John Stewart, 101
Shelton, Robert, 166–67
Shipley, Ruth, 118
Silber, Bernard, 166–67
SISS (Senate Internal Security Subcommittee), 84, 90, 108, 166–68. *See also* contempt-of-Congress cases
Sixth Amendment rights, 38, 72, 141–42, 156. *See also* witnesses: right to confront
Slagle, Laverne, 244n23
Slochower, Harry, 84
Smathers, George A., 88
Smith, Howard W.: HR 3 anti-preemption bill, 78, 86–89, 107, 110, 123–24, 142–43, 160; and labor-law, 220–21n42; and Smith Act, 21, 87
Smith Act (1940), 21, 86–87, 96, 150–52, 172–73, 245n41
Smith Act cases: *Dennis*, 25, 37, 44–47, 173; indictment of CPUSA leaders, 16, 24–25, 201nn34–35; and *Kremen*, 96–97; *Lightfoot*, 244n31; *Mesarosh*, 94; *Noto*, 152, 245n41; and pretrial bail, 56; and *Sawyer*, 140–41, 240n62; *Scales*, 144, 150–52, 173, 244–45nn33–34; and self-incrimination, 40; *Yates*, 91, 94–97, 106, 175
Sobell, Morton, 208n50
Soboleff, Simon E., 72
Social Security benefits, denial of, 128, 135–36
Souter, David, 175
Southern Conference for Human Welfare, 216n47
Southern Democrats, 78, 87–88, 110
Soviet Union: and CPUSA deportees, 204n12; espionage by, 13–14, 17, 19, 183–84n3, 208n50, 237n9. *See also* Rosenberg, Ethel and Julius
Spector, Efroim, 50, 204n12
Speiser, Lawrence, 120–21
Spellman, Francis Cardinal, 92
Stassen, Harold, 17

state anti-subversive statutes, 22, 86–90, 98–99, 238n27. *See also* preemption of state laws
State Department, 101, 117–20, 233n49. *See also* passports
statute-of-limitations issues, 53, 95
Steinberg, Sidney, 96
Stennis, John C., 88
Stern, Joseph, 130
Stevens, John Paul, 182n38
Stevenson, Adlai E., 19–20, 187n33
Stewart, Potter: appointment of, 127; background information, 129; on Harlan, 69; and *Scales*, 152; on Warren, 65
Stewart, Potter, published opinions: *Bates* opinion, 133; *Braden* opinion, 146–47; *Brawner* opinion, 159; *Cramp* opinion, 163; *Deutch* opinion, 148; *Russell* opinion, 167; *Sawyer* concurrence, 140–41; *Shelton* (NAACP) opinion, 145–46; *Wilkinson* opinion, 146–47
St. Louis Post-Dispatch, 34, 196n44
Stone, Geoffrey, 15, 108, 172
strict constructionism, 10–11, 182n37
Subversive Activities Control Board (SACB), 21, 37, 78, 81–83, 153–55, 160, 173
"subversive" organizations, attorney general's list of. *See* attorney general's list of "subversive" organizations
summary-termination statute, 107
Supreme Court: about, 189n50, 196n40; impeachment of Justices, 4–5, 62, 178n11; number of justices, 7, 180n21; packing the court, 7; refusal of executive branch to enforce decisions, 7–8; retreat of, 3, 12, 108, 127–43, 160, 173–75; vulnerability of, 3, 8, 12, 175. *See also* court-curbing legislation; jurisdiction-stripping legislation; *specific justices*
Sweezy, Paul M., 98–99

Taft, Robert A., 17, 185n12
Taft-Hartley Act non-Communist-affidavits: about, 23–25; *Douds*, 35–37; *Gold*, 79–80, 103; *Jencks*, 91–92, 104–7, 227n63, 248–48nn6–7; *Killian*, 162–63, 248–49nn6–7; *Mine-Mill*, 103; repeal of, 247n60; *Travis*, 156; *Zucca*, 81
Talmadge, Herman, 75
Taney, Roger B., 7
Taylor, Charles Allen, 137
Tenney committee, 41–42, 200n22
Thomas, J. Parnell, 16

Thompson, Lula Mae, 246n53
Thompson, Robert G., 96, 201n34, 242n1
travel, right to, 117–20. *See also* passports
Travis, Maurice, 103, 156, 226n57
Truman, Harry S.: 1948 election, 16–17; and the Internal Security Act, 21, 36; and the Loyalty Review Board, 72, 85; and Navy authorizations, 159; and passport proclamation, 118; presidency of, 15–17; Supreme Court appointments, 24–25, 28–31; on Warren, 65
Trumbo, Dalton, 33
Tydings, Millard E., 19

Ullmann, William Ludwig, 79
undisclosed "confidential information," 22, 80–81, 119, 128, 136–37, 143
Unitarian churches, 121
United Public Workers union, 129–30, 237n13
Uphaus, Willard and *Uphaus* case, 128, 132–33, 145, 168
Urofsky, Melvin I., 26, 30, 42

vacation stays, 61–62
Van Devanter, Willis, 25
Veterans and government benefits, 34, 120–21
Veterans' Preference Act, 85
Vietnam War era, 170–72, 253n6
Vinson, Fred M.: appointment of, 28, 29; background information, 29–30; and conservative majority in "Communist" cases, 24–25, 29, 229n1; death of, 64, 211n1; private meeting with Brownell, 60, 209n61; and the Rosenberg case, 60–62
Vinson, Fred M., published opinions: *Bryan* opinion, 32–33; *Dennis* opinion, 45, 201–2n37; *Douds* opinion, 35, 197n49, 197n52; *Feiner* opinion, 42; *Fleischman* opinion, 32, 195n35; *Osman* per curiam, 197n52; *Rogers* opinion, 41; *Rosenberg* opinion, 62; *Stack* opinion, 56
Vinson court, 24–36, 190n5
Vitarelli, William Vincent, 138, 239–40nn51–52

Waldron, Francis, 195n30. *See also* Dennis, Eugene
Walker, Doris Brin, 83, 219n2
Wallace, Henry A., 14, 42, 207n36
Walsh, Fr. Edmond A., 18
Walter, Francis E., 86, 107, 120, 137

War Brides Act, 34
War on Terror, 2
warrantees searches, 96–97
Warren, Earl: appointment of, 64, 222–23n8; background information, 64–65, 212n5; Black tribute, 169; and "Communist" cases, 65–66, 68; criticism of, 5, 88, 162, 175; dispute with ABA, 106; and Frankfurter, 67, 99, 145, 213n16; impeachment drive, 5; and individual rights, 65, 212n5; on influence of public opinion, 3; liberal alliances, 67–68, 79, 93, 144; and unanimity in school-desegregation cases, 74, 127; vice-presidential bid, 186n19; and Whittaker retirement, 164
Warren, Earl, published opinions: *Brown I and II* opinions, 74–75, 175; *CPUSA v. SACB* dissent, 154; *Emspak, Quinn* and *Bart* opinions, 70–71, 214n27; *Gold* per curiam, 103; *Greene* opinion, 137; *Jay* dissent, 80; *Lerner* dissent, 114; *Levy* per curiam, 73; *Mesarosh* opinion, 94; *Nelson* opinion, 86–87; *Peters* opinion, 72; *Sacher* per curiam, 67; *Sweezy* opinion, 99; *Watkins* opinion, 98; *Zucca*, 81
Warren court, as activist court, 10
Watkins, John T., 98, 224–25n29
Watkins contempt-of-Congress case, 91, 97–98, 106, 113, 123–25, 147, 160
Wheeler, W. M., 62
White, Byron R., 164–65
Whitman, Alden, 166–67
Whitney v. California, 172
Whittaker, Charles E., 92–94, 161, 164, 240n59, 249n13
Whittaker, Charles E., published opinions: *Bonetti* opinion, 116; *Deutch* dissent, 148; *Harmon* per curiam opinion, 122; *Heikkinen* opinion, 116; *Killian* opinion, 162; *McPhaul* opinion, 148; *Nowak* dissent, 117; *Slagle* opinion, 149
Wiecek, William M., 17, 18, 29
Wiig, Jon, 140
Wilkinson, Frank, 146, 243n7
Winston, Henry, 112
Witkovich, George I., 102
witnesses: *in camera* inspections of witnesses' reports, 92, 104–7, 141–42; credibility of, 94; and *Jencks* legislation, 106–8; rights of, 98; right to confront, 38, 137–38, 141–42, 239n50; undisclosed "confidential information," 22, 38–39, 80–81, 119, 128, 136–37, 143

World Fellowship organization, 132–33
World War I era, 2, 8–9
World War II era, 1–2, 9. *See also* Japanese internment
Wyman, Louis C., 106, 132–33, 145, 238n27

Yakovlev, Anatoli, 208n50
Yalta and Potsdam, 13, 15, 185n12
Yates, Oleta O'Connor, 110–11, 230n7

Yates bills, 105–6, 110, 123–25, 142, 160
Yates contempt-of-court case, 110–11, 230n10
Yates Smith Act case, 91, 94–97, 106, 172, 175
Young Progressives of America, 42

Zydok, John, 204n9

ROBERT M. LICHTMAN, a Washington lawyer for nearly thirty years, has practiced in San Francisco since 1986. He is coauthor of *Deadly Farce: Harvey Matusow and the Informer System in the McCarthy Era.*

The University of Illinois Press
is a founding member of the
Association of American University Presses.

University of Illinois Press
1325 South Oak Street
Champaign, IL 61820-6903
www.press.uillinois.edu